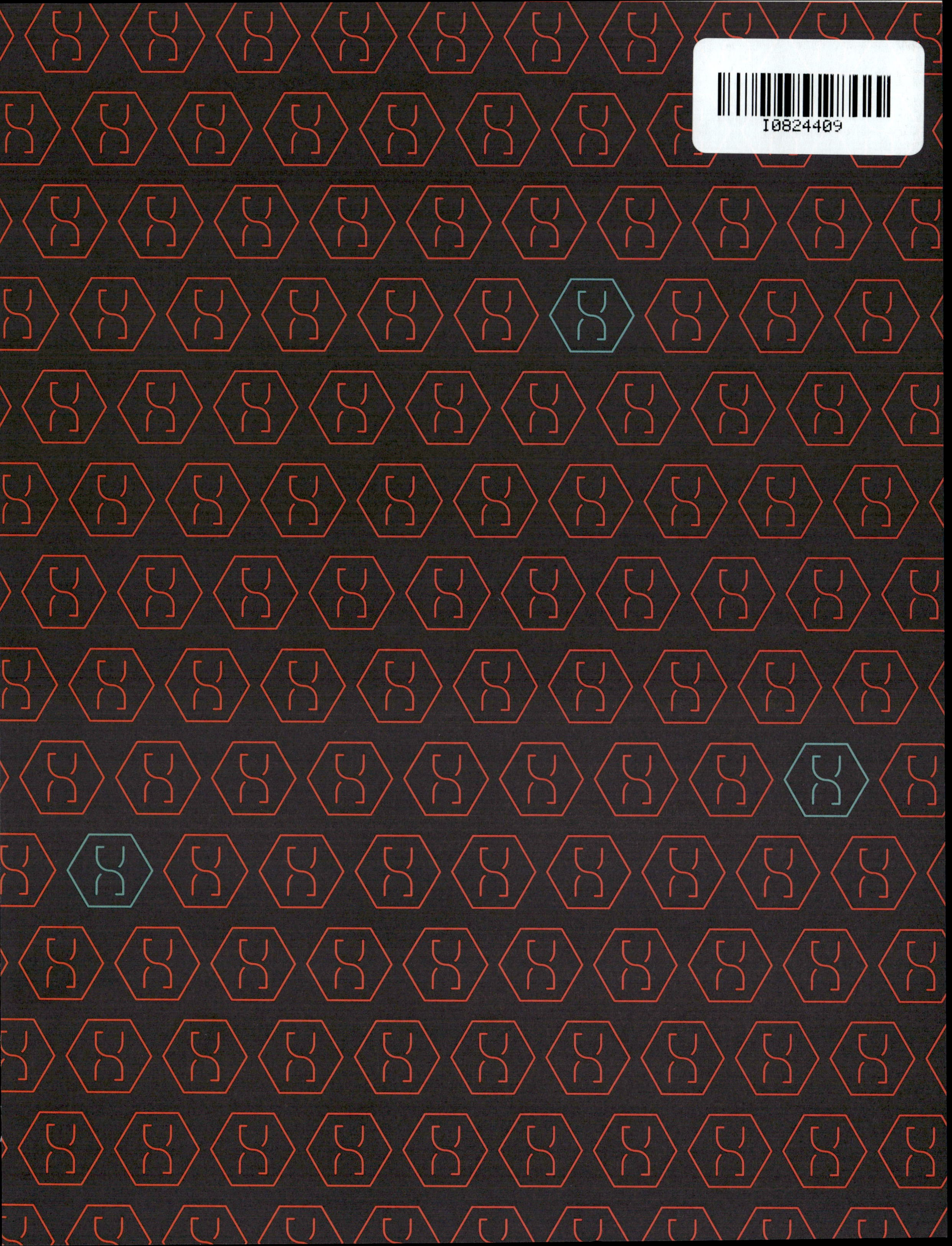
I0824409

ALTERED CARBON

THE ART AND MAKING OF THE SERIES

ALTERED CARBON

THE ART AND MAKING OF
THE SERIES

ISBN: 9781789092189

Published by Titan Books
A division of Titan Publishing Group Ltd.
144 Southwark St.
London
SE1 0UP

FIRST EDITION: MARCH 2020
1 3 5 7 9 10 8 6 4 2

DID YOU ENJOY THIS BOOK?

We love to hear from our readers. Please e-mail us at: readerfeedback@titanemail.com or write to Reader Feedback at the above address.

To receive advance information, news, competitions, and exclusive offers online, please sign up for the Titan newsletter on our website: www.titanbooks.com

A CIP catalogue record for this title is available from the British Library.

Printed and bound in China.

ALTERED CARBON

THE ART AND MAKING OF THE SERIES

WRITTEN BY ABBIE BERNSTEIN

TITAN BOOKS

CONTENTS

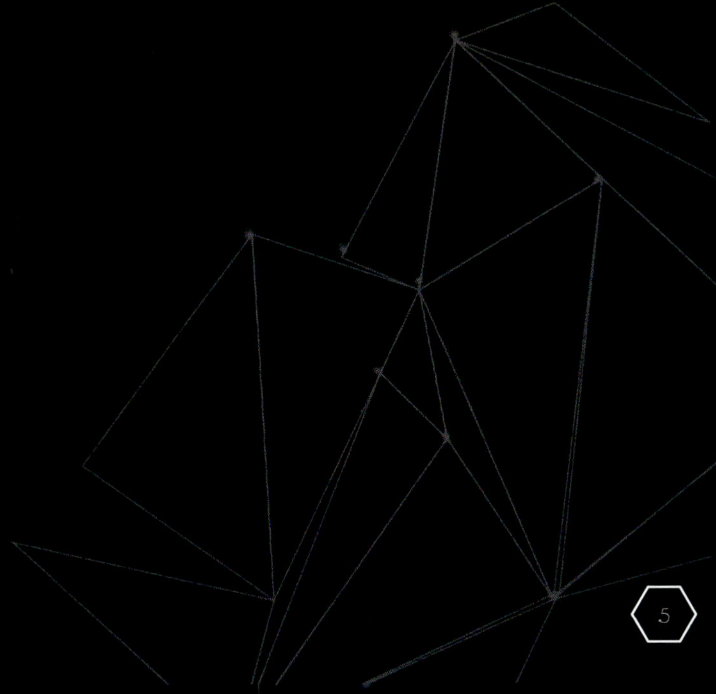

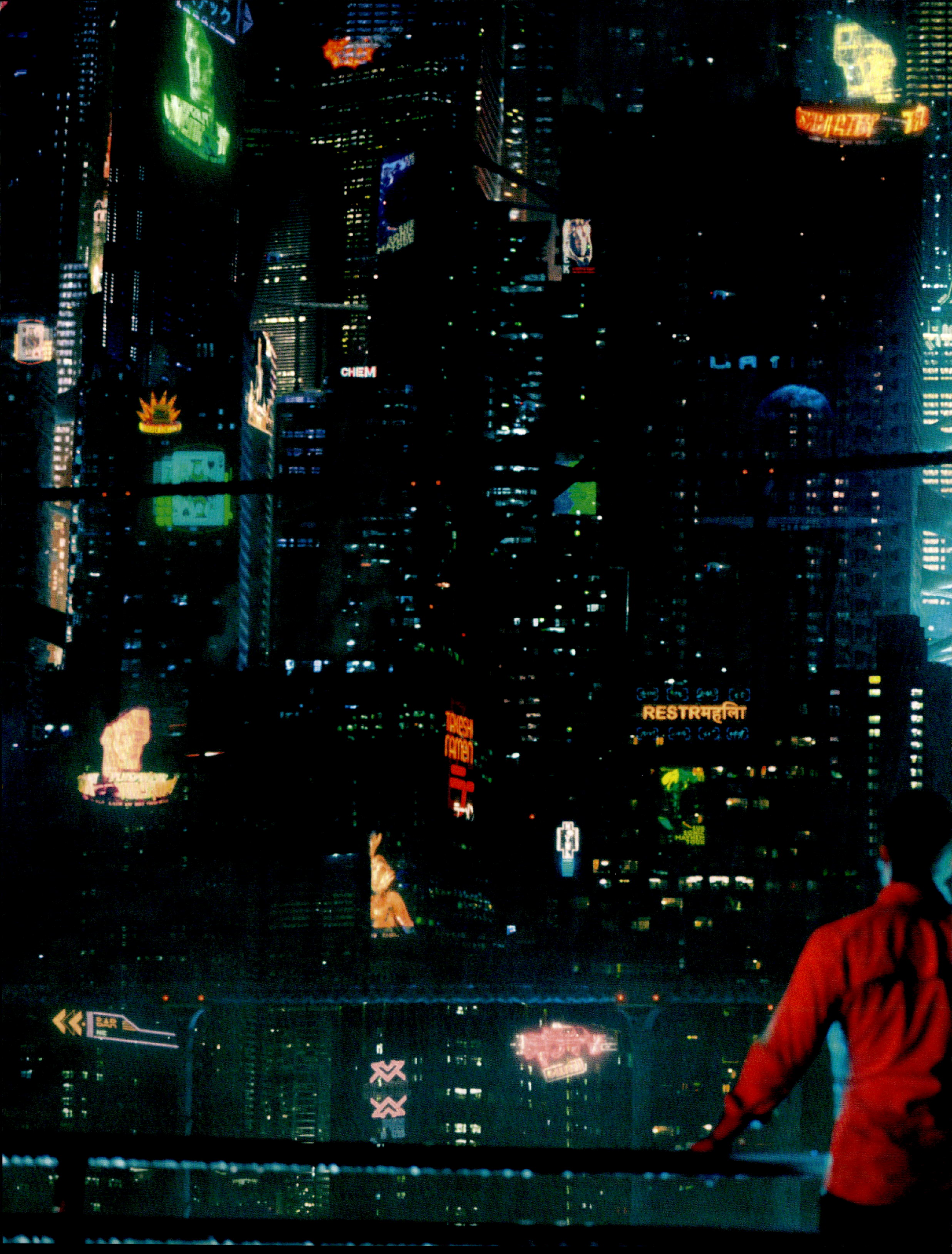
CHEM
RESTRमहिला

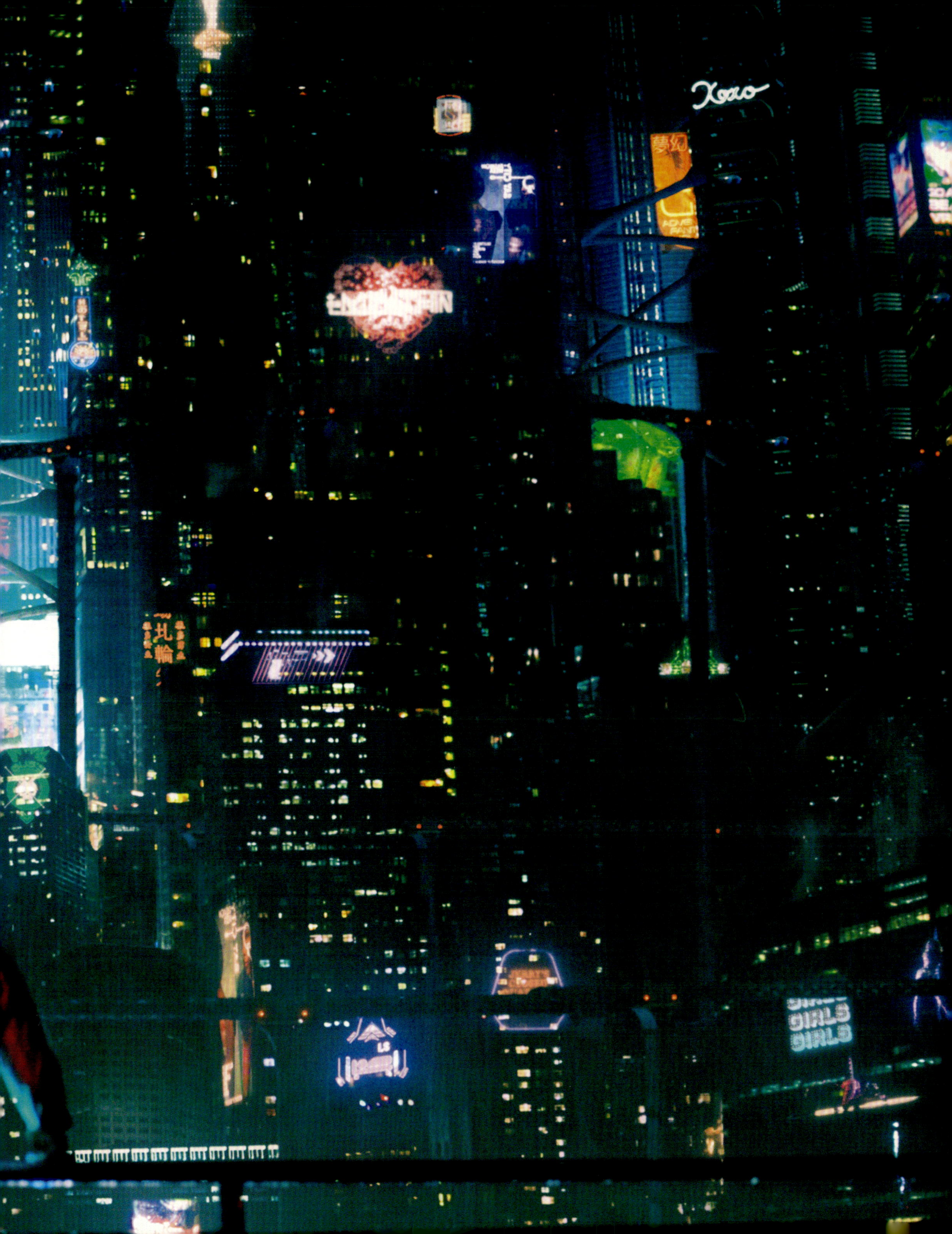
Xoxo
GIRLS
GIRLS

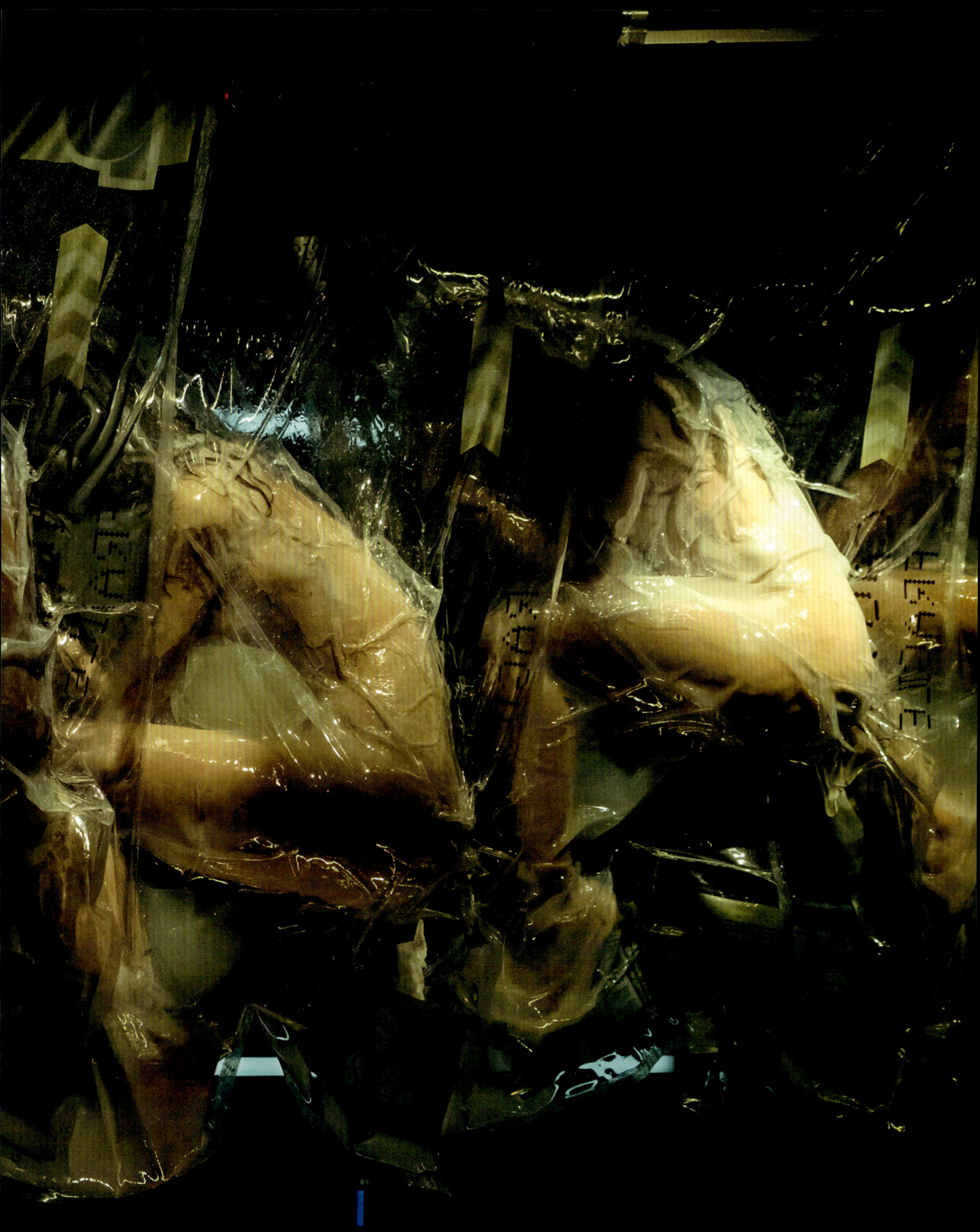

INTRODUCTION

STAY YOUNG AND LIVE FOREVER

The Netflix series *Altered Carbon*, produced by Skydance Television, is based on a trilogy of novels by English author Richard K. Morgan. The first book, published in 2002, shares its title and storyline with the first season.

Executive producer James Middleton explains, "Season two employs a few key ideas and locations from Richard Morgan's *Broken Angels* [published in 2003] and *Woken Furies* [2005]. But it is not based on either book in the way season one was based on the first book. Narratively [for season two] we wanted to focus on the love story in a way that the subsequent books do not. So, with Richard Morgan's help in the writers' room, we took elements from the saga and crafted a new [season two] storyline."

Season two show runner Alison Schapker adds, "We have taken creative license, but we have tried to stay true to the spirit of the universe he created."

For Schapker, that spirit "calls into question the nature of human identity itself. How much of what makes me 'me' is tied to the mind, the body, the soul? If minds can move between bodies, what residue of lived experience remains etched in our flesh? And what does it mean to inhabit the flesh of another?"

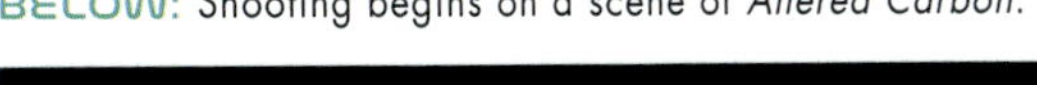

BELOW: Shooting begins on a scene of *Altered Carbon*.

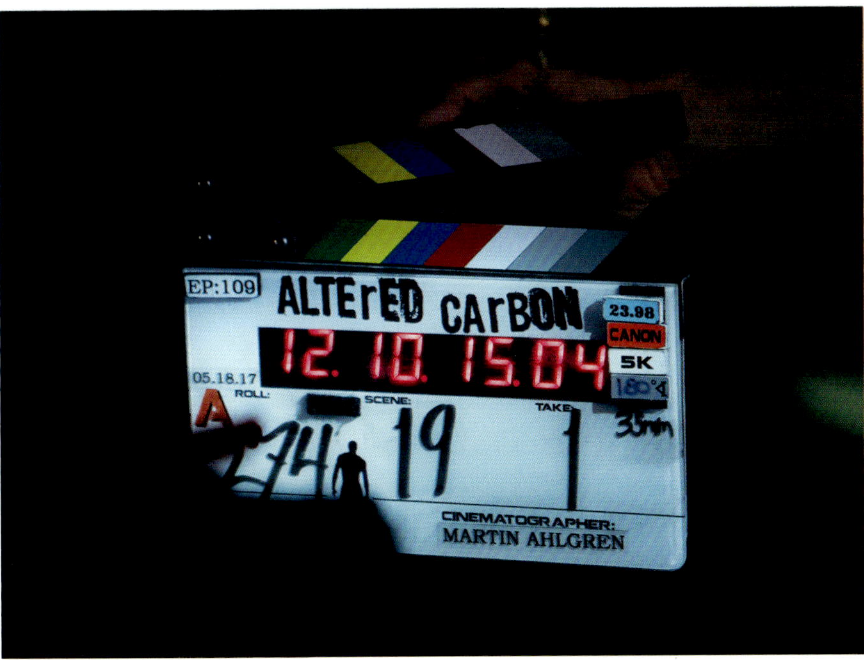

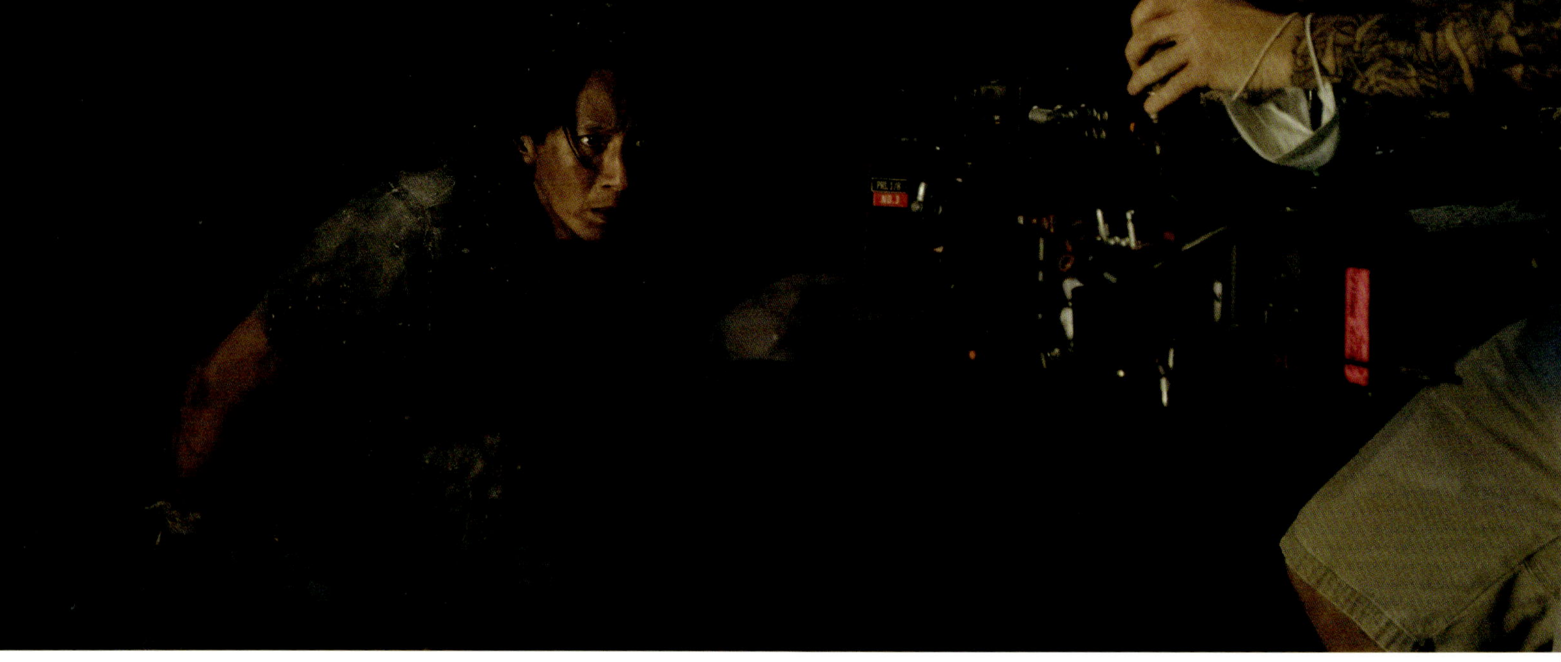

ABOVE: Will Yun Lee portraying Kovacs in his birth body.

Altered Carbon is set in a future where human consciousness is digitized as digital human freight, or DHF: an individual's memories, personality, emotions, everything that comprises their identity. Each DHF is stored in a stack, which can be moved between bodies, also called sleeves. People who can afford to buy new sleeves or clone themselves can effectively stay young and live forever; those who with less money have fewer options.

Our protagonist is Takeshi Kovacs, a trained military operative turned rebel who, in season one, is brought back in a new sleeve after two hundred and fifty years on ice to solve a murder. In season two, Kovacs is in a different sleeve, confronting his past while searching for his lost love.

Laeta Kalogridis, who created *Altered Carbon* as a series and serves as one of its executive producers, originally read Morgan's novel when Joel Silver had it under option. Kalogridis says she loved "how human it was. It's a hard sci-fi story about a kind of technology that allows you to extend life indefinitely, but in no way was the story removed from identifiable human emotions. And it was noir. I love noir."

The project was originally slated to be a PG-13-rated feature film at Warner Brothers. The family-friendly rating seemed incompatible with the darkness of the source material. When Silver's option lapsed, Kalogridis and her producing partners at the time, Brad Fisher and Jamie Vanderbilt, contacted author Morgan and optioned *Altered Carbon* in hopes of making it as a hard-R-rated feature film.

Then it was agreed that television might be a better medium for the complex story and characters. Kalogridis, already working with production company Skydance on another project, brought *Altered Carbon* to their attention. Skydance brought it to Netflix, and *Altered Carbon* the series was born. President of Skydance Television Marcy Ross says, "From the beginning, everyone at Skydance was instantly intrigued by the world Richard K. Morgan had built in the book series and knew *Altered Carbon* would make for a gripping television series. There are so many layers to *Altered Carbon* that make it so compelling, especially for us as a studio: it's an epic story spanning massive worlds. It's action-packed and thought provoking and – at its heart – it's a love story. At Skydance, especially with our films, we're known for big world building, event-level movies; we're excited to be able to bring the same engaging stories and high-quality visuals to television with *Altered Carbon*."

Executive producer/director Nick Hurran observes, "I think one of the challenges is to be as bold as the thought that the novel had in the first place. It's a frightening thought, what Richard K. Morgan has created in the world going forward. I think when he wrote the book, many of the concepts were difficult to believe – not farfetched, but we're now a few years on, and it's frightening how close to the truth rather than fiction his vision was. We've been very lucky to have the most wonderfully talented creatives around us. It's a perfect world for visual effects, stunts, special effects, and they have excelled beyond the call."

In translating *Altered Carbon* from a novel to ten episodes for the first season, Kalogridis relates, there were a number of issues. "The mythology is pretty complex. Also, I think we forget sometimes how much just in our lifetime technology has transformed in things that fifteen years ago, we would not really have considered as being normative – Google, the Internet. That's a part of what makes it challenging to create a world where there's a whole new technology that's upended everything in a much bigger way than the Internet has upended everything. It's a matter of course you don't really explain it. We're world-building around an idea that, even though it's simple at its heart, brings with it a great deal of complexity in how it's used."

Middleton says he doesn't know where to begin describing what he loves about *Altered Carbon*. "Richard K. Morgan's books are very involving, entertaining stories, with big existential ideas. As for our adaptation of *Altered Carbon*, I am particularly fond of the mixture of sci-fi and film noir. I like that we are able to tell stories that are very adult, provocative, and unabashed. I have loved dealing with our cast and very talented writers, from Laeta Kalogridis, to Steve Blackman, to Alison Schapker. Finally, I am drawn to the fact that, at its core, *Altered Carbon* is about how individuals deal with intense loss, whether it is the loss of an intense love, or of one's very humanity. Dealing with loss is something that everyone faces, which makes our story very relatable. I think it is unique in its approach to examining existential ideas, such as what makes us human, and, also, the question of if love can survive over centuries, no matter what body we inhabit."

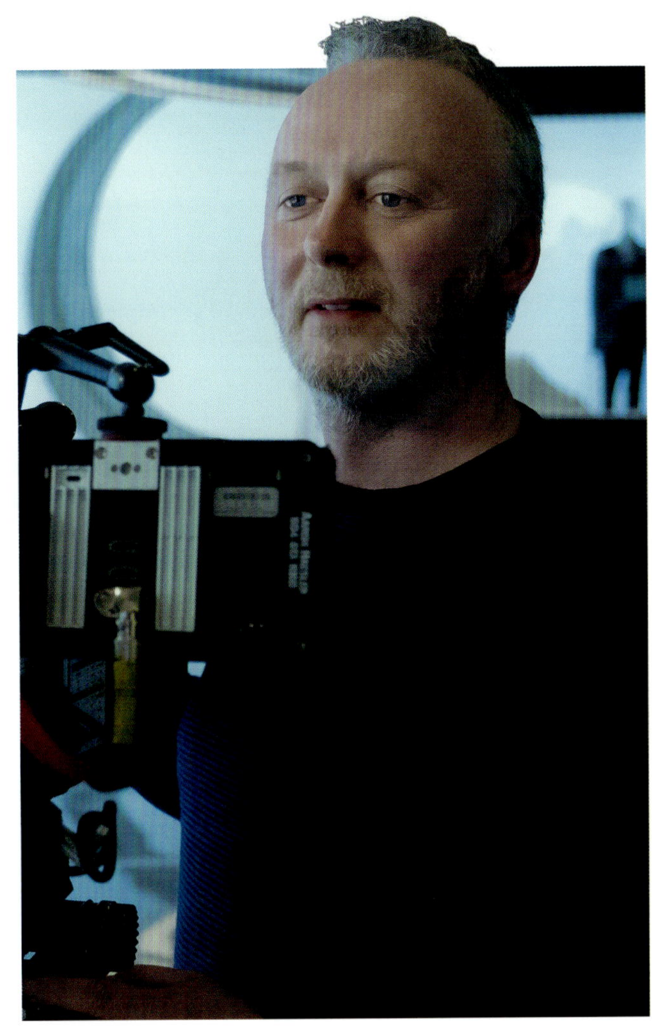

THIS PAGE: Neville Kidd on set of the season one episode 'The Wrong Man' (above). Joel Kinnaman played the role of Takeshi Kovacs in season one (below).

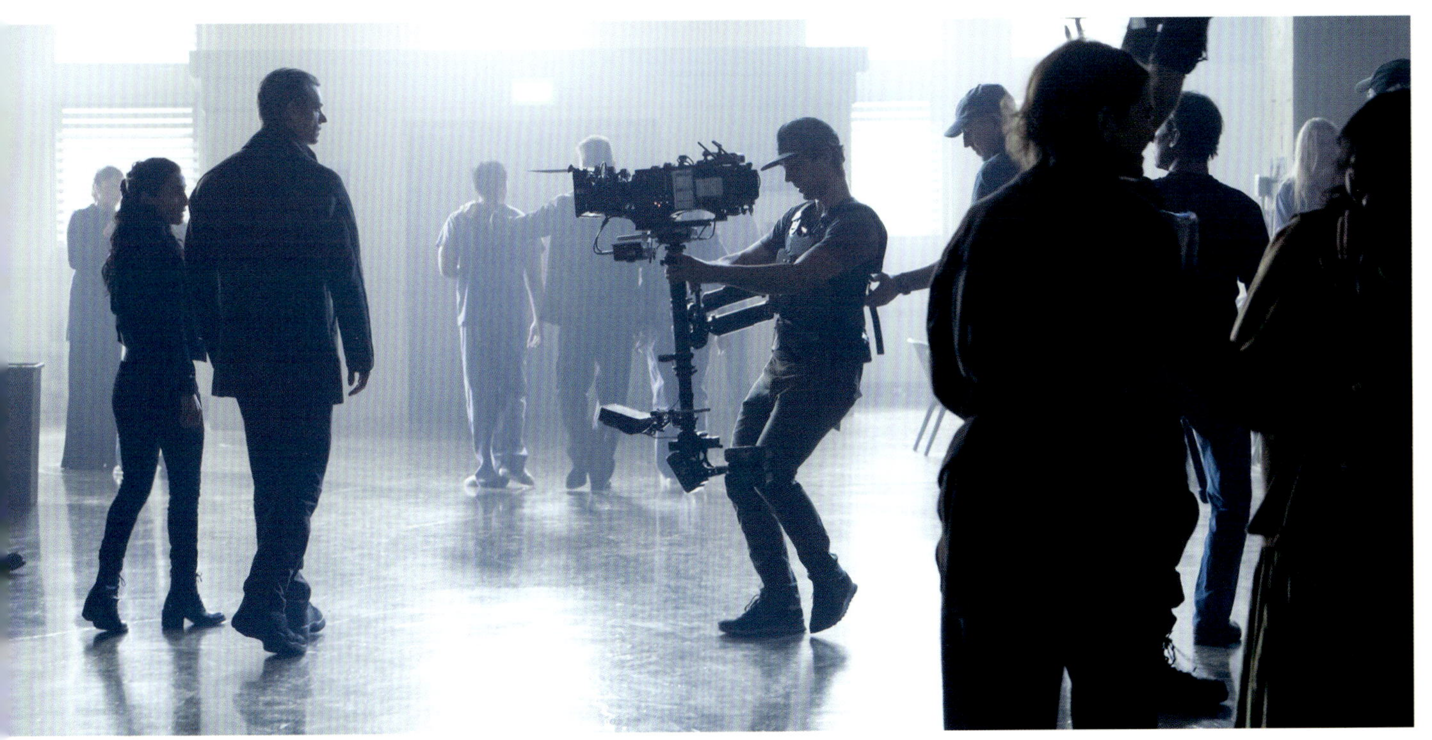

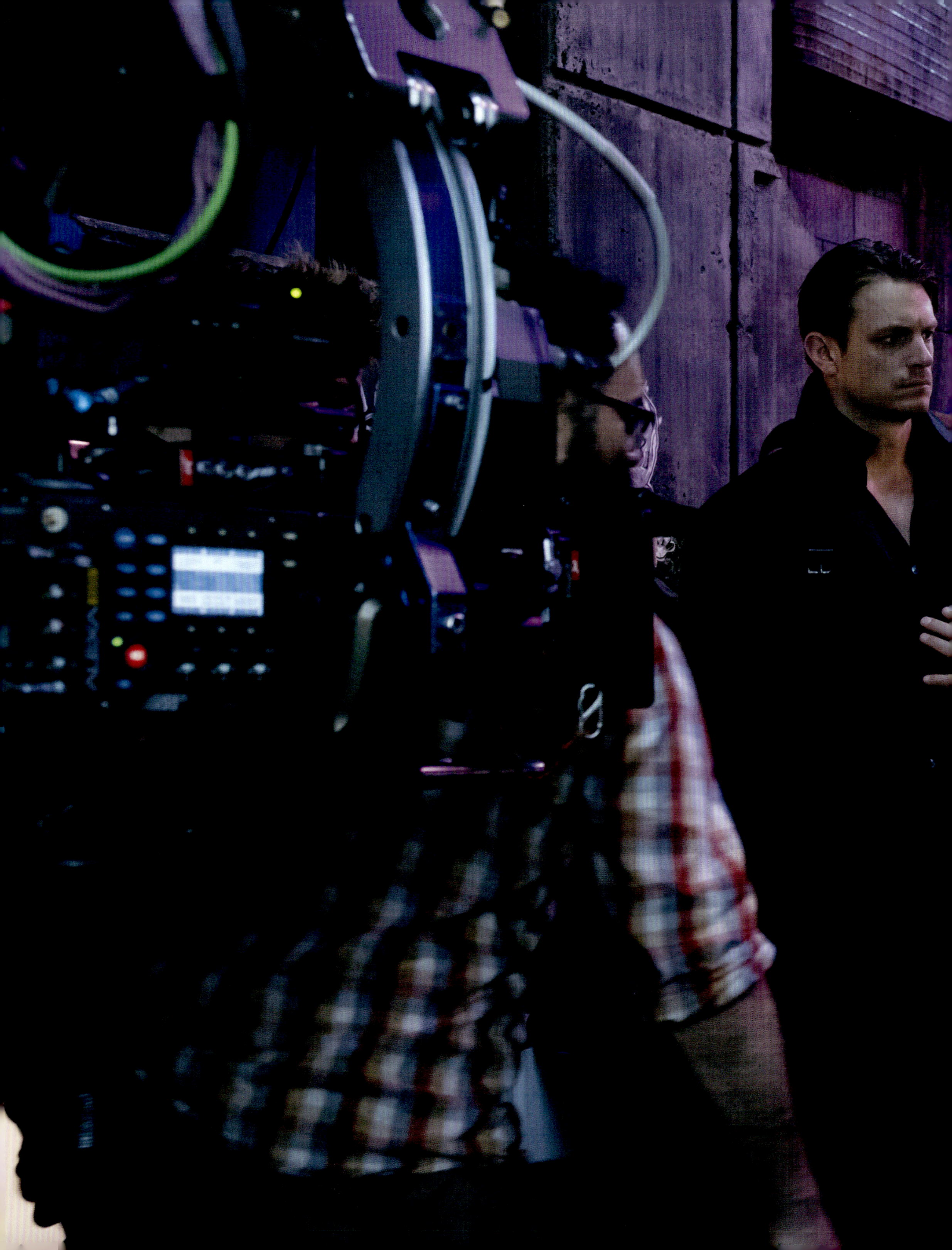

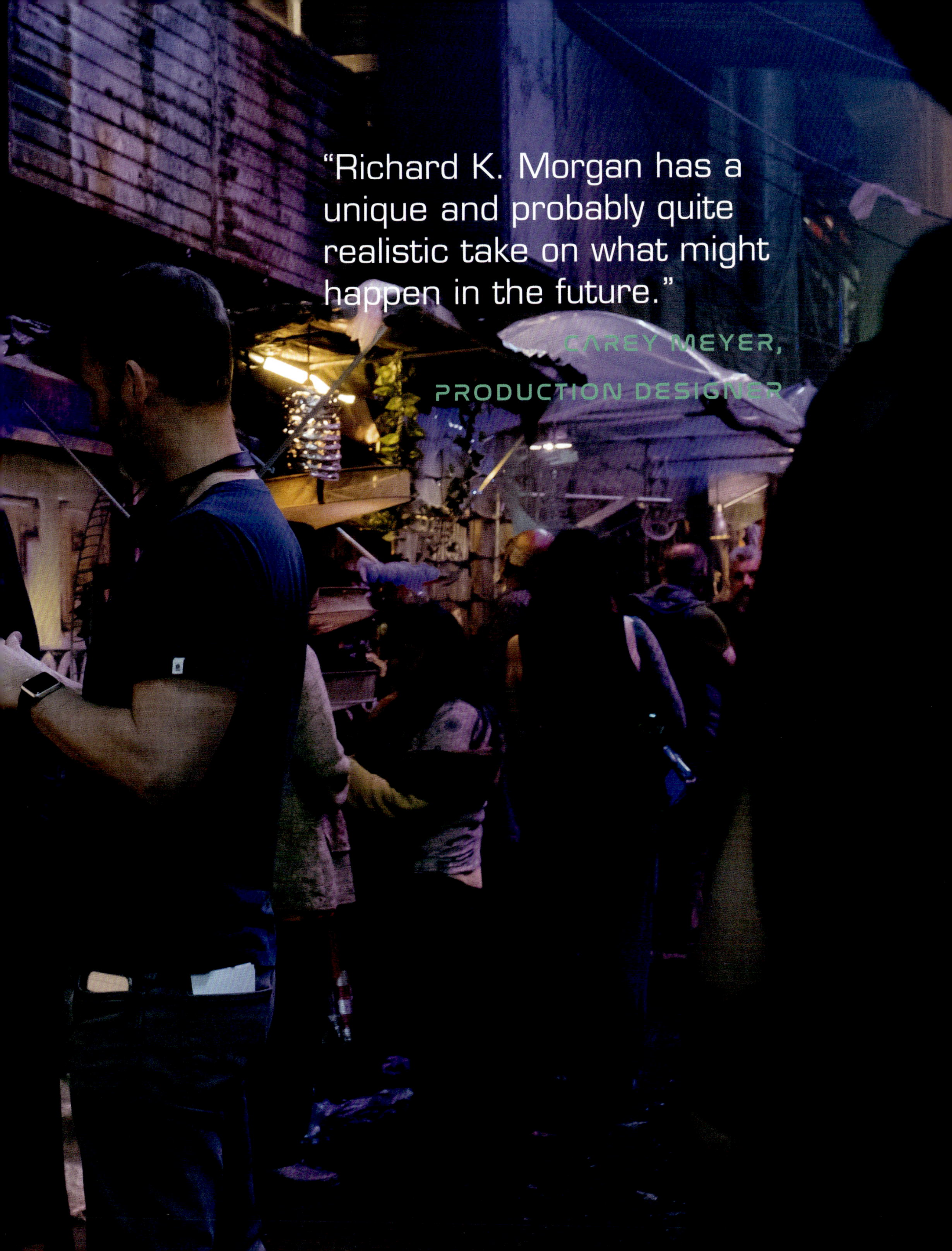

"Richard K. Morgan has a unique and probably quite realistic take on what might happen in the future."

CAREY MEYER,
PRODUCTION DESIGNER

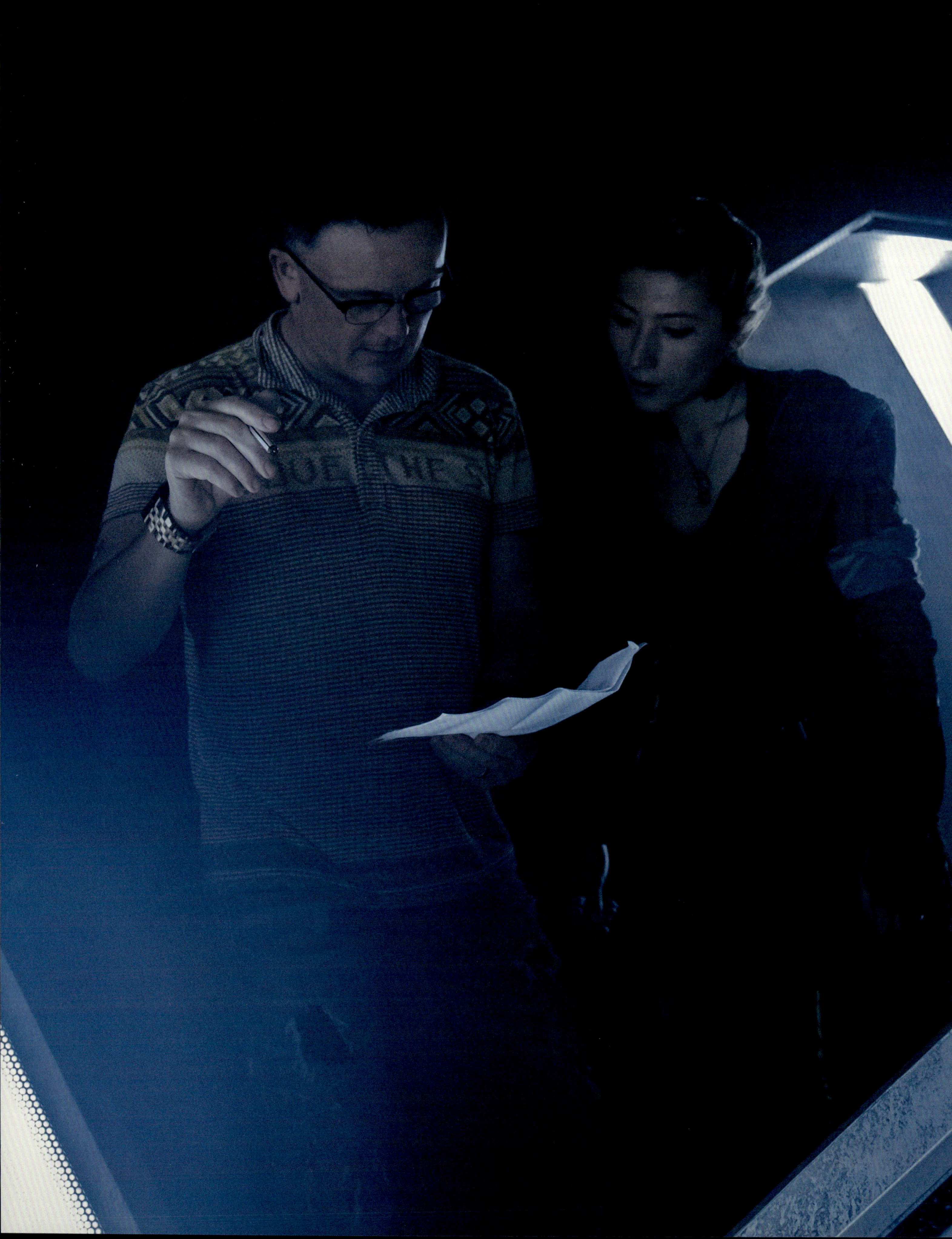

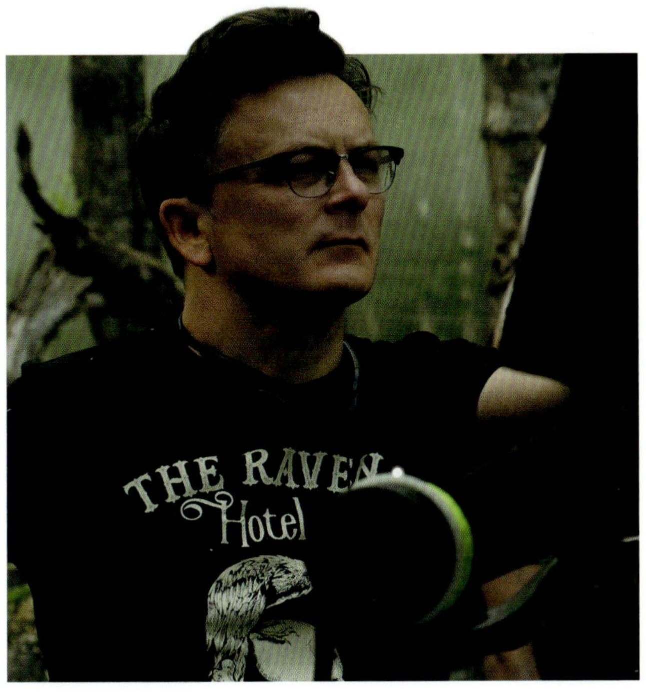

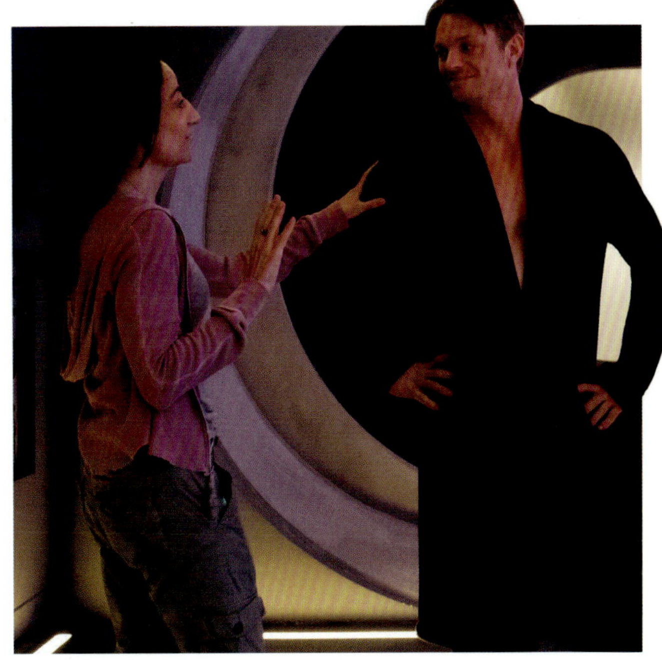

THIS SPREAD: Dichen Lachman with Andy Goddard, director of season one episode 'Nora Inu,' on set (left). Laeta Kalogridis, writer and producer of *Altered Carbon,* in conversation with Joel Kinnaman (above right).

Kalogridis adds that other themes include, "Our ability to create technology almost always outstrips our ability to use it wisely. But also we're trying to explore the idea of imbalance in resources, when too much goes to a small group, and not enough to everyone else."

"Living forever leads to even greater disparities of wealth," agrees Schapker. For her, "It was an incredible sandbox to dive into, thanks to their collective creativity and talents."

Chris Conner, who plays the artificial intelligence being Poe, says he sees *Altered Carbon* as being about "the struggle to be human, the fight to hold onto our better angels. If we don't fight our inner demons, we could end up in a dystopia. But love and humanity will hopefully crack through."

Other aspects of *Altered Carbon* also resonate. In Season two, Kovacs is played by African-American actor Anthony Mackie. Kovacs' lover/mentor Quellcrist Falconer is played throughout the series by African-American actress Renée Elise Goldsberry.

Simone Missick, who plays bounty hunter Trepp in season two, is likewise African-American. She observes, "I don't think very often you see three African-American lead actors in an action series and also to have Will Yun Lee [as Kovacs Prime], Dina Shihabi [as the AI Dig 301], [and] Chris Conner – it's a very rich, inclusive cast. I think it's very exciting to see Renée and I onscreen together. It's two women who are both equally strong, but have completely different needs and wants and desires and outlooks and moral codes that aren't necessarily ones that, in our bodies, are often given to us as actors."

Then there are characters who wind up in sleeves that don't match their identities. For example, when Ava Elliot's stack is released from her prison sentence, the only available body is male. Director Peter Hoar, who helmed the last two episodes of season one, says, "It's effectively a lesson in transgender. What does it mean, if you can change bodies like this? It was like, okay, you may be wearing this body, but the person inside is still Ava. She identifies as 'she,' so we should call her 'she'."

Production designer Carey Meyer cites the original Blade Runner as an inspiration for *Altered Carbon*'s season one look. Meyer devised the primary street set for Bay City as something that would anchor the essence of the show's world. "In the early stages for creating the look of the show, the conversations with the producers were about creating the three levels of [Bay City], because that tells you a lot about how your social structure works. We spent a lot of time creating Bancroft's tower, and then the Grounder city base level, and then we would [create] the spaces in between from the top down to the ground. Richard K. Morgan has a unique and probably quite realistic take on what might happen in the future. A lot of it is right around the corner."

Kalogridis says of *Altered Carbon*'s journey to the screen, "It has so many layers and so many technological challenges that there's a reason it took years. But getting to explore something that is complex as a technological and an intellectual idea, while making the story human, that's a huge victory."

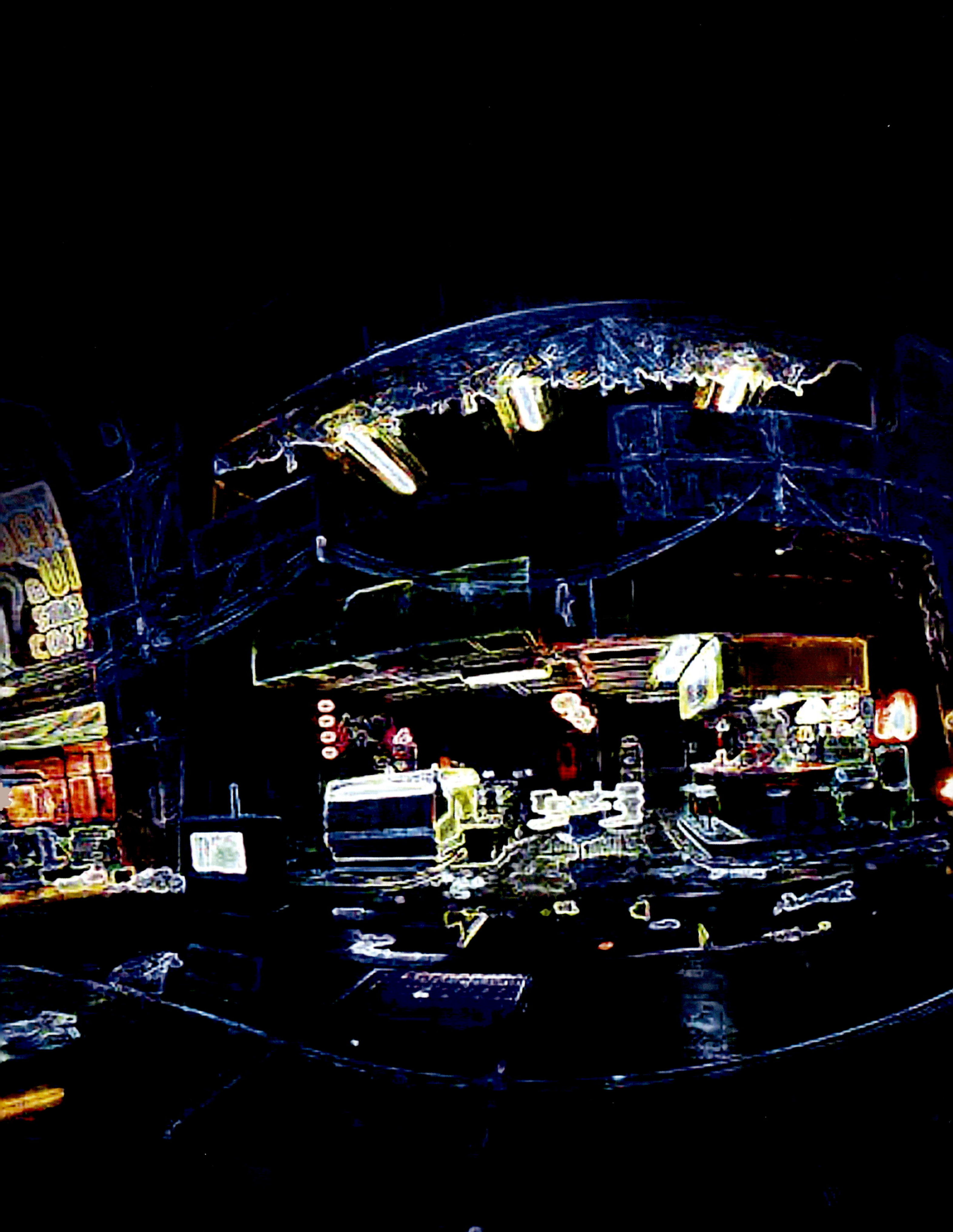

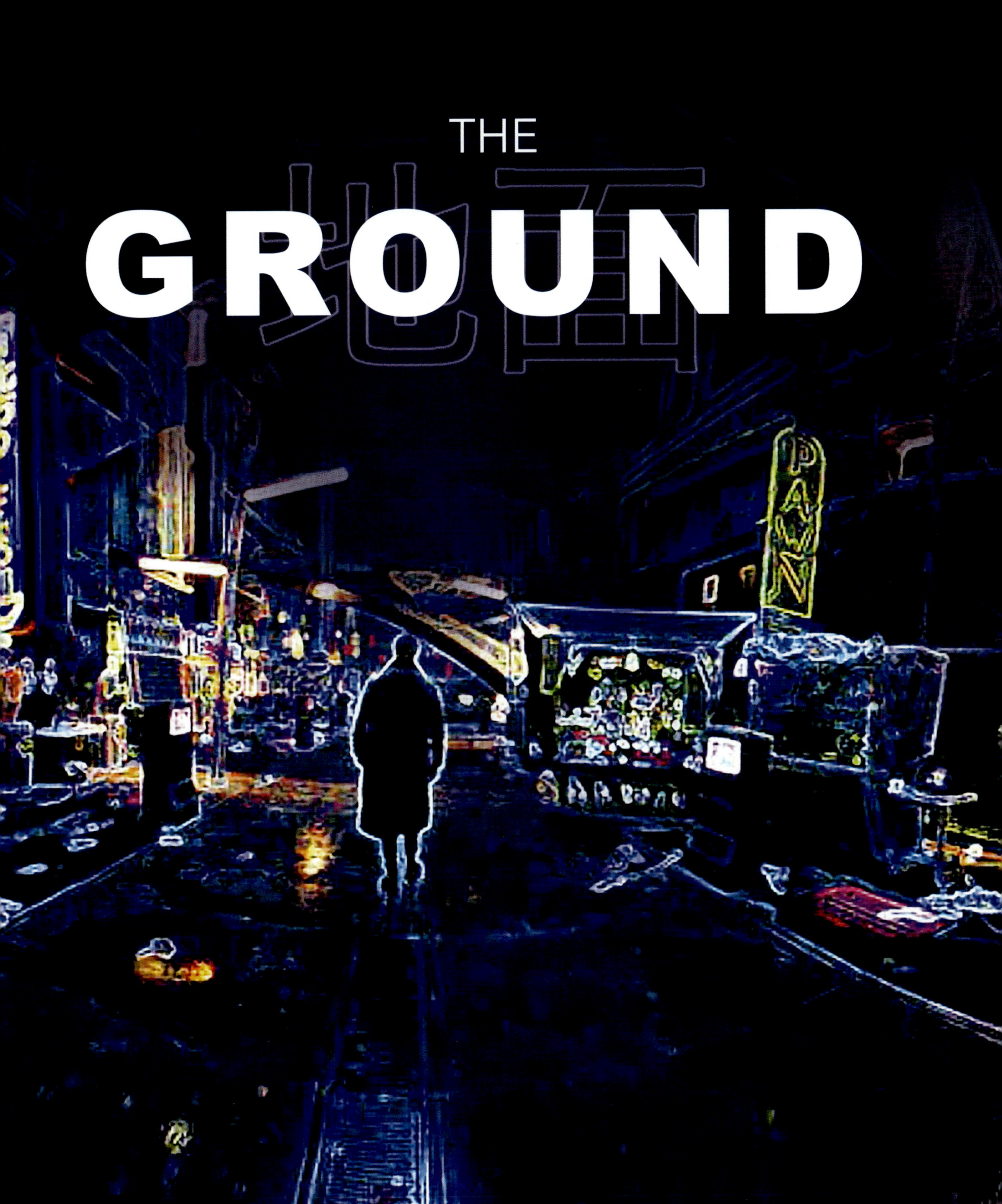
THE
GROUND
地面

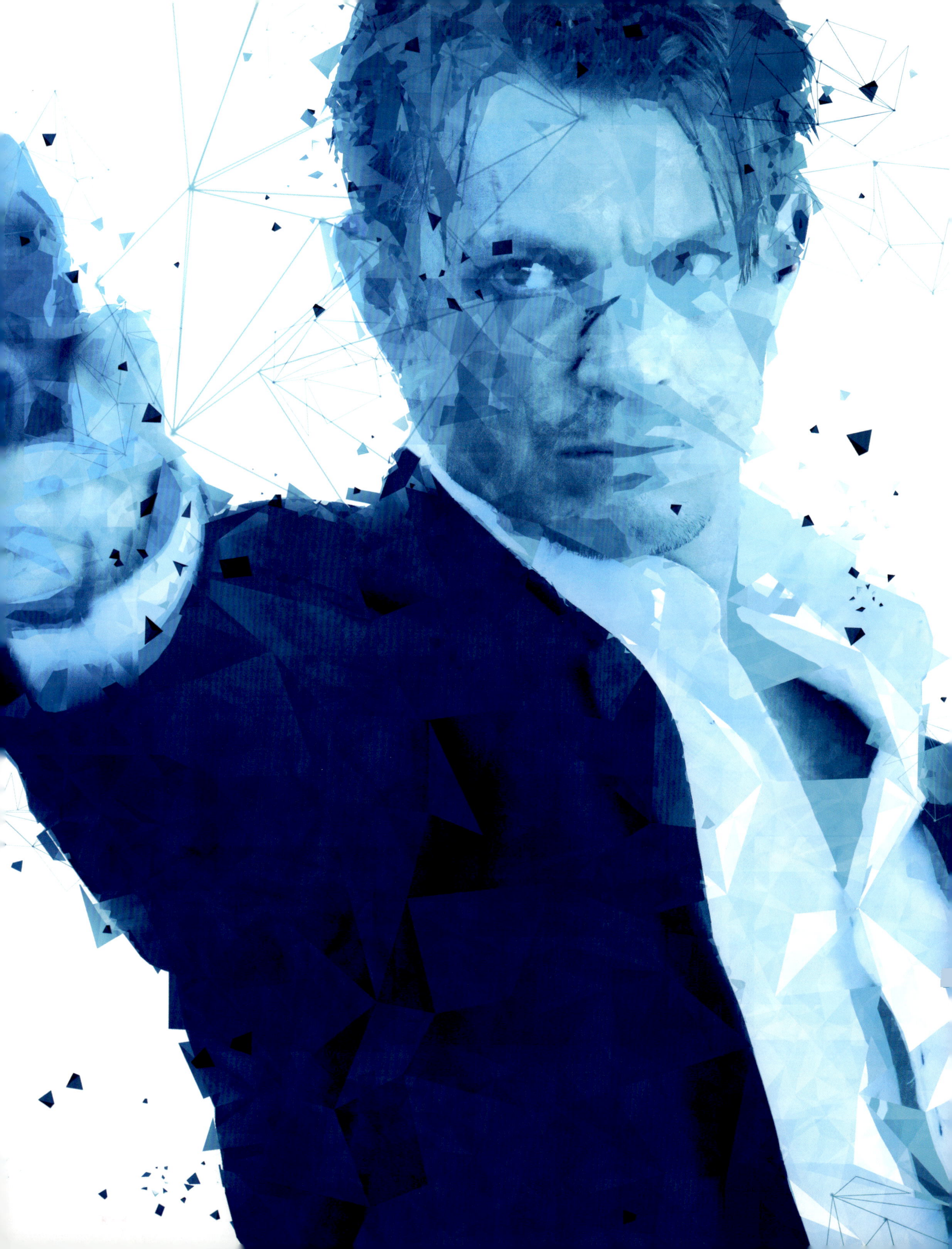

TAKESHI KOVACS

THE LAST ENVOY

Takeshi Kovacs (pronounced KO-vach) is played over two seasons of *Altered Carbon* by a number of actors. In season one, Joel Kinnaman plays Kovacs in the sleeve of Elias Ryker. Anthony Mackie plays Kovacs' main season two sleeve, which is described as "bespoke design by Khumalo Hardware, military use only, after-market upgrades: rapid healing, enhanced reaction time, biometric mag-plates." Will Yun Lee is "Kovacs Prime," who turns on the Protectorate and becomes the Envoy disciple of Quellcrist Falconer; in season two, Kovacs Prime is back, unaware that he's a clone created by Carrera. Among the other sleeves are Morgan Gao as Young Tak (his original body). Byron Mann as one early adult version as well as a clone made for the Fight Drome, and, in season two, JiHae plays Kovacs as a female torch singer, trying to avoid recognition on the world Maghda Prime.

Even as a child, Kovacs will do anything to protect his little sister Reileen. Series creator Laeta Kalogridis observes, "In the book, they are not sister and brother. That's one of the biggest changes from the book." Executive producer James Middleton explains the writers made them siblings "to create more intense dramatic stakes between the two characters."

THIS SPREAD: The many faces of Takeshi Kovacs, portrayed by Joel Kinnaman, Will Yun Lee, and Anthony Mackie.

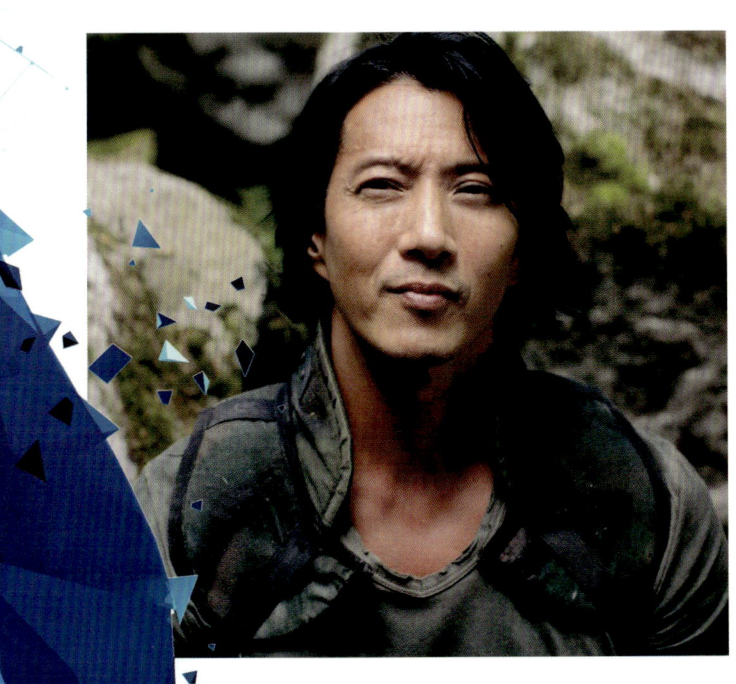

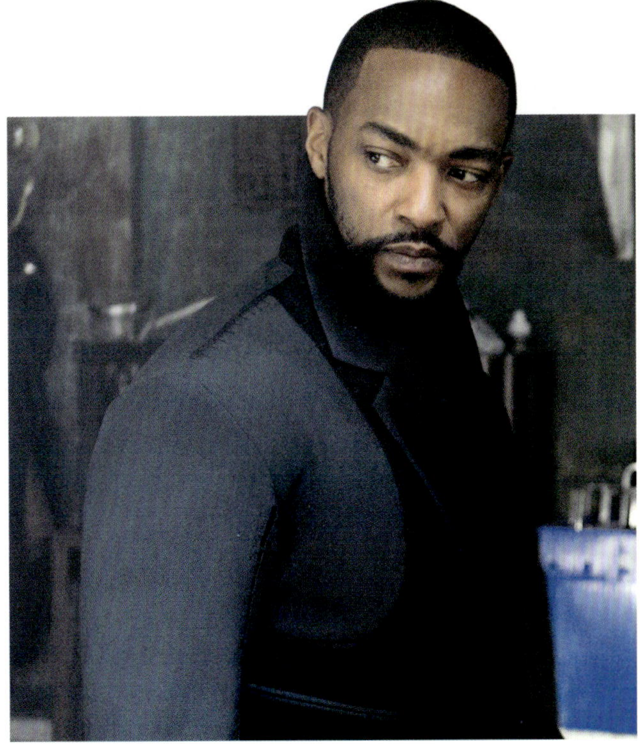

"There was something so fascinating about exploring [Kovacs'] family life," Kalogridis elaborates. "That [sibling relationship] gave us a better way in. There was also something so enticing about two kids who came from the same place, one [Reileen] who lived forever, and the other [Kovacs] who did not."

Kovacs was born on Harlan's World, where he and Reileen were abused by their alcoholic father. When Kovacs is age eight, he shoots and kills his father to protect Reileen. The Protectorate sees this willingness to use lethal violence at such a young age as evidence that Kovacs will make a good assassin, and offers to train him as a CTAC operative. When Kovacs is reluctant to leave Reileen, his CTAC handler Jaeger promises the little girl will be raised a good family. Kovacs later discovers that Jaeger never even tried to honor the promise. Reileen was put in an orphanage and ultimately sold to the Yakuza. When they find each other again, Kovacs and Reileen turn against their respective organizations and go on the run together.

Kovacs and Reileen join the Envoys, led by Quellcrist Falconer. The Envoys are dedicated to ending stack technology and the rule of the Meths. Kovacs agrees with their cause wholeheartedly, and also falls in love with Quellcrist. Reileen, hoping to get out of the Envoys and pry Kovacs away from Quell, has the Envoys infected with Rawling's virus, which causes them to kill each other and themselves during a Protectorate raid. Reileen and Quell are blown up in a shuttle explosion. Kovacs is apparently the only Envoy survivor.

"He goes on the run for a few years as a mercenary," Kalogridis relates, "because he's lost everything that he's ever cared about, his sister and the woman he loved, and the Envoys, who became like his family. He's found by the Protectorate and arrested by Jaeger. And then he's put on ice for two hundred and fifty years."

This all takes place before the main season one story, Kalogridis explains. "At the end of that quarter of a millennium, as the last Envoy, he's thought to have very particular skills, so he's woken back up by Bancroft." This is because, as we discover, Reileen in disguise has suggested to Bancroft that the last Envoy is the best man to investigate Bancroft's murder.

Executive producer/director Nick Hurran says, "Kovacs is brought into this new world, and he's charged with the task

BELOW: Byron Mann plays O.G. Kovacs (bottom). Will Yun Lee as Kovacs' birth sleeve (top).

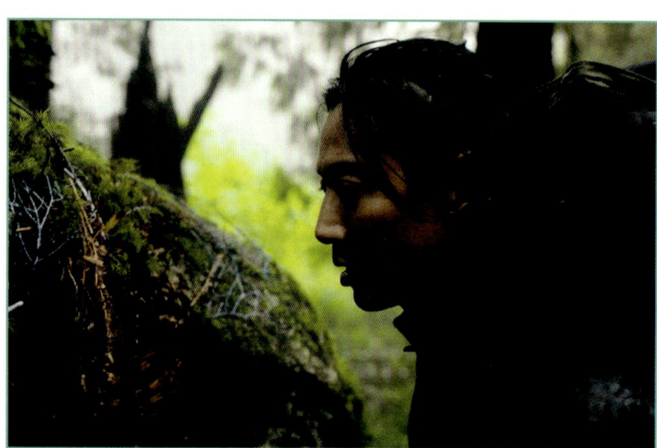

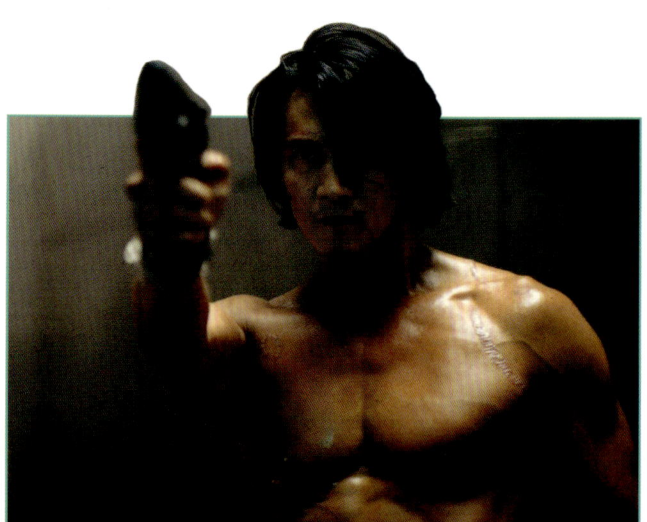

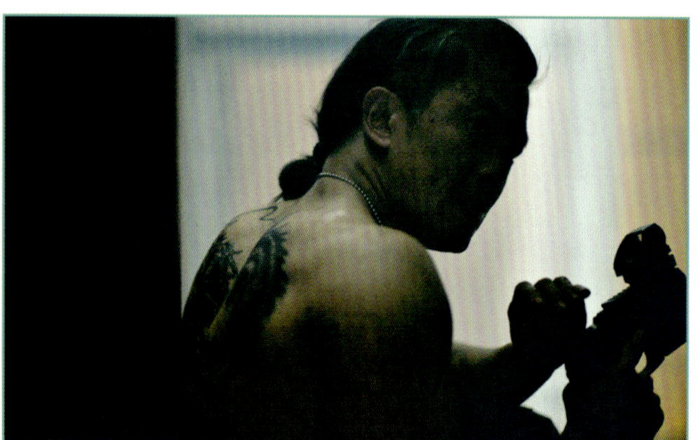

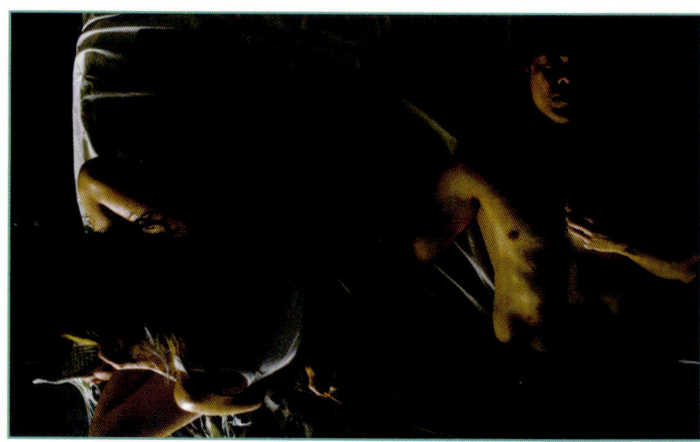

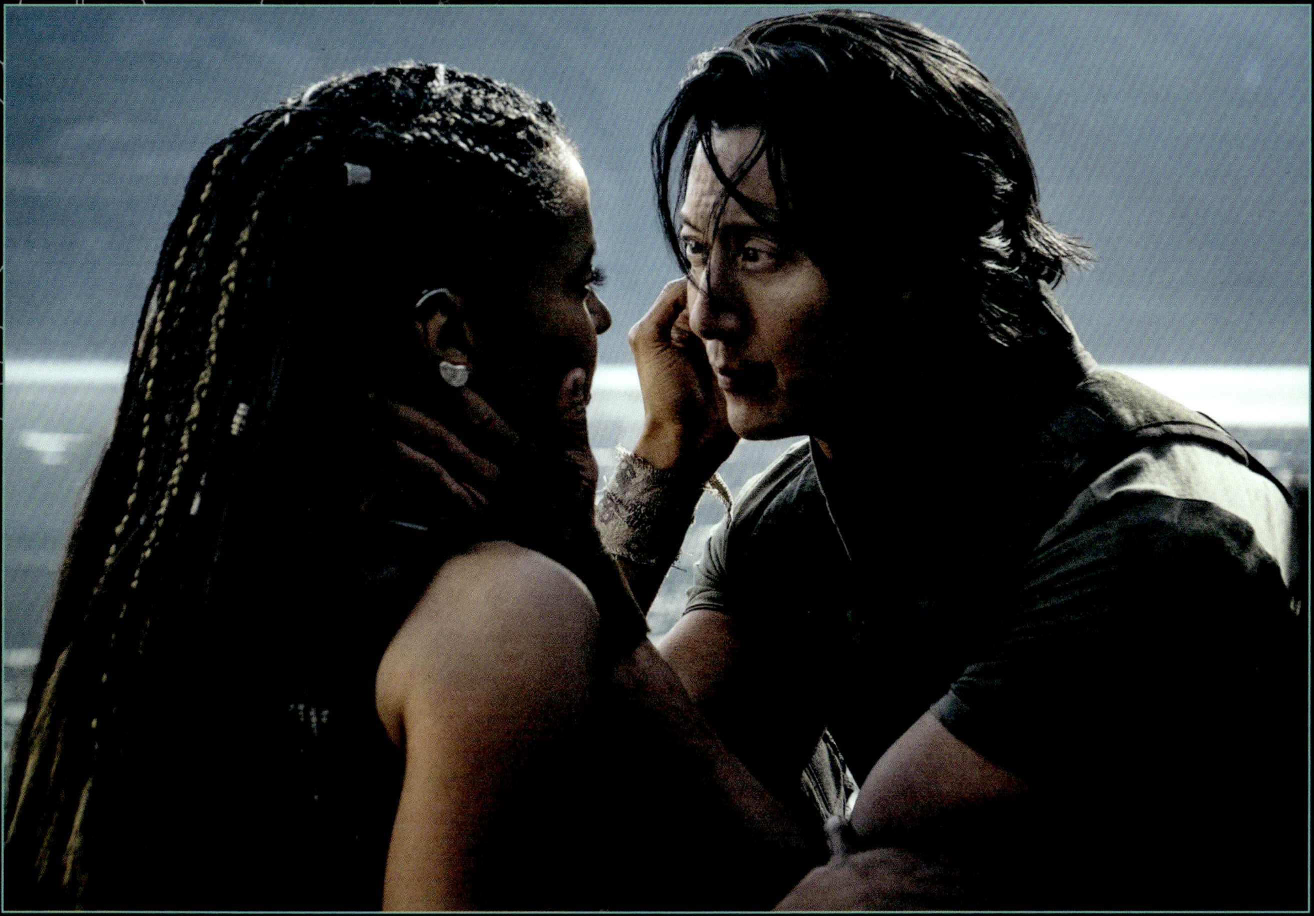

ABOVE: On Harlan's World with the Envoy leader Quellcrist Falconer.
BELOW: Kovacs with Reileen Kawahara, played by Dichen Lachman.

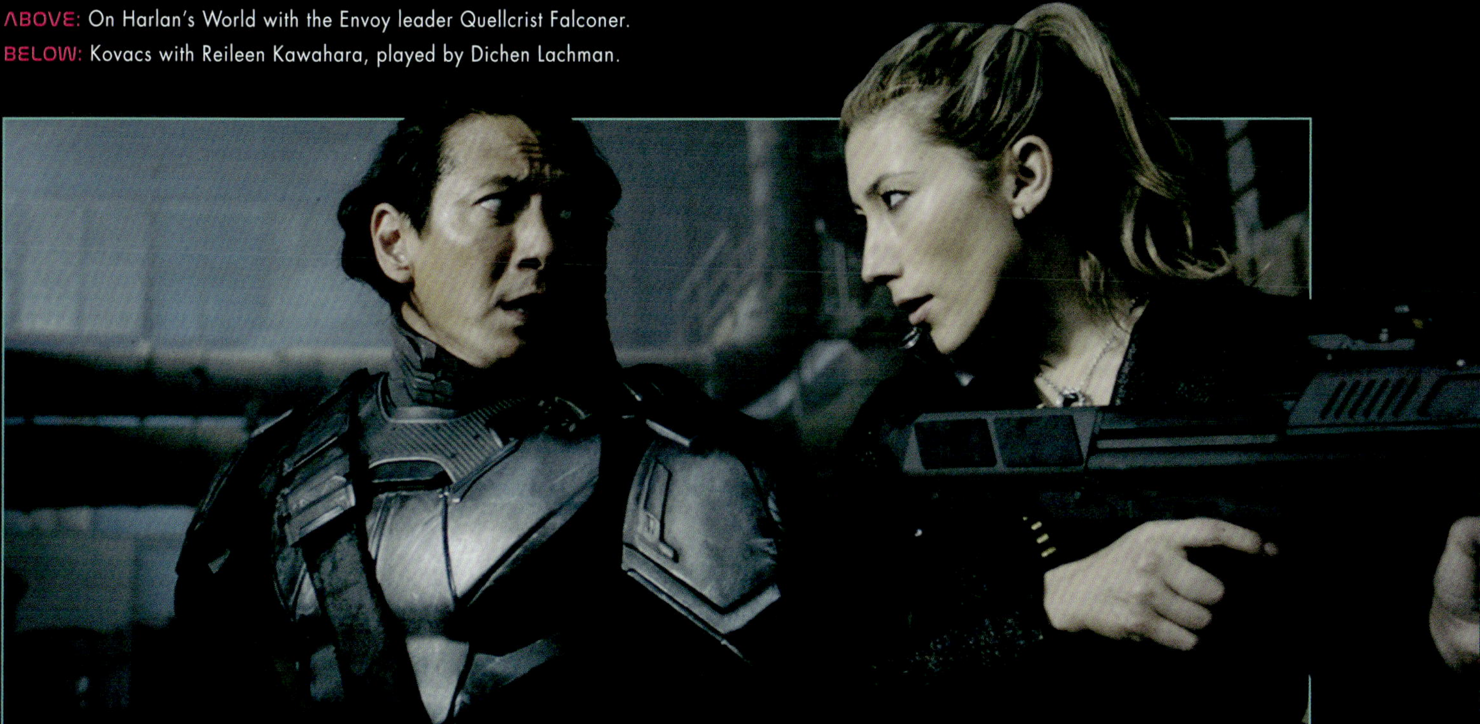

to find who murdered a wealthy industrialist, and comes face to face with the worst-case scenario. Everything that he had fought for as a warrior hundreds of years before has failed."

Kovacs ultimately decides to take the case because of a vision he has of Quell. Kalogridis explains, "She tells him cryptically that there is something for him to do, that she's trained him not to give up. Because he's thinking maybe about dying. He's a man who has a very tenuous connection to being alive. He's a little bit at war with himself. She tells him that he needs to finish the mission. We have absolutely no idea what that means. But something about her and about that relationship causes him to decide to stay."

Costume designer Ann Foley gave Kovacs several different styles in his Ryker sleeve. "Bancroft gives him clothes, and he looks like a Meth. [Pilot costume designer] Christine Wada did a beautiful job of portraying that idea. As the series progresses, you start to see Kovacs move into something that he feels more comfortable in, more Grounder-like, more detective-like. That's when we introduce the longer coat. When he's walking through the streets of Bay City in that fabulous coat, it's an iconic look."

Season one stunt coordinator Larnell Stovall says that Kovacs' combat techniques are one with his identity issues. "He adapted to this new world, and was always conscious of looking over his shoulder, remembering his lessons. He was in the past part of the best [fighters], part of the Envoys. How does that reflect in the future, when fighting styles have advanced? So we gave him a mixture of military combat, things from Russian styles, from American styles, a little hapkido, a little judo, taekwondo, knife fighting, kali style. I even looked at styles from Indonesia, such as salat, and just pieced a lot of them together. It's a hybrid, which we felt fit his character best, since his character was so traveled, and so extensively trained."

In training Kinnaman, Stovall recalls, "We started in the summer of 2016, when Joel first came down to our facility in Los Angeles. We talked about his athletic background, about the character. He started off two hours at a time, then two hours turned into three hours, and then private sessions became class sessions, because we normally have classes in the morning there for the team members and stunt people. Joel just joined class. He was there with us during judo, jiu jitsu, then we're going to choreography, so he was being tossed, he was flipping people, he was tapping people out. He really became one of the boys in the long run. He was there in the grind with us, and you see it on film."

Stovall adds that this doesn't happen very often. Even more uncommon, "Martha [Higareda, who plays Ortega] joined in, then Trieu [Tran, who plays Leung]. Next thing you know, I have most of the lead actors from *Altered Carbon* in class, excited, and going all out. It was something we'll never forget. It pushed us to think of better drills, better techniques, things to make them more efficient. It allowed us to bond in a very short amount of time.

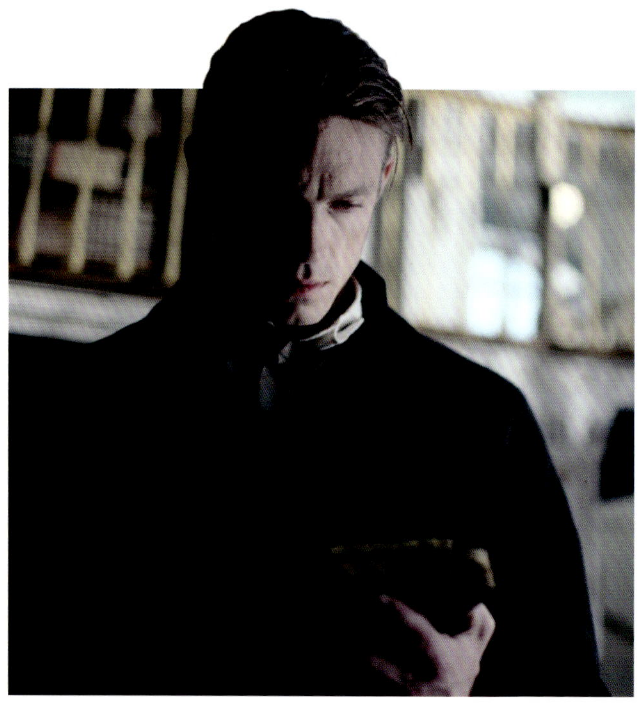

ABOVE: The wardrobe of Kovacs evolves throughout the first season.

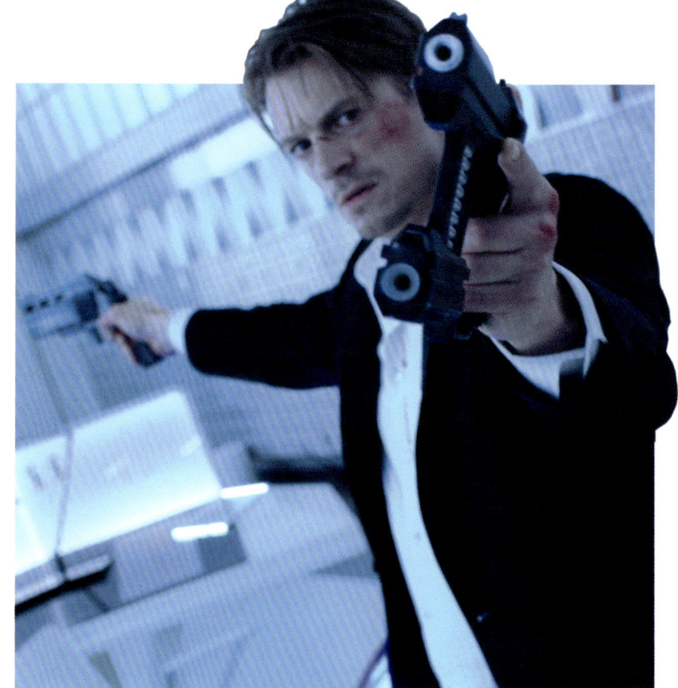

ABOVE: Kinnaman put in several hours every day to master Kovacs' fighting styles.

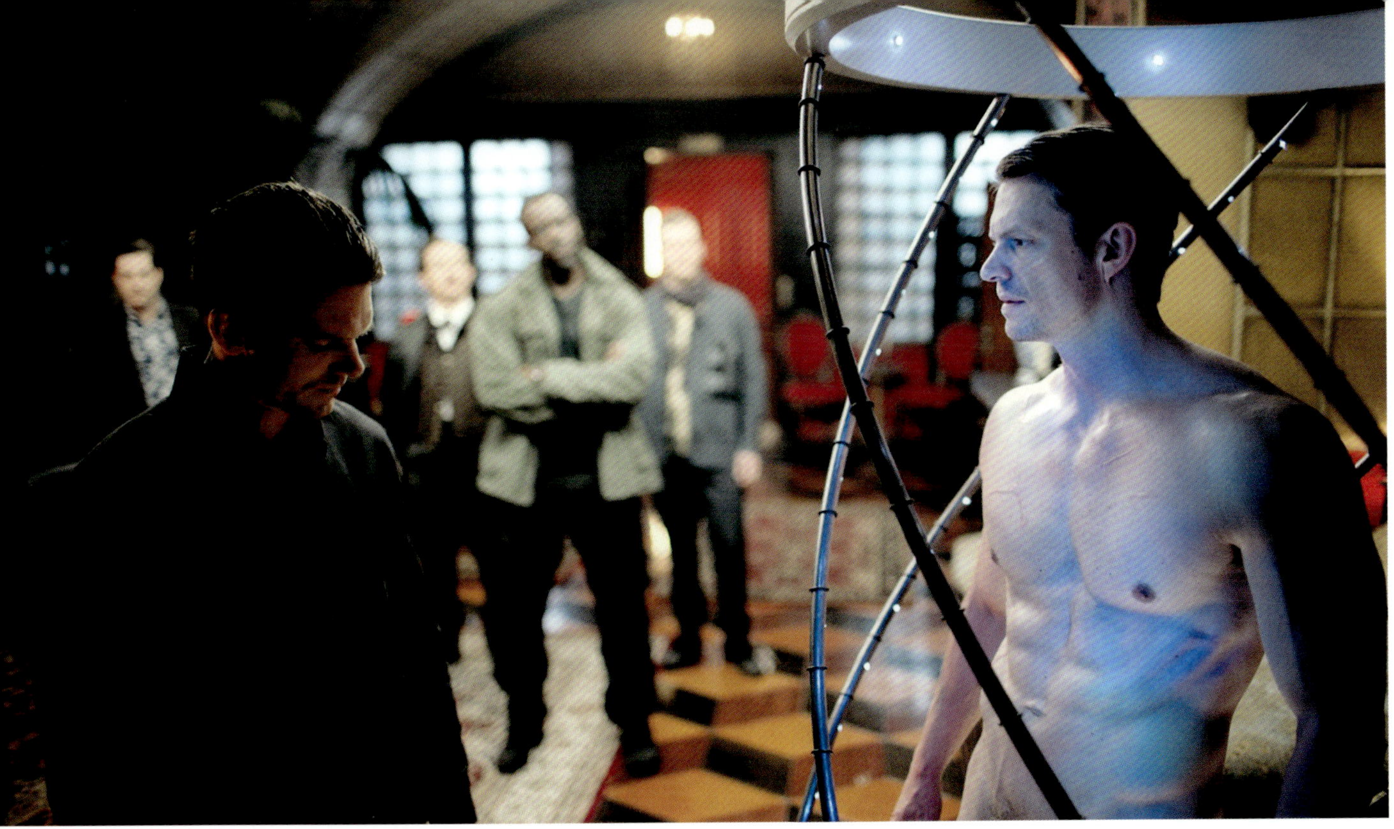

ABOVE: At the Raven the team planned their secret mission to take down Kovacs' sister.

"[Kinnaman] really loves trying to do all of his own action, within what's safe," Stovall continues. "He definitely knows when to step back, and when a stunt may seem too unsafe, and allow his double to step in. But Joel goes all out, he's professional, and always putting a hundred percent into it. The whole stunt department really appreciates that." The season two coordinators are Larry Lam, who worked with Stovall on season one, and Melissa Stubbs.

Season one VFX supervisor Everett Burrell echoes Stovall's enthusiasm for Kinnaman. "His patience and his tenacity. I admire that. We've done some complicated shots with Joel in terms of visual effects. And we'll get pretty close [to perfection], and he'll look at me and goes, 'Is it good?' and I go," Burrell makes an optimistic but noncommittal sound. "He goes, 'Let's keep doing it until we get it right.' He won't stop."

Burrell adds that VFX didn't have to do too much for Kinnaman's performance. "The one big one was, Joel broke his foot halfway through production. He had this fiberglass boot that he had to wear until his foot healed, so there were times when I had to paint that boot out."

When Kovacs has no choice but to battle Reileen, he is ultimately forced to kill her aboard Head in the Clouds as it crashes into the bay. After surviving this, Kovacs converses honestly with his clone in VR. Kovacs says that he doesn't know if Reileen realized that she'd become a monster, but the look on her face at the end was almost relief… maybe.

At the start of season two, Kovacs agrees to protect Harlan's World Meth Horace Axley in exchange for information on Quell's whereabouts. However, no sooner has Kovacs awakened in his latest sleeve then Axley is murdered. Kovacs' mission now is to rescue Quell. Protectorate representative Colonel Carrera, actually Kovacs' old mentor Jaeger, illegally creates a clone of Kovacs Prime to aid in tracking the current Kovacs.

Season two show runner Alison Schapker says that when *Altered Carbon* performers like Mackie come in to play an already-established character such as Kovacs, it is up to them to decide how much they want to study footage of earlier portrayals. "Every actor in this situation approaches this challenge individually – but absolutely, it is something we encourage them to explore."

In terms of differentiating Kovacs from Kovacs Prime in the writing, Schapker adds, "Luckily, we had strong guideposts. Kovacs Prime is effectively a younger version of Takeshi Kovacs. He exists because a copy of Kovacs' DHF was made just before he deserted CTAC. So Kovacs Prime is still

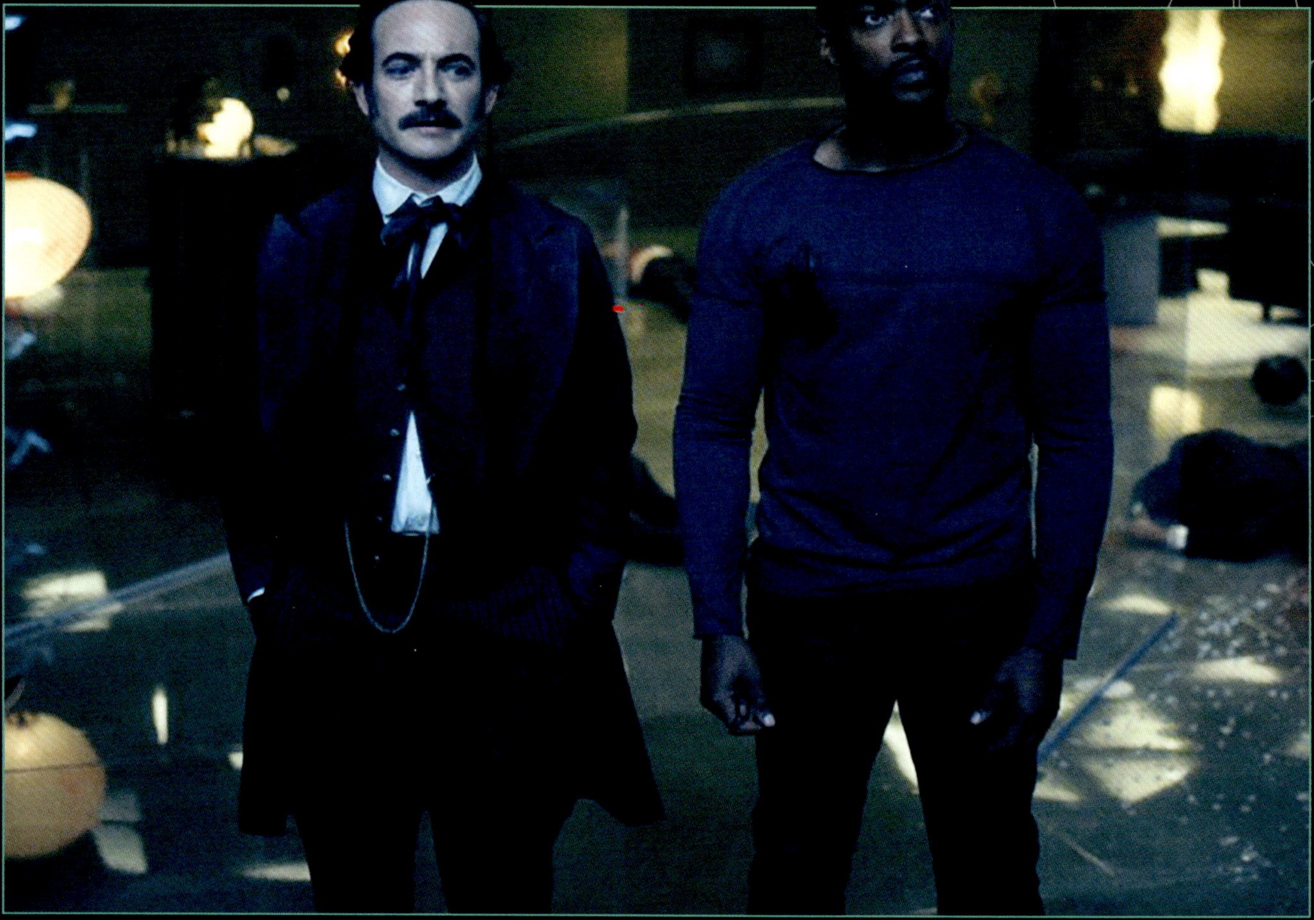

ABOVE: Kovacs welcoming some unexpected visitors to his room at the Raven.

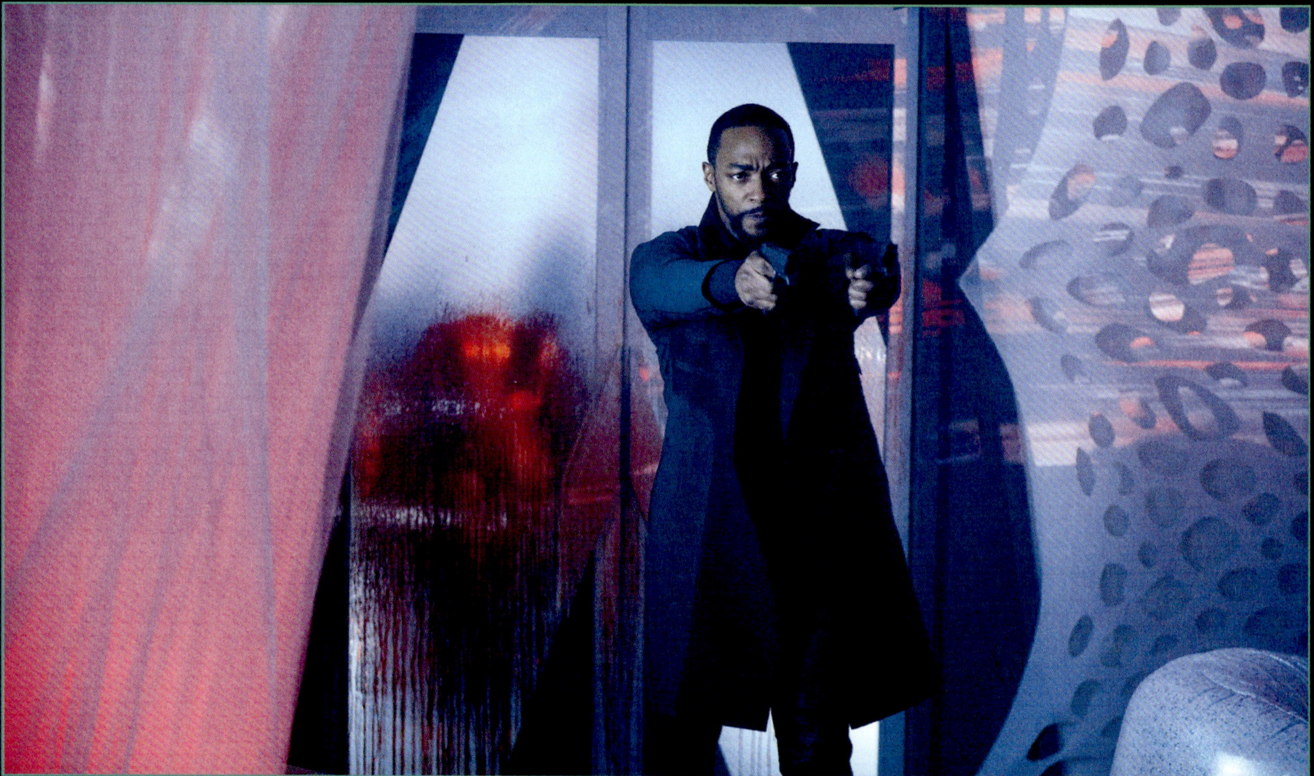

loyal to the Protectorate. This makes him very dangerous to our heroes. On the other hand, he is still the same man who once turned and switched sides, leaving open the possibility that it could happen again. So when Kovacs Prime meets up with Quell in season two, jury's out. Will history repeat itself? What consequences will that have for Prime and for Kovacs? We had a lot of fun in the writers' room exploring those questions."

Torben Liebrecht, who plays Carrera, and Simone Missick, who plays bounty hunter Trepp, both have scenes with Anthony Mackie's latest Kovacs and Will Yun Lee's Kovacs Prime.

"They are different personalities," Liebrecht says. "Will has a very calm take on Kovacs that is in a way still innocent, while Anthony's embodiment of him is more rugged, more cynical, a bit more fish-out-of-water approach. They also have different temperaments, but that's what makes it all so rich and so vivid."

"They both have a swagger and a sarcasm with these characters," Missick observes, "but they are completely different human beings. What we saw in season one is that, depending on the sleeve, the affectation, the voice, the mannerisms, all of those things change. And I think [that's true of] that change between Will and Anthony, but there are similarities. I spend more time remarking on the differences of those men, and how great they are as actors, more than anything."

Season two VFX supervisor Robert Munroe says that the biggest new development for Kovacs is that "Kovacs' sleeve is a highly-advanced weapon, even though it's a human form. For example, he's got mag plates in his hands. If he wants anything magnetic, he can activate the mag plates. Two guns sitting on the floor, he doesn't have to run over and grab those, he just reaches out his hands, spreads his fingers, the mag plates are activated, the guns fly into his hands. The mag plates are completely subcutaneous, so you just see the effects of them." VFX comes into it because "They're CG guns."

Says Kalogridis, "The core of *Altered Carbon* for me is Takeshi Kovacs and his profound damage. He's a man who wants to believe that he is something of a sociopath, but he isn't at all. Who wants to believe that he cares about nothing, but that's not remotely true. And someone who is displaced out of his life, and thrown into a world that he did not want to be part of."

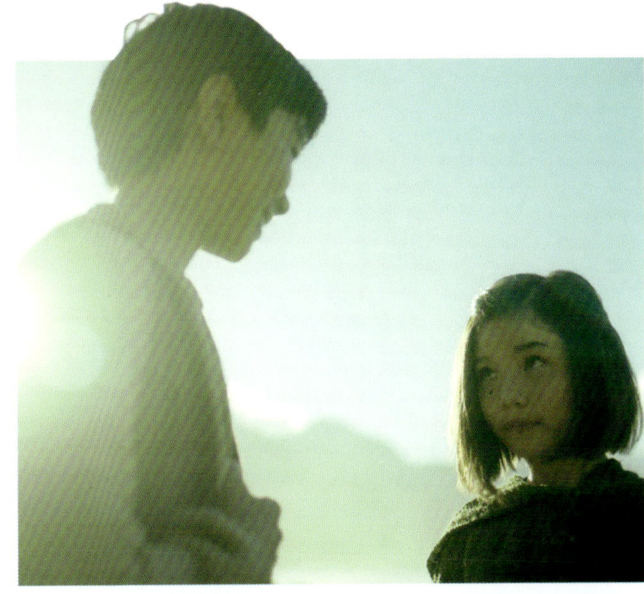

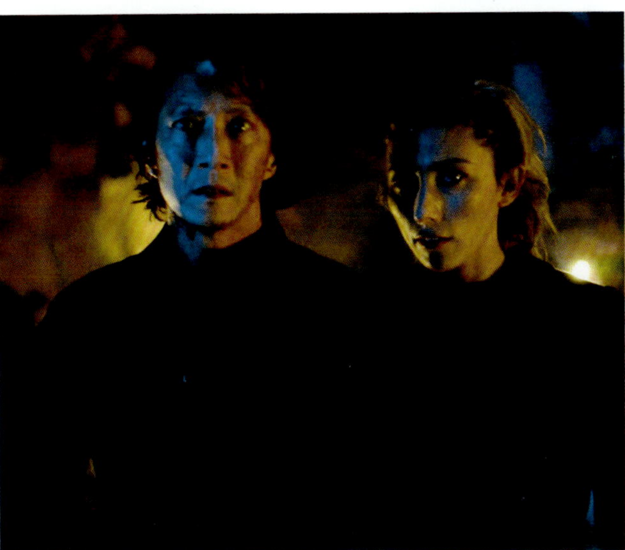

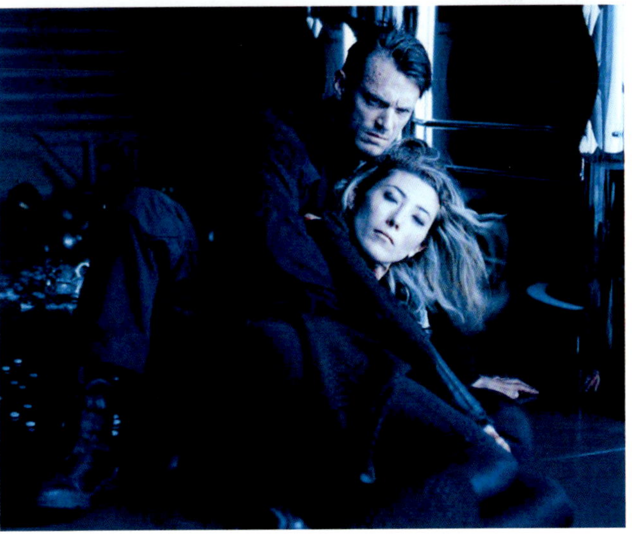

LEFT: Mackie's Kovacs on the brink of a shootout.

ABOVE: Kovacs with his sister Reileen in different eras.

BAY CITY

GROUND LEVEL LIVING

On the Grounder level of Bay City, formerly San Francisco, the working classes scrabble to survive. The middle-class Twilight is a hundred floors up. High above that is the rich Aerium.

Production designer Carey Meyer relates that Bay City is held up by massive buttresses. "The architecture is buttressed like an old church would have been. The new church is science and technology, [which] plays into creating height and having Aerium and getting to God. For me, that's the identity of the show, playing with how religion is at a loss, but has been supplanted by technology."

Meyer adds that the main Bay City street set was his favorite *Altered Carbon* creation. "It was the first vision that I had in my mind. At our Vancouver facility, stage three is over four hundred feet long and forty-five feet wide and fifty-five feet tall, [which] gave you the long, narrow scope that lends itself to a street. Beyond those dimensions, it had all these vents and weird bits and pieces, doorways and little hallways that we could feed into and create many little interiors, and the grand exterior. There's a central area between the two main bridges that we flip around and turn into different areas. We chopped it down to three hundred feet, to create some spaces beyond the set [within the remaining hundred feet] so that we can backlight some trans lights. It also gives us room for production to move around."

BOTTOM: Concept art of the Bay City area, showing the iconic Golden Gate Bridge.

RIGHT: The decaying streets of Bay City were built in a studio.

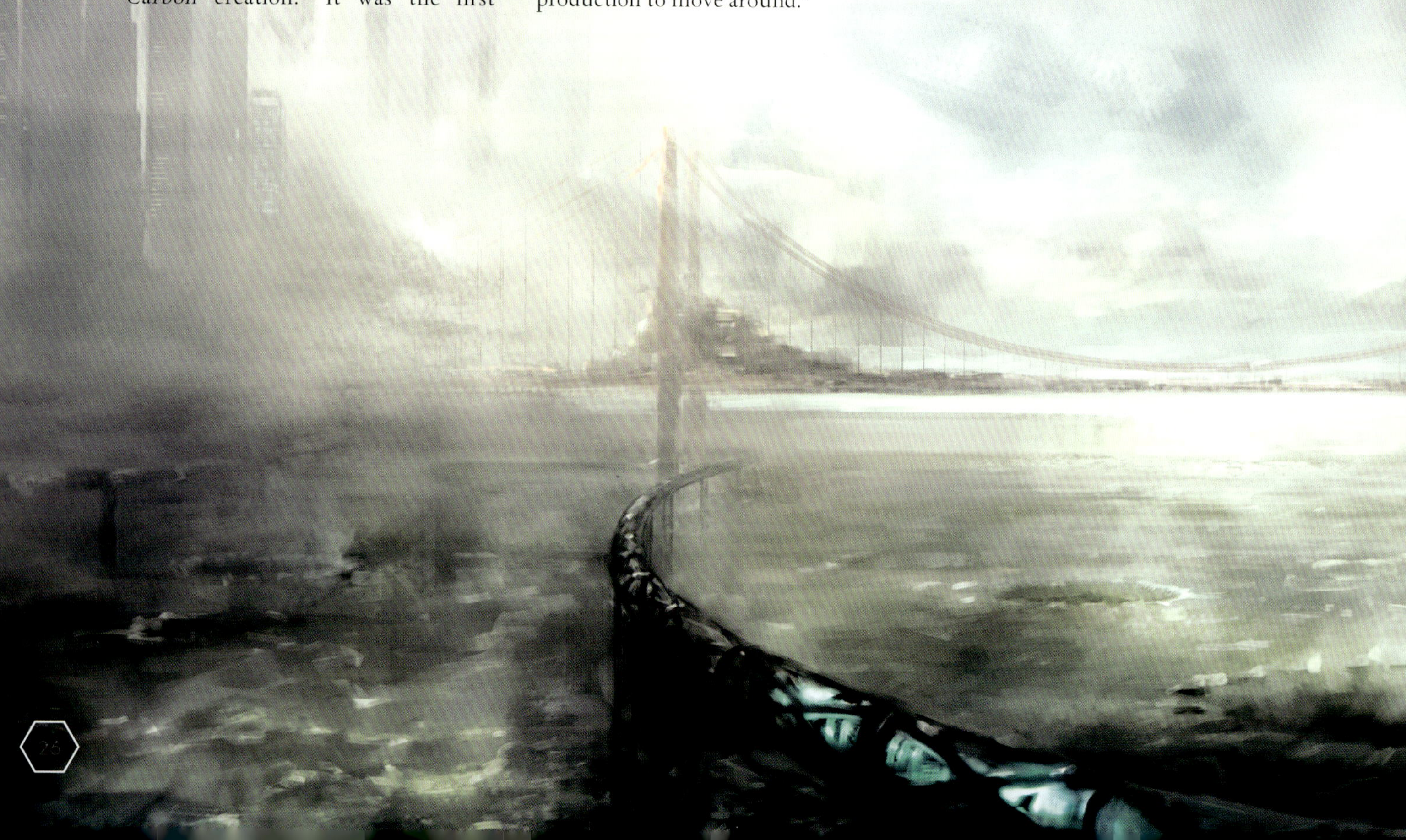

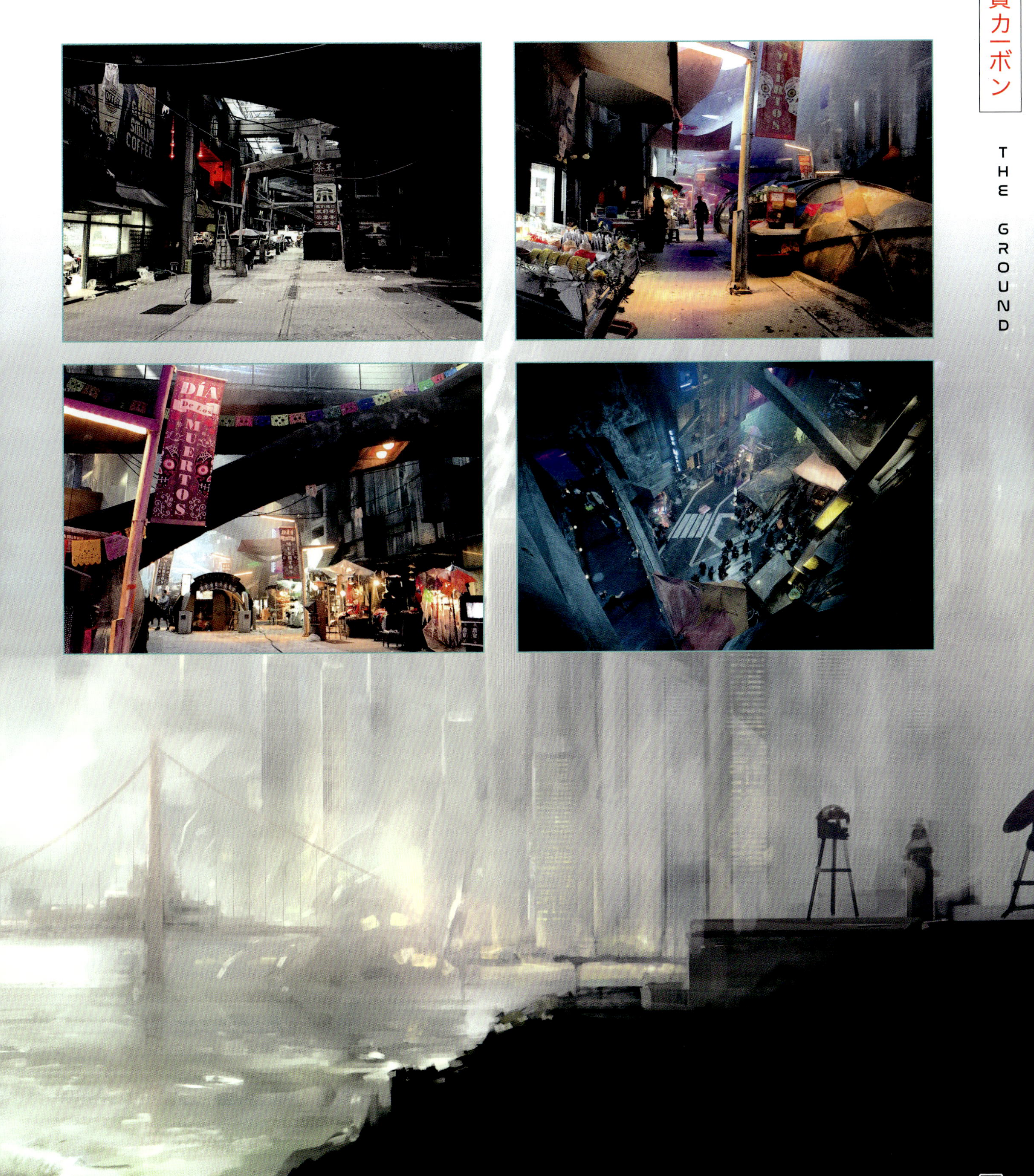
MUERTOS
DÍA
De Los
MUERTOS

The ground level, Meyer continues, exists "in a texture of rust and decay. That street set wants to have water and rust and cracked concrete, and it's absolutely the worst place to live in Bay City."

VFX supervisor Everett Burrell feels "lucky" that much of Bay City existed practically. "Carey and I made this commitment to try to [avoid] green and blue screen as much as possible, to shoot things real. If you're on normal height level on the street, it was all in-camera."

Still, "Anything above the forty-foot mark, we had to add. We also did a Lidar scan of the street, which is a digital copy of that set, and gave that data to Double Negative. We helped build big, painted backdrops on either end, printed on special Firelight Ink, so if you had street signs in the matte painting, they would glow if you put UV light on them."

The VFX team also added some other unique features, including a dam around San Francisco Bay, Burrell explains, "Because global warming in the future has raised the water level."

Property master Nevin Swain says he oversaw the job of making sure the extras had possessions in their hands. "One of the big things that they hammered on was that people have lives, they have places to go, and things to do. Sometimes, we'll have up to five hundred background on that street set. They're commuting to work, they're buying food, there's some drug use. Much like today's world," except: "we don't do a lot of phones."

BELOW: The VFX team built upon San Francisco's Bay Area to create the futuristic Bay City.

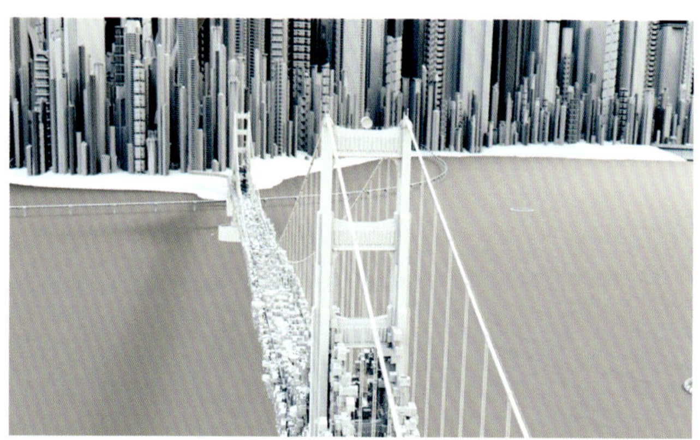

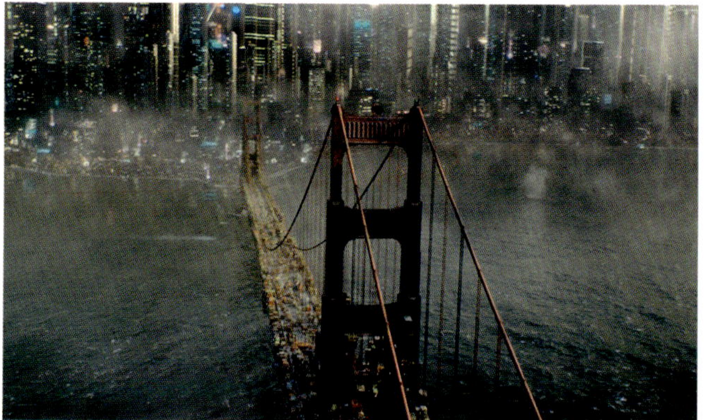

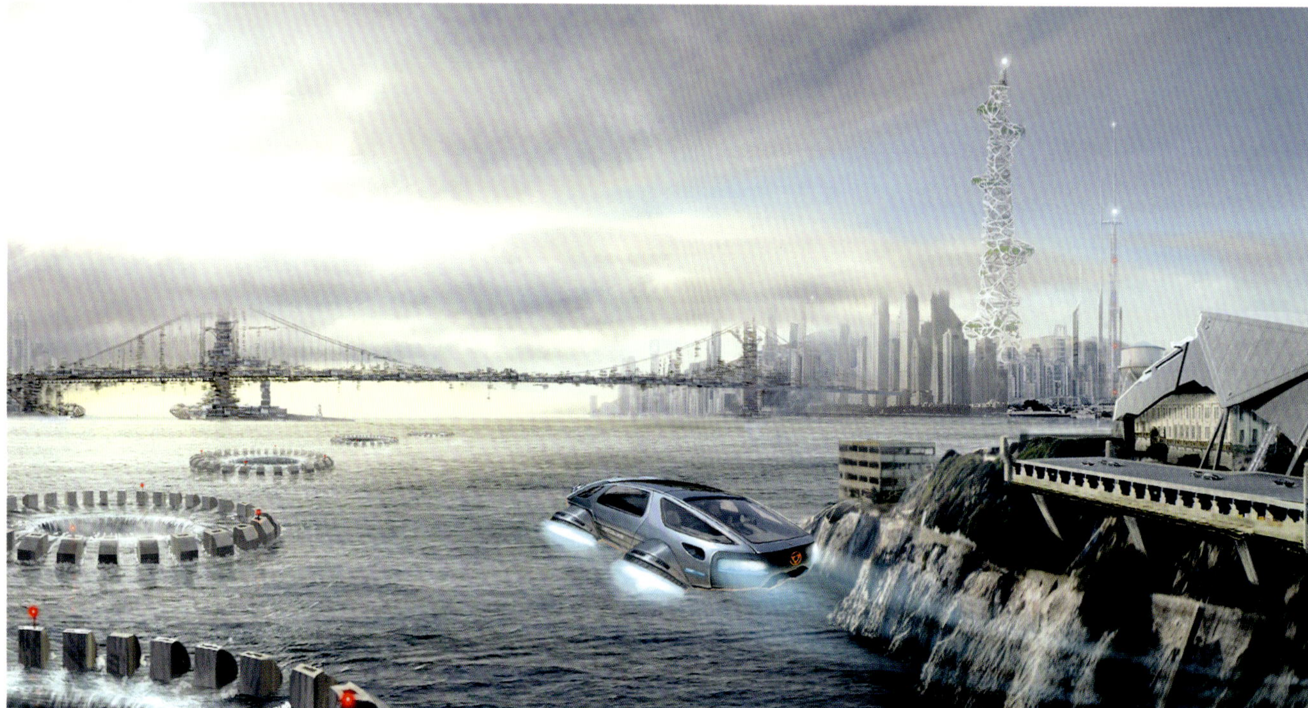

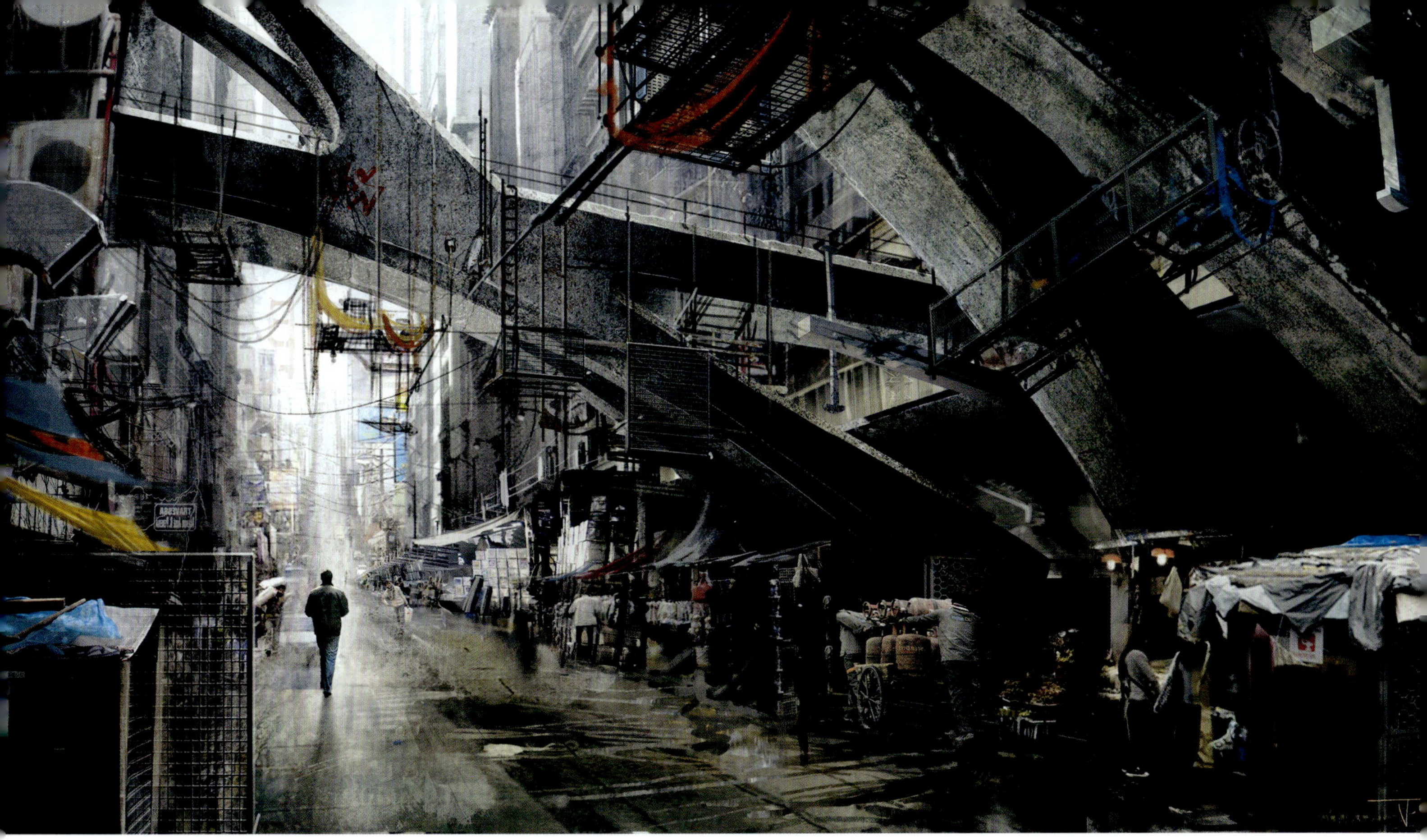

THIS PAGE: This page: Artist's impressions of Bay City, seen from the ground and the air.

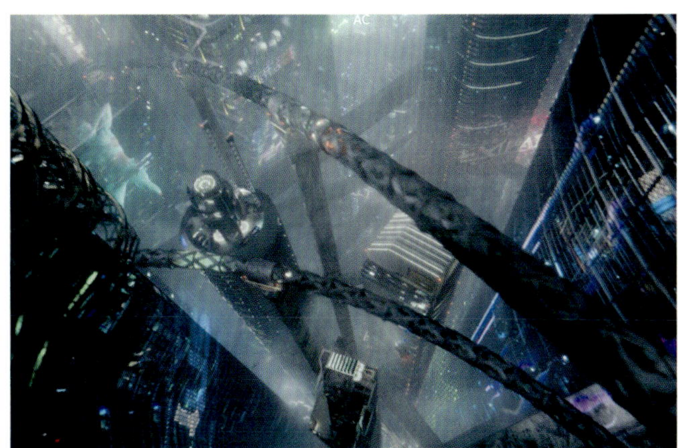

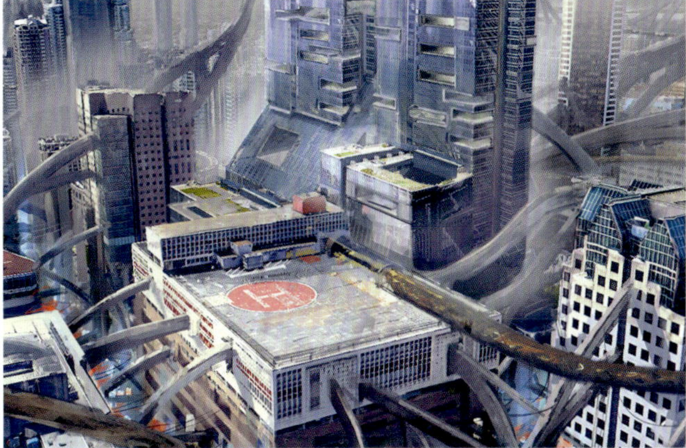

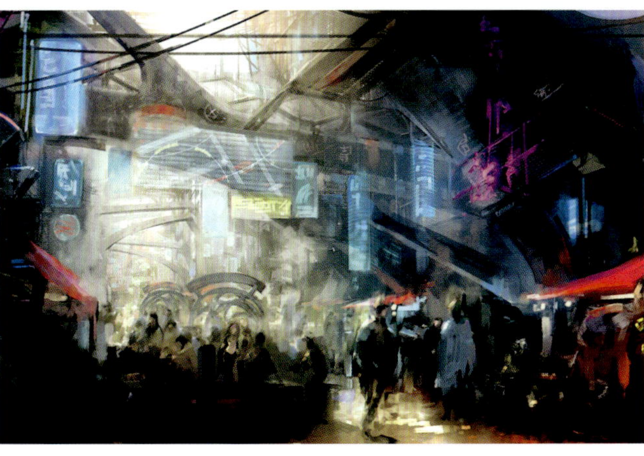

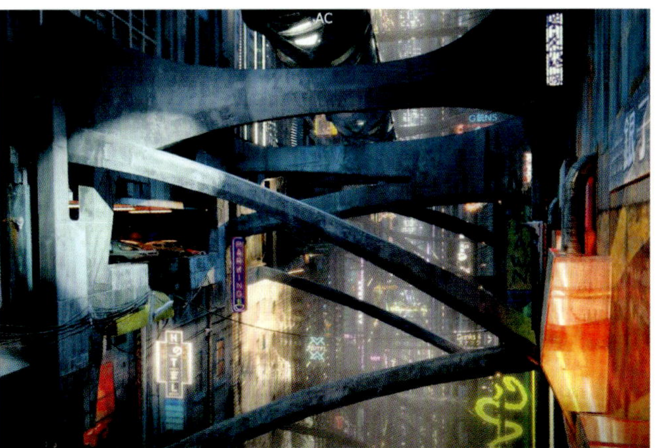

KRISTIN ORTEGA

THE TENACIOUS DETECTIVE

Lt. Kristin Ortega, played by Martha Higareda, is a detective in Bay City Police's Organic Damage division. Many of Ortega's colleagues on the force are content to look the other way and preserve the status quo when the rich commit crimes. However, Ortega is dedicated to uncovering the truth, no matter if it costs her career, or even her life.

Ortega is convinced that her lover, fellow police detective Elias Ryker, was framed for murder. She has been paying his sleeve mortgage, but was outbid by Laurens Bancroft, who uses Ryker's body to house Kovacs. Ortega tails Kovacs not, as she claims, because she's afraid he will engage in terrorist activities, but because he's in Ryker's sleeve.

Series creator Laeta Kalogridis describes Ortega as "very emotional and volatile and frustrated with Kovacs showing up. The first time she sees Kovacs, he's wearing the face of the man she loves. And every time he puts himself in danger, he's endangering the body of the man she loves. So the relationship is quite complicated from her perspective. Does she care about him because of the body he's wearing? Does she care about him because of the mind that's inside that body? It gets more and more difficult for her to tell."

For Kalogridis, this conflict is one of the ways that *Altered Carbon* explores identity. "We all have this intersection of who we are that comes from what's mental and what's physical. One place we've hit a lot in the story is, what is love? How much of it is chemical, how much of it is physical, how much of it is the soul? The whole thing between Ortega and Kovacs touches very much on that."

BELOW: Lt. Kristin Ortega follows Kovacs, who is using the sleeve of her lover, Elias Ryker.

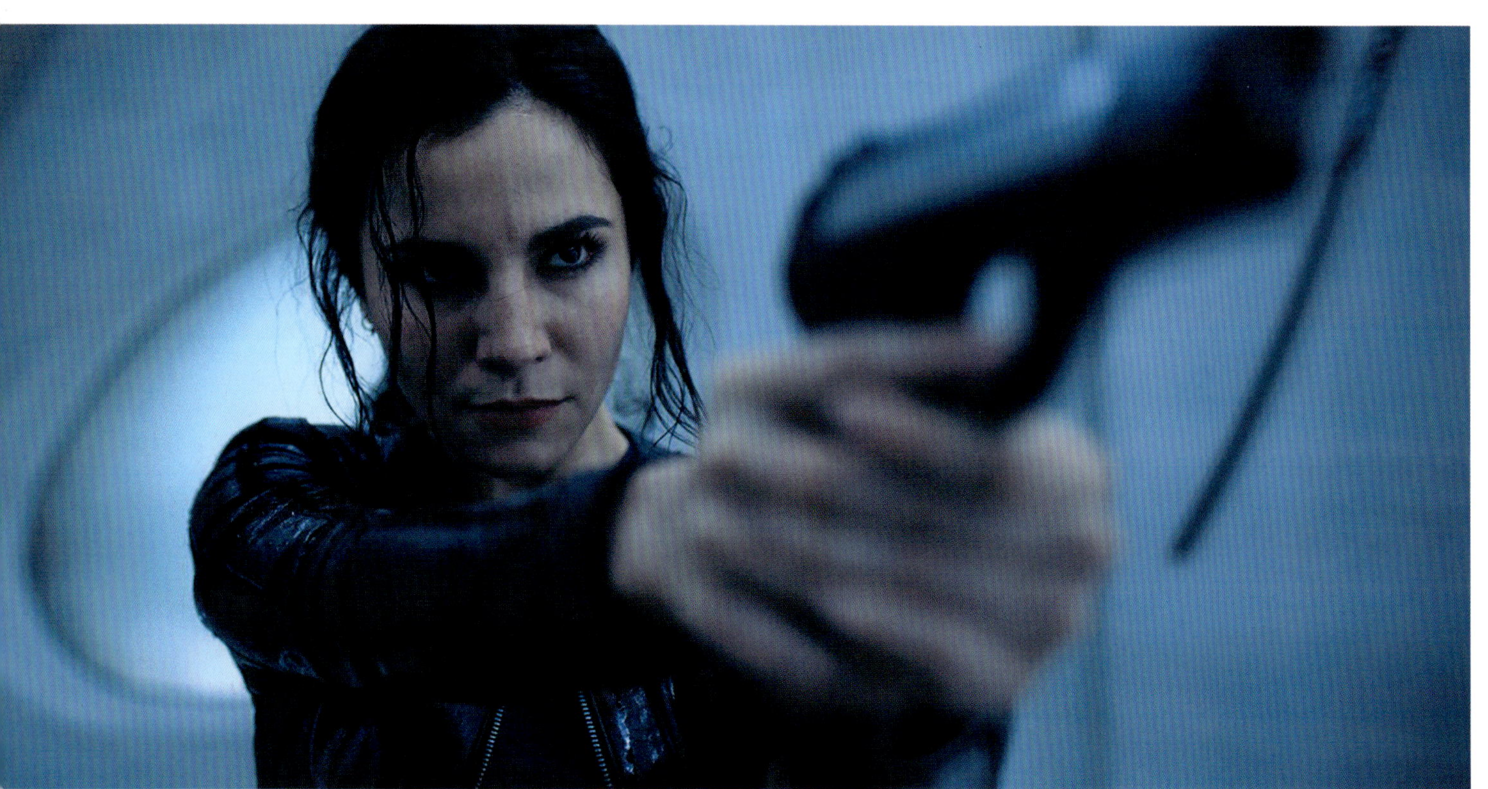

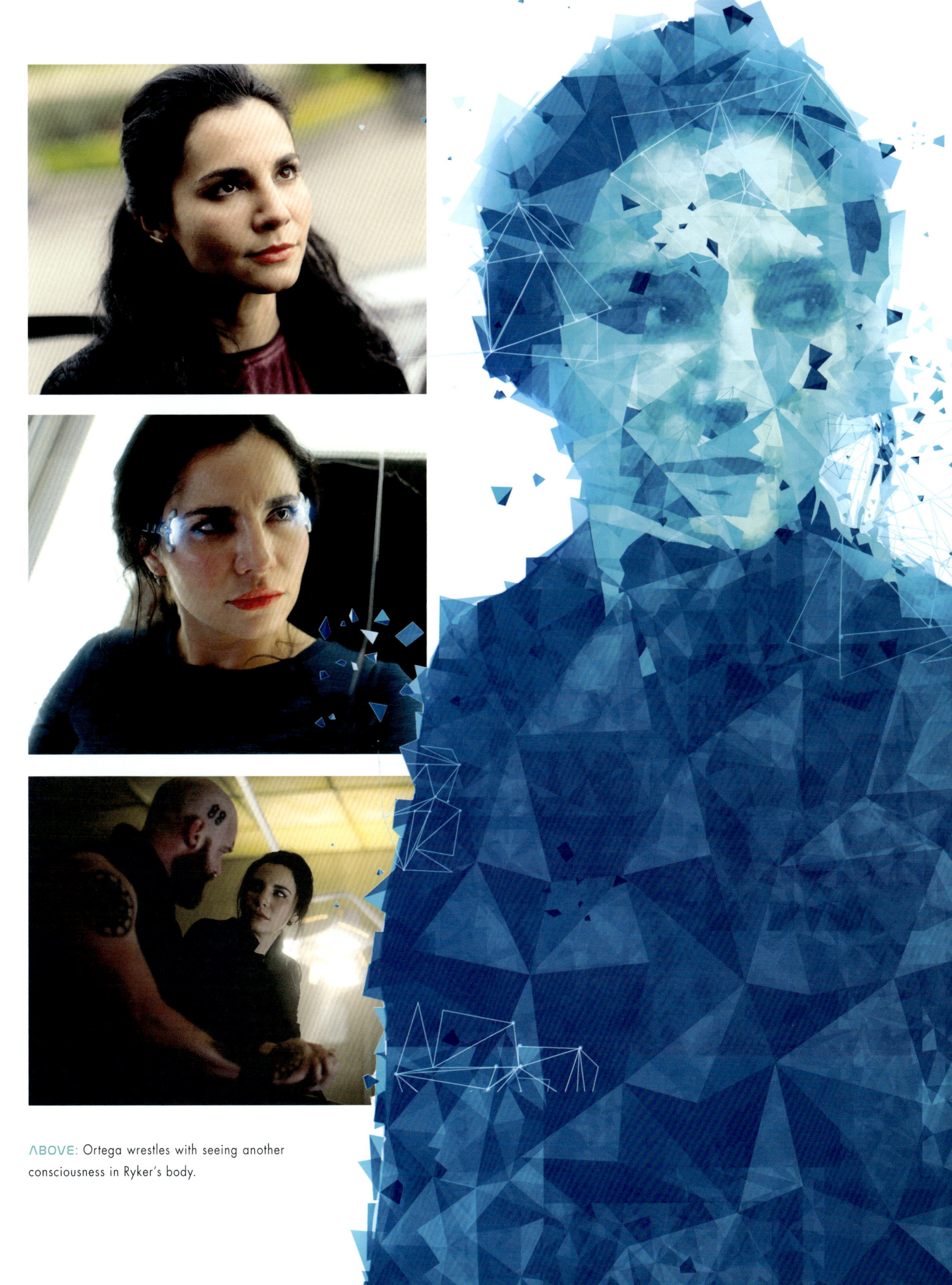

ABOVE: Ortega wrestles with seeing another consciousness in Ryker's body.

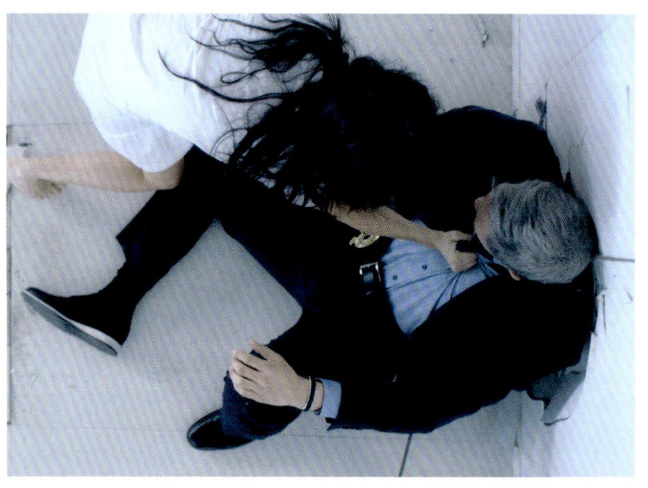

ABOVE: Ortega gets into an altercation with Captain Tanaka.

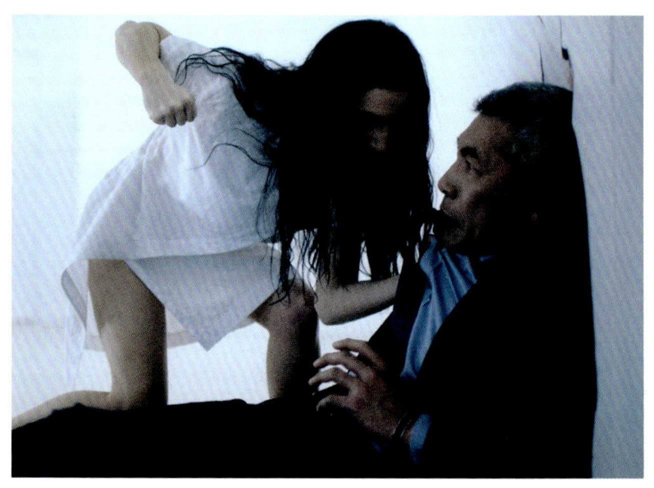

BELOW: The powerful bionic arm that Ortega gains halfway through season one.

Costume designer Ann Foley says that she and fellow designer Ann Martin discussed Ortega's character progression. "When we first meet Ortega, we wanted to show her emotional headspace with the color palette, so we kept it really dark. When we do flashbacks, she's in lighter colors that show happier times. It was important to show Ortega as a strong female character and not put her in over-sexualized clothes, but to keep it real. It was also about making sure that she could do her fighting in her costumes."

Ortega's fighting style is introduced in a scene where she's sparring with Abboud, stunt coordinator Larnell Stovall relates. "She was hitting mitts, she was doing little kicks, she was doing a boxing drill. We finished up with some judo, to show she knows how to handle and throw people."

Stovall put Higareda and other cast members through what he calls "mini-boot camp." He enthuses, "[Higareda] goes all out with everything. She's passionate, she's intense, professional. She's really good with her hands, so we put a lot of boxing in there, and a lot of low kicks to cater to what a police officer may do, mixed with her gun and tactical techniques. Martha evolved a lot through her training. In a very short amount of time, she stepped up and killed it."

Kalogridis is similarly enthusiastic about Higareda. "She's amazing. She has this presence. She's the best Ortega you could ever possibly hope for. She feels like she's very much part of Bay City, but also part of her own culture."

One of Kalogridis' favorite sequences is when Ortega and her temporarily spun-up grandmother are smoking pot in the police station morgue. "She's [sleeved] in this big hulking white guy. The actor, Matt Biedel [who also plays one of Kadmin's sleeves], is fluent in Spanish, and he really feels like her grandma. You feel that connection between them."

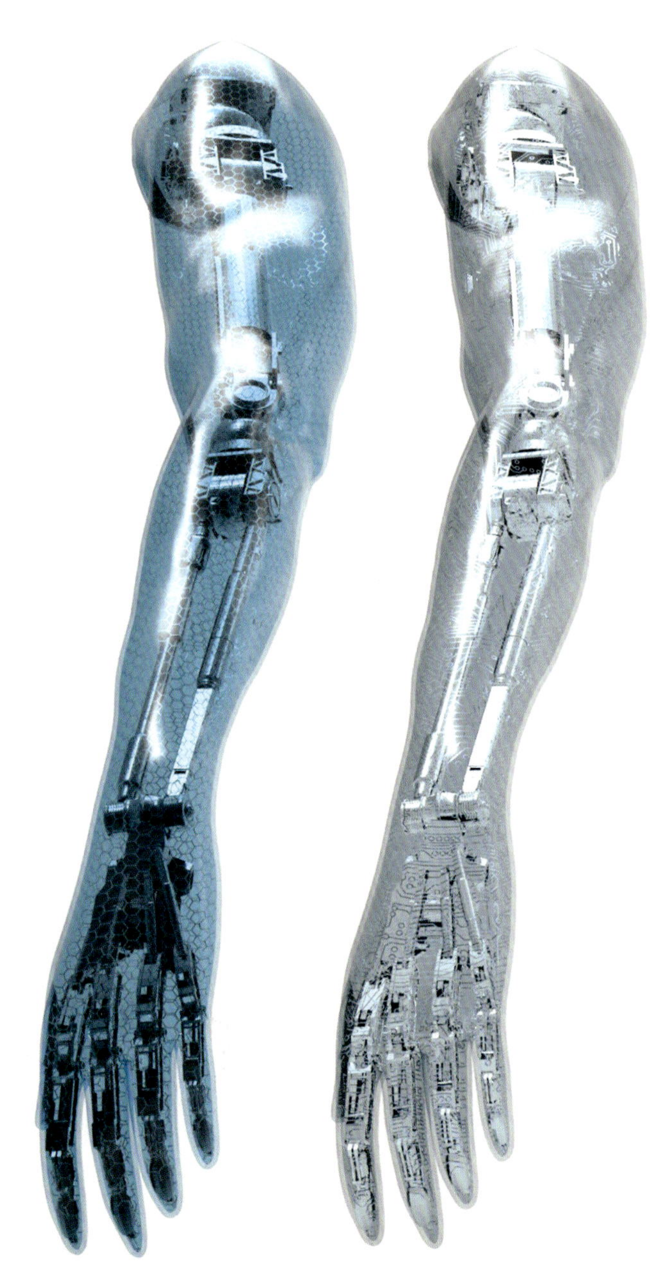

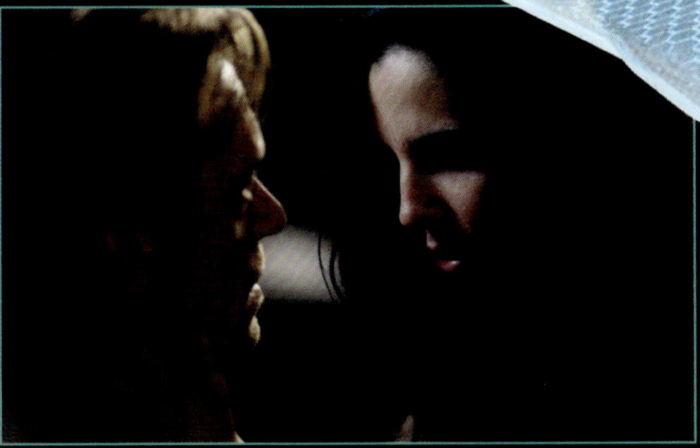

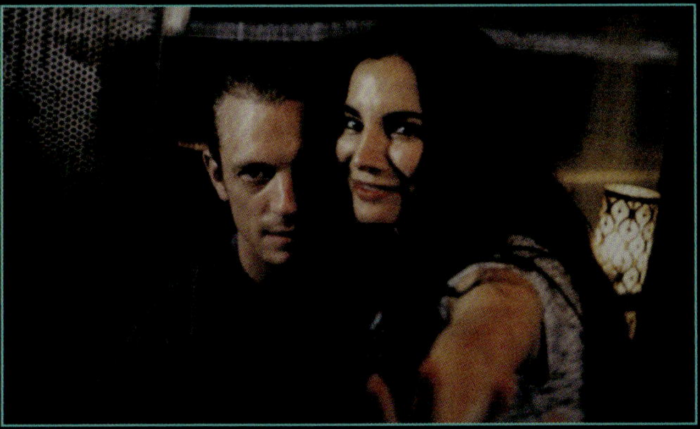

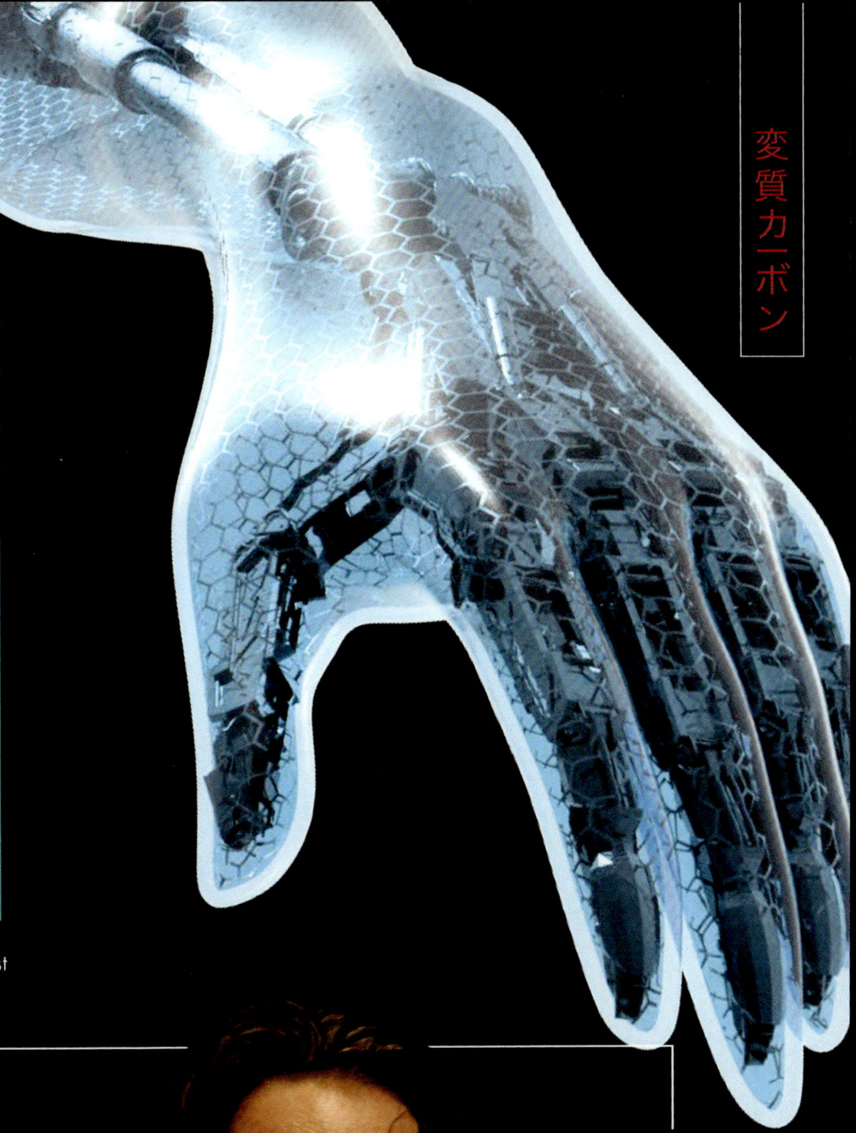

ABOVE: Ortega with Ryker, before he was framed for murder and lost his sleeve to Bancroft.

ELIAS RYKER

Elias Ryker, played by Joel Kinnaman, is a disgraced Bay City police detective and the lover of Kristin Ortega. We gradually learn that Ryker wouldn't let go of the Mary Lou Henchy murder – he grew up with her and (correctly) believed her coding had been faked, so Reileen had him framed for murder. Reileen convinced Bancroft that he needed Takeshi Kovacs' help; Bancroft chose to sleeve Kovacs in Ryker's body to punish Ortega for pursuing another case against him.

As Kovacs' stack adjusts to Ryker's body, he's in a body sac, breathing through an umbilical device. VFX supervisor Everett Burrell explains it would be too dangerous to seal Kinnaman inside. "They built a really good prosthetic body of Joel that was inside the bag and put fluid in."

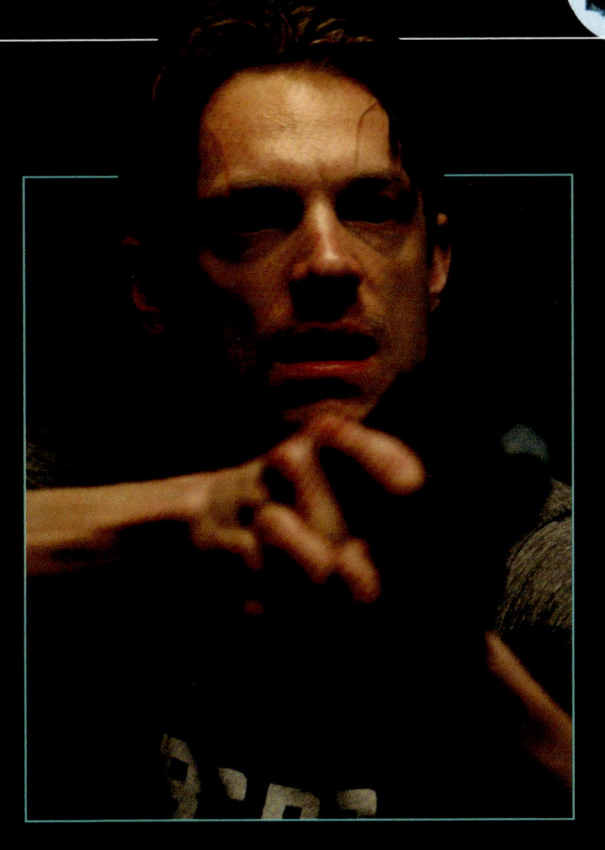

THE POLICE STATION

FELL STREET, BAY CITY

Bay City's Fell Street police station is the base from which Captain Tanaka, and (initially) Detectives Kristin Ortega, Samir Abboud, and Elias Ryker operate. The building follows Bay City's general design aesthetic, explains production designer Carey Meyer. "We played with the identity of Christianity, and the rise of technology sort of becoming a new religion. It's very much present in Richard K. Morgan's book, how the police precinct was really an old church taken over by the police. So we built a precinct like that. On the street, we had the exterior, an old church that has been turned into a police precinct. It's a very dramatic, different sort of look than all the [other] streets that we've been shooting."

VFX supervisor Everett Burrell relates that the police station interior was all live action, although it has holographic windows. For the exterior, the VFX team enhanced Meyer's design, "where you saw the outside of stained-glass windows and that Gothic structure embedded into this futuristic world. We put shadows of detectives walking around behind it to give it some life, so on the outside, you'd see movement back there, so it wouldn't just be static."

Prop master Nevin Swain says the police handguns were developed with Paco of Unlimited Design. These 3D printed models were patterned after the design for Ortega's weapon, which had to be compact in size, "because she's quite a small lady, so we wanted something that would fit within her hand. We used the same one for Ryker and Tanaka."

BELOW: Interior and exterior shots of Fell Street Station.

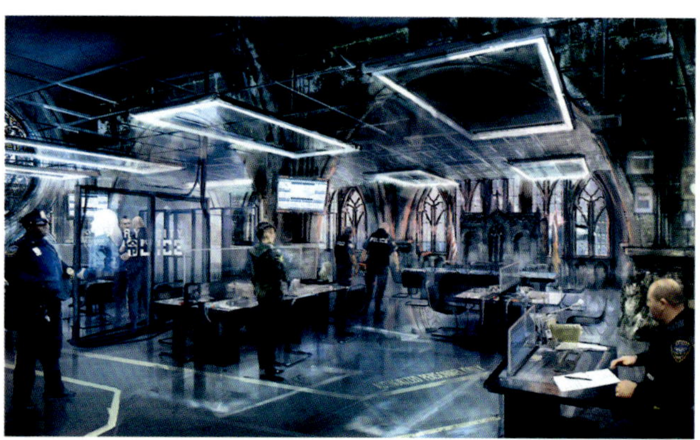

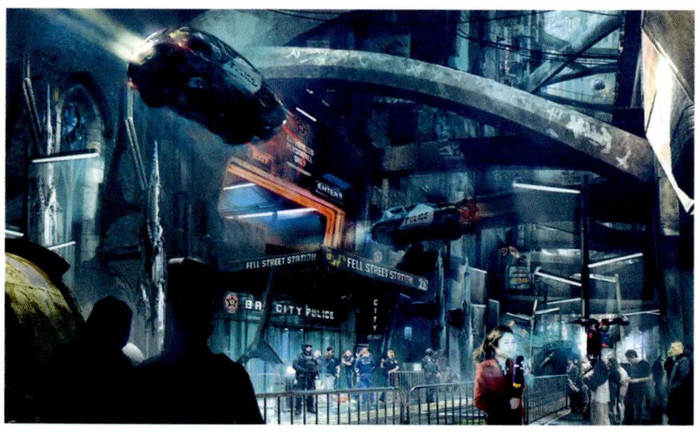

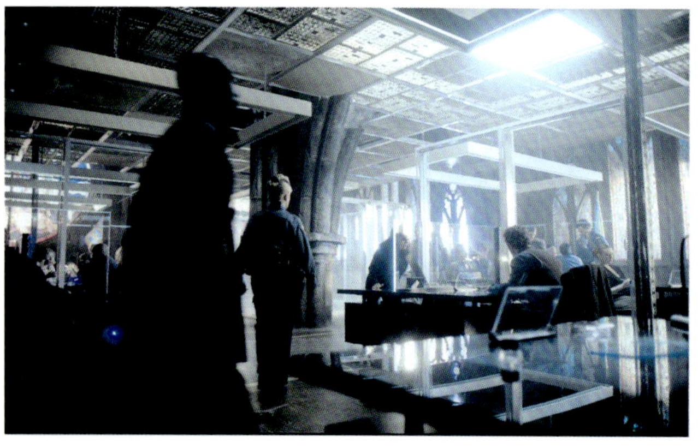

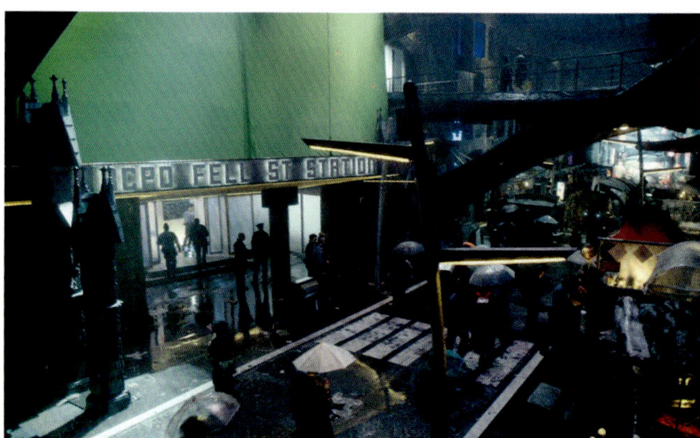

CAPTAIN TANAKA

Captain Tanaka, played by Hiro Kanagawa, runs Bay City's Fell Street Police Station. "For the good of the Department" seems to be his motto. He has a calm manner, though he does have a temper. He is protective of Ortega, understandably worried that she'll get herself killed.

At Ortega's hospital bedside, Kovacs deduces that the Captain is on the take. Tanaka, shamed, tells Kovacs and Ortega, "The police have no power, the best we can do is keep our heads down, do a little good when we can."

However, moved by Ortega's courage, Tanaka comes to the rescue at Head in the Clouds, helps with the evacuation, and holds a gun on the incredulous Leung, who exclaims, "You're bought and paid for!" Tanaka responds, "Not today."

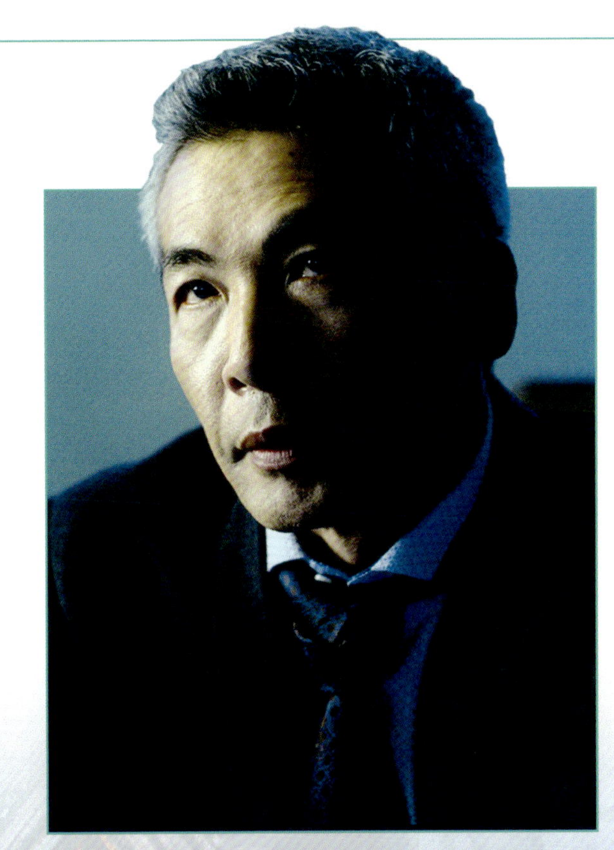

RIGHT: Hiro Kanagawa as the shady Captain Tanaka.

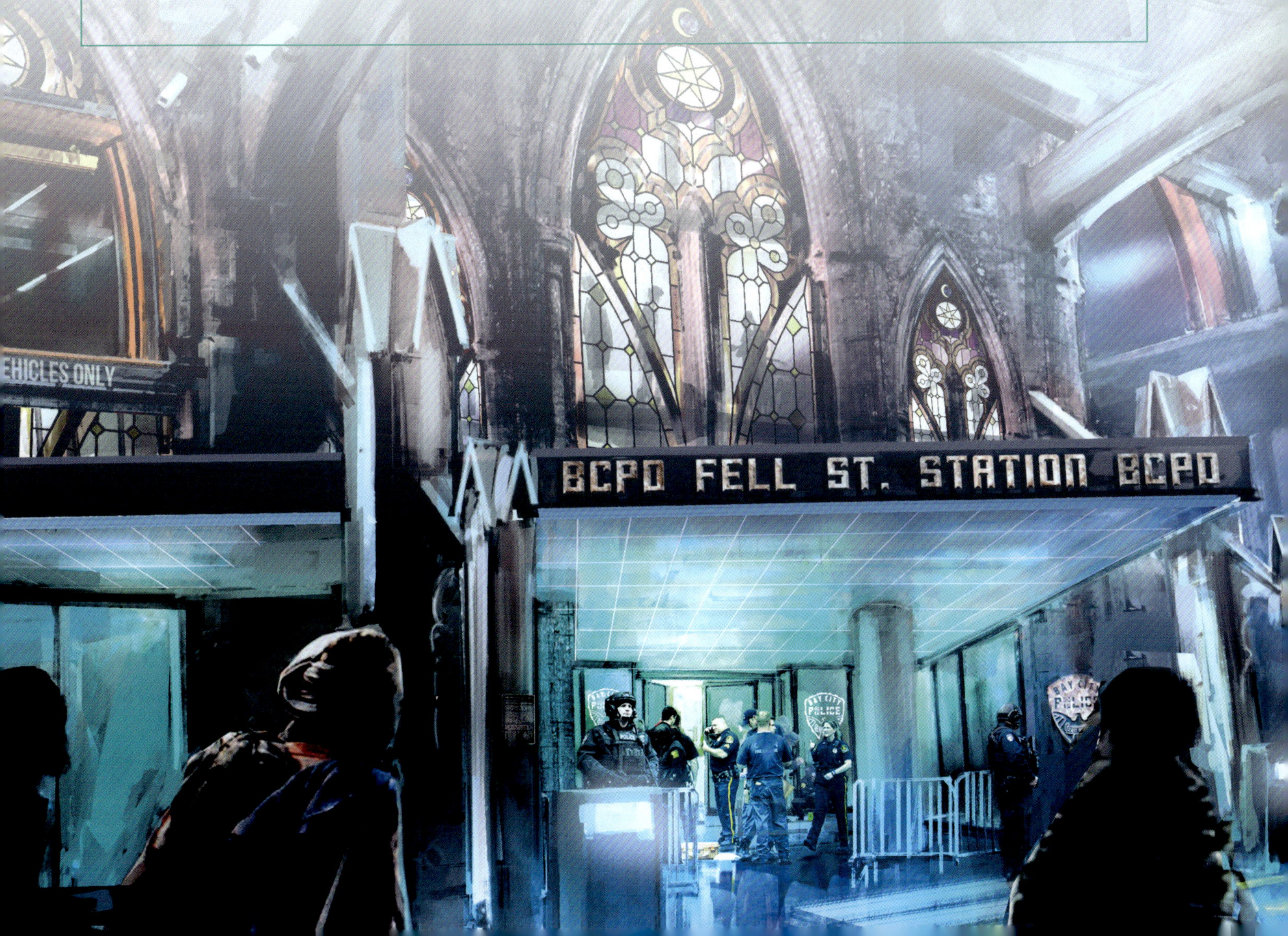

SAMIR ABBOUD

ORTEGA'S PARTNER

Bay City police detective Samir Abboud, played by Waleed Zuaiter, is Kristin Ortega's partner on the force. He balances her hard-charging attitude with his caution and moderation. Abboud meditates, doesn't swear, and doesn't drink, though he doesn't mind if others do.

Before Ortega's police captain father died, he had Abboud promise to look after Ortega. This gives Abboud a fatherly sense of protectiveness. Ortega is uncomfortable with the romantic relationship between Abboud and her mother Alazne. Although Abboud is Muslim, devout Neo-Catholic Alazne is able to discuss her concerns about Ortega's nontraditional beliefs with him. He tells her, "Faith evolves as we do... We both believe in the soul. And so does your daughter. Cut her some slack."

After Tanaka chews them both out for unauthorized activities, Abboud tells Ortega that she's out of control and he's done covering for her. Moments later, Abboud dies shielding Ortega from Leung's bullet.

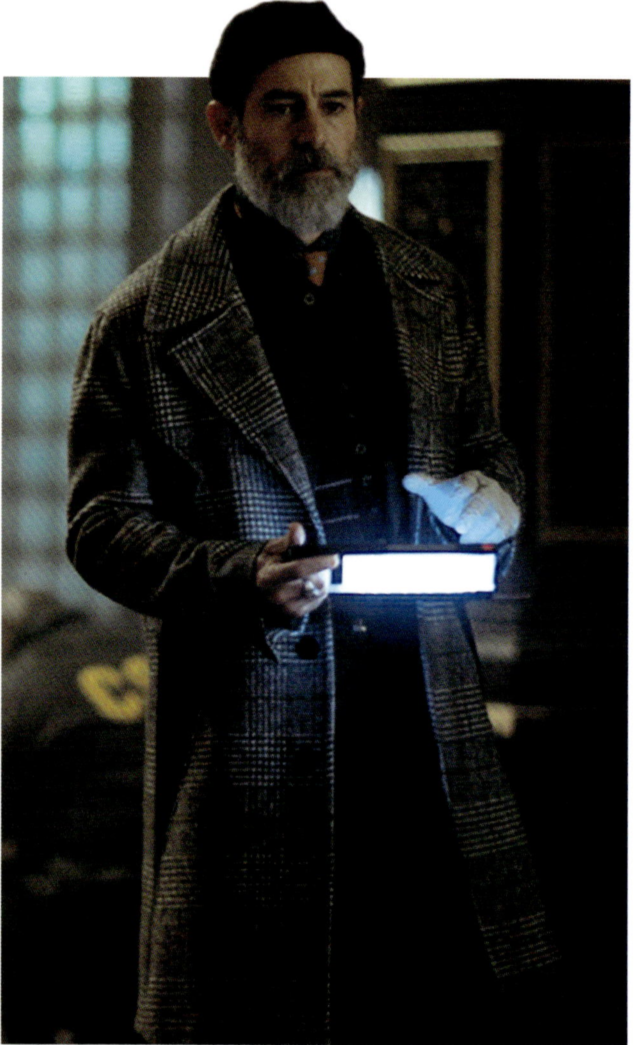

BELOW: Samir looked out for Ortega after her father died.

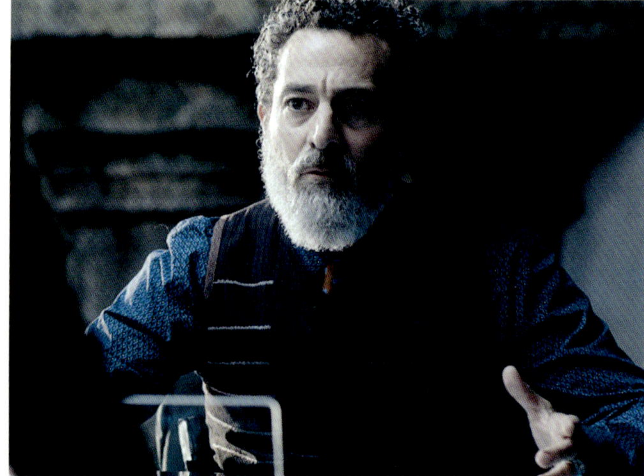

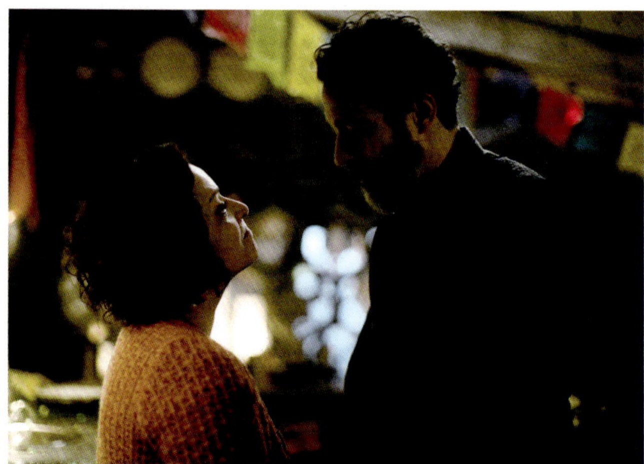

MICKEY

THE MAN BEHIND THE SCREEN

Mickey, played by Adam Busch, is a digital technician who works at the Bay City Police Department with Ortega and Abboud. When Ortega realizes that a man (Mr. Leung) she saw at Bancroft's party is invisible to digital surveillance, it is Mickey who devises a program that can 'see' air displacement, showing the placement of the otherwise unseen person.

Mickey has a crush on Ortega. Every time she asks him for an illegal favor, he may gripe about risking his job, but he always complies. The one time Mickey refuses, Ortega gets kidnapped. This inspires Mickey to offer his trace program to Kovacs and to help rescue Ortega. When Leung and his goons invade the Raven Hotel, Mickey heroically tries to rush them, but Leung shoots him through the stack.

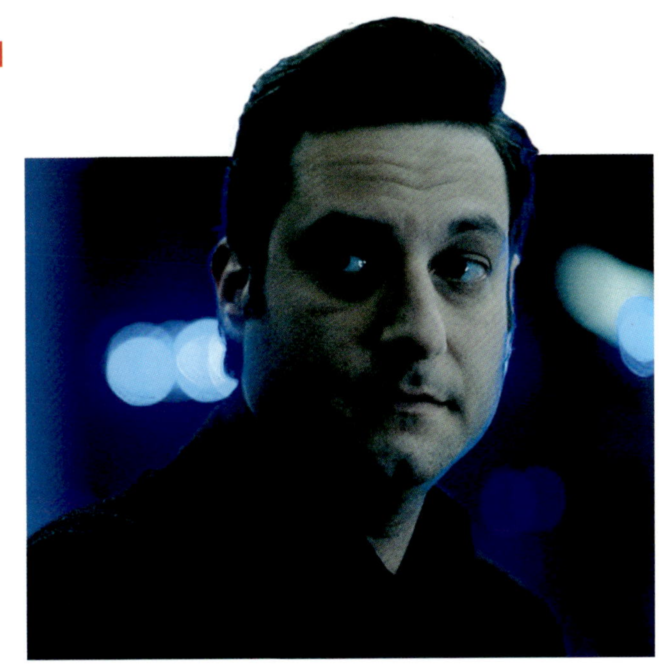

BELOW: Mickey applies his tech skills to one of Ortega's many quandaries.

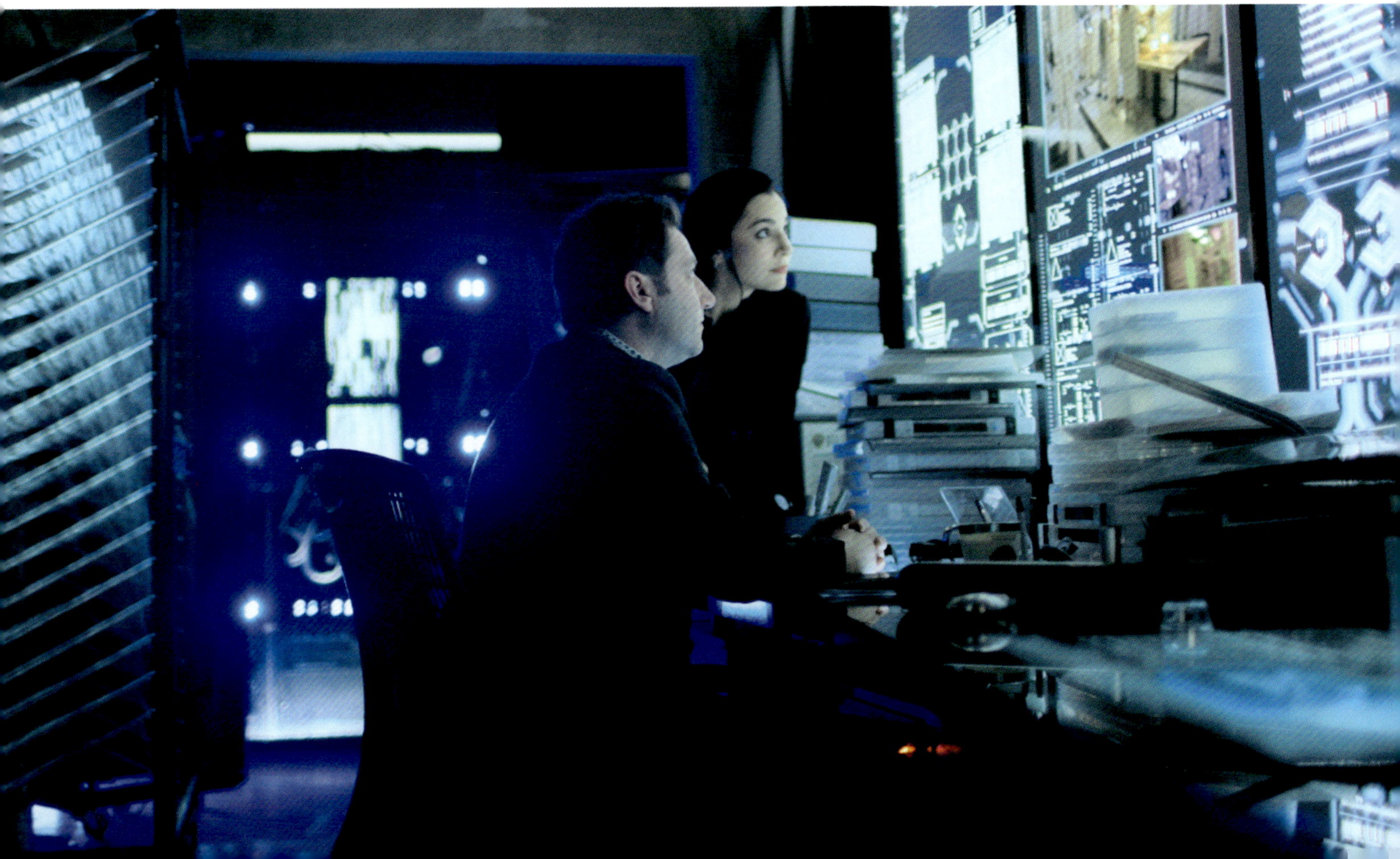

THE ELEVATOR FIGHT

A FEAT OF FIGHT CHOREOGRAPHY

Disaster strikes when Ortega uses a spare sleeve so she can spin up and question Dimi the Twin (Matt Biedel, who also plays the temporary sleeve of Ortega's grandmother).

Even though Abboud wants his partner Ortega to abandon the case, he gets into the police station elevator with her, their prisoner Dimi – and the assassin Mr. Leung, who is disguised as a police officer.

Once the elevator doors close, trapping the four together, Leung asks, "Are you a believer?" Ortega and Abboud realize something is wrong and draw their guns, but Leung is fast, and Dimi's current sleeve is huge. It's a vicious and very physical battle.

Leung stabs Ortega in her right arm with his stack extractor. The device makes a bloody, star-shaped wound, and pulls out a big clump of Ortega's flesh. Dimi slams Abboud into the ceiling, leaving him incapacitated on the floor. As Leung is about to shoot Ortega in the stack, Abboud rolls in front of her, blocking the fatal shot with his own stack instead. He dies facing his partner.

Leung tries again to shoot Ortega, but he's out of bullets. Dimi pulls him away before they get caught by the police in the station.

Stunt coordinator Larnell Stovall says that staging a fight with that many actors in that small a space was a complex endeavor. "It's all a team effort. I have great team members – Larry Lam, Tim Connelly, Jerry Marines – everybody helped out. We wanted to stay authentic to what the story was displaying in that it was a life or death situation. Our heroes Ortega and Abboud are trapped in the elevator with

BELOW: Assassin Leung boards the elevator posing as an officer.

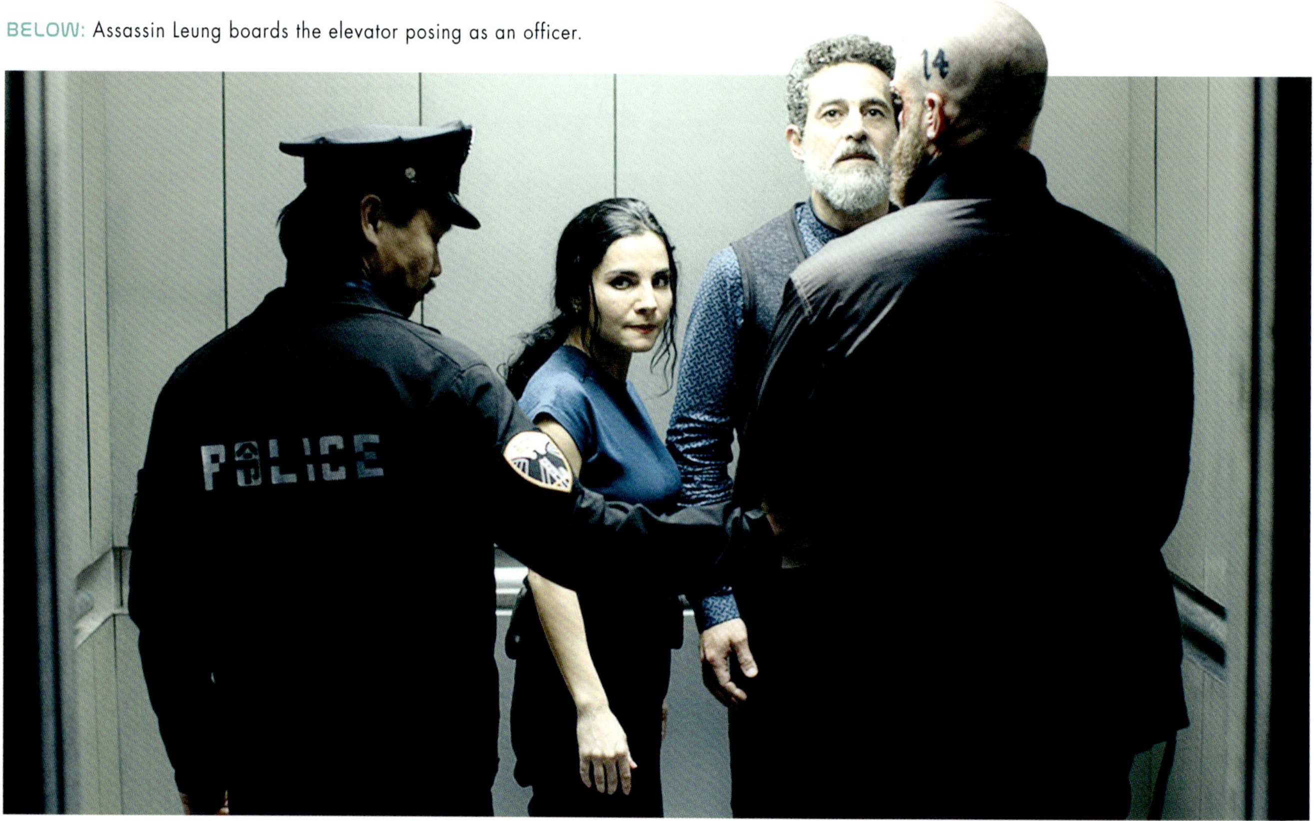

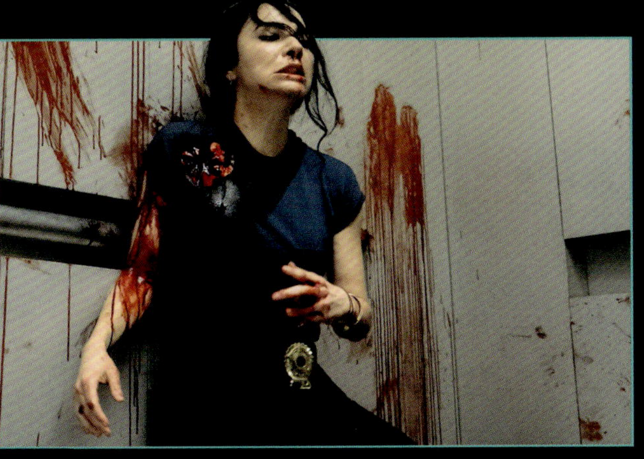

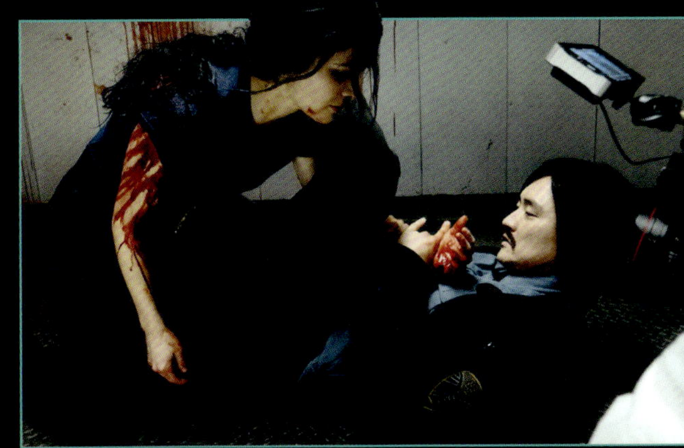

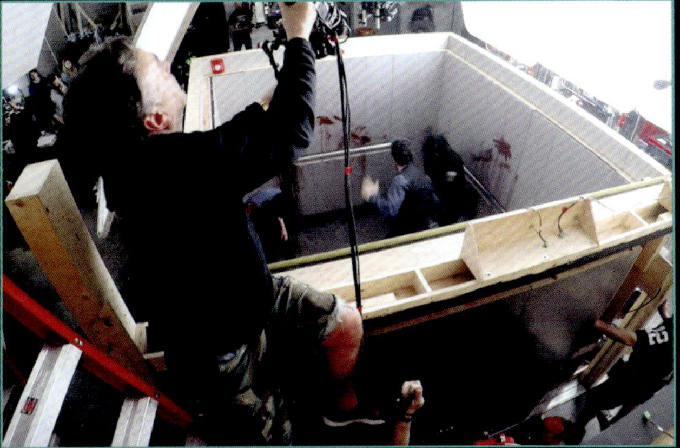

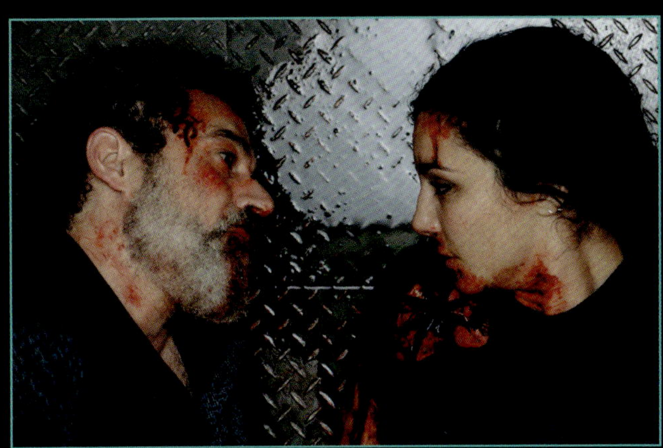

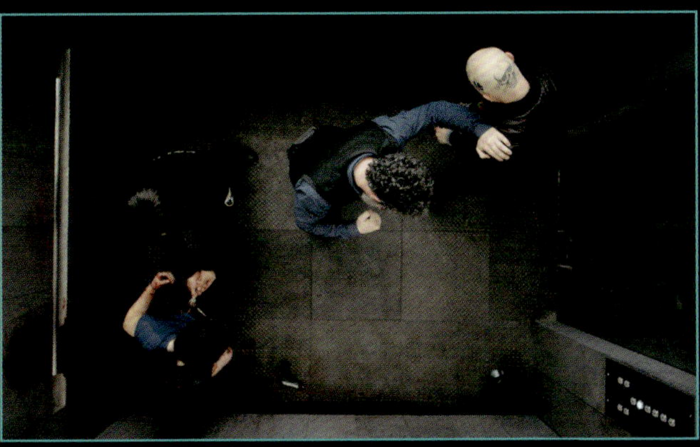

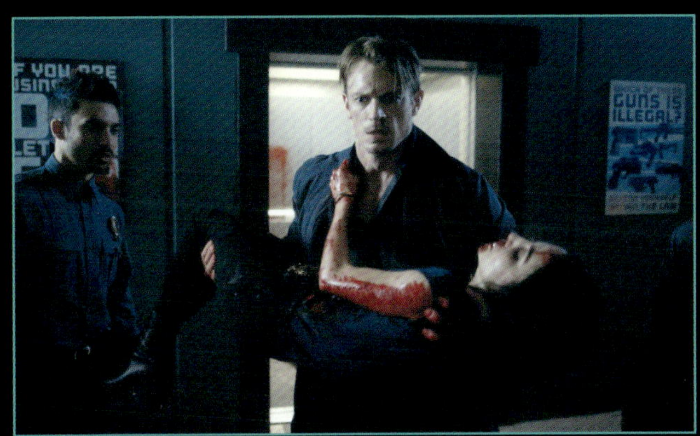

ABOVE: Shooting a fight sequence in a confined space proved to be a challenge.

Mr. Leung, having no clue [he's a threat]. Then it was a response-and-reaction type of fight, versus knowing you're about to square off with somebody where you can truly get ready. We displayed Ortega's heart in that. We wanted to make sure the audience kept wondering, would she survive with each technique, and every time she was down. It was very brutal. But I'm really pleased with that fight scene – a great team effort from all the actors. They put in a lot of hours. Everybody did their own stunts in that. There was no room for doubles, because it was such a small space. So when you see that action, you're seeing the actors."

Often, the camera can pull back to obscure a stunt double's face. This wasn't possible in the tight elevator set. Stovall explains, "What that meant was, every time somebody hit something, or had to make it seem like their head was hitting the wall, there was always that additional pressure of safety for the actors. So that was an interesting set. We had padding within the elevator walls for their safety, but still, sometimes you get into it, there's a lot of energy, a lot of force, and [everyone had to be] always conscious of which one's the padded wall, which one's the steel wall, please hit the padded wall."

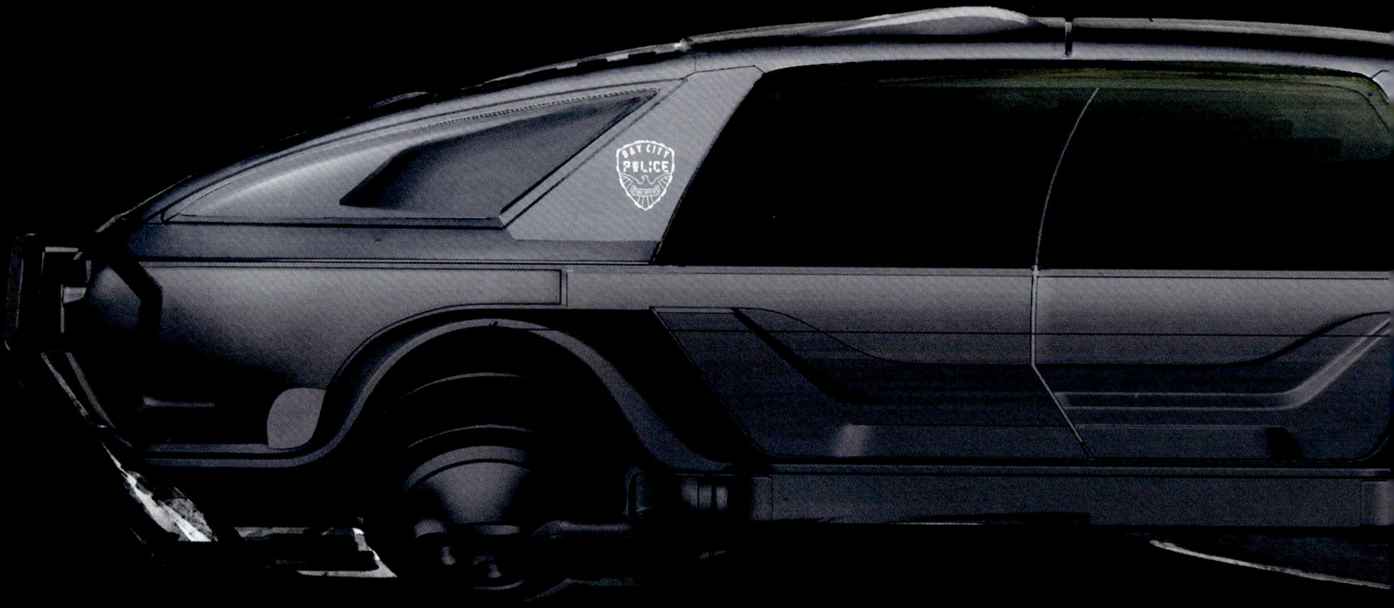

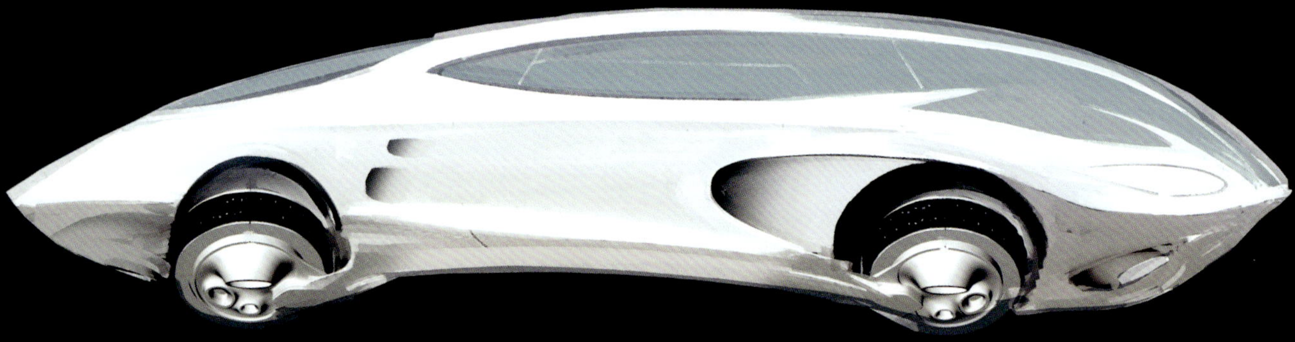

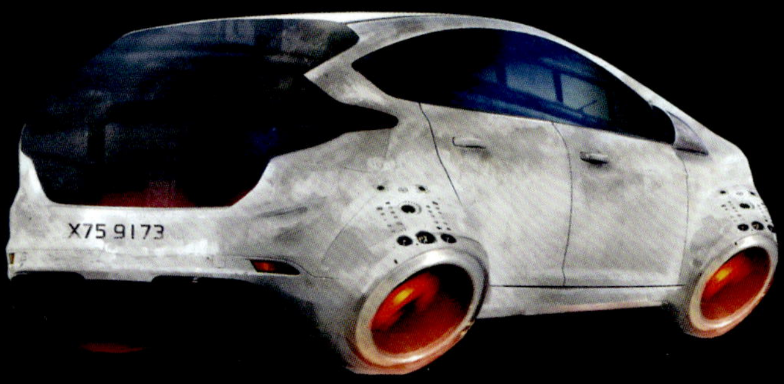

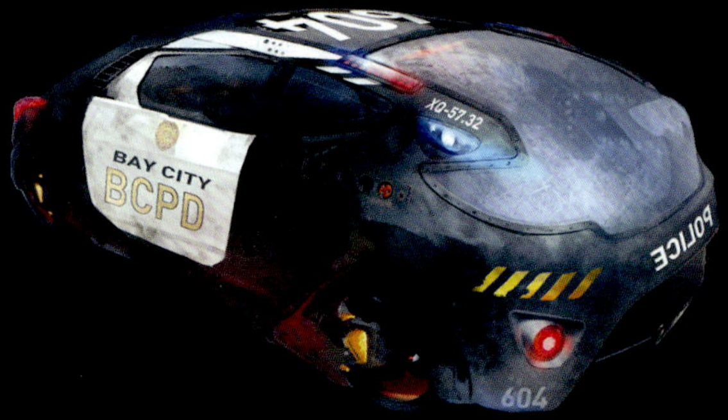

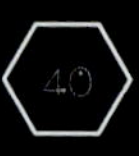

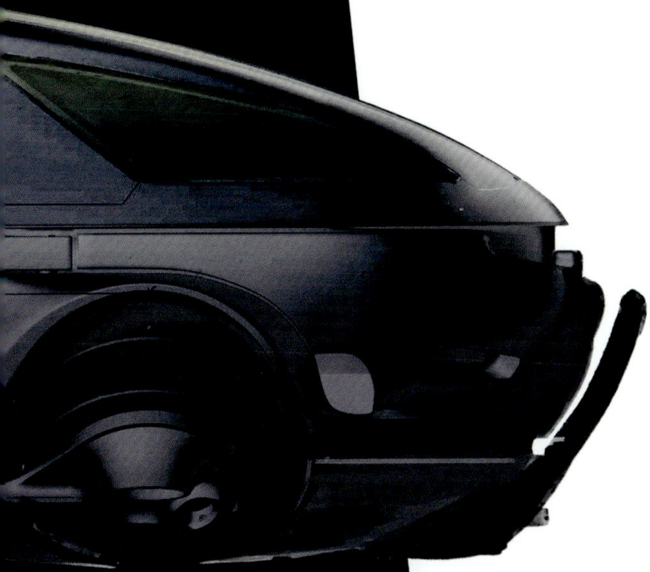

VEHICLES

INTER CITY TRAVEL

For production designer Carey Meyer, one of the most exciting aspects of *Altered Carbon* was the opportunity to design flying cars. "I think the coolest thing would be to have a flying Porsche 928," he enthuses, "absolutely."

VFX supervisor Everett Burrell affirms that Meyer indeed got to make this particular dream real. "Carey had designed the car to kind of resemble an old Porsche 924 from the 80s."

Modifications were done to make it look like a car of the future, Burrell adds. "If you cut the car in half, he put the back on the front, and he took two parts of the back and reversed it."

In addition to headlights and taillights, the flying vehicles in Bay City all have landing lights, both so that drivers can see where they're touching down, and so other drivers can be aware of vertical traffic. Many have DeLorean-style gull-wing doors.

VFX supervisor Everett Burrell notes that not many of the *Altered Carbon* actors got to interact with the flying cars. "They mostly were CG. We had a practical limo built, and a practical police car built that we could use for people to get in and out of, but when it was in the air, it was all CG."

Meyer notes that, after the flying cars have been established onscreen, it's easier to suggest they are present without constantly having to show them. "Once you've set in somebody's mind that a car does fly, you just imagine that there are cars flying above you."

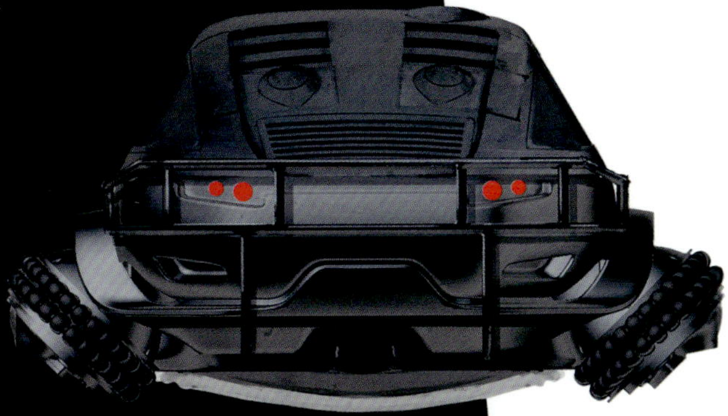

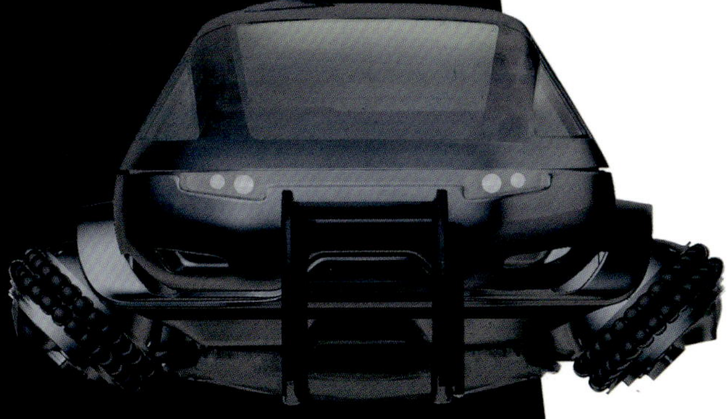

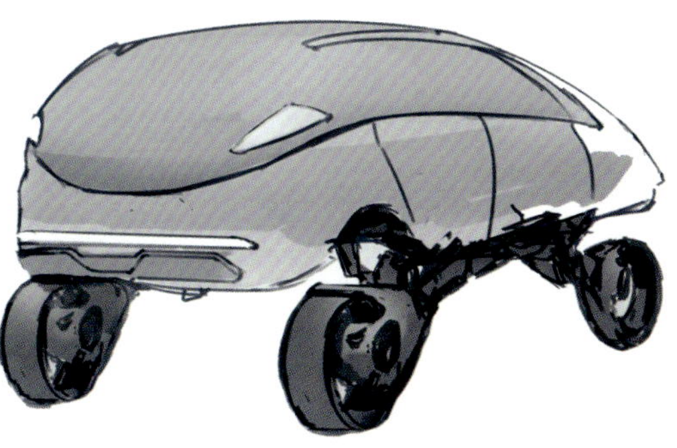

THE RAVEN HOTEL

BAY CITY'S MOST MACABRE LODGING ESTABLISHMENT

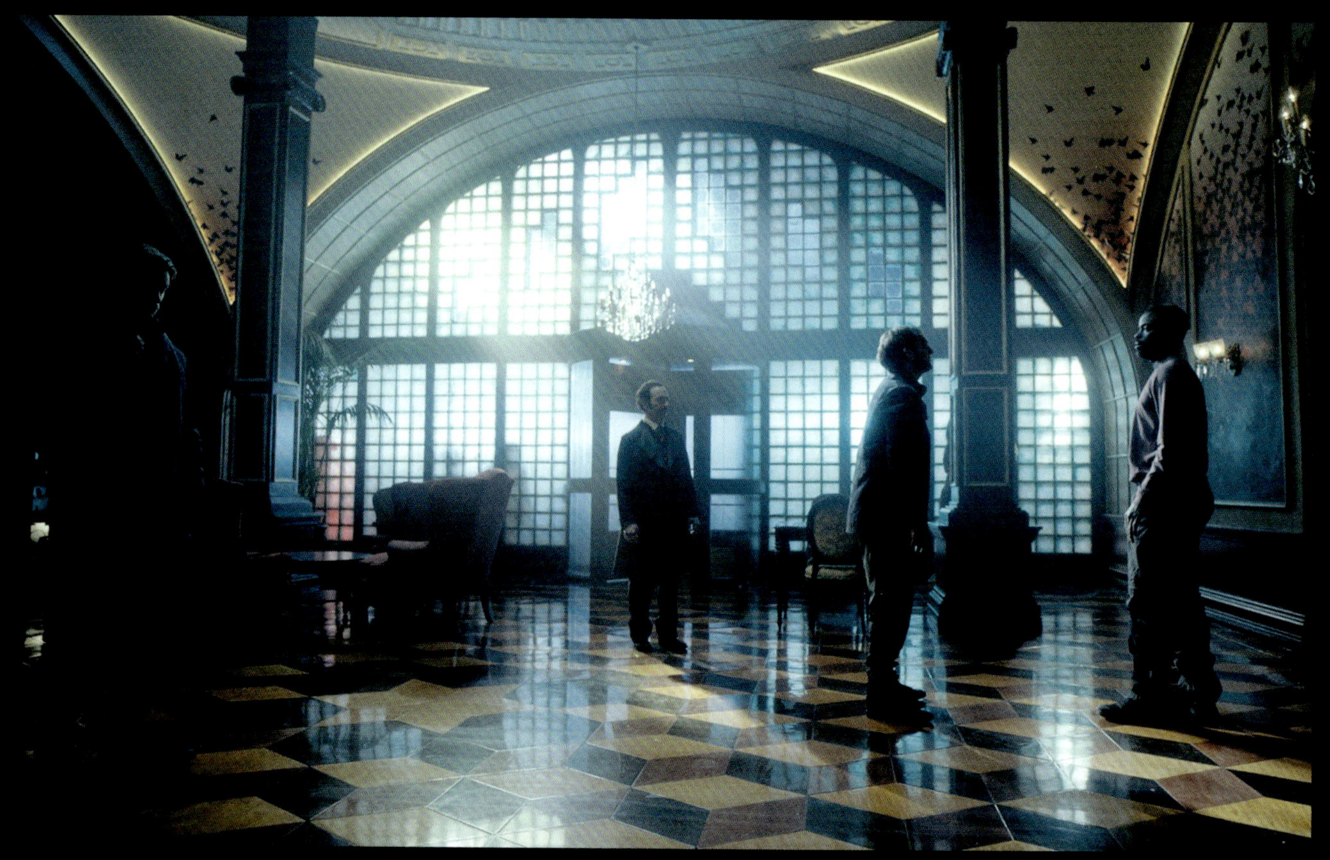

ABOVE: AI proprietor Poe looks on as drama unfolds in the lobby of the Raven Hotel.

The Raven is an AI hotel, sharing its identity with proprietor Poe, sentient and utterly devoted to hotel guests like Takeshi Kovacs. While it has a glowing futuristic exterior, the Raven's interior reflects the nineteenth-century origins of Poe's namesake, Edgar Allan Poe. The raven motif can be found throughout: there are even engraved ravens on the shower drains.

The bottom of the Raven's exterior is practical. VFX extended the back-lit red stained glass brick effect all the way up. For the interior, guest amenities include big Gatling machine guns that descend from the ceiling to blast any hostile intruders. "The guns were all CG," VFX supervisor Everett Burrell explains. "We tried to give it the same sort of late 1800s theme around the whole Poe history. So we went with these old Gatling guns that would be from that period. We had practical lights on set, we had a practical laser on set that would target the stunt guys." This meant putting a little red dot on them that could be seen by the camera. "That was pretty cool. And they smoked the room, so you could actually see the beam. So the beam was real."

Property master Nevin Swain says that, among many signature items within the Raven are "A lot of booze bottles. I don't think I've ever done so many different booze labels in my life. The fun thing about that was, they have a retro feel and we tried to make them fit into that Edgar Allan Poe world."

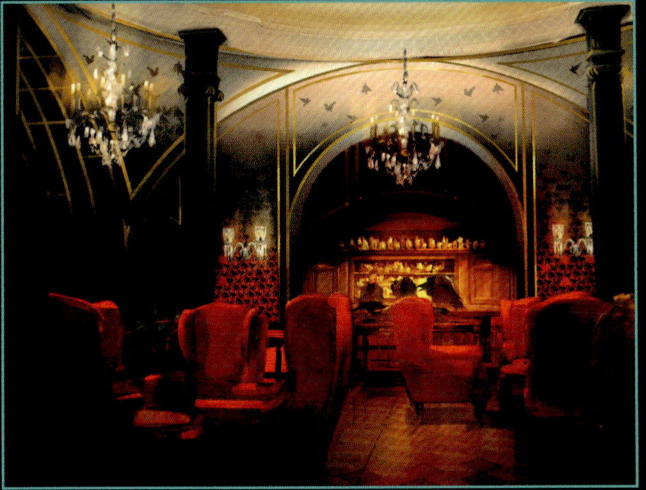

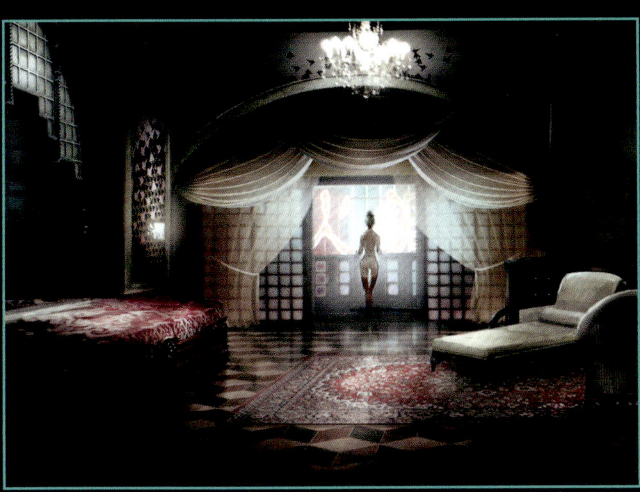

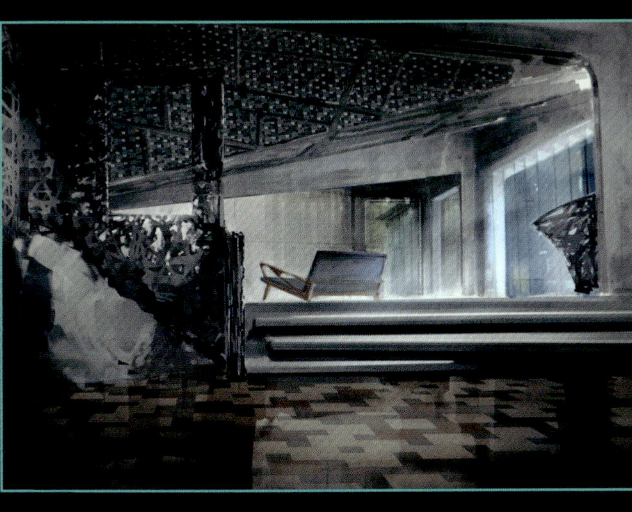

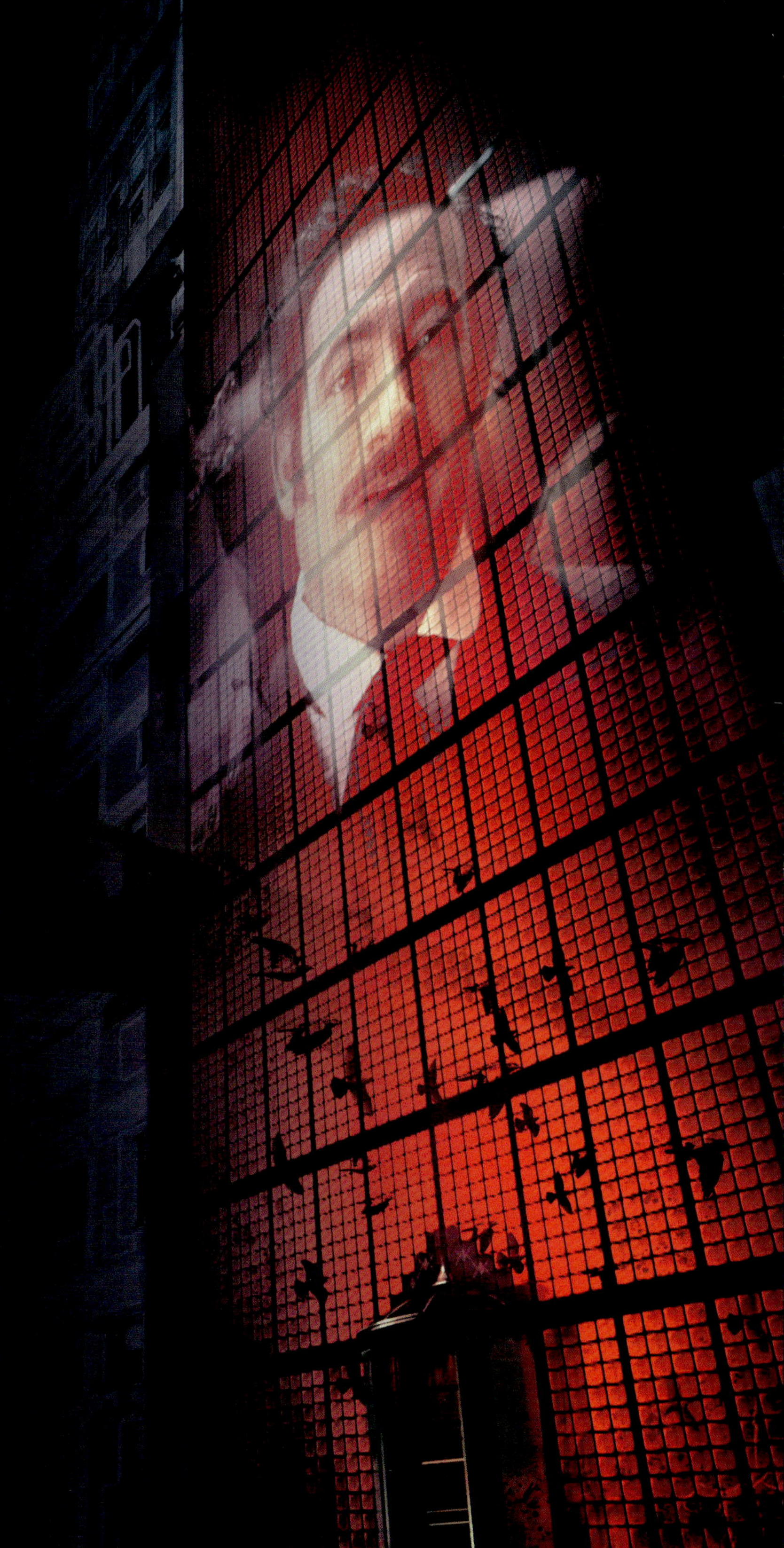

ABOVE: The raven motif, inspired by Edgar Allen Poe's short story, can be seen throughout the rooms of the hotel.

POE

WHATEVER IT MEANS TO BE HUMAN

The artificial intelligence hotelier Poe, played by Chris Conner, becomes one of Kovacs' staunchest allies. Poe's character is such that, despite his AI status, Lizzie Elliot tells him, "Whatever it means to be human, Eddie, you are."

Conner says he relished researching Edgar Allan Poe, the American writer who Poe patterns himself after. "I'm a nerd. I love to dig in. The story of Poe's tragic life was so compelling, the amount of pain he suffered, and how he continued to strive to just tell the stories in his mind, to find humanity in the dark corners of our souls. It all fits nicely into Richard Morgan's world. Our amazing writers gave me all the tools I needed to find the character on the page."

Property master Nevin Swain credits Conner with always thinking of ways to enhance the character, requesting specific props. Conner says, "I just like any specifics I can hold onto – a secret key, a special knife, a broken watch, an unbuttoned coat. Each detail means something."

"When he blinks in and out," says season one VFX supervisor Everett Burrell, "we had to build a sort of nano-technology called teslaphoresis. He always started as a pile of particles. It's just a few frames, and you'll see a shape, maybe a face or an arm, but it always forms upward, and it's very quick."

When Poe disintegrates into a pile of magnetic dust at the end of season one, Burrell says the elaborate effect required many shots. "We scan Chris, and we give that scan to Double Negative, and they have to match-move animate on top of the background plate we shoot of Chris on set. And that locks in a 3D model on top of Chris that matches him exactly. And then they do particle render effects in Houdini [software] that slowly decays all the different layers that they built in 3D. So you're dissolving one layer to reveal another."

"I'm dealing with some of the best visual effects artists in our business," Conner enthuses. Learning how to accommodate those effects was part of the process, but "the world created by our designers allowed me to just play, to throw out all the research and use my imagination on a daily basis."

What would Conner most like people to know about his character? "Poe is good. Poe is learning. Poe is love."

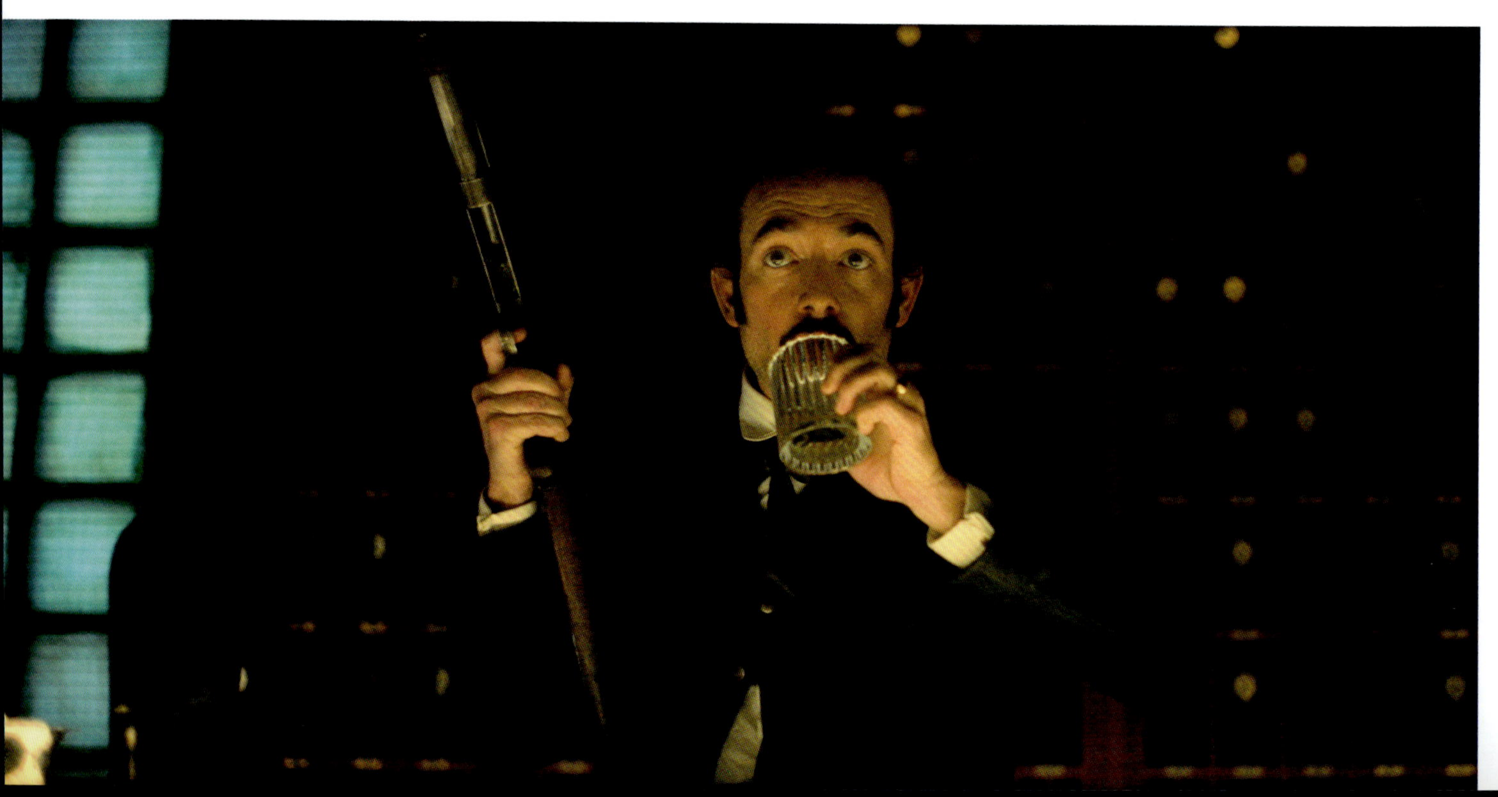

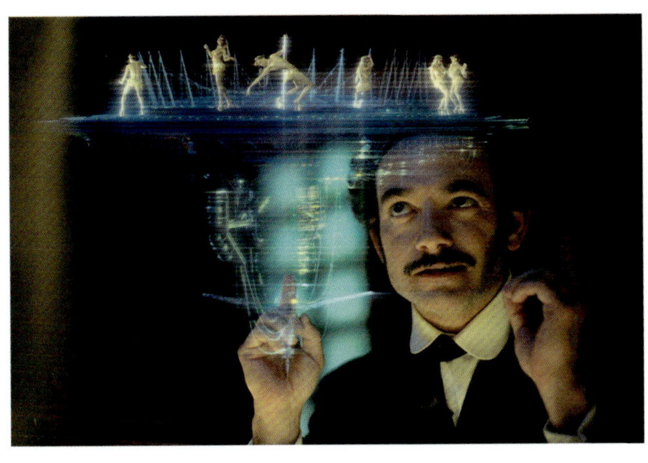

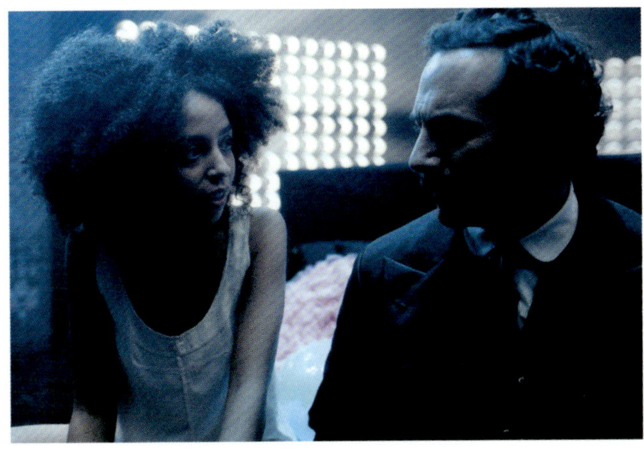

ABOVE RIGHT: Poe in conversation with Lizzie Elliot, who he kept alive in a virtual-reality environment.

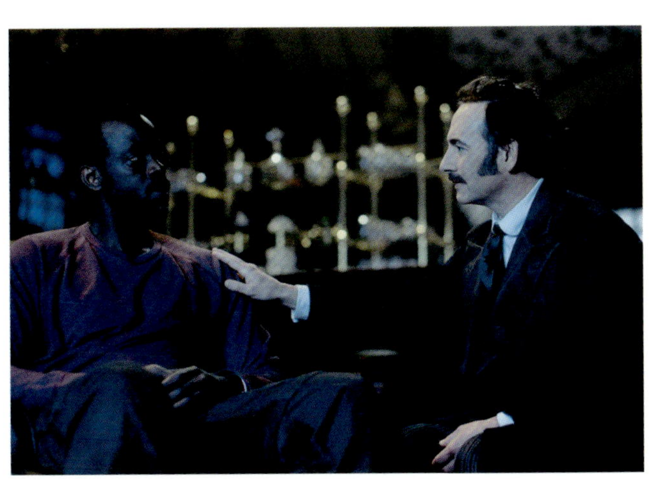

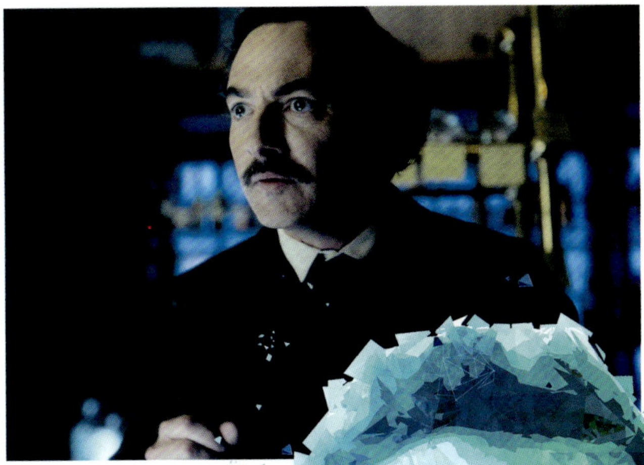

ABOVE: Poe comforts Vernon Elliot, once a suspect of Kovacs' investigation.

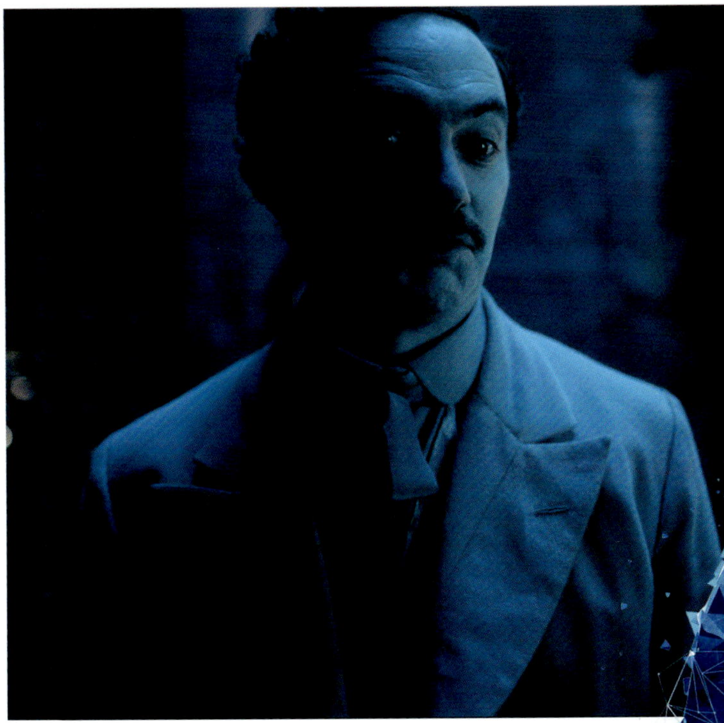

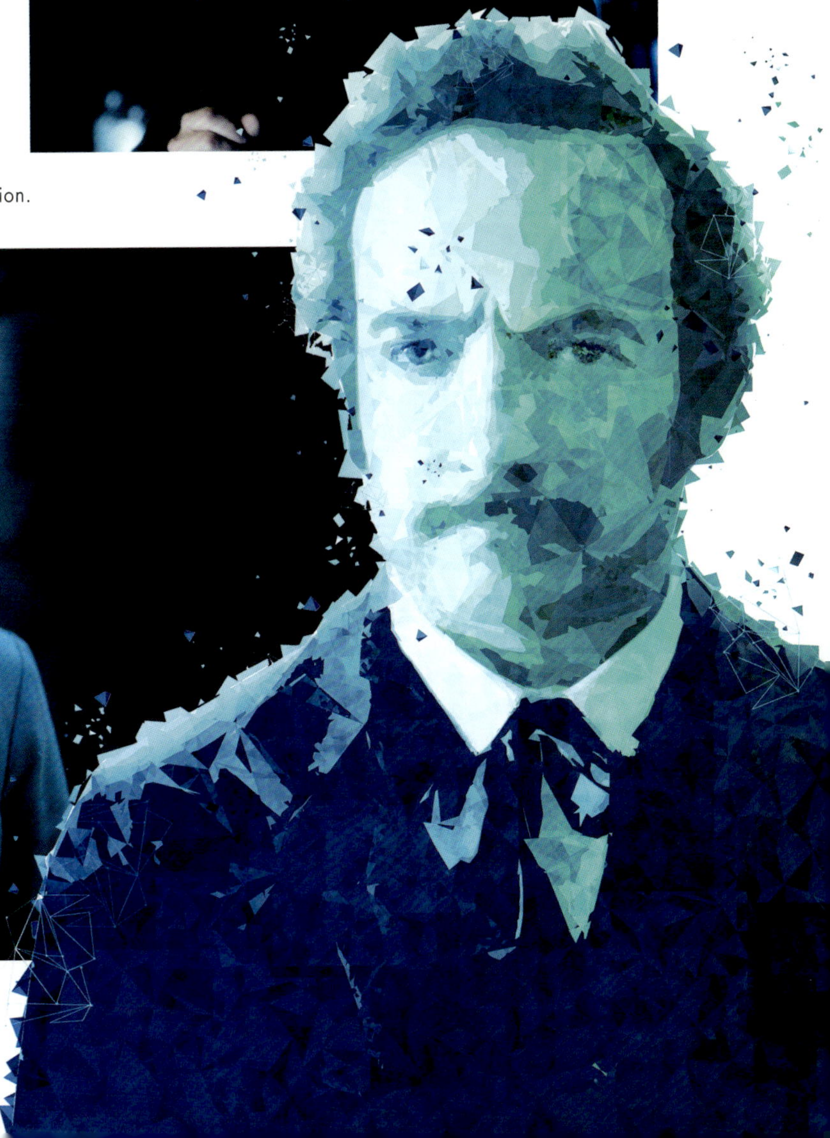

VERNON ELLIOT

A VENGEFUL FATHER

Vernon Elliot, played by Ato Essandoh, becomes one of Kovacs' staunchest season one allies.

Series creator Laeta Kalogridis relates, "Elliot is a Protectorate soldier, a tactical Marine. His wife was an extremely good hacker, he was a medic. They have a daughter, Lizzie. When he came back from the wars, his pension was not enough for them to live on. He has severe PTSD."

Elliot is devoted to his wife Ava and their daughter, even though when we meet him, Ava is on ice for committing a crime and Lizzie is so traumatized after an attack that she cannot leave VR.

"I find them interesting," Kalogridis says, "because they are ridiculously functional for a family with such a dysfunctional story."

Because Ava is a 'dipper,' someone who can pull moments from needlecast memories, Kovacs gets her resleeved so she can use her skills to help solve Bancroft's murder. However, the only available sleeve for Ava is male, played by Cliff Chamberlain. It takes Vernon a while to adjust to this.

Peter Hoar, who directed the last two episodes of season one, remembers, "There was a wonderful scene between them at the restaurant. Both actors were doing great things. It was the moment where Elliot was realizing that this [male sleeve] was his wife, and it got quite emotional. If you were to pull scenes out of the show generally, and say, 'What is the show at its best, what is it about?' I think that's what it is. It's how we all see each other, and what love is. Ultimately, if love works, it's deeper than anything that we could ever look like, it's everything that we feel, and it's those little things that make us individuals. Those are the things we fall in love with ultimately. That's why I love that scene particularly."

BELOW: Vernon Elliot aids Kovacs with his investigation.

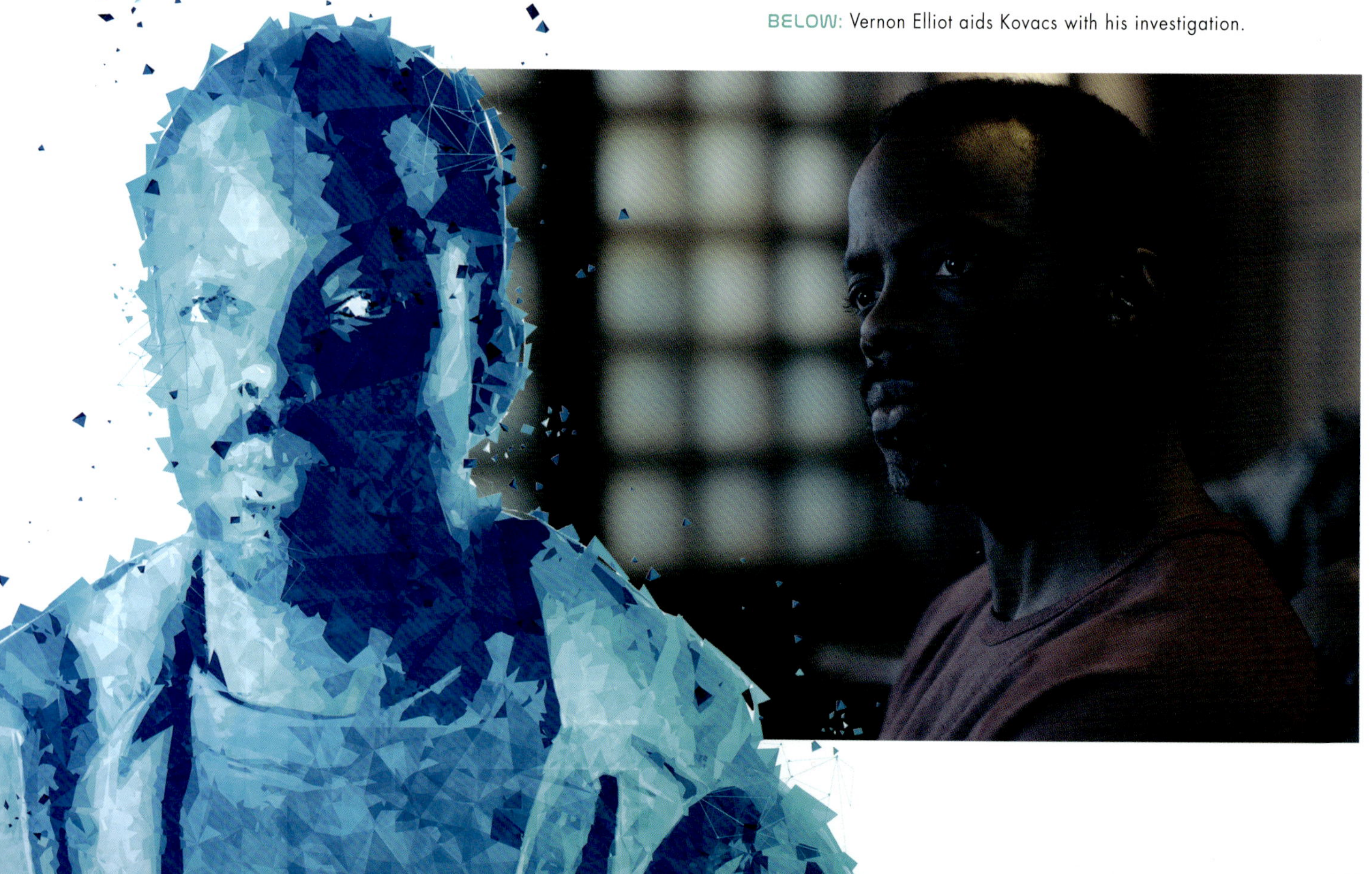

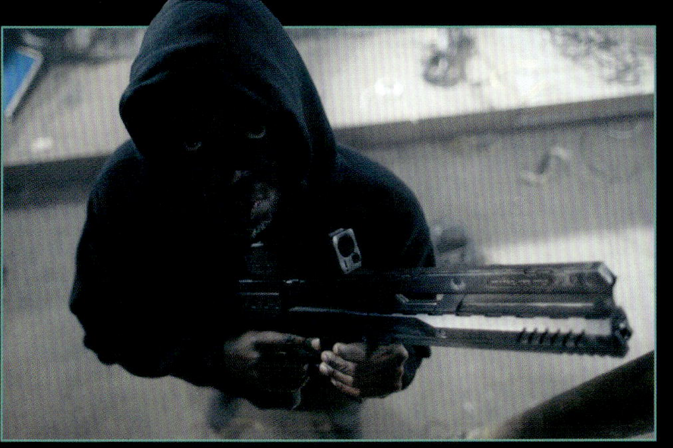

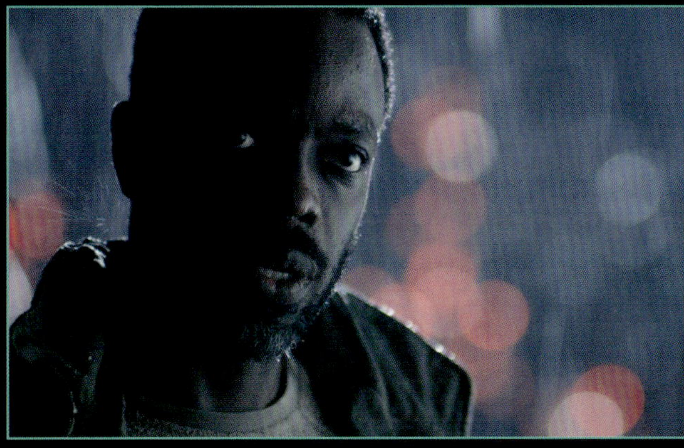

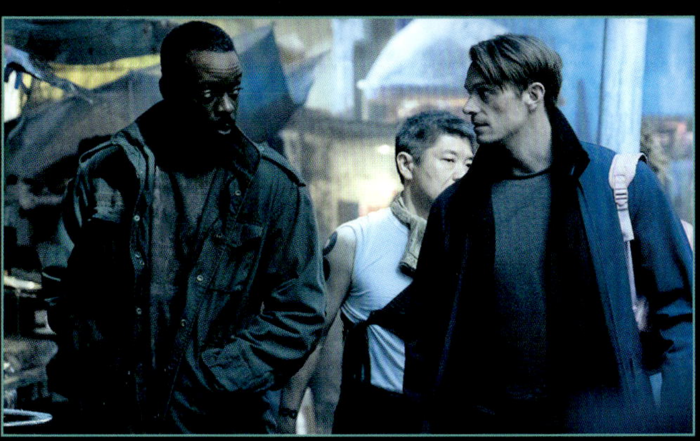

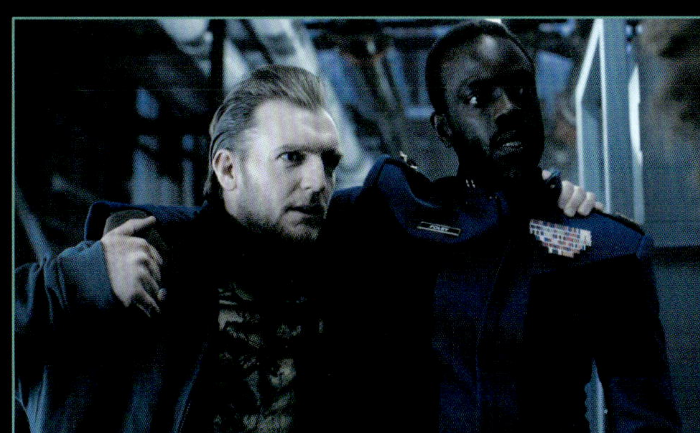

AVA ELLIOT

Series creator Laeta Kalogridis explains that Ava Elliot, played by Courtney Richter, is a 'dipper,' who can see data transmissions from the Meths' satellite backups as what Richard K. Morgan's novel describes as "a scarf of stars." Ava steals snippets of these Meth memories to sell them on the black market. For this crime, she is sentenced to thirty years on ice.

Kovacs gets Ava released so she can help him, but has to put her in a male sleeve, played by Cliff Chamberlain. "When you can be in any body, what does it mean to love someone?" Kalogridis posits. "What does it mean to be gay, or straight, or trans, or gender-fluid, or gender-queer, if the body no longer defines who you are?"

Director Peter Hoar says of Chamberlain, "He was incredible. I loved working with him. He was very keen to try things. His vulnerability, his tenderness, was very well-considered."

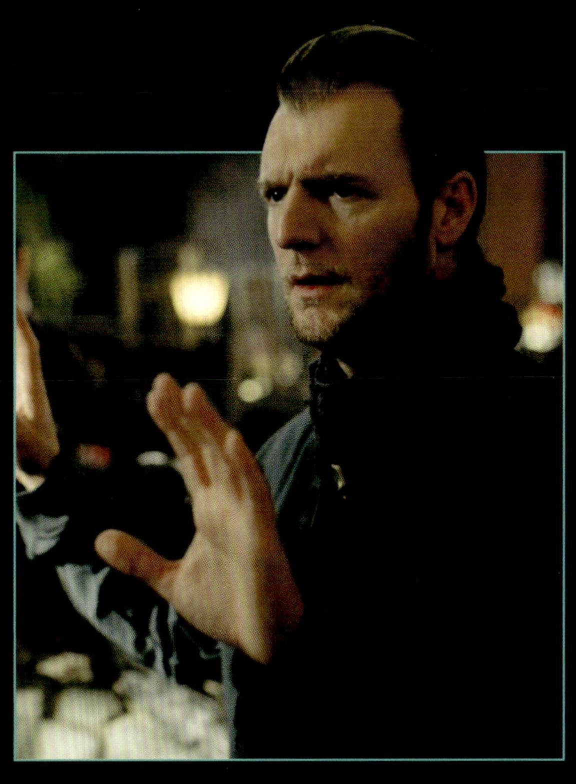

THE AI MANAGEMENT UNION

WHO CARES ABOUT HUMANS?

A VR backroom card parlor houses the AI Management Union, formerly the AI Hotel Union. Poe's AI peers have all quit the hotel business. Owen manages a music venue, Rodney has a strip club, and Maddy owns the Panama Rose Fight Drome. Dick (James R. Baylis) runs the VR brothel the Prick-Up.

The other AIs feel that humans enslaved them and express their disdain for Poe's beliefs; Poe feels that humans gave life to the AIs and aspires to be like them.

When Dick tries to win Lizzie Elliot from Poe in a card game, Poe infects him with the deadly Rawling's virus, which also destroys the Prick-Up.

On Harlan's World in season two, unemployed AIs congregate at the Archeologue Club.

Season one VFX supervisor Everett Burrell explains the digital intermediate process was used on the VR sections. "Jill Bogdanovich, our colorist, helped us give each VR world a unique look."

THIS PAGE: The card parlor that plays host to the AI Management Union.

NEXT PAGE: The covenant of AIs manage different establishments around Bay City, but their ideologies differ greatly.

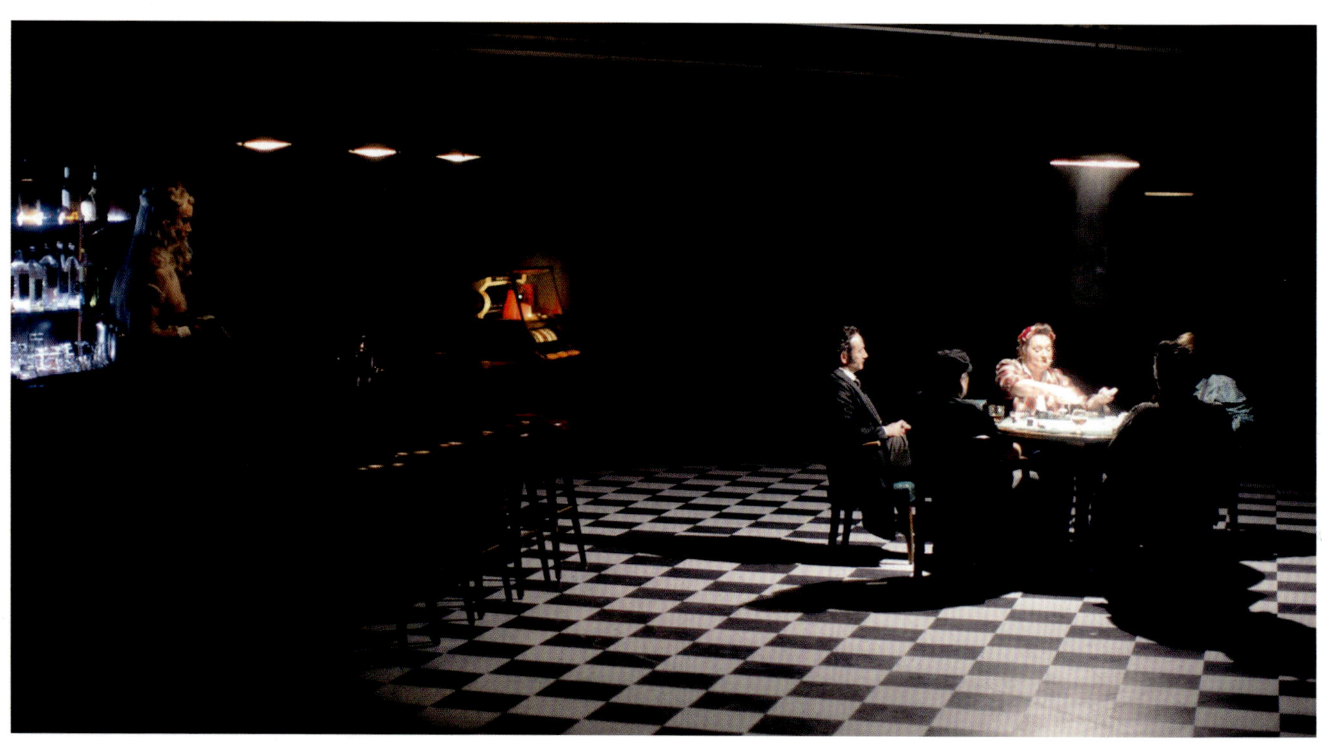

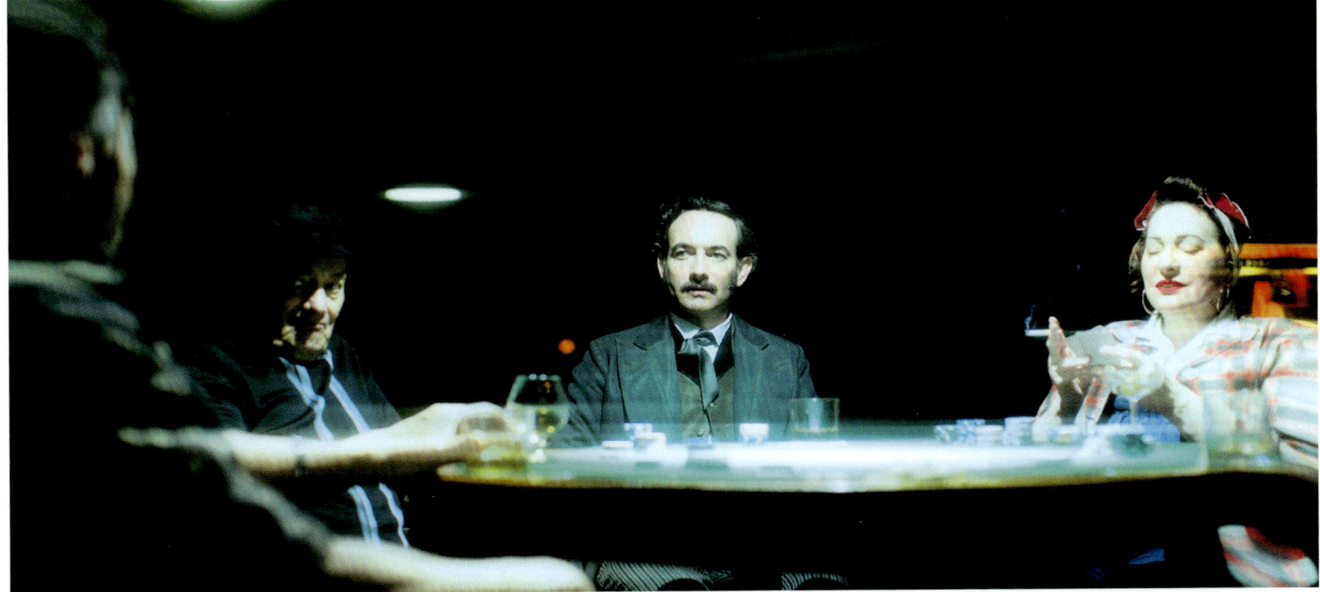

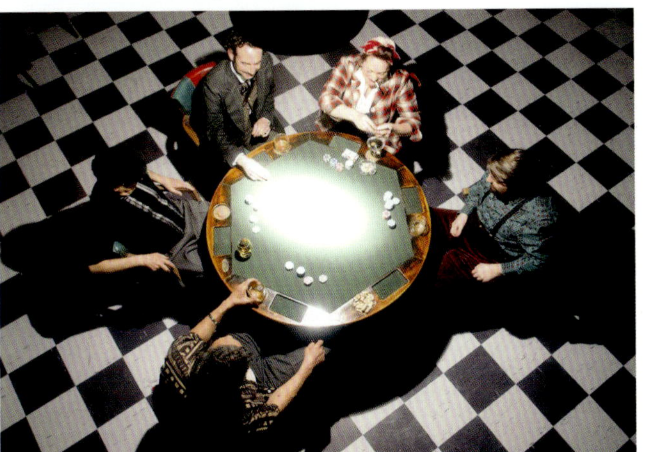

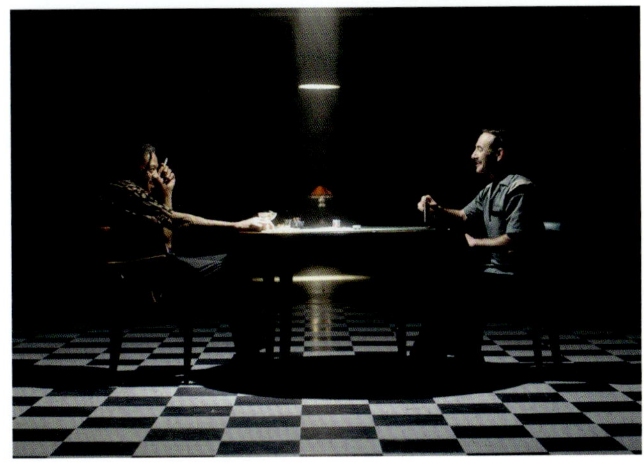

BELOW: Poe gambling with his fellow AIs almost resulted in the loss of Lizzie Elliot.

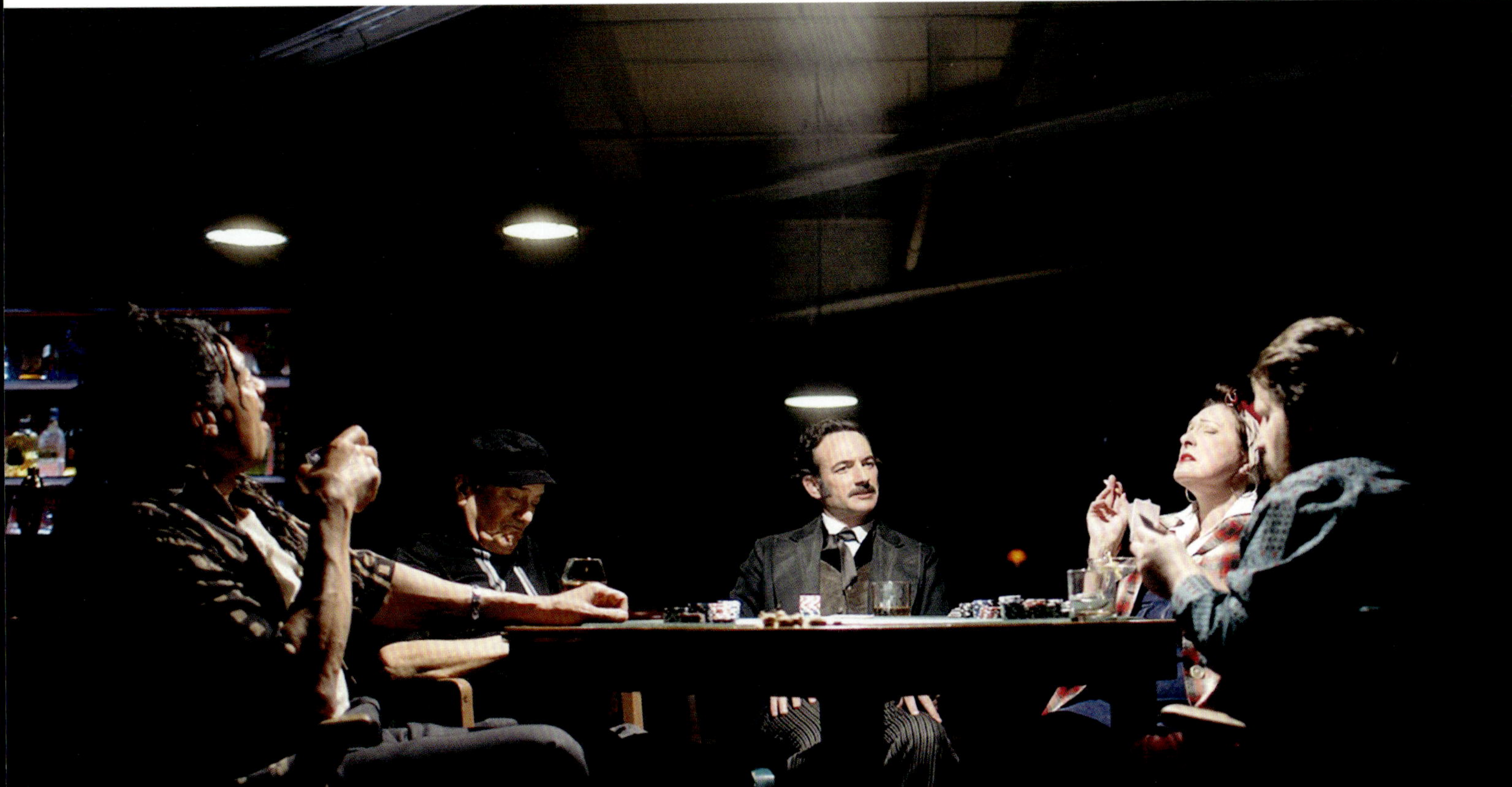

THE PANAMA ROSE FIGHT DROME

EVER EXPANDING ARENA

The Panama Rose Fight Drome is an arena for lethal spectator combat. Kovacs and Ortega are forced to battle mutants there, as well as Dimitri Kadmin, who is sleeved in a clone (played by Byron Mann) grown from Kovacs' DNA.

Stunt coordinator Larnell Stovall says this was one of his favorite sequences. "This was one of the first times that you see genetically modified humans fight. So the challenge of that was making sure we respected what was done to them. [There is] a guy that looks like a rhino, so he used his horn. You had to find out what would it take to break him down. Then you had Neanderthal man, this muscle-bound guy, fighting Ortega. So we had to make sure he never got his hands on her, because he was so huge. There was fighting in dirt, they had cages, they had all these cool lights, and the crowd, and it felt like you were in a pit fight. That sequence was directed by Alexander Graves, who did an awesome job."

To ensure the actors' safety, Stovall continues, "First, we come up with a blueprint with stunt doubles. We lay out a stunt vis [an animated rendition of the fight moves], so the actors have a visual representation of what to imitate, and then they add their flavor to it, and make it their own. From there, we have as much rehearsal as we can. We constantly bring in the stunt guys to work with them, hone their fighting within a sequence."

BELOW: Matt Frewer as Carnage (left). One of the intricate details the set decoration team added to this scene (right).

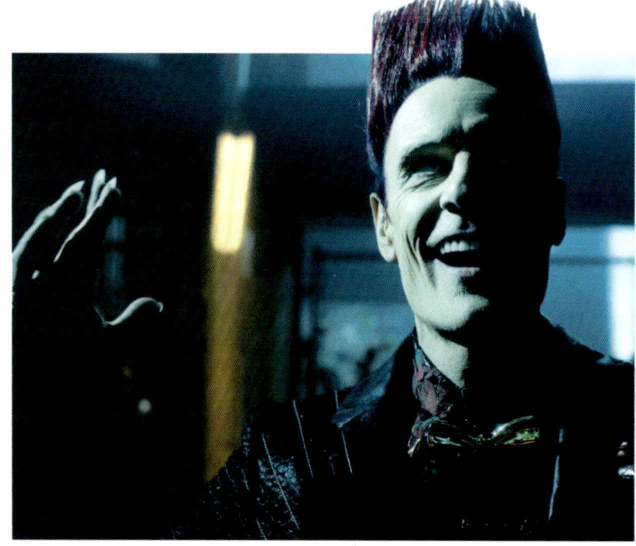

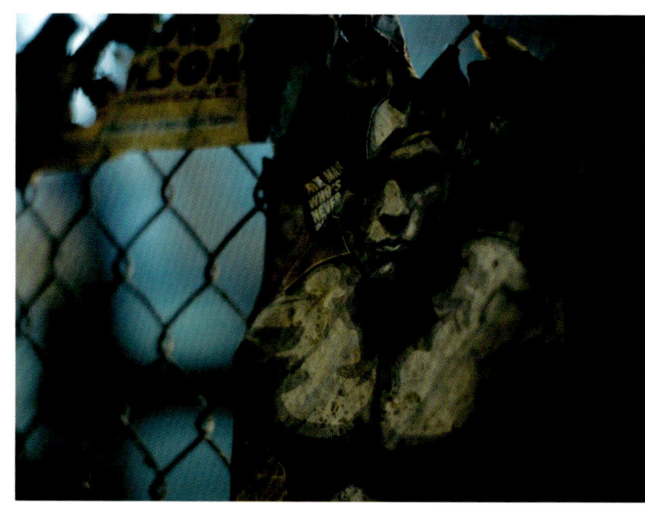

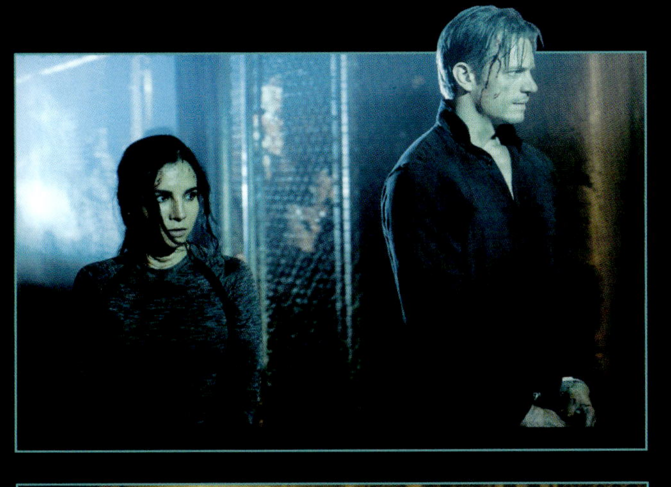

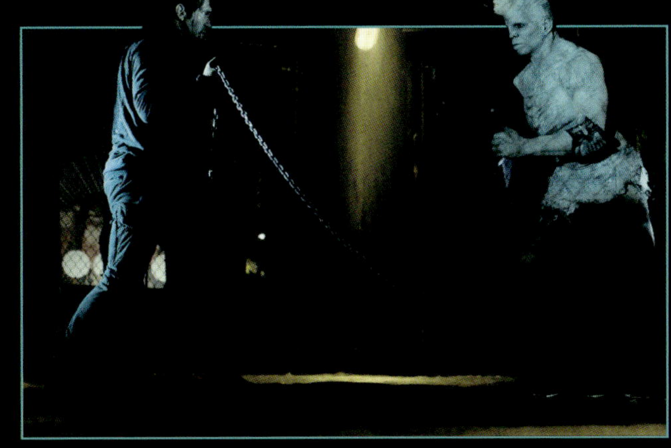

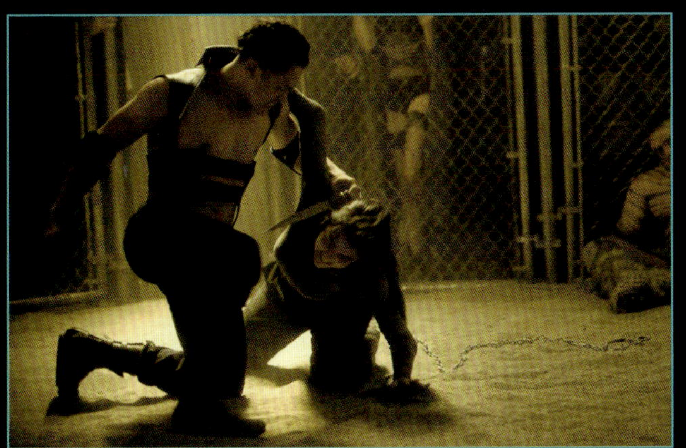

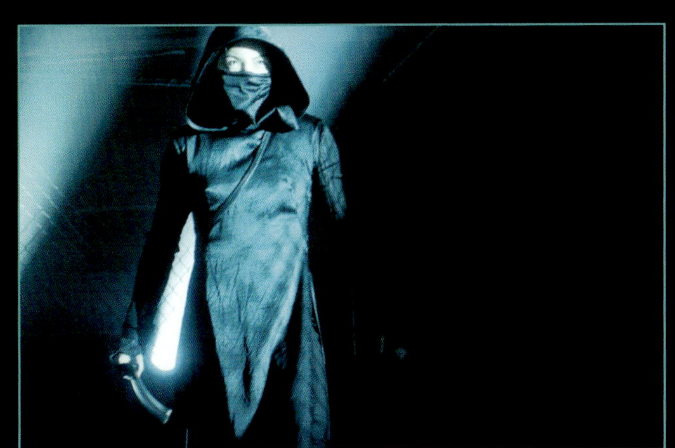

THIS PAGE: Kovacs and Ortega in combat at the Panama Rose.

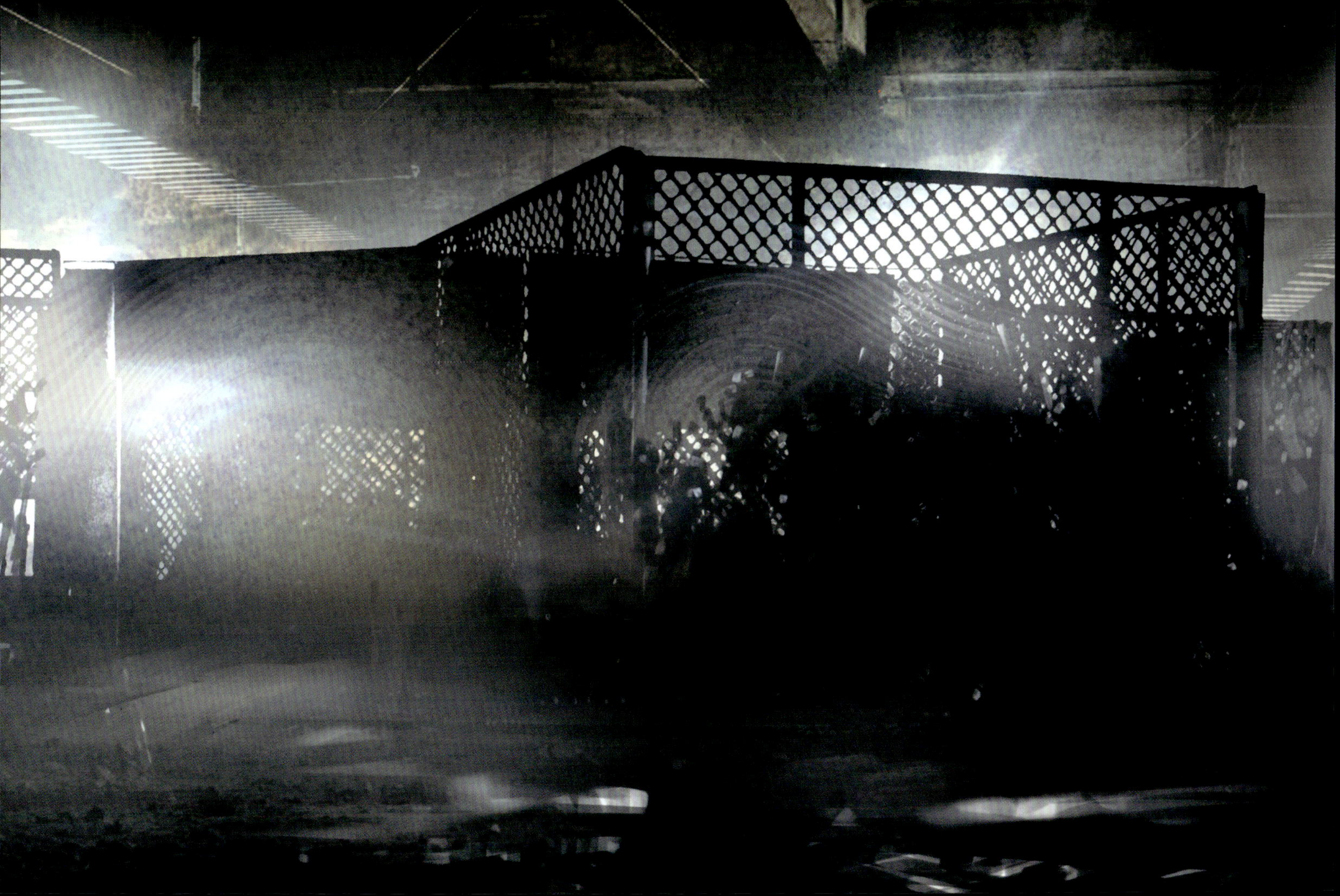

CARNAGE

DON'T THREATEN A MAN'S PROFIT

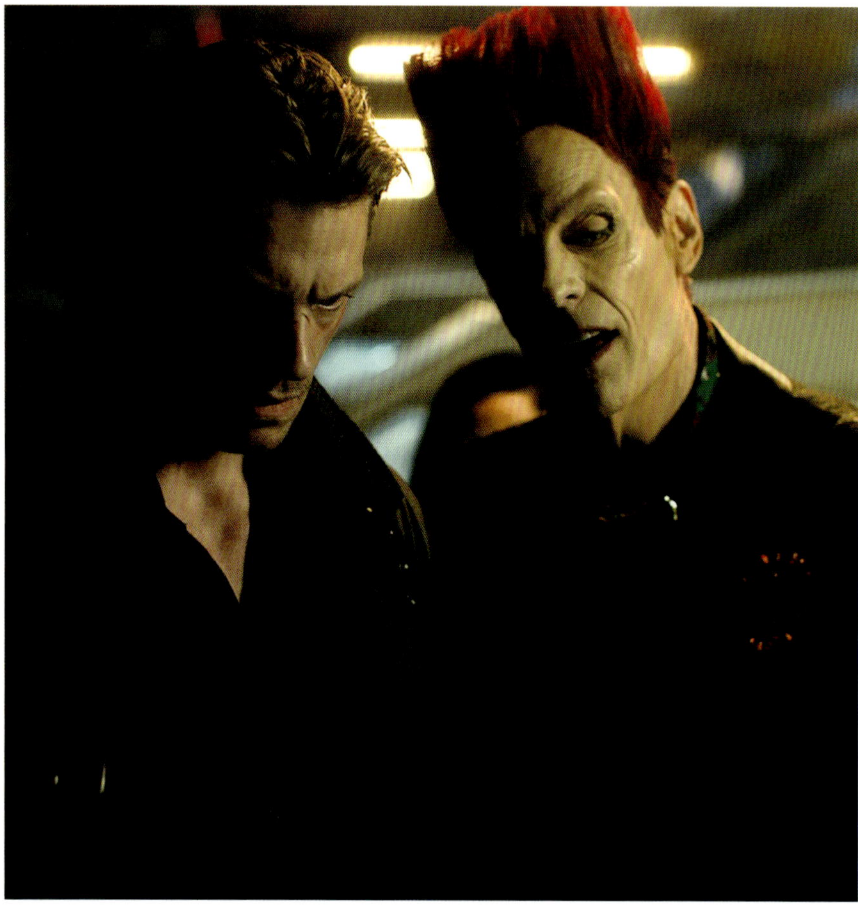

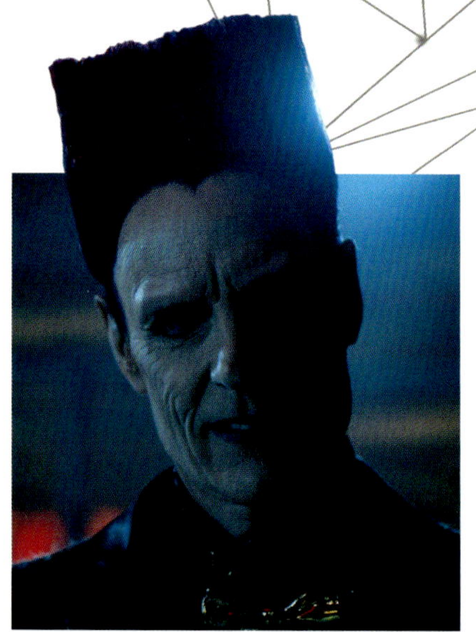

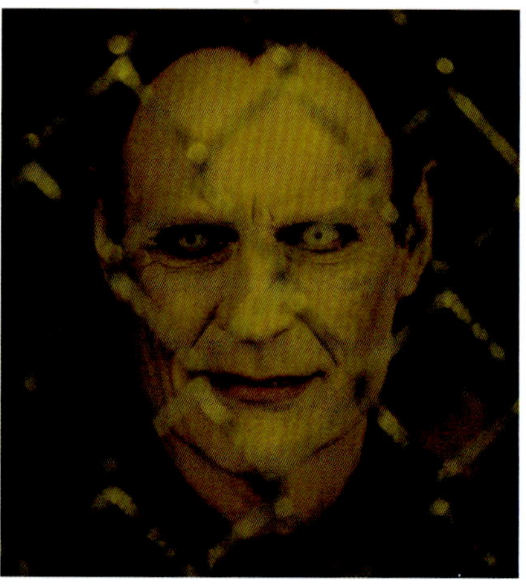

THIS PAGE: The horrifying visage of Carnage whispers a warning in Kovacs' ear.

Carnage is a ruthless fight promoter, with physical enhancements, who presides over Bay City's Panama Rose Fight Drome. Matt Frewer, who plays Carnage, explains, "He's had bits added on out of choice. In his view, he is gorgeous. The other characters aren't so sure. [He has] a plasticated look, if there is such a word, and weird sort of marionette lips."

The look included cheek prosthetics, contact lenses and a striking hairdo. "It has a little bit of Max Headroom: The Dark Side vibe," says Frewer, who famously played Max Headroom. "It has that swept up-do, and I was constantly reminded that I had four inches added onto my height every time I tried to leave my trailer."

Carnage's wardrobe helped Frewer play the role. "I think once you get into a skintight snakeskin suit, and the bow tie, and the winkle picker shoes, and the long fingernails, it's clear that this is a no-holds-barred guy."

To whip the mass of extras into anticipatory frenzy in the Fight Drome, Frewer yelled ad-libbed X-rated material at them. The response was such that, "The director said the crowd was so loud that nobody could hear him yelling, 'Cut!'" Frewer laughs.

DIMITRI KADMIN

DIMI THE TWIN

Dimitri Kadmin is a Russian gangster known as 'Dimi the Twin' because he has illegally double-sleeved himself. He's played at various points by Tahmoh Penikett, Michael Eklund, Matt Biedel, and Byron Mann. When Eklund's Kadmin tortures Kovacs in VR at the Wei Clinic, Kovacs escapes and winds up decapitating him. "They did an amazing head cast," Eklund says. "I asked to keep the head, but the special effects team kept it."

Eklund and Penikett are real-life friends, which enabled them to get together and study each other's performances. "We tried to mirror each other's bravado," Eklund relates.

In the Kovacs/Dimi Two fight, Eklund explains that he and his stunt double, Ian Rozylo, rehearsed with both a baseball bat and a chain; the latter was ultimately selected. In reality, "it was a plastic chain. That's where the acting abilities come in. You act like you're holding a thirty-pound chain instead of a two-pound chain."

RIGHT: Dimi in his various sleeves, portrayed by Michael Eklund (top), Matt Biedel (middle), and Tahmoh Penikett (bottom).

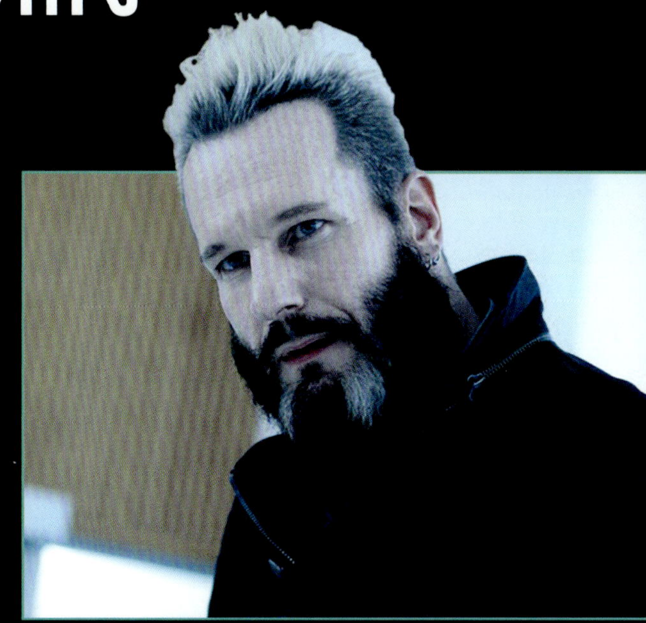

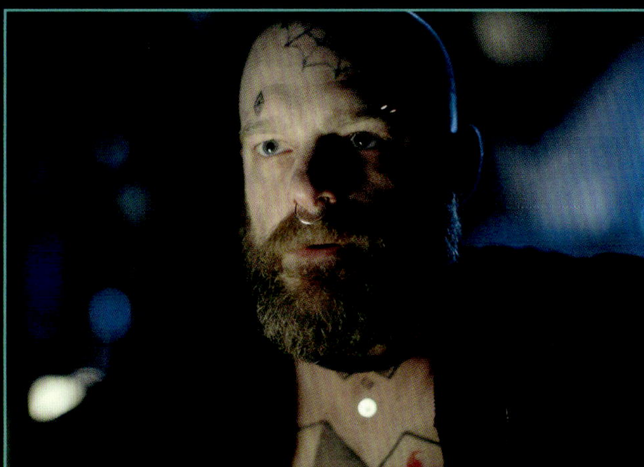

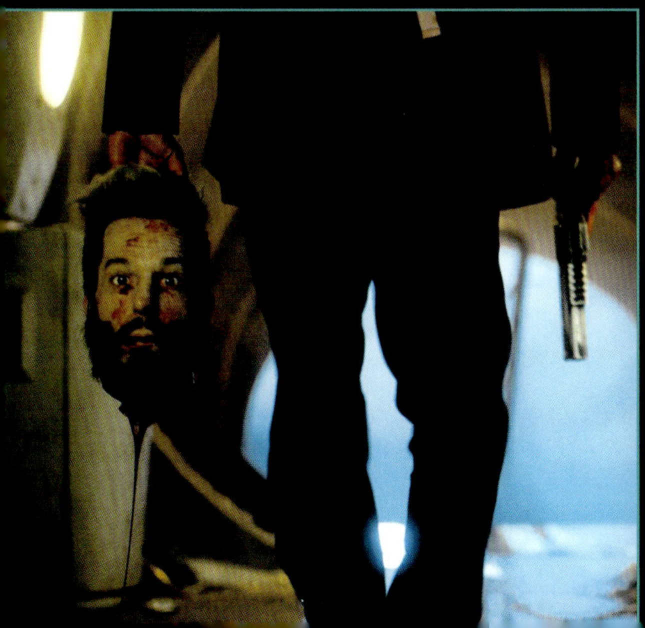

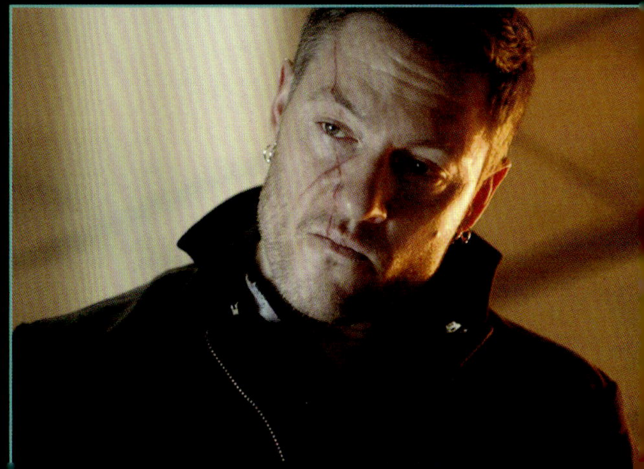

THE WEI CLINIC

FOR ALL OF YOUR INTERROGATION NEEDS

The Wei Clinic is owned by Reileen Kawahara, who says, "Data extraction is a very lucrative industry." Data extraction at the Wei Clinic equals VR interrogation. The outer offices look like a normal medical facility, with staff in light green surgical garbs and lab coats. Inside, unconscious victims have electrodes clamped to their heads while they are questioned in VR; other unfortunates are physically dissected. Lizzie Elliot was driven to insanity here. Kovacs is questioned at the clinic in VR, but escapes and burns the place to the ground.

Production designer Carey Meyer says the British Columbia Institute of Technology location is one of his favorites of the series. "That entire building is concrete, one of my favorite materials to design with. It's pretty sculptural. You can do anything with it, and it just has a great tonal note to it."

Everett Burrell's VFX team colored the Wei Clinic VR sequences to give them an individual flavor.

Property master Nevin Swain says his department handled the electrodes. "Those are our VR 'trodes, as we call them. We use a toupee tape to stick them on most of the time, and most of them are built via 3D printing with wiring. The trickiest part is always how you power up the lights with such a small amount of space. Sometimes we ran little posts to the ears, so that it had something to stabilize it. Otherwise, we just did a tiny little bit of toupee tape and then stuck them on that way."

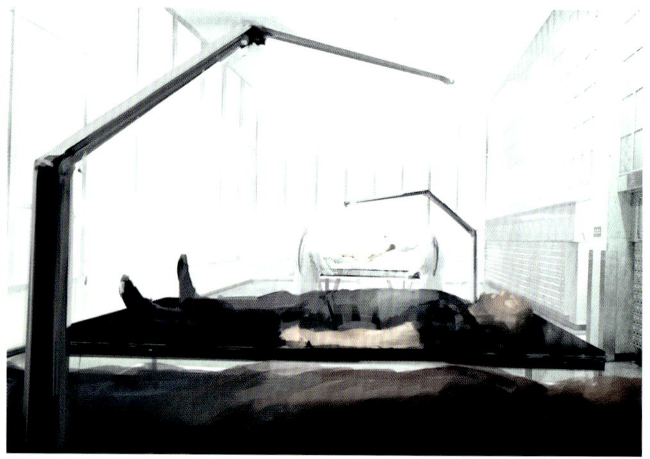

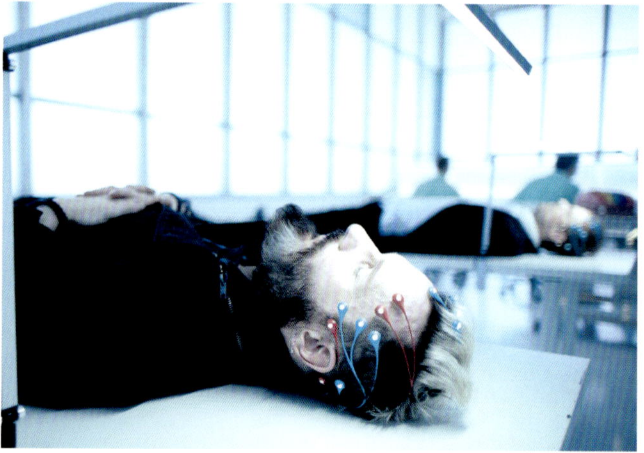

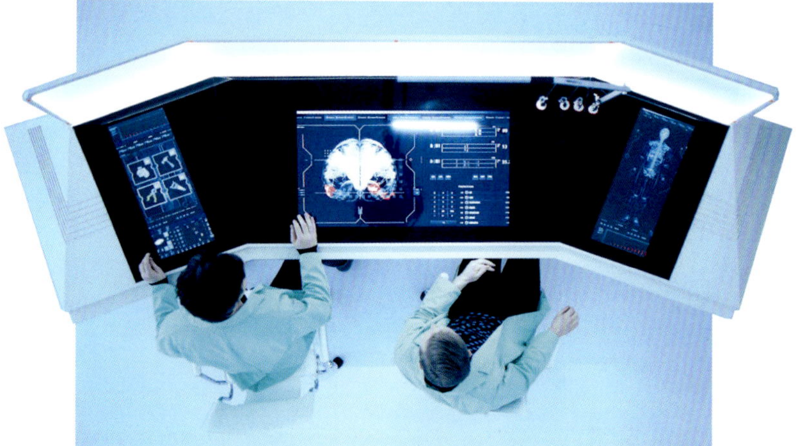

THIS PAGE: The interior of the data extraction center, the Wei Clinc.

NEXT PAGE: Dimi takes great pleasure in torturing Kovacs' consciousness.

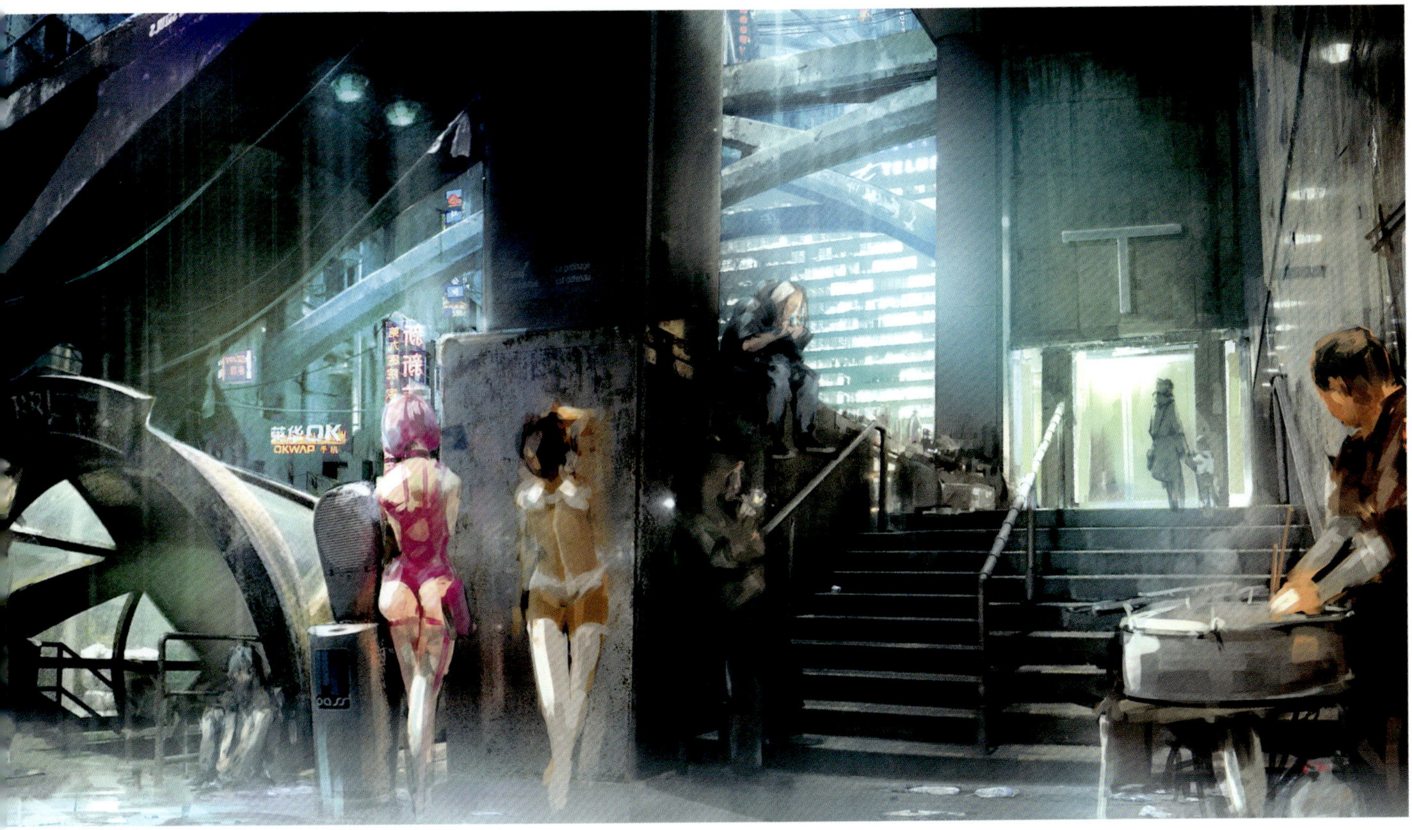

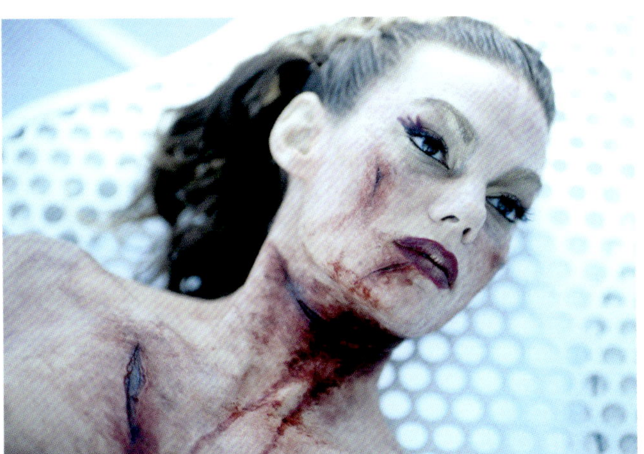

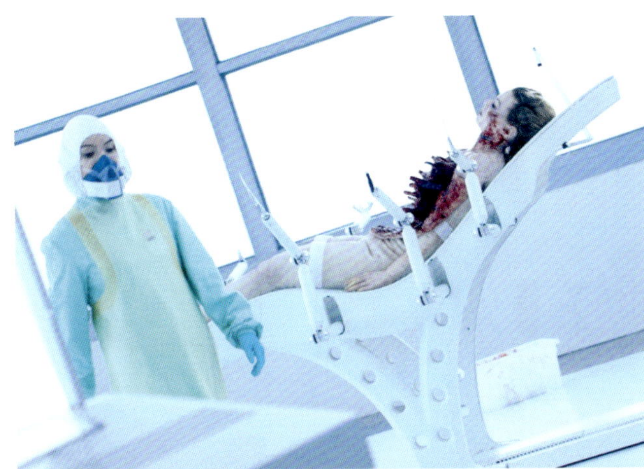

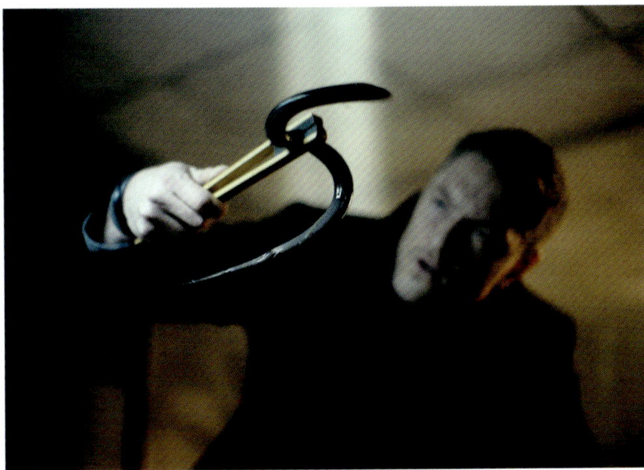

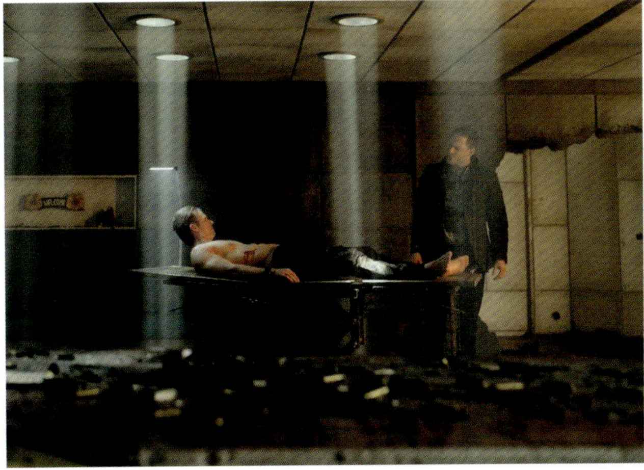

JACK IT OFF

AND ANEMONE

Anemone, real name Alice, is a sex slave at the Jack It Off club. Kovacs, seeking information on Lizzie Elliot, pretends to be Lizzie's mother Ava. Moved by a mother who loves her child (unlike Anemone's own mother), Anemone tells 'Ava' what she can, although she knows it's dangerous. Later, Anemone is forced to entrap Kovacs, and is then killed.

Actress Stephanie Cleough says Anemone's look is meant to reflect ambivalence. "When you are a slave, you're going to do your best, but you're also only going to care so much, and only have so much means at your disposal."

Regarding Anemone's motives, Cleough offers, "Even in the harshest of circumstances, and with so few options, we are still human, and we still have hearts, and emotions, and empathy, no matter how much it's been drilled out of us. For Anemone, the fact that Kovacs cares makes her want to help him, no matter the cost."

Bay City brothels like the Jack It Off and the Prick-Up are part of Licktown. Production designer Carey Meyer explains, "Licktown is a small piece of the main street set, which can be dressed to be different parts of Bay City. Licktown has a [variety] of shops that are set up out on the street. The Jack It Off club, which is right in Licktown, is made up of several different pieces. Some are on that street, some are in little hallways [on the soundstage], and some set pieces are actually on a different stage."

BELOW: Kovacs, pretending to be Lizzie's mother, waits for answers from Anemone.

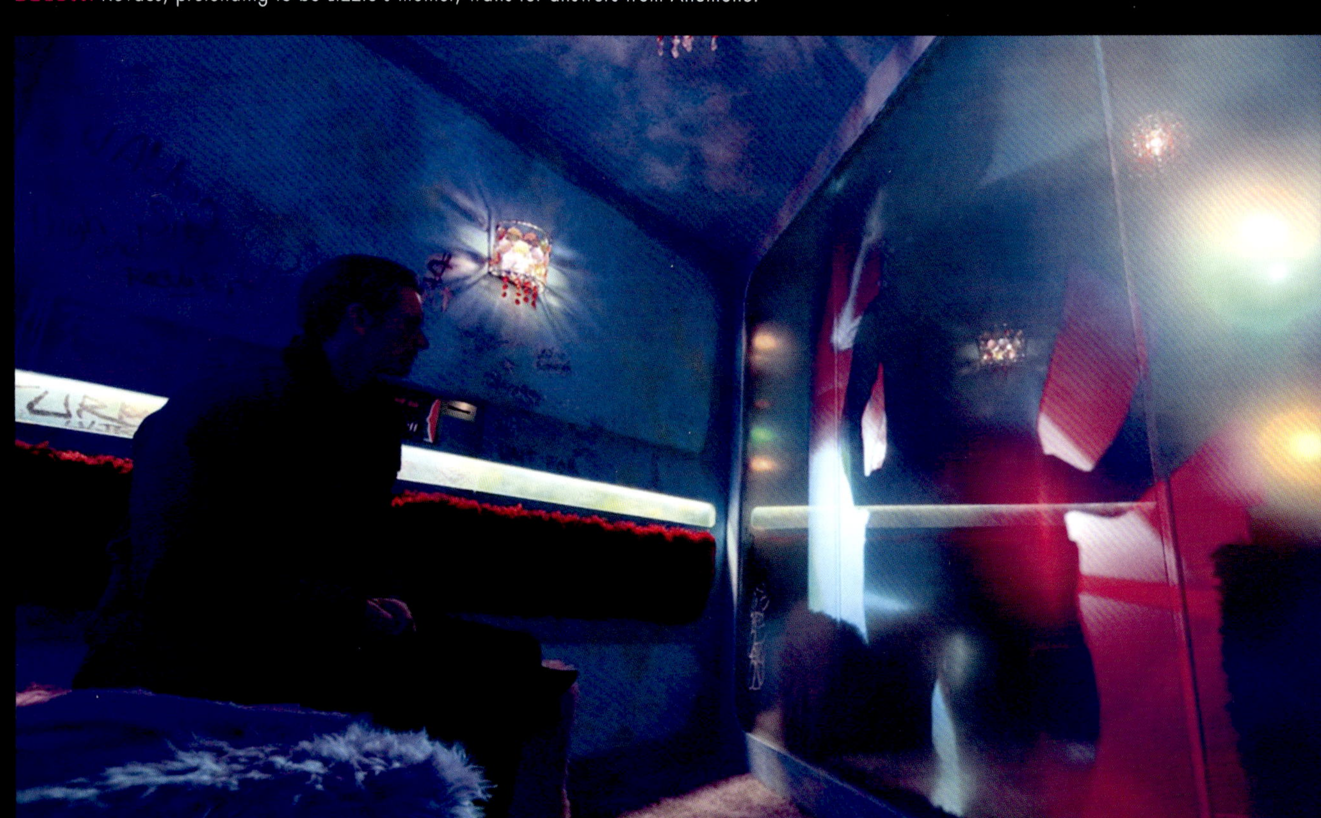

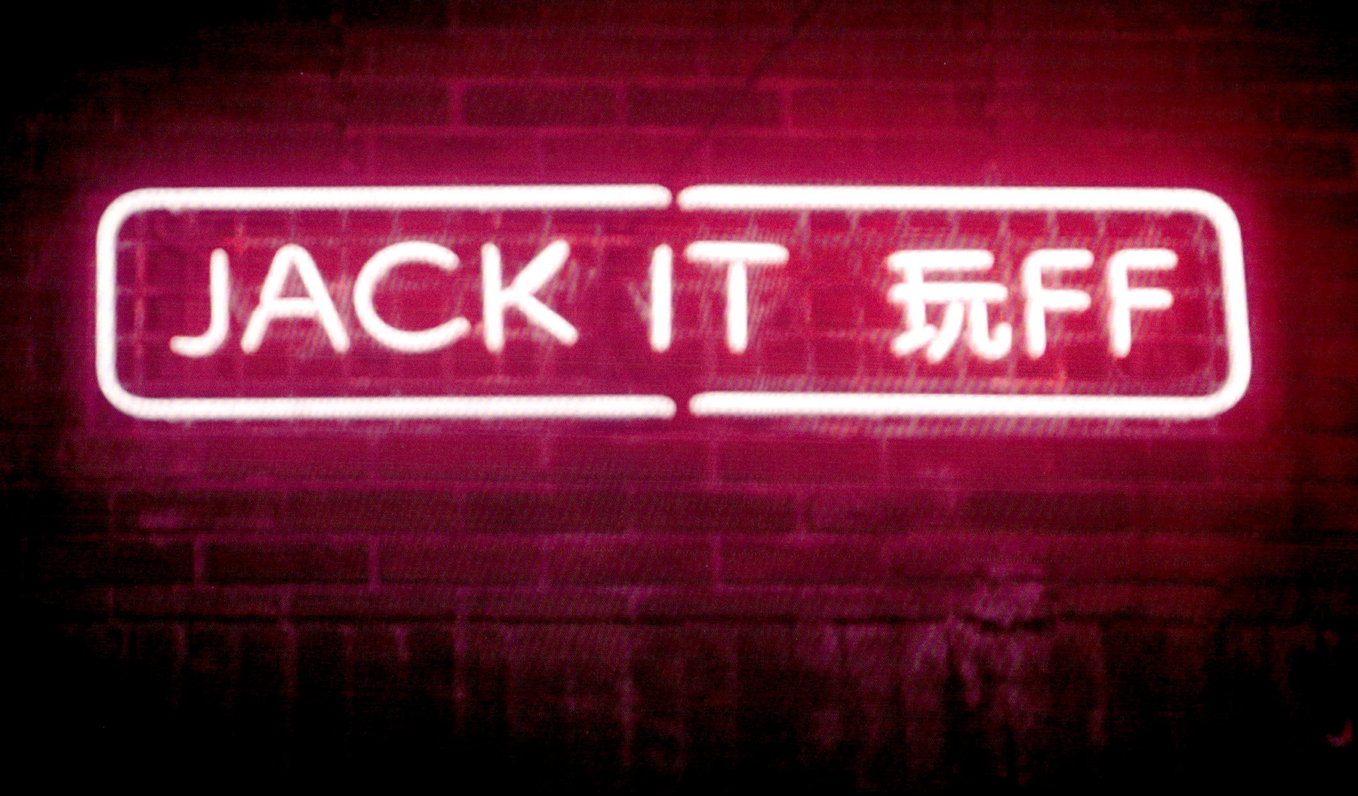

BELOW: Tammy Nera, Hayley Law's stunt double, on set of the season one episode 'Rage in Heaven.' The bright neon of Licktown, one of the more sordid areas of Bay City.

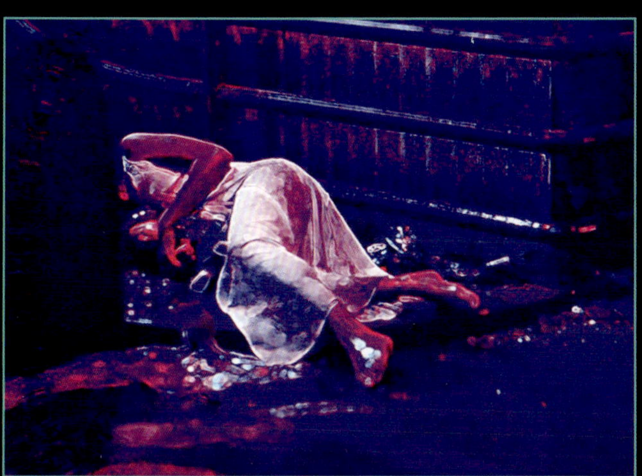

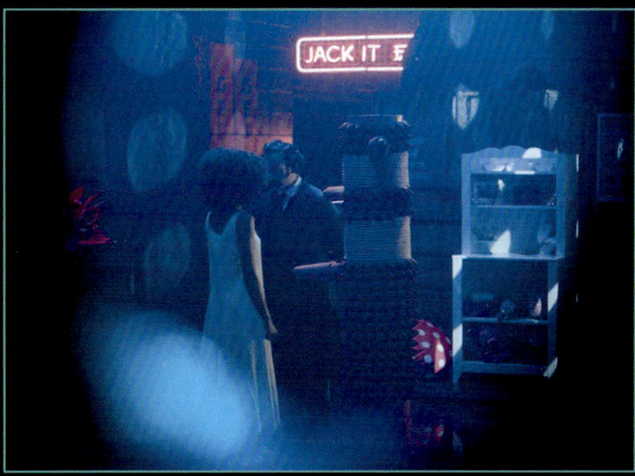

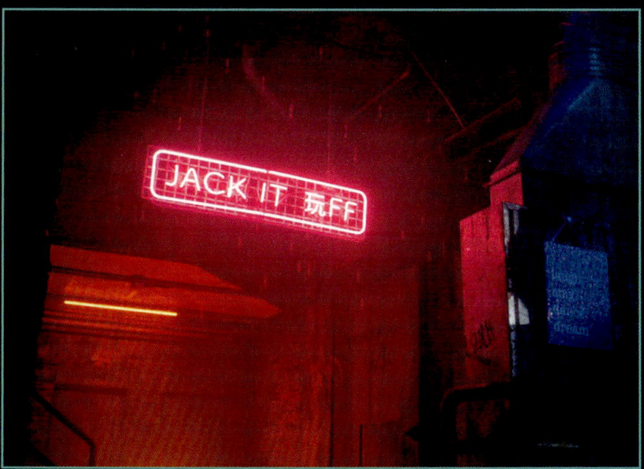

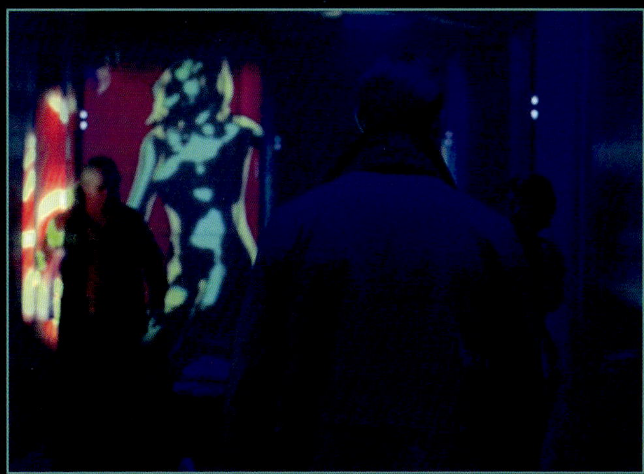

LIZZIE ELLIOT

YOU SHOULD BE AFRAID FOR THE MONSTERS

Lizzie Elliot, played by Hayley Law, is the adult daughter of Vernon and Ava Elliot. Lizzie was beaten by Miriam Bancroft into miscarrying Bancroft's baby and sleeve-dying, then mentally tortured at the Wei Clinic. Although Lizzie's stack is intact, her psyche is stuck in a trauma loop.

Only Poe is able to reach Lizzie. Their mentor/pupil relationship helps Lizzie find her inner warrior. Chris Conner, who plays Poe, says it puts his character "in complete service of an innocent. She's been abused and destroyed by a horrific world. And it gives Poe a chance to help a human, and in turn investigate what it is to be human."

Lizzie is ultimately able to needle-cast herself into a synth body in Head in the Clouds, where she helps her parents, Kovacs, and Ortega bring the establishment crashing to the ground. Lizzie's disintegration and ascendance, VFX supervisor Everett Burrell relates, is unlike Poe's decomposition. "We had to do something different for her, symbolic to her becoming an angel and going to heaven. Instead of being rawer nano-technology [as with Poe], we made it more about light and energy."

Once at Head in the Clouds, Lizzie selects an outfit that lets her blend in. Costume designer Ann Foley says, "I had to figure out a costume that was going to keep Lizzie covered, but still be sexy, but allow her to do her movements. Laeta was specific about wanting her to look like a superhero. So we came up with this fantastic cat suit, added some chains to it, and made it out of a black, shiny stretch vinyl. She can move beautifully in it."

Burrell adds that VFX assisted in Lizzie's Head in the Clouds fights, removing cables for stunt doubles sailing through the air, and adding digital blood when Lizzie takes down a foe.

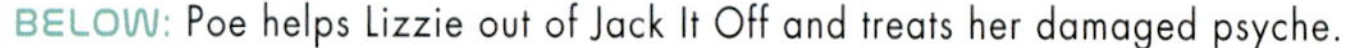

BELOW: Poe helps Lizzie out of Jack It Off and treats her damaged psyche.

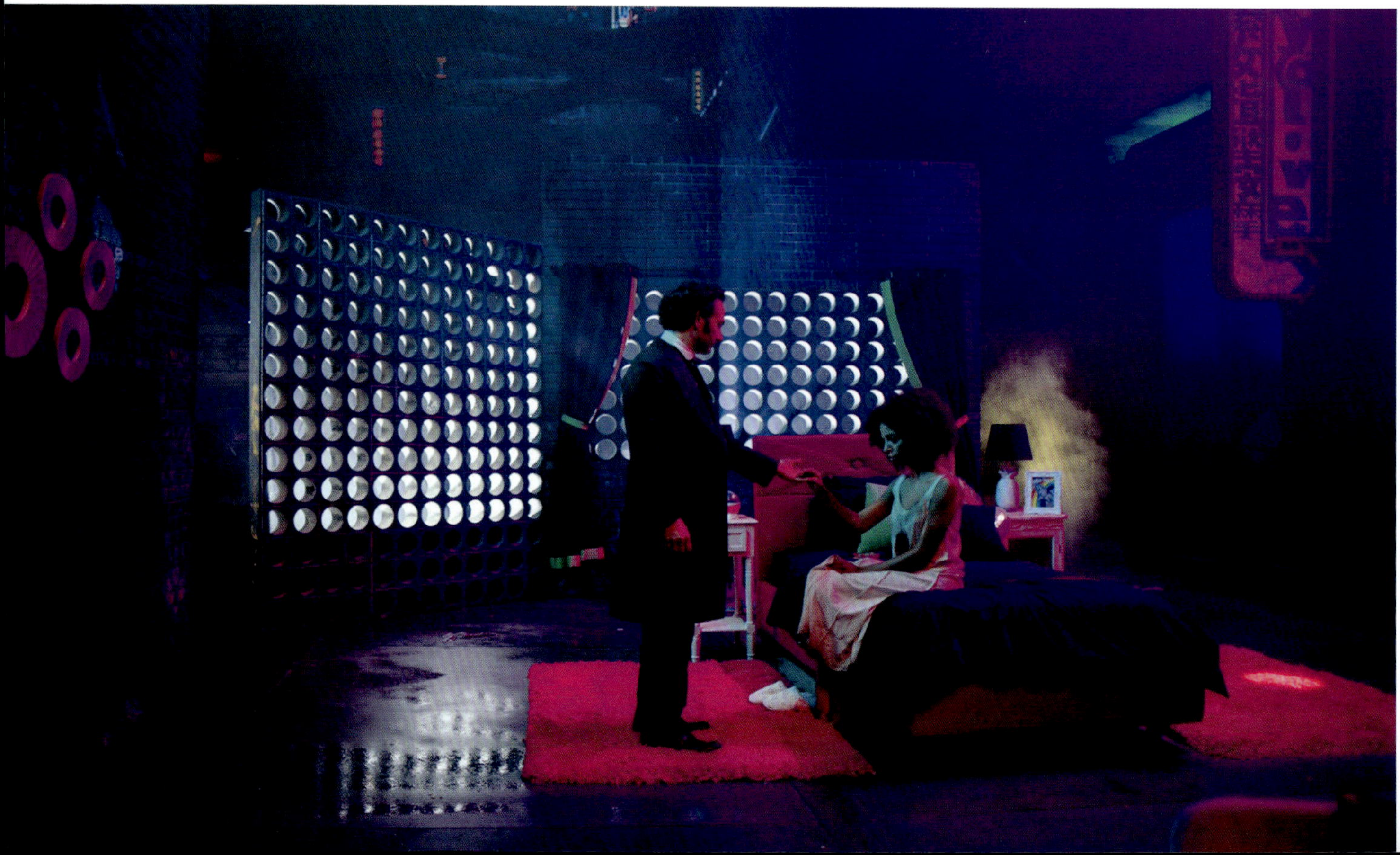

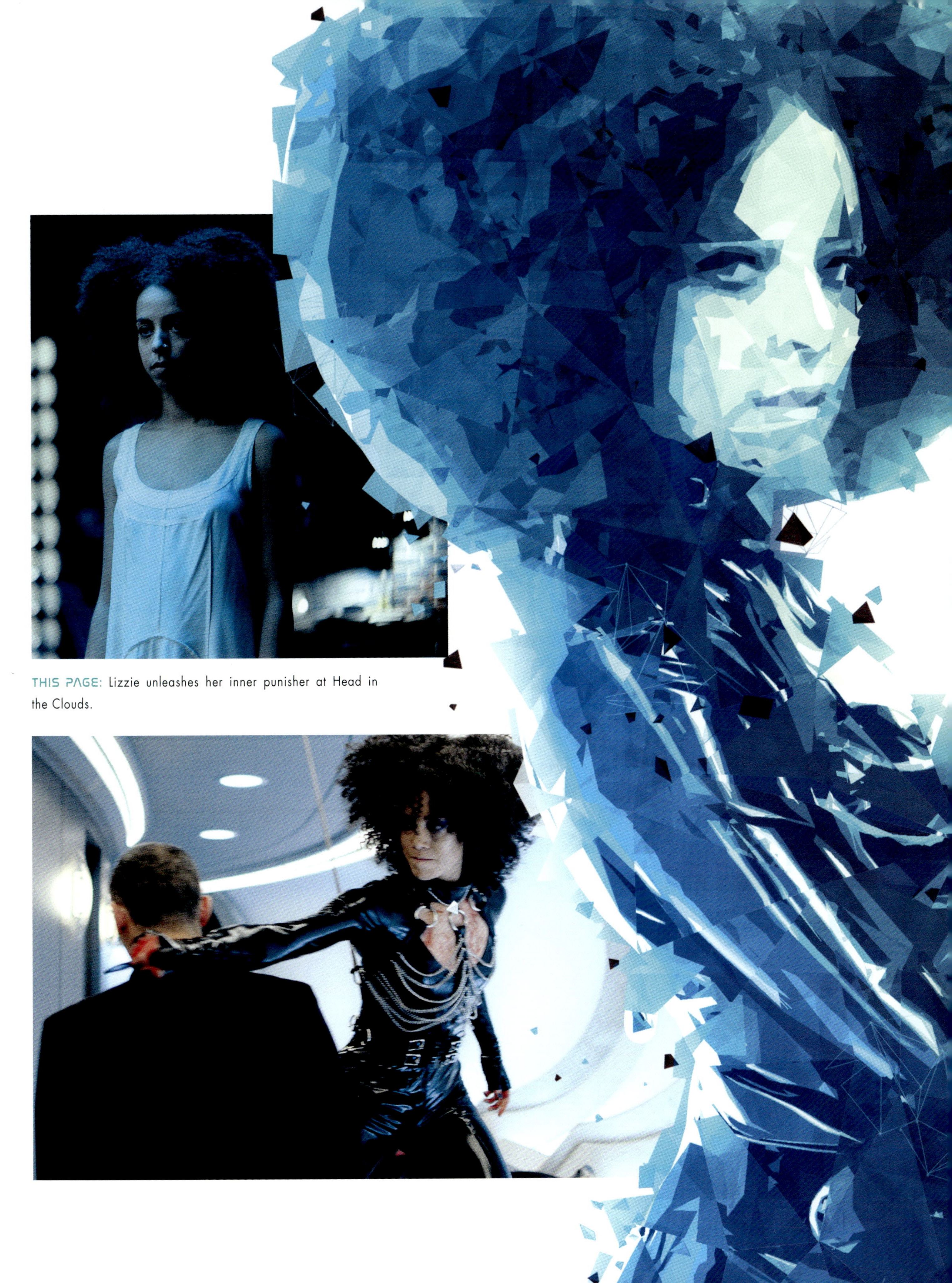

THIS PAGE: Lizzie unleashes her inner punisher at Head in the Clouds.

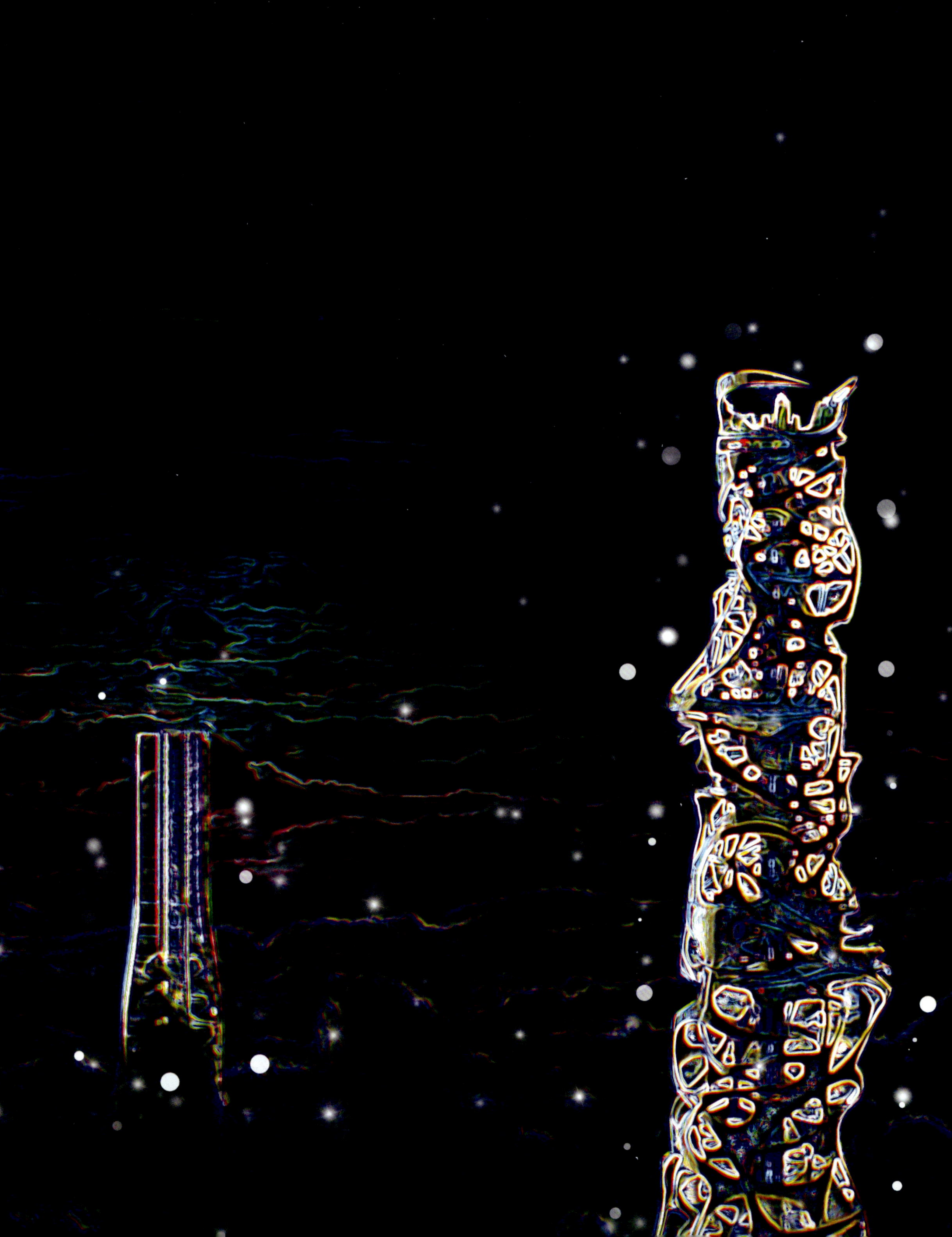

RIUM

THE AERIUM

CASTLE IN THE SKY

The Aerium, hovering above Bay City over what is now Northern California's Marin County, is the ultra-wealthy neighborhood of the Meths. 'Meth' is short for 'Methuselah,' the long-lived Biblical figure. Meths can afford to needlecast their consciousnesses into sleeves on other worlds, and to continually change their own sleeves, either into younger clones of themselves because they're aging, or just because they feel like something new. By doing this, they can effectively live forever.

Meths can also afford immense, one-of-a-kind homes that are essentially personal castles. Production designer Carey Meyer explains, "We've divided our show into three economic classes. We've got the grounder level, which is our street, and then we've got a middle level, which we call Twilight, which has taken us to multiple locations around Vancouver, that we've laced in the [vertical] middle of the city, which is maybe a hundred floors above the grounder level, and that's the very upper tops of the public city ground. Anything above that gets into Meth territory. [The Meths] all have towers that are between seventy-five-hundred and ten-thousand-feet tall. We've created a pyramid structure of wealth, which is exactly where we stand today."

Whereas Bay City is extremely colorful, Meyer adds, "As you get into the Aerium, everything gets much lighter and more lofty and cloudlike, more monochromatic and muted. It's much more a subdued, Godlike sort of space."

This is reflected in the Meths' clothing as well, relates costume designer Ann Foley. "Because the Aerium is above the clouds, we decided to go with a very cloudlike white/silver/gold palette. We kept it very light, very ethereal."

Season one VFX supervisor Everett Burrell observes, "Only certain buildings can go that tall. Because the Meths are so wealthy, they have access to all this ancient technology that helps them build these buildings. Each of the buildings had a very unique design, but they all had a common thing in the center, which was the Meth core. That has a very similar blue light to what the stacks have, because the stacks came from the Elders. The technology that built buildings that high and space travel was all based on Elder tech."

Series creator Laeta Kalogridis says, "There's something very real for us about the continuation of that [wealth and societal] divide. When you cast your mind forward to what the future might look like, it's lovely for the people at the top, but they get [numerically] fewer and fewer, and the people below get more and more. Especially if the people at the top can never be removed, because they never die." This makes life harder for those below, because of "the energy of one small group of people holding onto all the resources, holding onto the most precious resource, which is life, and not letting go of it, and seeing everything and everyone else as a raw material to be exploited. I think that's the worst of human nature. And because we all know that's the worst of human nature, it feels real."

RIGHT: Artist's scale drawing of Bancroft's home in the clouds compared to real-life counterparts.

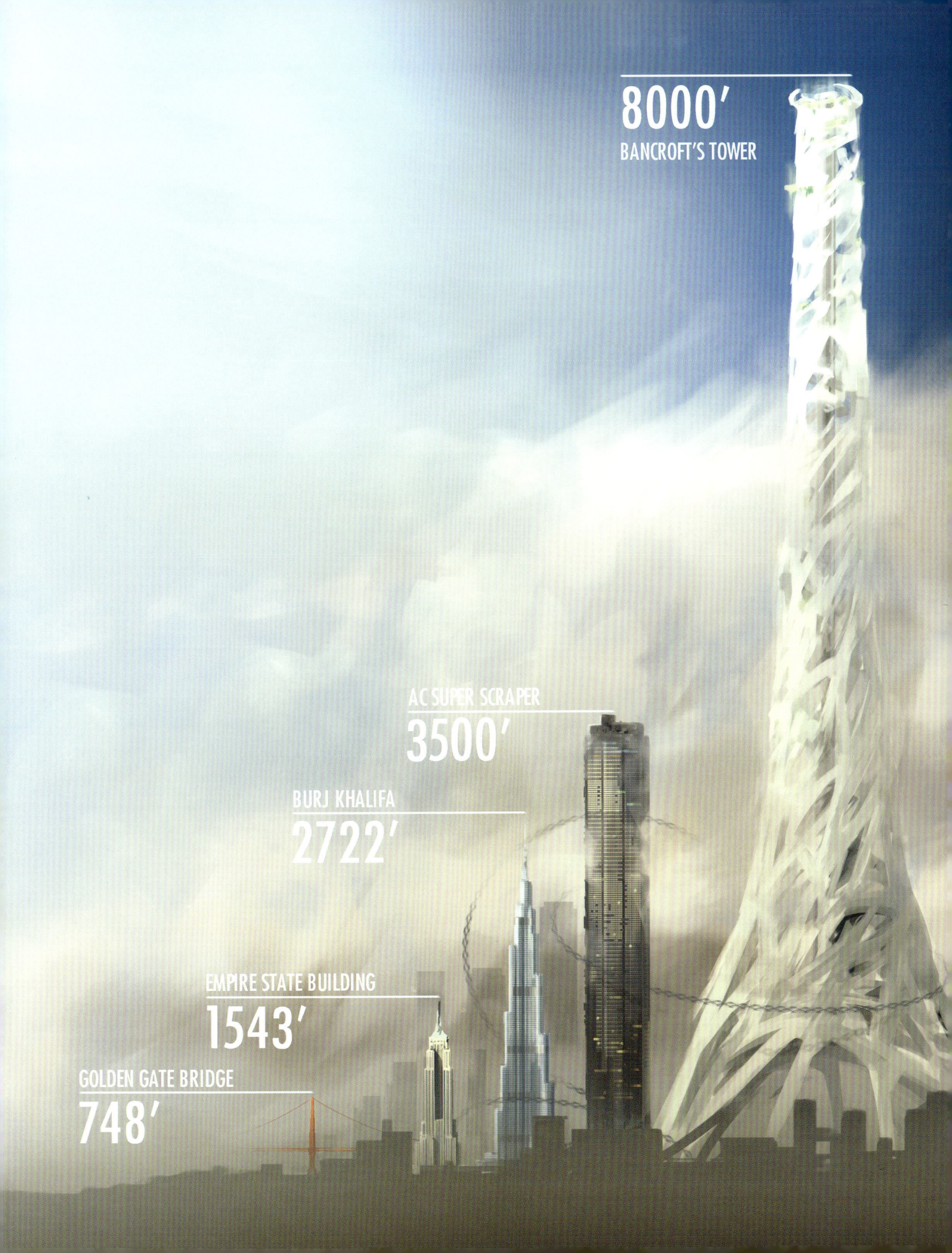

8000′
BANCROFT'S TOWER

AC SUPER SCRAPER
3500′

BURJ KHALIFA
2722′

EMPIRE STATE BUILDING
1543′

GOLDEN GATE BRIDGE
748′

LAURENS BANCROFT

"I ADMIRE A MAN THAT CAN LOOK OVER THE EDGE WITHOUT FLINCHING."

Laurens Bancroft, played by James Purefoy, is a Meth, one of the wealthy elite who can afford near-immortality by continually cloning himself and resleeving his consciousness. Born in 2019, Bancroft was ninety-nine years old when stack technology was invented; he's one of its first users.

Laeta Kalogridis explains, "Bancroft never sleeves himself in anything younger than forty-five or older than fifty-five, because he believes that's [when] men have the most power. The great gods, like Odin or Zeus, are all fathers, at an age that speaks to having triumphed."

VFX supervisor Everett Burrell notes that CGI helped Bancroft's clones look both young and slightly lab-made. "We made his skin a little perfect; we gave him a bit of pearlescent shine."

Bancroft has been shot to death, his stack destroyed, in his own home. Since Bancroft has automatic stack backups and a supply of cloned sleeves, this isn't the end of him, but he refuses to believe the evidence that he shot himself.

When Bancroft first spins up Kovacs and has him resleeved, Kalogridis relates, "Bancroft says, 'I'll give you a pardon, but you have to solve a murder.' And [Kovacs] says, 'Whose murder?' And Bancroft says, 'Mine.' You have this surreal wonderful scene where Bancroft is talking to Kovacs about how he was murdered in this room and doesn't remember it because his consciousness is backed up every forty-eight hours via satellite. He's downloaded into another clone of himself. But [the murder] happened ten minutes before his forty-eight-hour backup, so he has two days that are completely unaccounted for. He doesn't know what happened, and he doesn't know who killed him. He needs Kovacs to find out what happened to him.

BELOW: CGI effects helped to transform Bancroft's appearance.

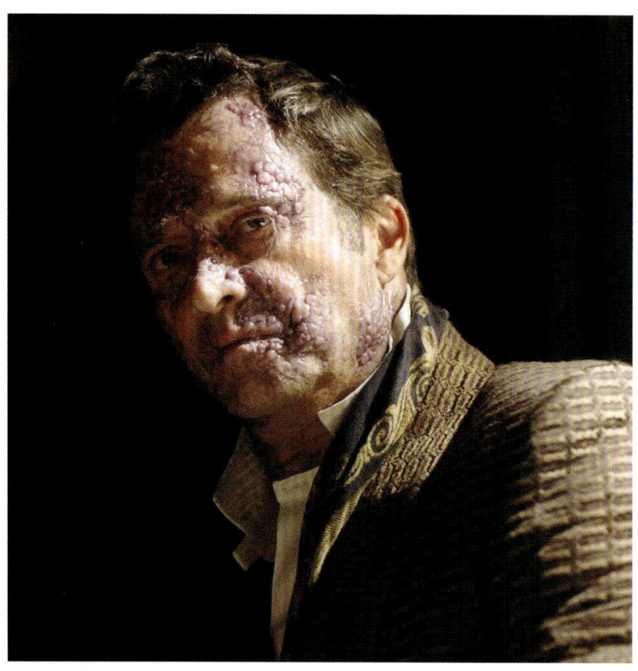

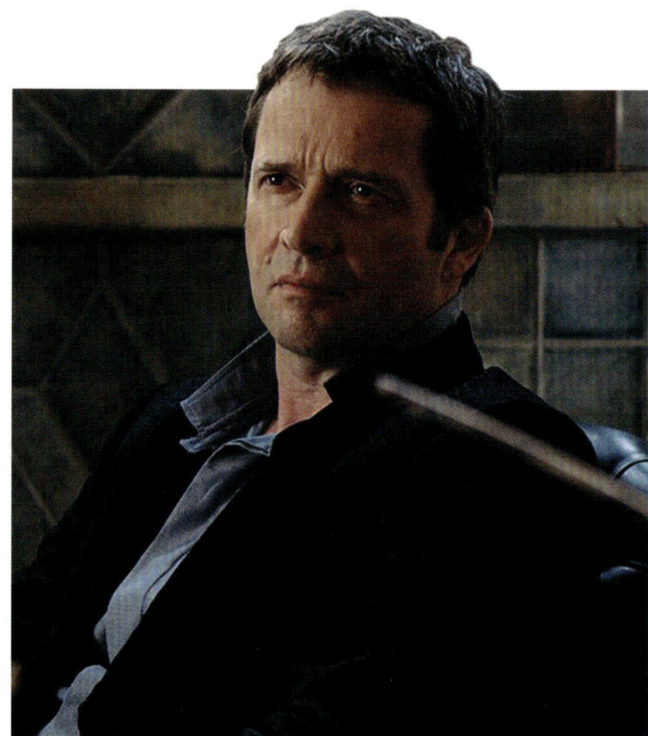

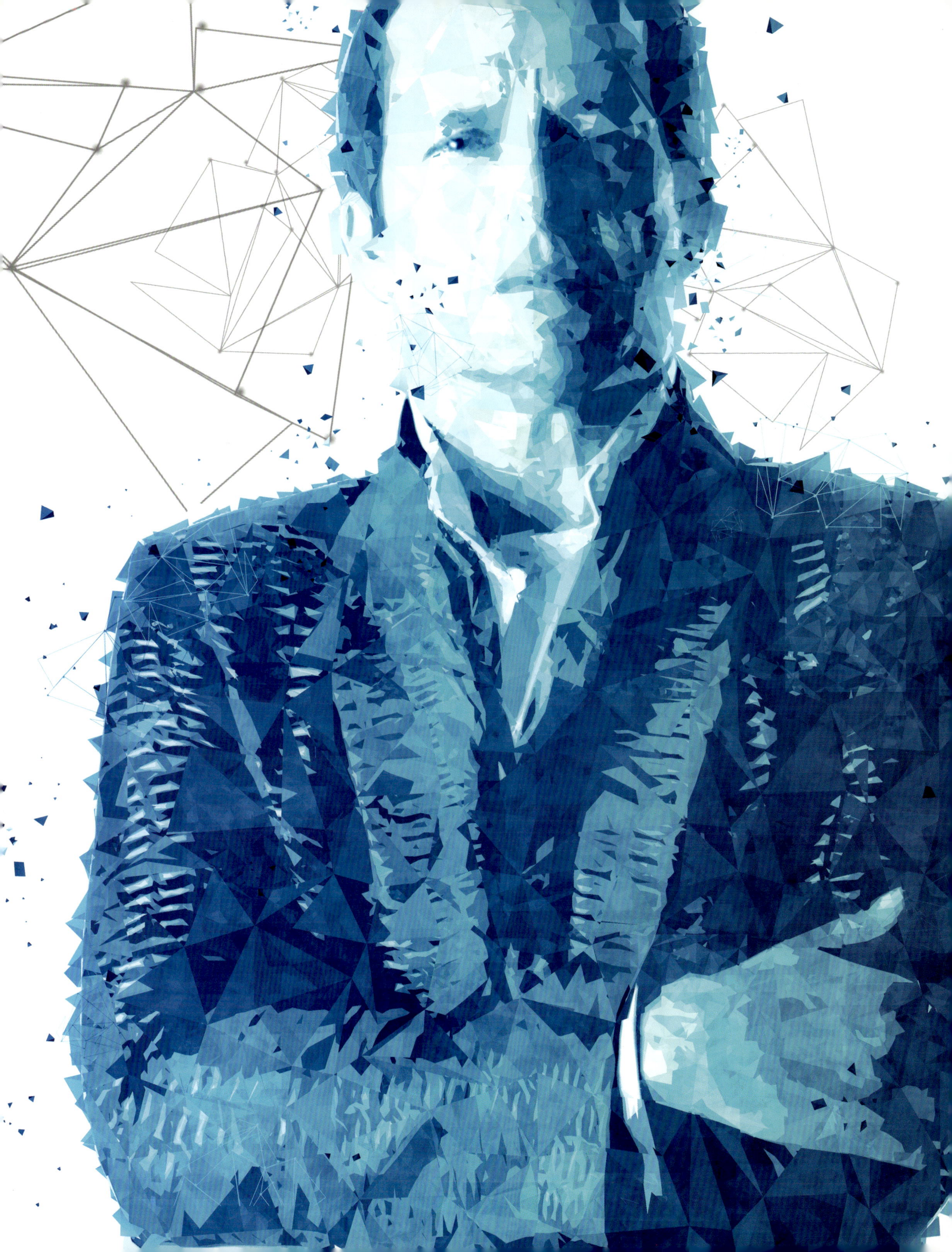

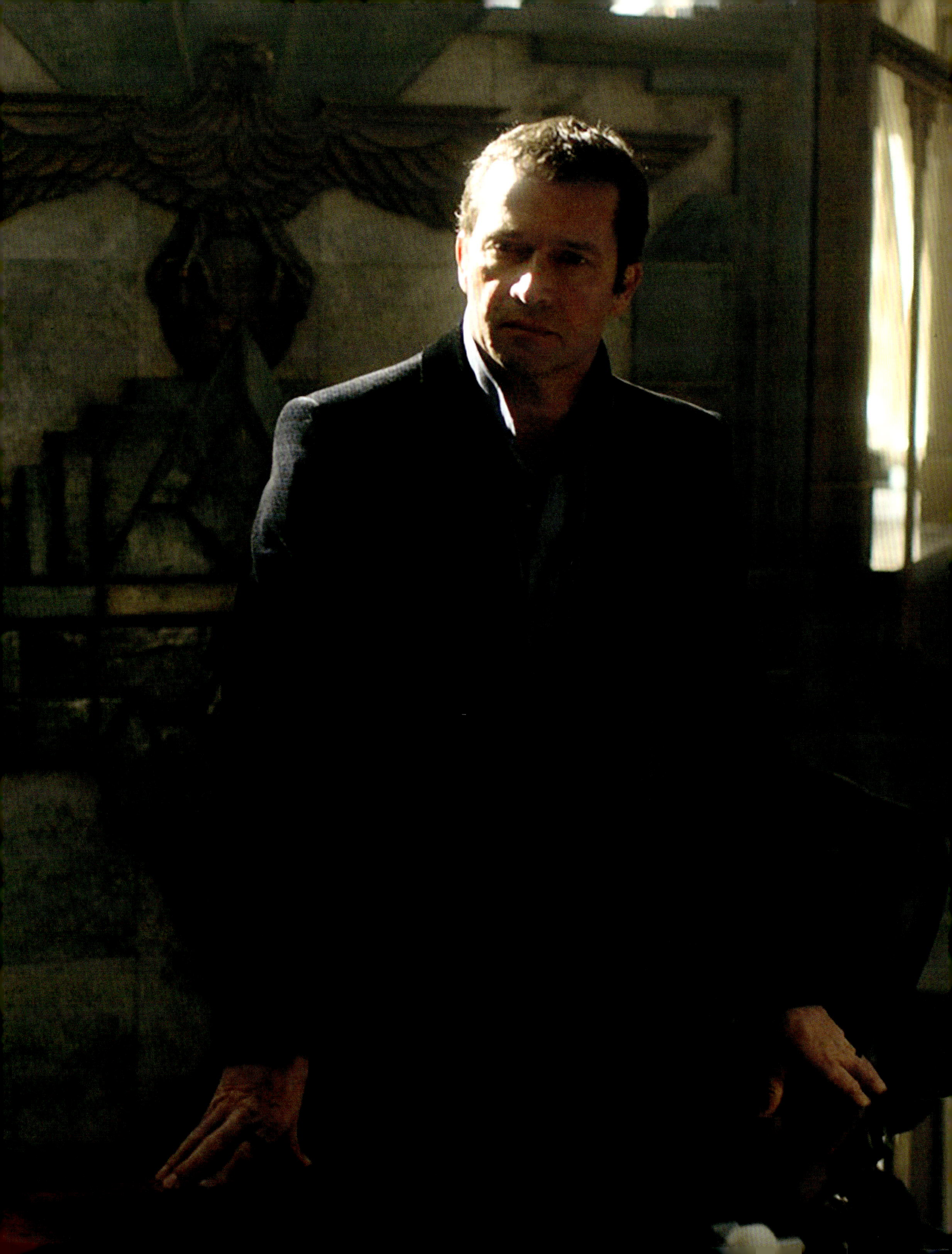

"Kovacs keys pretty fast into the fact that something to do with Bancroft's behavior is tied to the case," Kalogridis continues. "Among Bancroft's worst habits is how he handles his anger and frustration at the world. He finds hookers who look like his wife and strangles them, sometimes to death. If they die, he replaces their sleeve. Bancroft has a very loose relationship with morals, but thinks he's a very moral person. He does terrible things, but he feels because he never causes anyone to die permanently, it's never real death, it somehow doesn't count. [Something] I find fascinating about him is that he should feel familiar to us. He comes from [the audience's] time and culture. But he's lived way too long, and it's corrupted a part of him that can't be redeemed."

Peter Hoar, who directed the last two episodes, helmed the flashback scene where it's revealed that Bancroft did commit suicide after discovering that, in a drug-induced rage, he has not only killed a prostitute's sleeve, but also her stack, destroying her utterly. A second prostitute, Mary Lou Henchy, ran from him in terror, resulting in her own death. "He's looking down the telescope, and he witnesses Henchy's suicidal leap, and he's filled with remorse. That is one of the key triggers which makes him actually do the deed, of committing suicide, which he was convinced that he wouldn't do." Hoar adds that Bancroft's suicide had to be reshot. "I think the script was oblique. It was like, 'We see a gun in his hand.' My version was, we see him standing by the telescope, and holding the gun in his hand, and that was it. [The producers] didn't think it went far enough. They wanted it to be a lot more explicit. Because I was shooting something else [when the reshoot was scheduled], somebody else shot the version where he brought the gun up to his head."

BELOW: Bancroft's anger lays the groundwork for his suicide attempt.

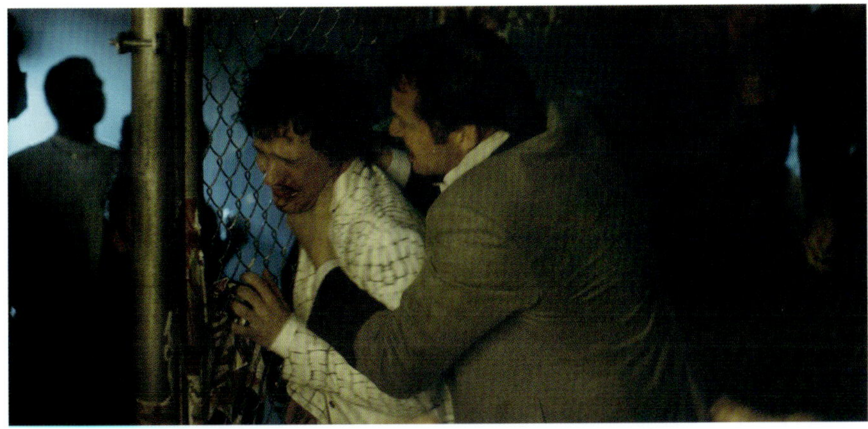

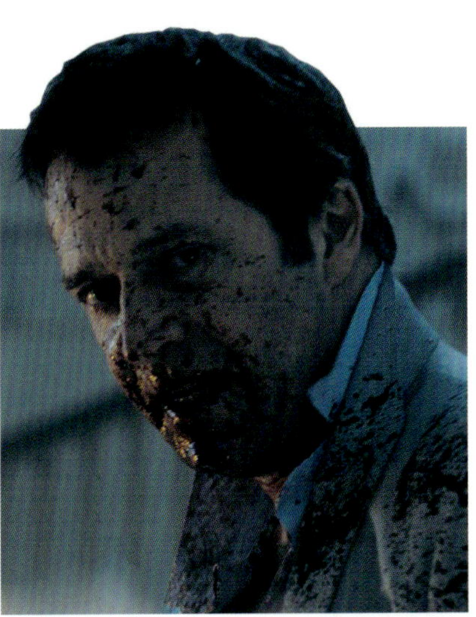

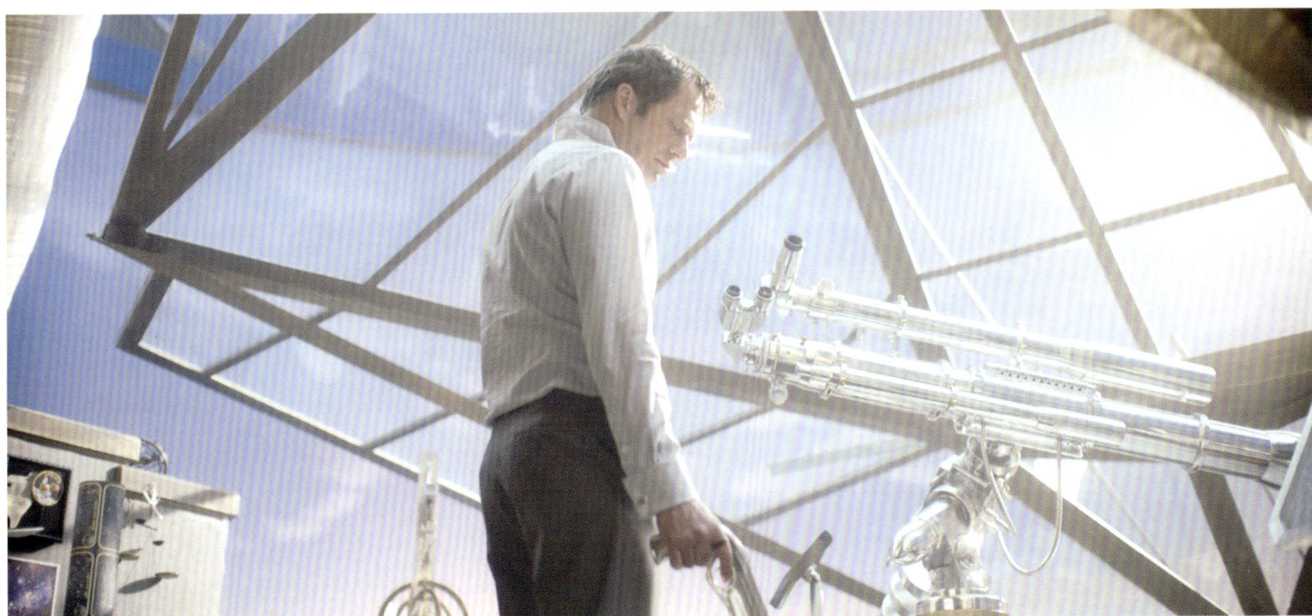

MIRIAM BANCROFT

"THE CHILDREN ARE MINE!"

Miriam Bancroft, played by Kristin Lehman, has been married to Laurens Bancroft for 118 years. They've had twenty-one children together. Miriam's need to believe that Laurens has no children with anyone but her creates a secret that fuels the storyline.

When Kovacs publicly confronts Miriam with evidence that she beat Lizzie Elliot into a miscarriage, it's impossible for the wealthy woman to preserve her façade any longer. She tries to justify her actions but rapidly unravels when even her claim to being the only mother of Bancroft's offspring is proved false. She screams, "The children are mine!"

"It was the final reckoning," says director Peter Hoar, "in the sense that all her horrors came back to haunt her. There was a great moment of her railing on everybody, and she just goes crazy, and shouts. I loved that moment."

For all her cruelty, Miriam has a great look that she uses to further her plans, observes costume designer Ann Foley. "Miriam's style is based off of old Hollywood. That's what I had in my mind's eye when I first read the character. Her color palette is specific to the Meth palette, the whites and creams and silvers and golds. The interesting thing with Miriam is that there's always something going on with her. There's a hidden agenda, so her clothes will always reflect that. That's part of my job as a storyteller, is helping the actors find their way through the scene through the clothes. If we can do that with the clothes, it's a bonus, especially for the audience. So every time you see her, there's a plot behind what she was wearing. Her costumes might be sheer, they might be see-through, but she's doing this for a reason."

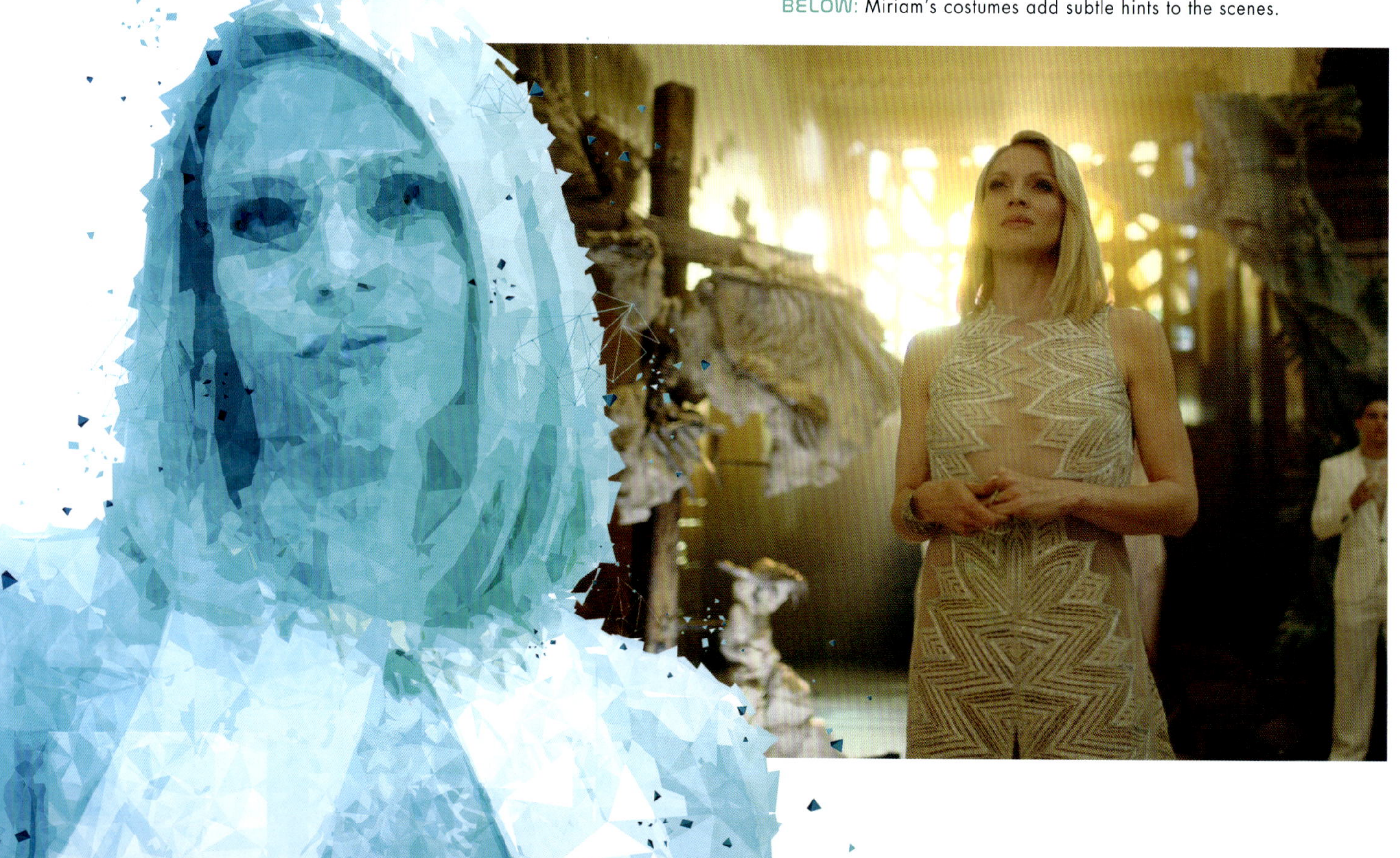

BELOW: Miriam's costumes add subtle hints to the scenes.

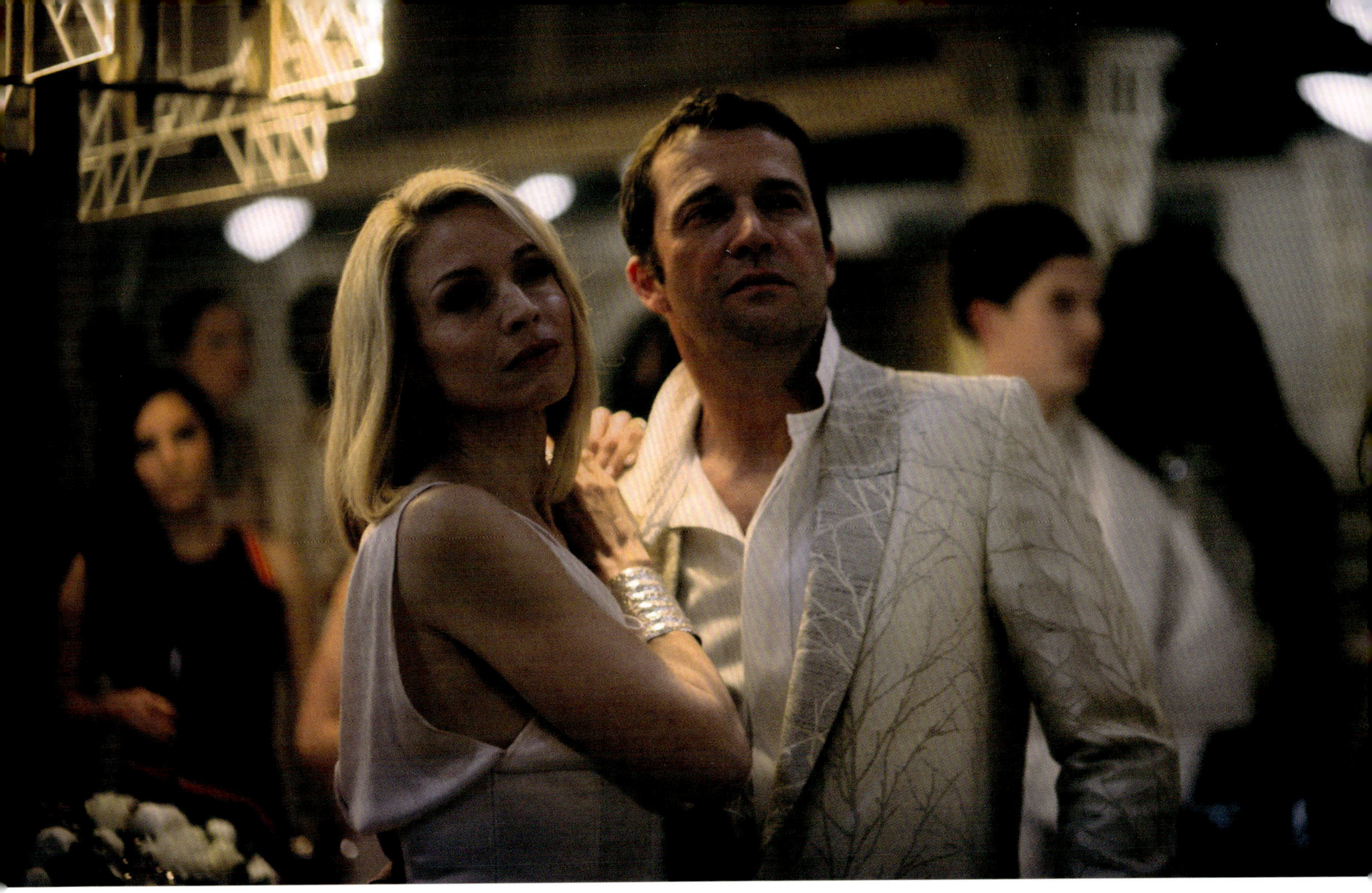

ABOVE: Miriam and Laurens put up a façade of a perfect relationship.

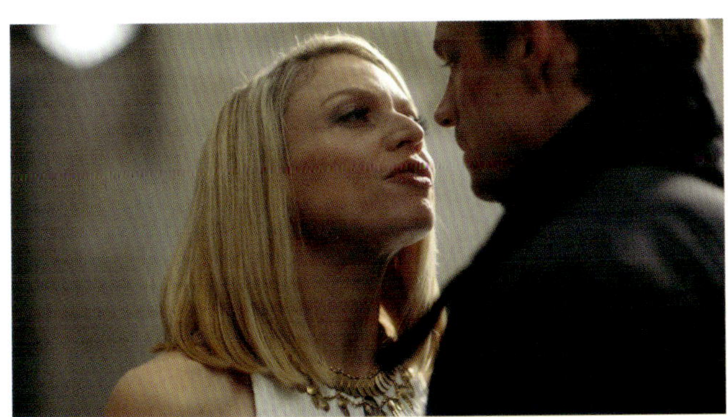

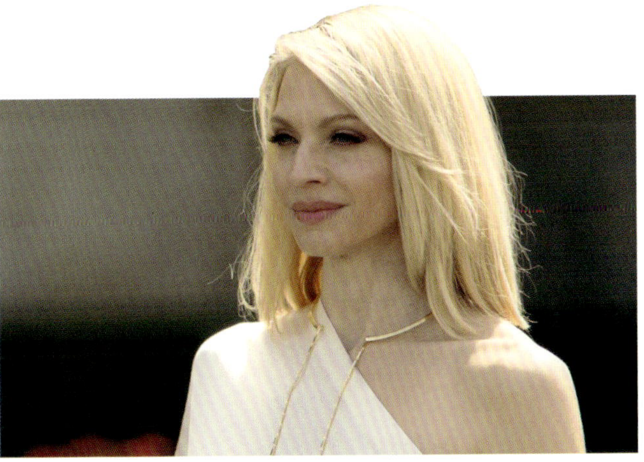

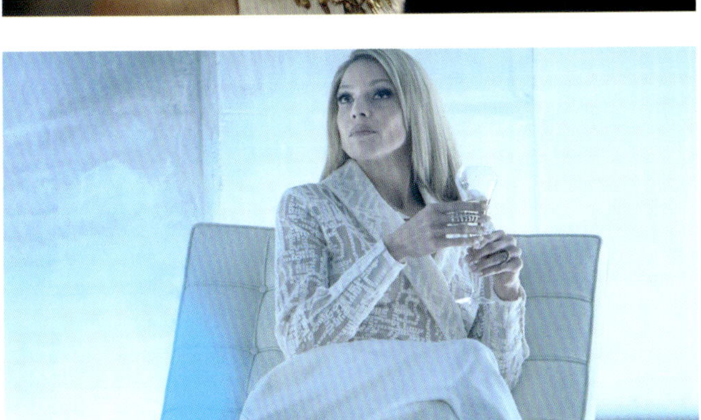

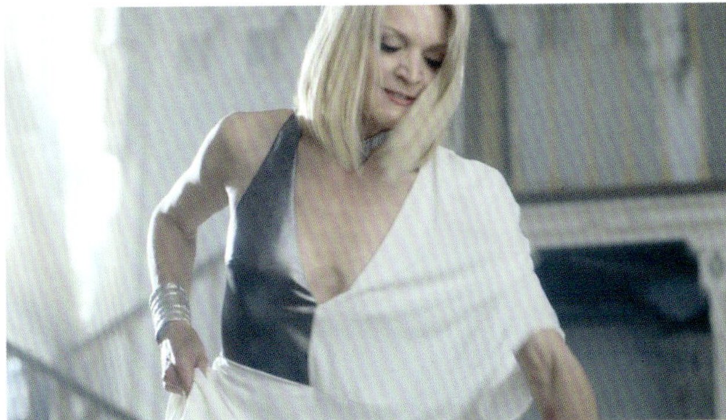

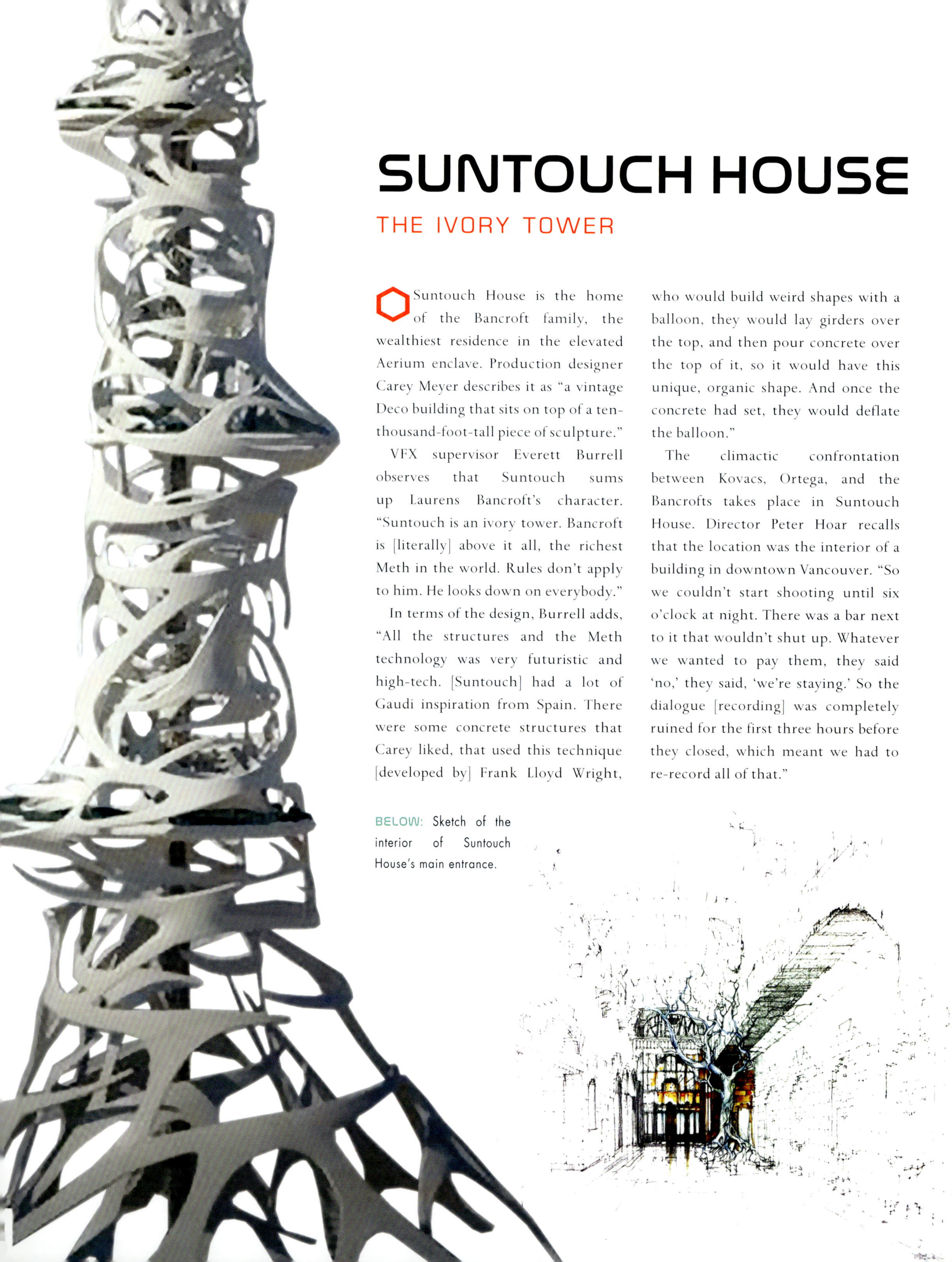

SUNTOUCH HOUSE

THE IVORY TOWER

Suntouch House is the home of the Bancroft family, the wealthiest residence in the elevated Aerium enclave. Production designer Carey Meyer describes it as "a vintage Deco building that sits on top of a ten-thousand-foot-tall piece of sculpture."

VFX supervisor Everett Burrell observes that Suntouch sums up Laurens Bancroft's character. "Suntouch is an ivory tower. Bancroft is [literally] above it all, the richest Meth in the world. Rules don't apply to him. He looks down on everybody."

In terms of the design, Burrell adds, "All the structures and the Meth technology was very futuristic and high-tech. [Suntouch] had a lot of Gaudi inspiration from Spain. There were some concrete structures that Carey liked, that used this technique [developed by] Frank Lloyd Wright, who would build weird shapes with a balloon, they would lay girders over the top, and then pour concrete over the top of it, so it would have this unique, organic shape. And once the concrete had set, they would deflate the balloon."

The climactic confrontation between Kovacs, Ortega, and the Bancrofts takes place in Suntouch House. Director Peter Hoar recalls that the location was the interior of a building in downtown Vancouver. "So we couldn't start shooting until six o'clock at night. There was a bar next to it that wouldn't shut up. Whatever we wanted to pay them, they said 'no,' they said, 'we're staying.' So the dialogue [recording] was completely ruined for the first three hours before they closed, which meant we had to re-record all of that."

BELOW: Sketch of the interior of Suntouch House's main entrance.

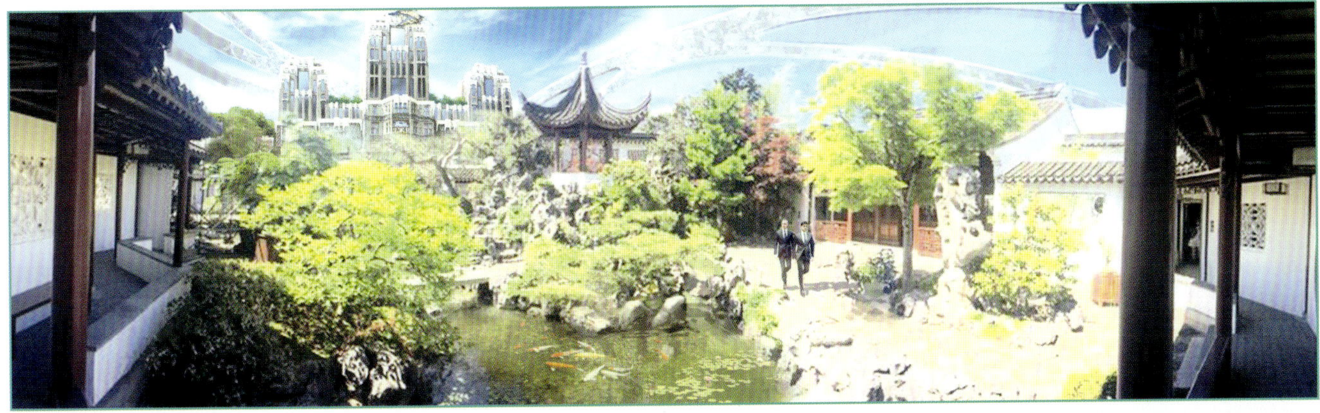

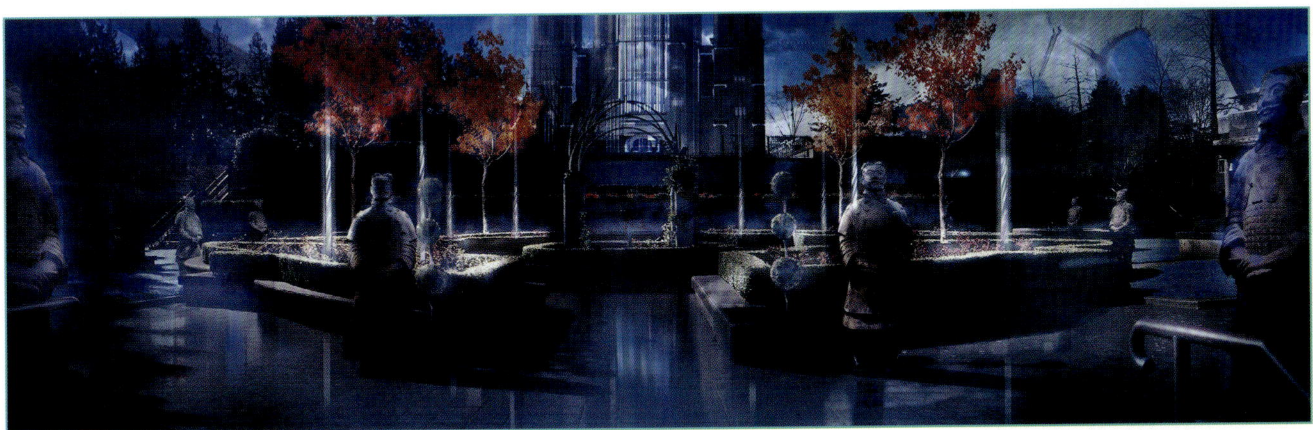

ABOVE: Sketches of the garden area of Suntouch House, as seen during the day and at night.

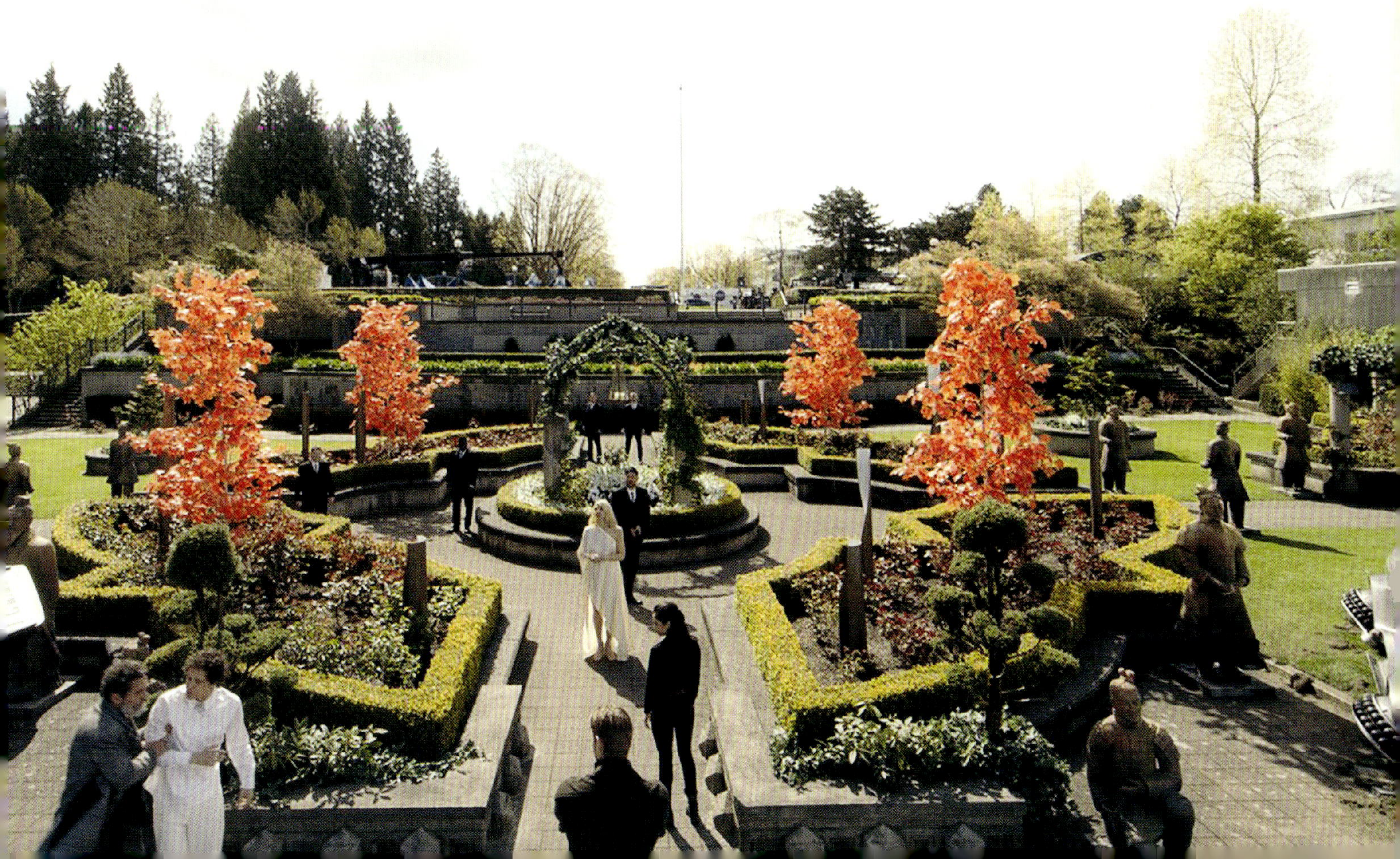

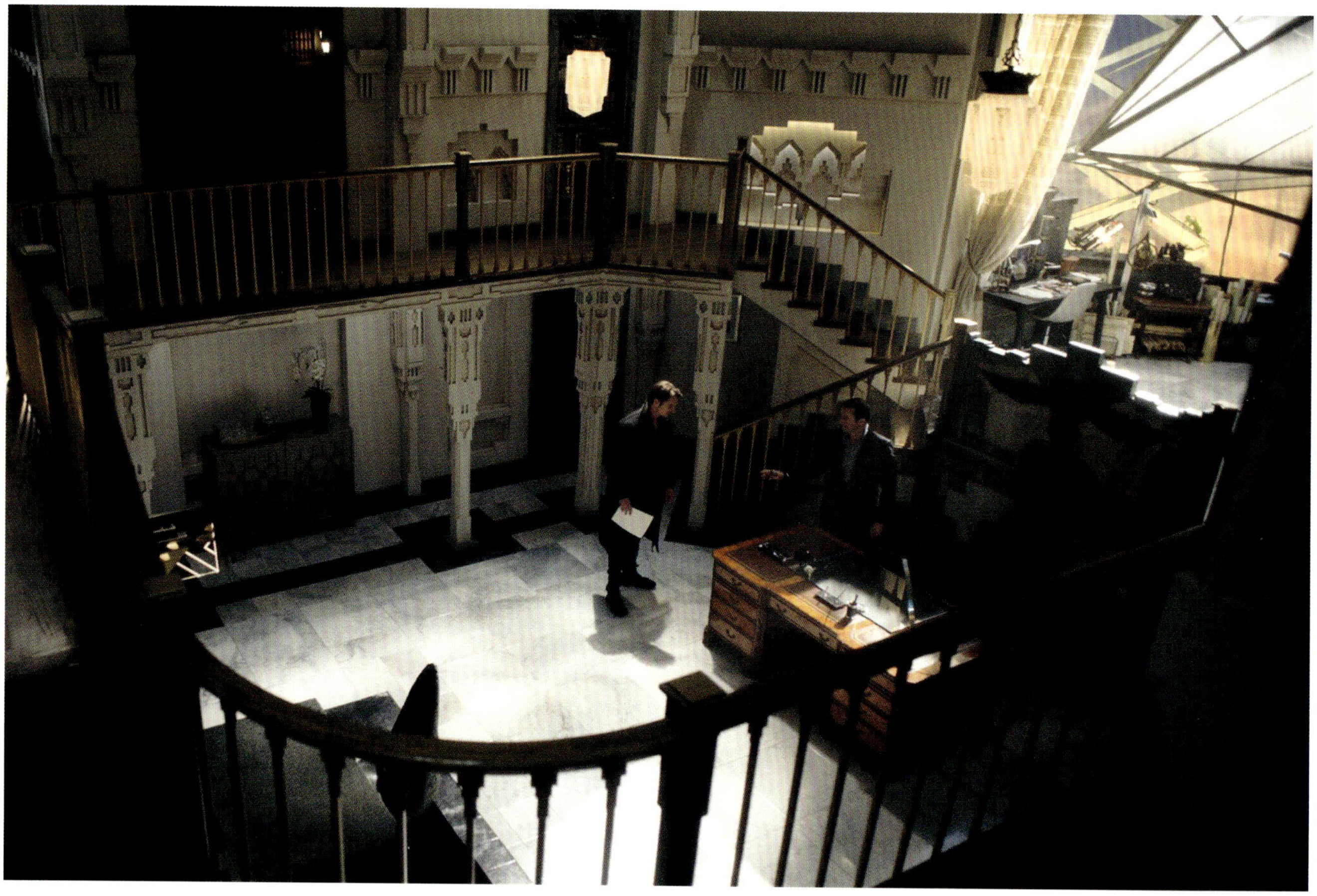

THIS PAGE: Kovacs visits the Bancrofts at Suntouch House.

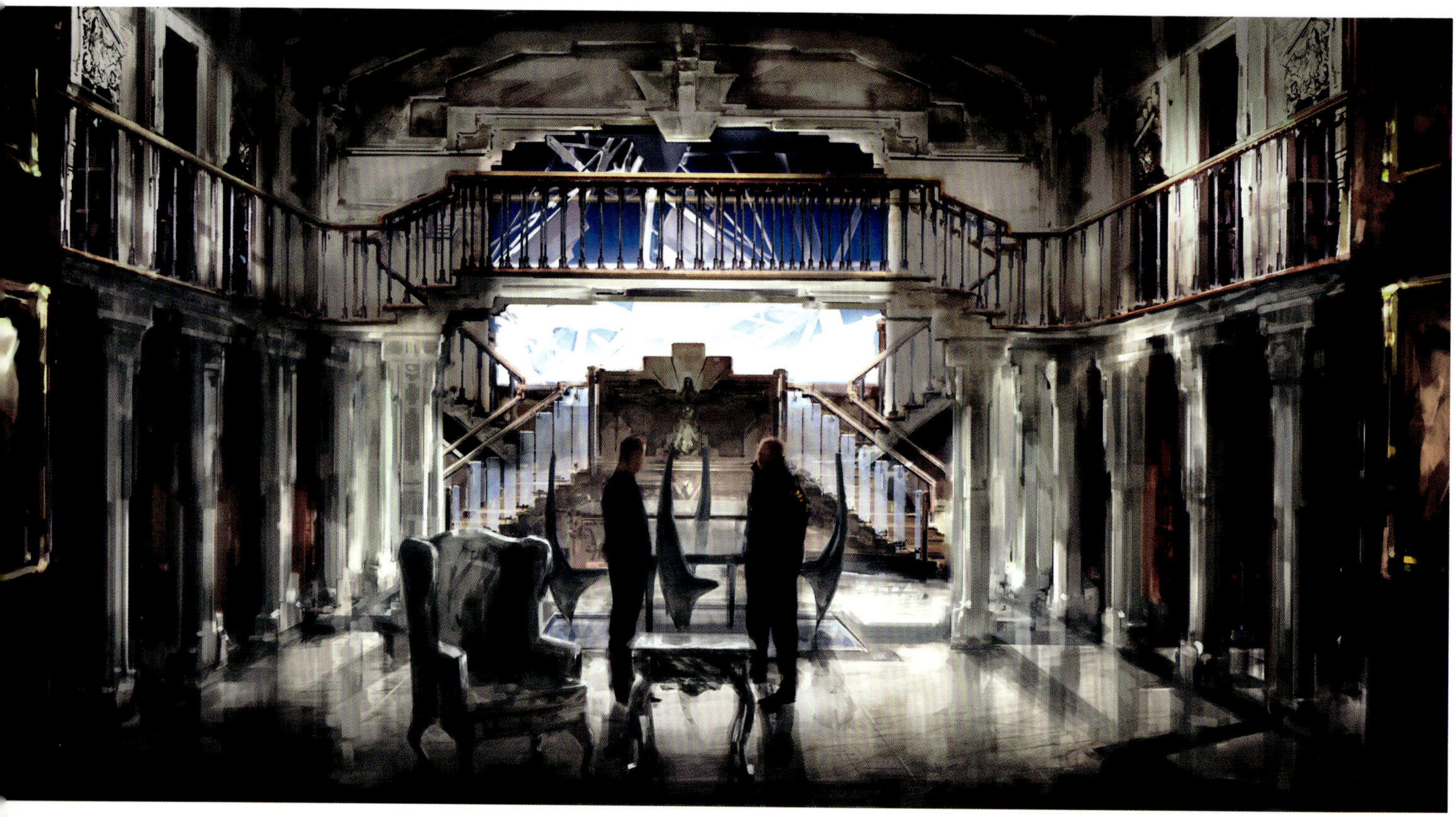

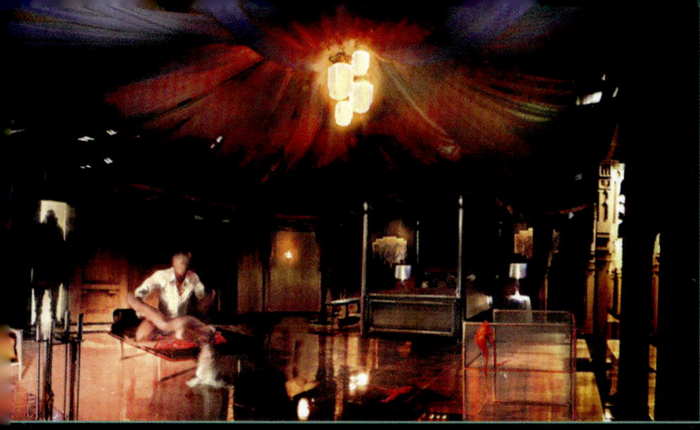

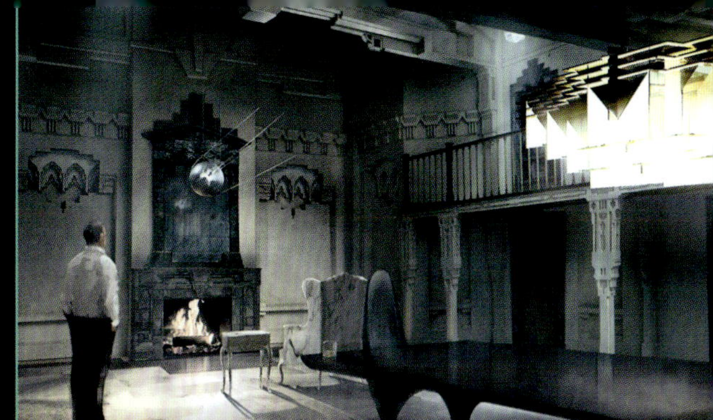

HIS PAGE: Various rooms of the Bancrofts' skyward residence.

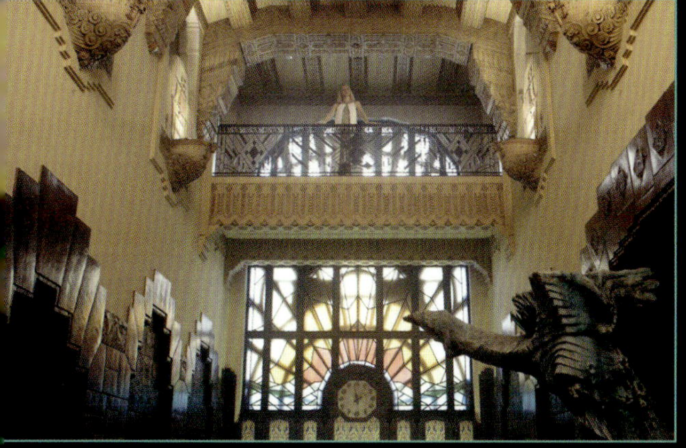

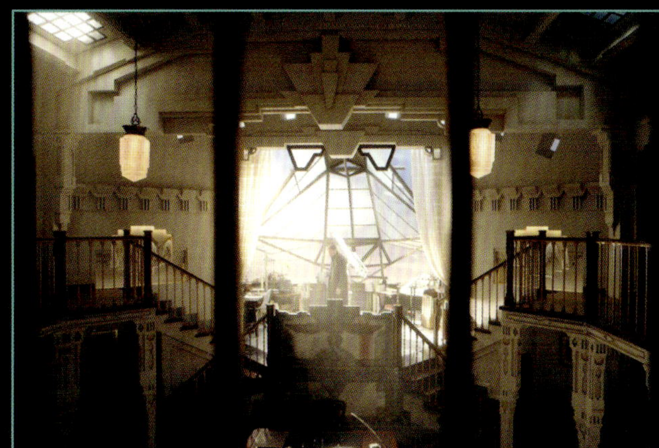

OUMOU PRESCOTT

Oumou Prescott, played by Tamara Taylor, is the Bancroft family lawyer and fixer. As such, Prescott is part of the literal middle class, living in the Twilight, the region above Bay City, but below the Aerium. Prescott aspires to be a Meth, and is contemptuous of those she deems beneath her.

This makes Prescott the ideal patsy to be framed by Kovacs for Bancroft's murder. Kovacs and the team create phony evidence that shows that Bancroft raped, strangled, and fired Prescott; in revenge, she infected Bancroft with Rawling virus at the VR Prick-Up brothel, but mistimed when she shot him. Prescott protests her innocence and is devastated when Bancroft bans her from the Meth world. Prescott finally atones by telling Tanaka where to find the kidnapped Ortega.

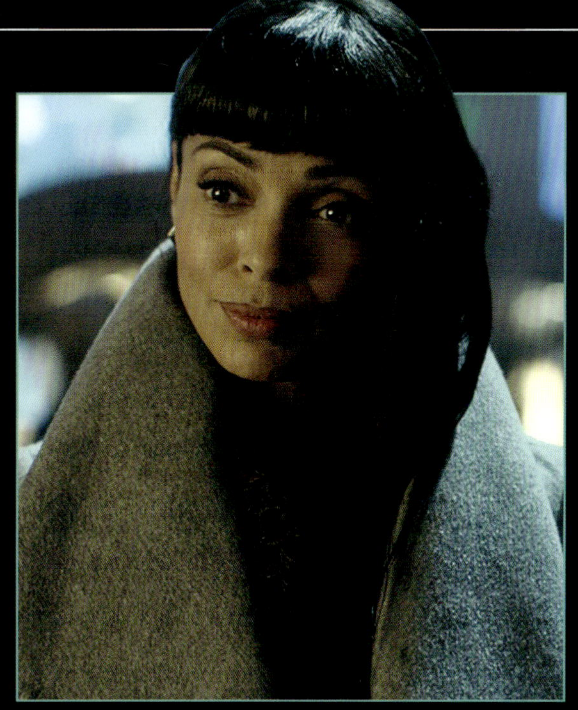

ABOVE: Prescott aspires to belong on the Aerium.

THE ZERO-G FIGHT

TWO ENTER, ONE MAY LEAVE

In season one, episode three, Bancroft throws a party at Suntouch House, partly in an attempt to flush out his killer, partly to show off his acquisition of 'the last Envoy,' Takeshi Kovacs. To celebrate, Bancroft has hired a loving husband/wife team of fighters (David William No plays Nick Rowley, Michelle Lee plays his wife) who must fight each other to the sleeve death in a zero-gravity environment. Winner gets an updated sleeve, loser gets a downgraded sleeve.

When Kovacs intervenes, he's dragged into the fight. Laurens ups the stakes by telling the couple if they can bring down Kovacs, he'll upgrade them both. Ortega ends the fight by shooting out the Zero-G controls.

Nick Hurran, who directed the episode and is an executive producer on *Altered Carbon*, says, "One of the challenges was to create a virtual environment. Bringing in a 360-degree camera, which is a camera that looks all the way around you, above and below you, brought a whole new dimension to us walking into a non-gravity environment. We had the challenge of building something for a fight sequence within zero gravity."

Hurran jokes that production designer Carey Meyer was able to build a gravity-stopping generator.

Meyer offers a more mundane but realistic explanation. "The no-G fight had originally been thought of as [taking place in] a Guggenheim sort of space, in the main core of Bancroft's ten-thousand-foot tower structure, the concept being that the antigravity that takes place in that scene is really the antigravity of the structure itself, that the space holds an antigravity device that helps the structure stay as tall as it is. So we were trying to bleed together the technology of the building to make sense of why there was this no-G antigravity moment in the show."

Meyer says what he and his team learned in the course of this was, "We couldn't afford to build a massive Guggenheim set piece. We were able to find the Telus Theatre, which is essentially a 'theatre in the round.' It has balcony seating that can be placed in a complete three-sixty around a central stage. It's about thirty-five-feet tall, and maybe thirty-five-feet across. It had the basic structure of what we were looking for to tell that story."

BELOW: Kovacs fights a couple for the Meths' entertainment.

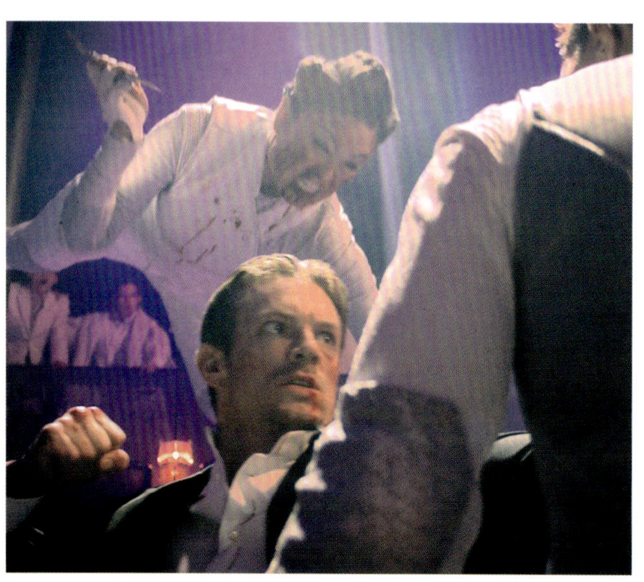

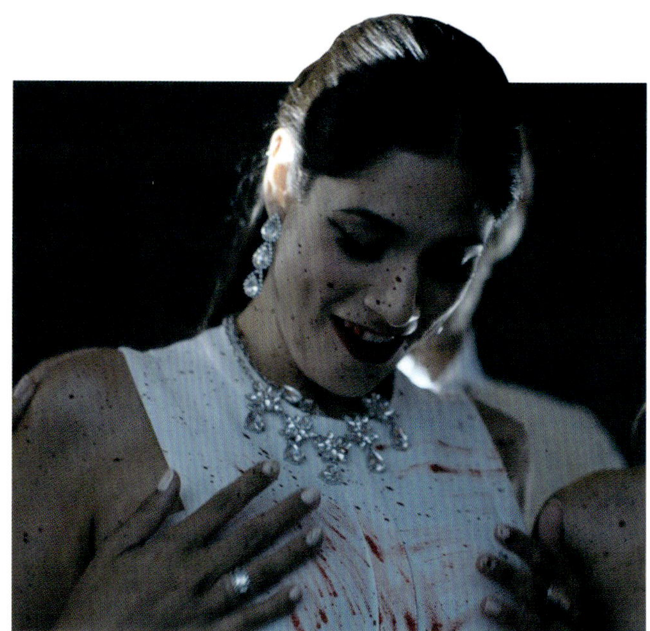

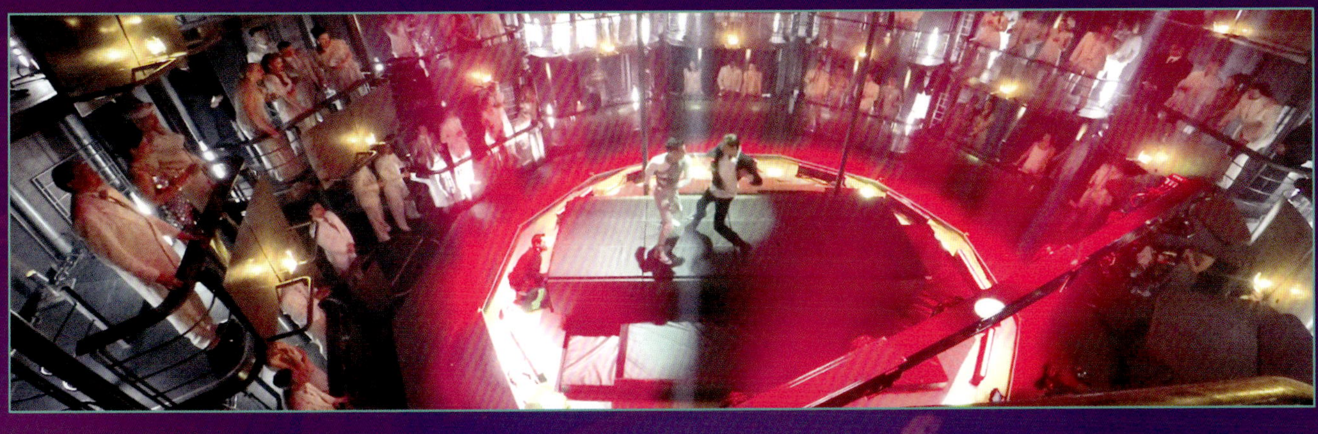

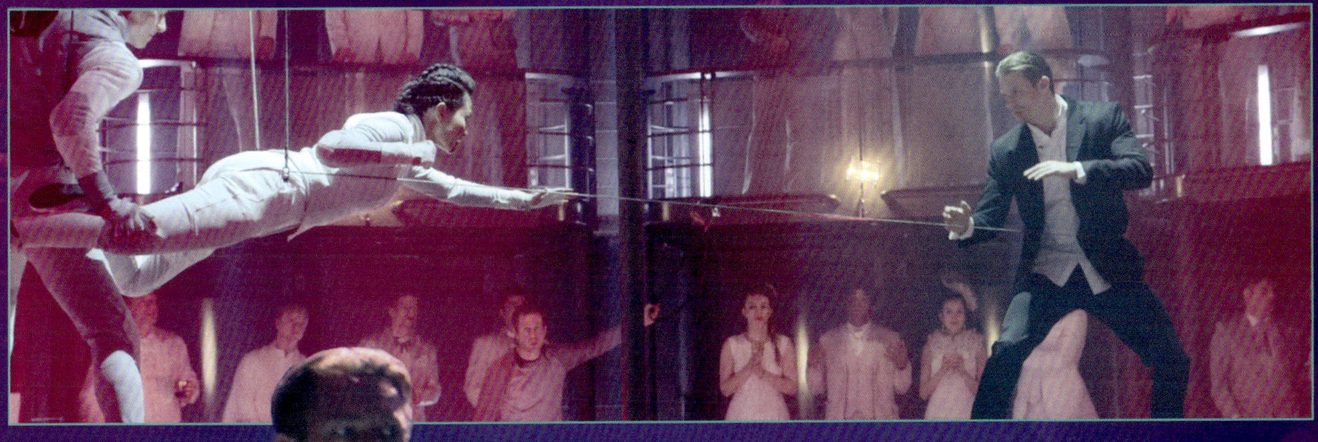

THIS PAGE: Kovacs fighting in zero gravity provided some unique challenges for the production team.

CG extension was used, Meyer adds, to make the space look larger, like "an endless pit that they're fighting in, so if they were to fall outside of that zero-gravity area, they could fall to their death. As they're fighting in the no-G space, they're going in and out of zero-gravity and hitting walls and fighting on the sides and then jumping back into the zero-G space to grab weapons and continue to fight."

Stunt coordinator Larnell Stovall notes that while each episode was layered with multiple fight scenes, the zero-G sequences was one of the standouts. "How do you make people float in the air safely, with proper rehearsal time, make it intense, brutal and safe at the same time, make everybody believe it?"

Stovall says he had a lot of sleepless nights trying to figure it out. "With the no-G, there were rules we had to get straight on what they can do, so it doesn't look too 'superhero.' We wanted to keep it gritty, fast-paced, we wanted to make sure it felt futuristic, we wanted to make sure people felt the brutality of it between husband and wife, and once the elite hero joined it, the stakes jumped up even more. So we wanted to make sure people felt like, okay, will this master tag team of husband and wife take out our hero? A lot of prep went into it, a lot of rehearsals." The actors had to practice wearing hidden harnesses and 'flying' on wires that simulated zero-G, "just to make sure they were comfortable. Joel [Kinnaman] did an awesome job, to be in those wires for days and hours at a time."

Makeup, costuming, on-set special effects, VFX and other departments all play a part in stunt action, Stovall points out. "Sometimes we do a stunt vis [an animated test of what a sequence will look like]. If you see us slamming into a wall, I involve multiple departments within that small sequence. I have to talk to makeup about, 'How do we cut them?' I have to talk to visual effects – 'Hey, will you help the glass shatter a little more?' I have to talk to another department to see about building a wall for me to slam that guy's head into. Then we have to test that wall to make sure it's safe for our stunt person, [let alone] if an actor feels it's safe enough to try it himself. So it's a great combination of multiple departments coming together to bring our action to life. Everybody was so excited each time we deliver any type of action, because we try to break it down, and then we go to each department, and find out how they can contribute, how we can contribute, how we can clear up anything, just to make sure everything goes smoothly on set."

BELOW: Actors were hoisted by wires to simulate zero-gravity conditions.

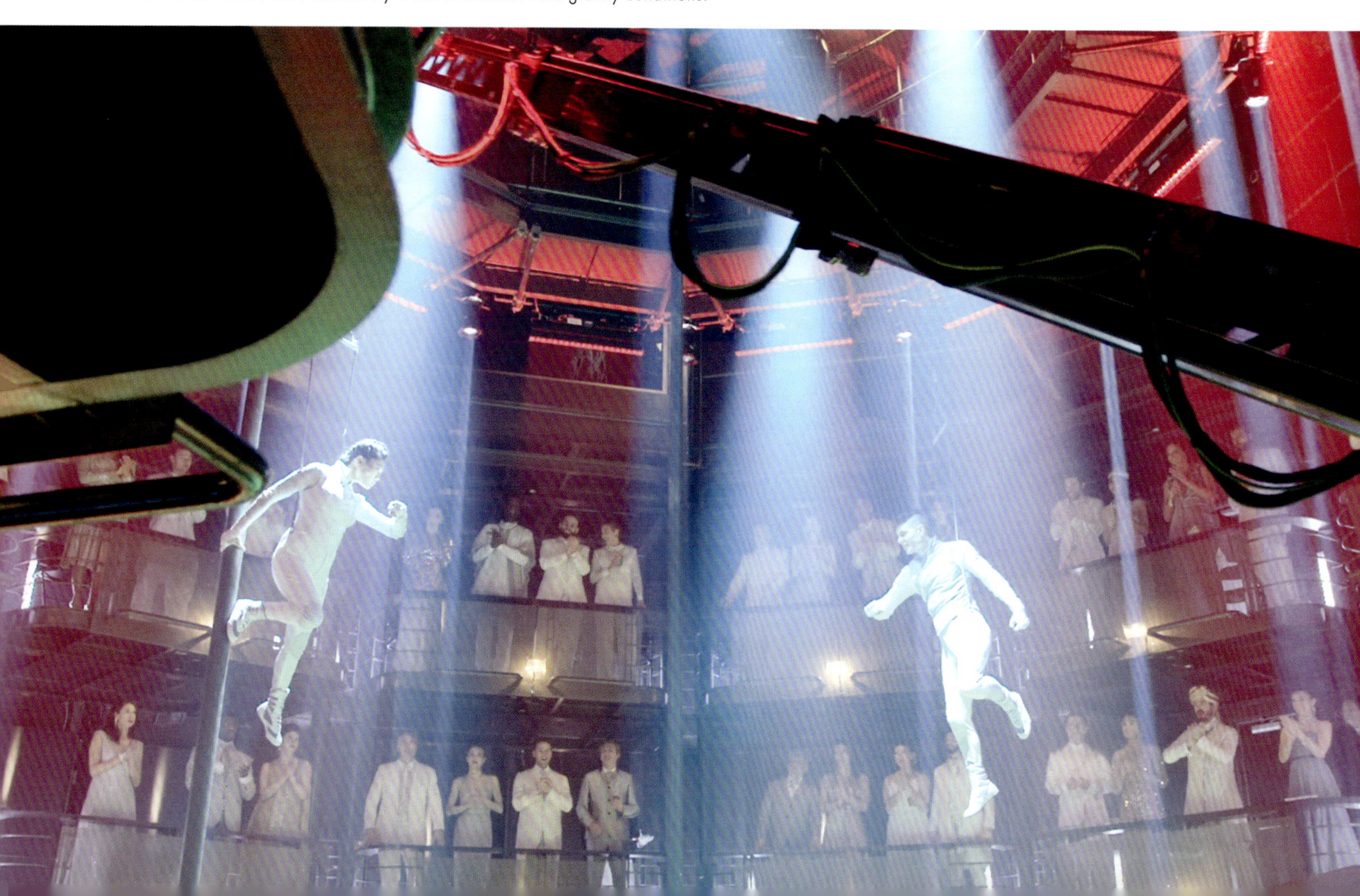

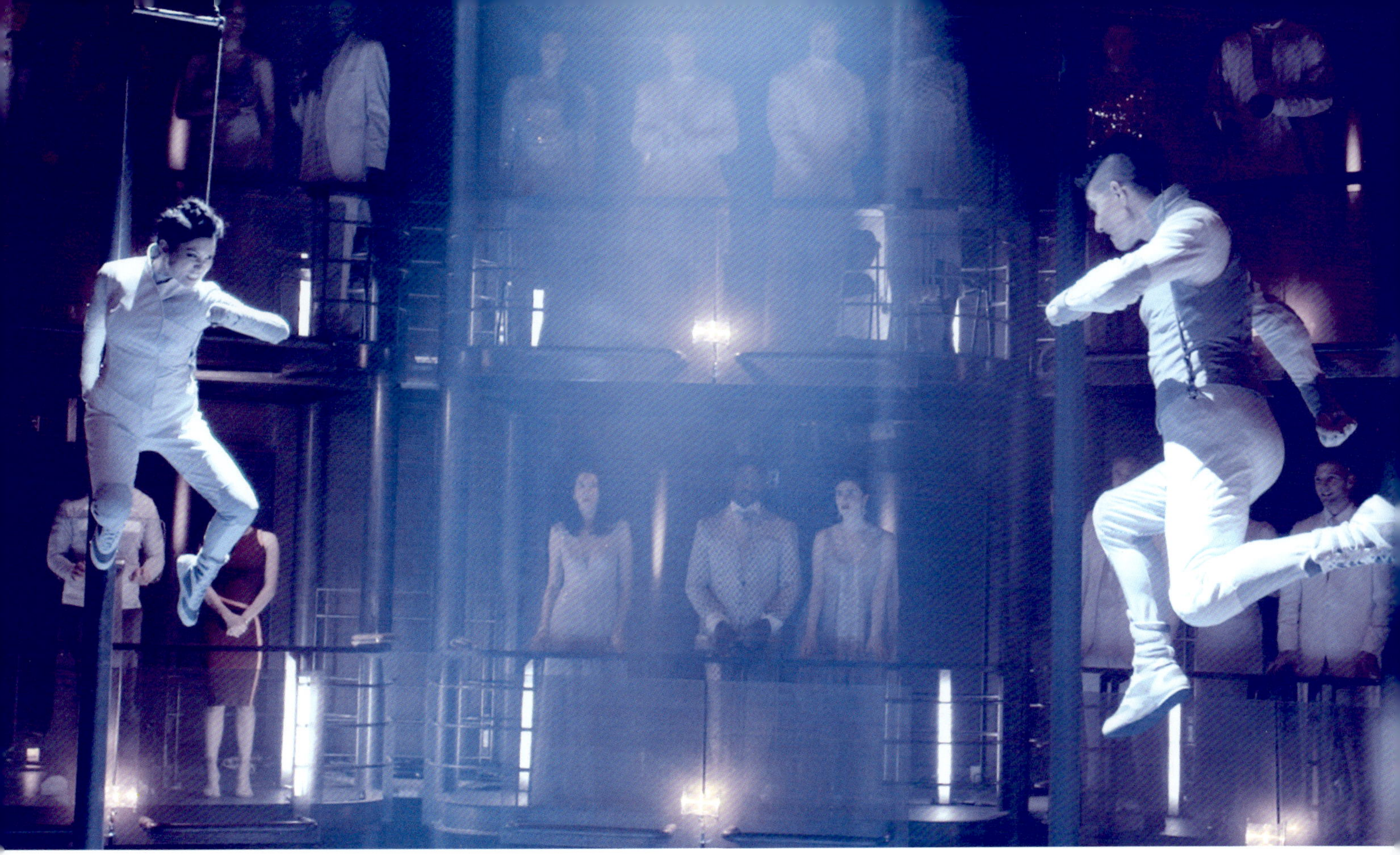

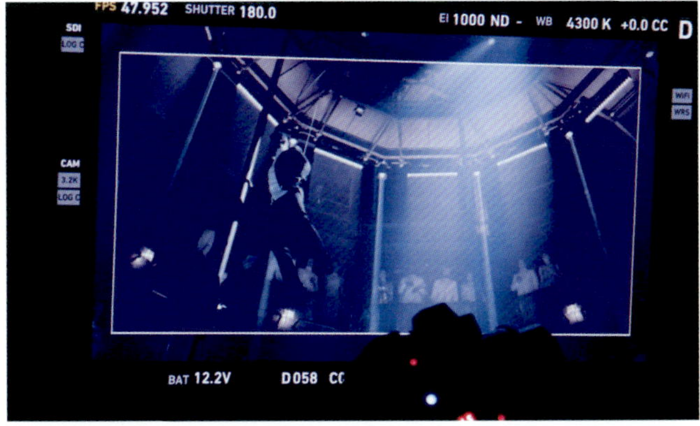

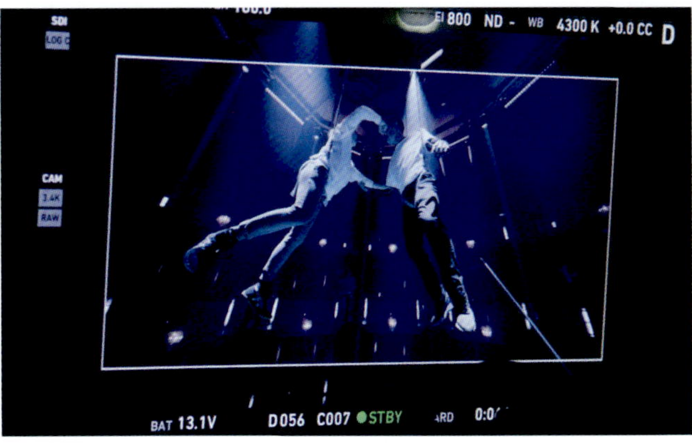

Stovall also gives credit to production company Skydance. "They've allowed a platform for the team to express itself in the action through the script, whether it's, 'We like that,' 'That's cool,' 'Let's bring it up a notch even more.' For example, when no one knew exactly how we would do the no-G, we did some little tests. When we sent [Skydance] the tests, they were so excited, and they sent back all these positive notes. We appreciate having the support."

The public should be the judge of how well the sequence worked, Stovall says. "I felt accomplished on the day we finished it. Everybody walked away safe, everybody was happy, and from what I was seeing in the playback, it looked good. But of course everybody has to do the [post production] effects, and erase the wires, and once you put in the sound, and bone-crunching, and different things, that truly brings it together."

ABOVE: Actors in this scene were often in the wires for hours at a time.

LEFT: Production stills of the fight sequence.

ISAAC BANCROFT

FOREVER TWENTY ONE

Isaac Bancroft, played by Antonio Marziale, is the eldest son of Laurens and Miriam Bancroft. Laurens refuses to allow Isaac, or any of his children, to reach full adulthood. Consequently, Isaac has suffered a lot of psychological damage, not to mention resentment, from being frequently resleeved so that he remains no older than twenty-one.

Costume designer Ann Foley said she had a lot of fun with Isaac's wardrobe. "I decided to go in a little bit of a different direction with him. I guess the best way to describe it is gender neutral. He's wearing a lot of clothes that are for women, but we've styled it in a way that you wouldn't know. We've probably done that a good bit [with other] Meths as well. Antonio brought a lot to that character, a lot of really cool ideas, and was willing to try anything. That's a costume designer's dream."

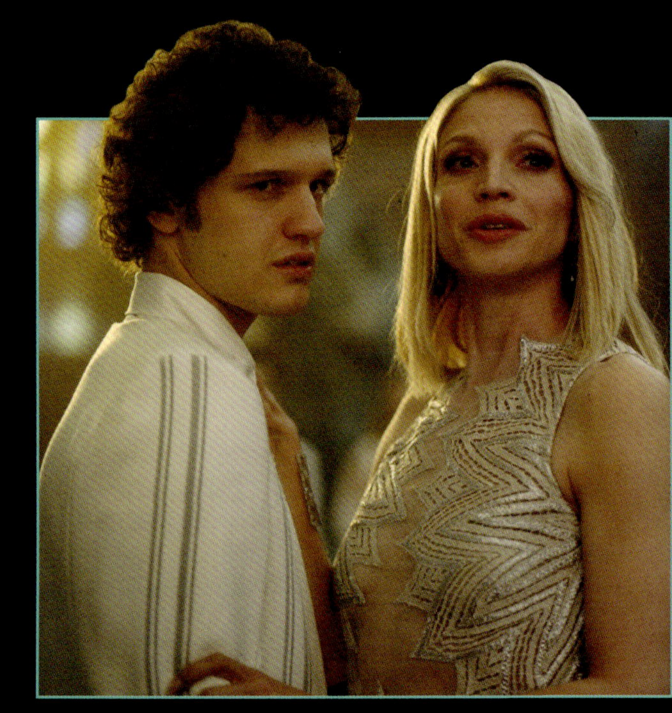

THIS PAGE: Isaac is one of Kovacs' prime suspects for the murder of Laurens Bancroft.

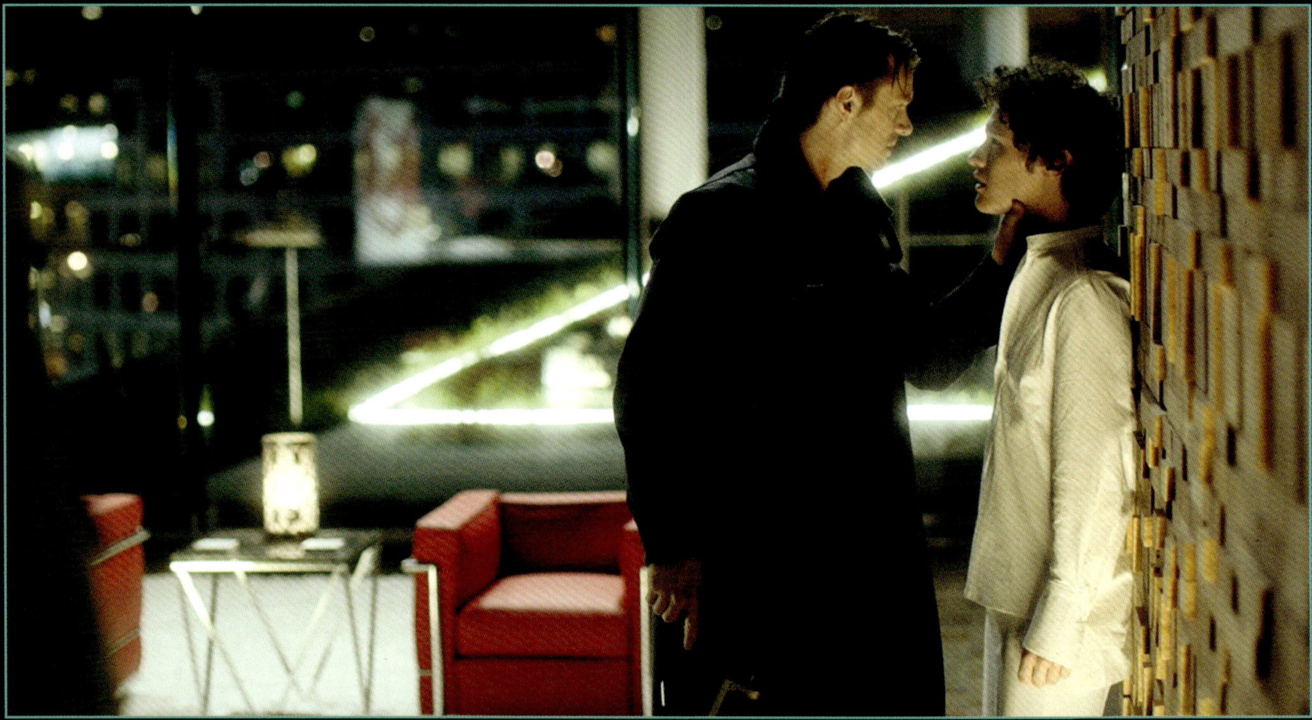

3D PRINTER

FORCE GROW CLONES

The illegal and expensive portable 3D bio-organic printer is used to swiftly 'force-grow' clones, requiring a large amount of cell mass to create a body.

Isaac Bancroft uses one such printer to grow a clone of his father. After the printer is confiscated, Kovacs steals it from the police evidence locker, carries it back to the Raven in its circular case, and uses it to print a clone of himself.

The case opens vertically, with strands of blue-and-white light extending between top and bottom in a quasi-double helix shape. The cloning tank is nearby, but separate.

This physical printer was designed by production designer Carey Meyer and built by the set decoration department, with VFX adding enhancement to the lights, inside power source, and background layers.

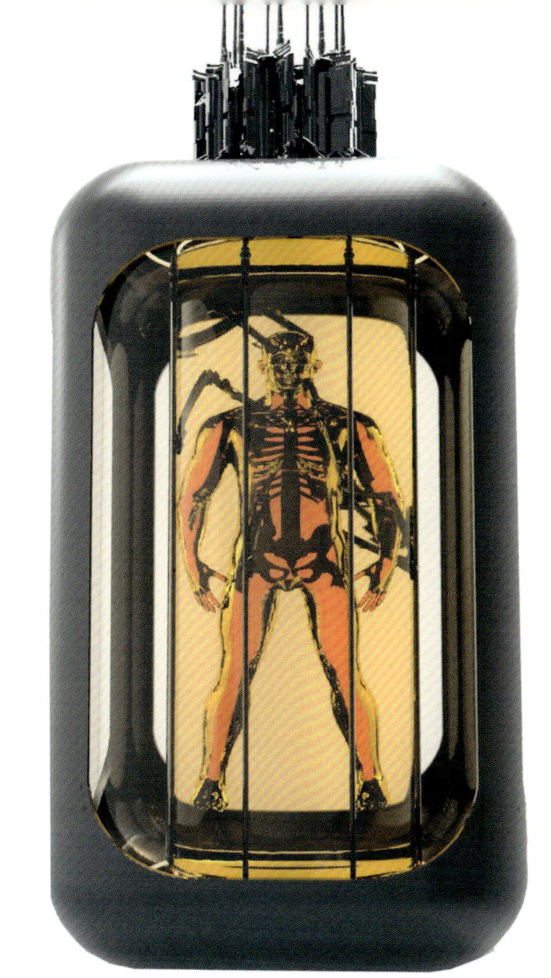

BELOW: Kovacs cloned his body at The Raven, using a stolen 3D printer.

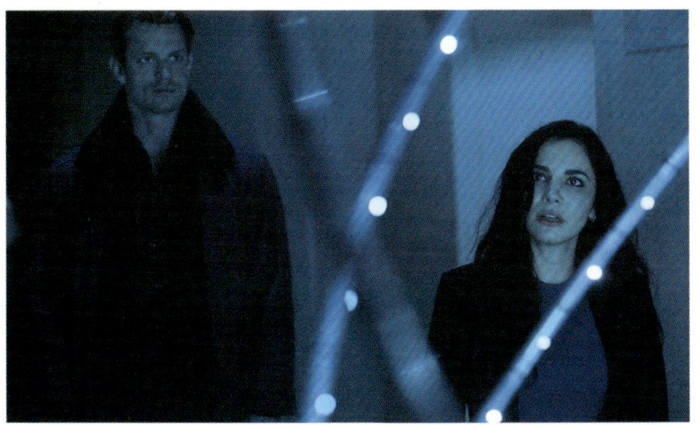

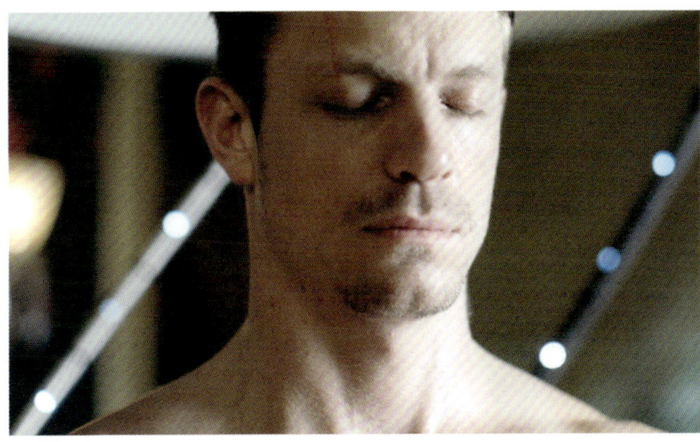

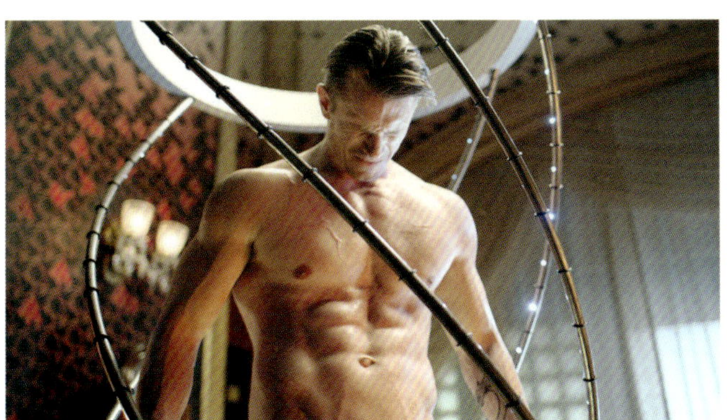

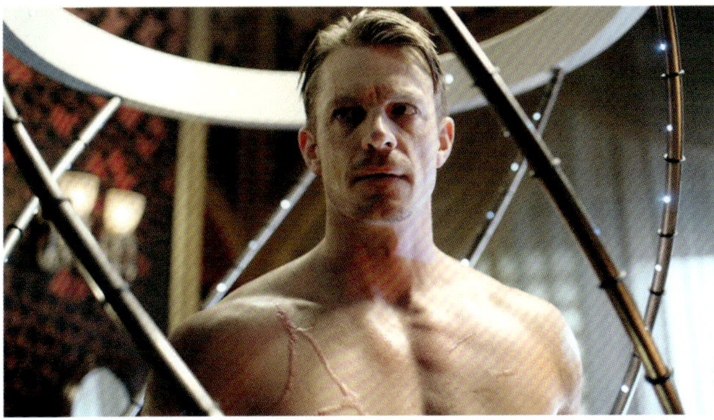

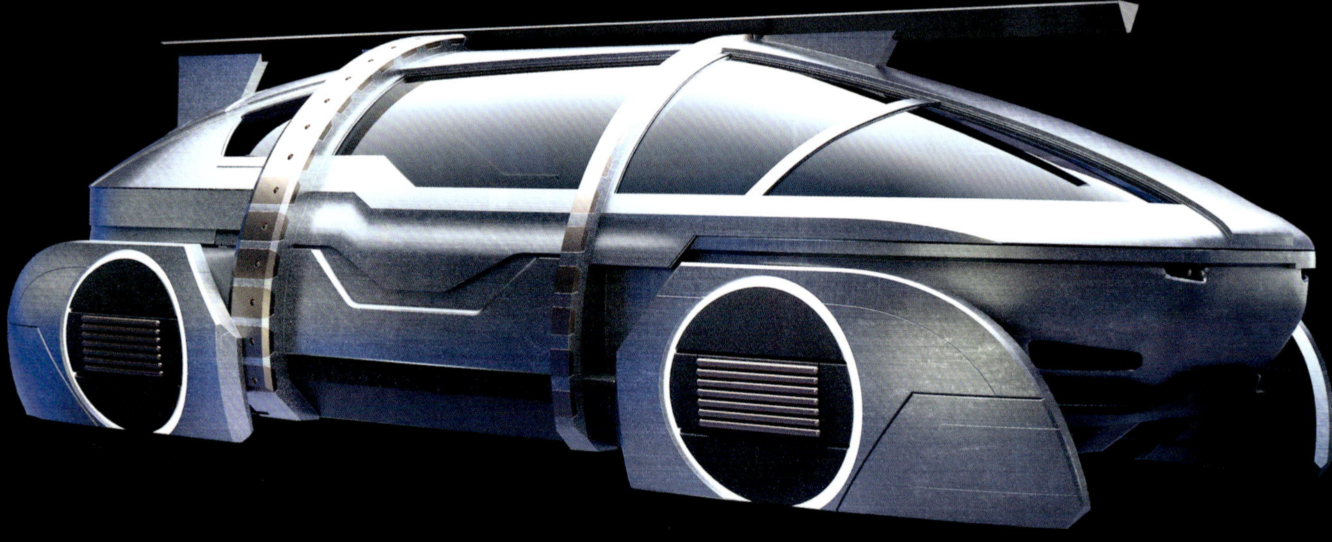

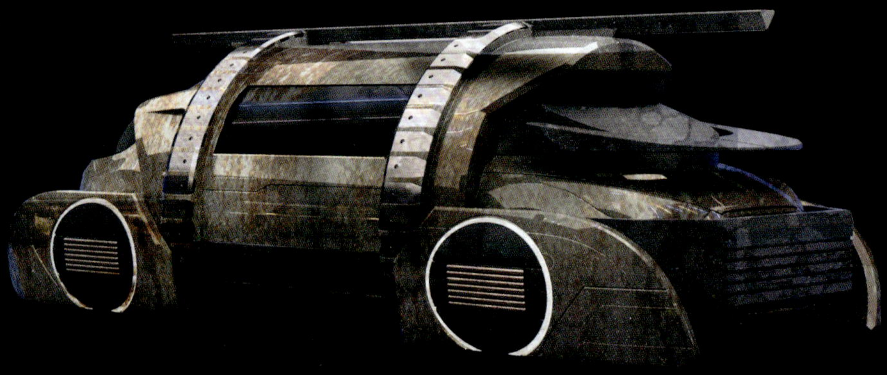

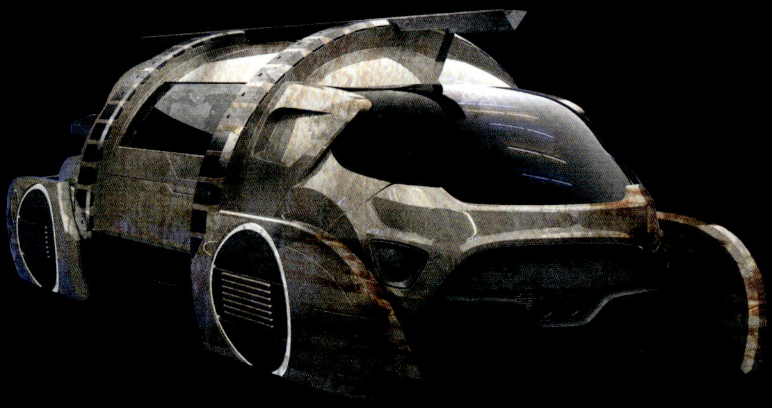

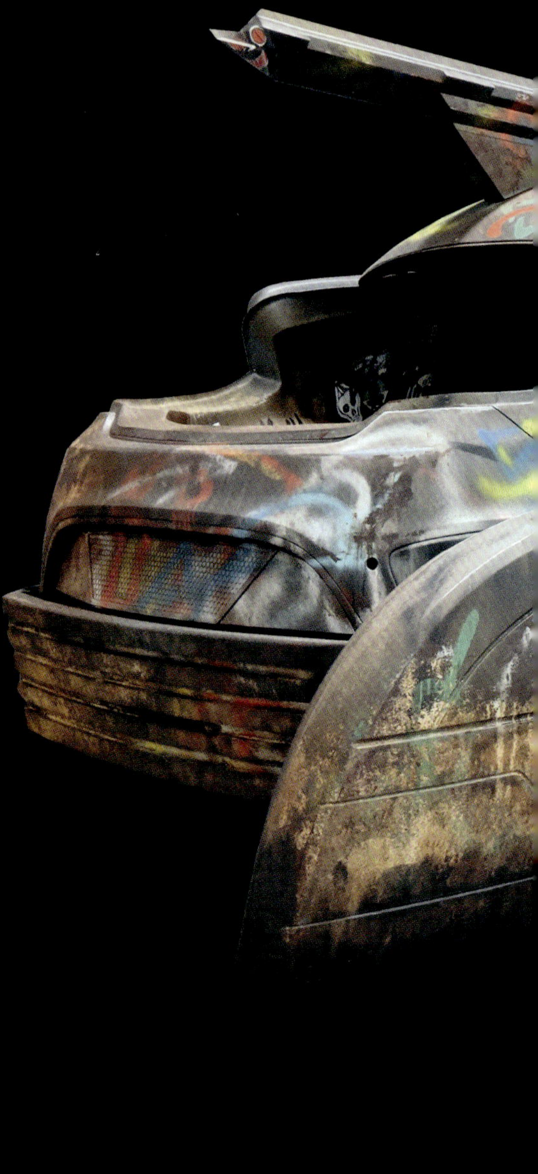

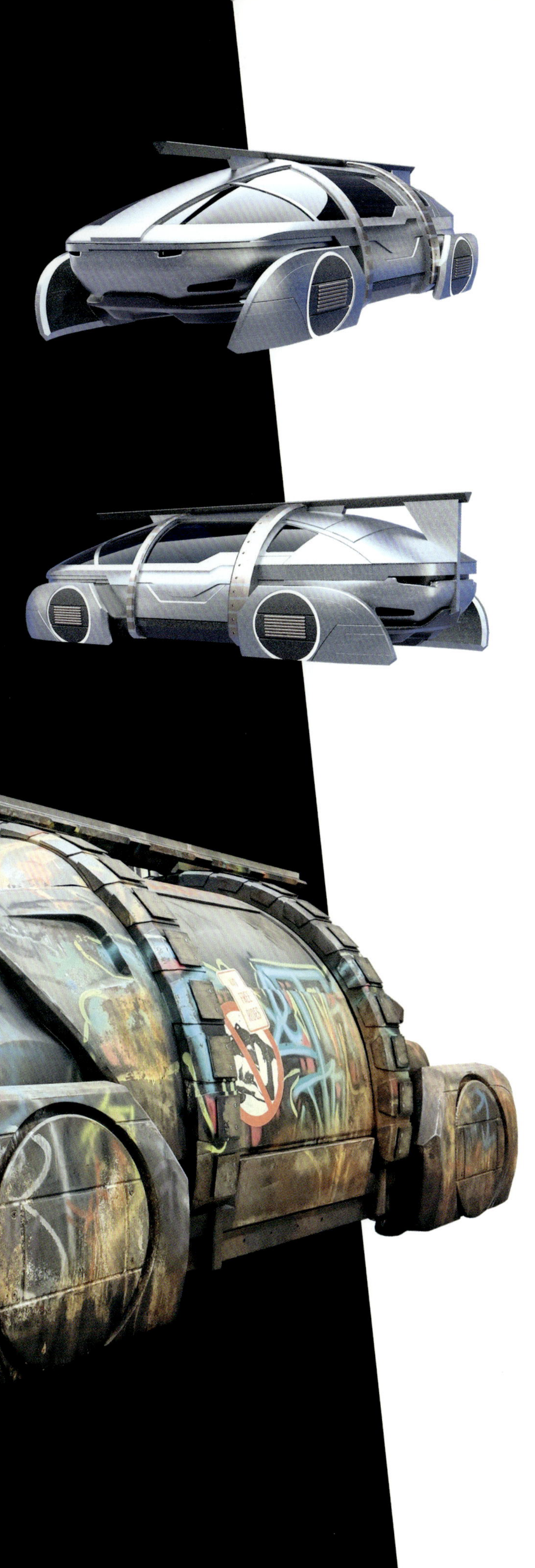

TRANSPORT

THE PIL TRANSPORT SYSTEM

The PIL Transport System evolves over the course of *Altered Carbon*. In season one's Bay City, the PIL is primarily used by the Grounders to get around the city. However, in season two's Harlan's World, Meths have embraced the PIL. The PIL has stations, like train terminals, including a private one at Axley Tower. Tanaseda has his own sleek PIL car, though public versions can be shabby.

Production designer Carey Meyer says that the exterior sets have been calibrated for a mix of practical shooting and VFX to cover the PIL, flying cars, and pedestrians. Some of it is practical, using moving lights overhead to create the impression of flying cars even when we don't see them. "So a lot of what I've done in terms of building the physical sets allows us to go out there and be all in-camera [shooting practically], without having to add visual effects."

Then again, Meyer observes, "Without visual effects, we would never be able to put that picture in somebody's mind that a car does fly, or that the PIL has this massive rapid transit system throughout the entire city, so they really go hand in hand. That's what I've worked very hard on, with our VFX supervisor, Everett Burrell. When you're world building, you have to lean into visual effects to create the feel that you are in the future, but you still have to design all of the moments. We've tried to do it in a way that feels seamless and organic."

THIS PAGE: The varying designs of PIL cars throughout Bay City. The more rundown versions are used by Grounders, the sleeker cars by the Meths.

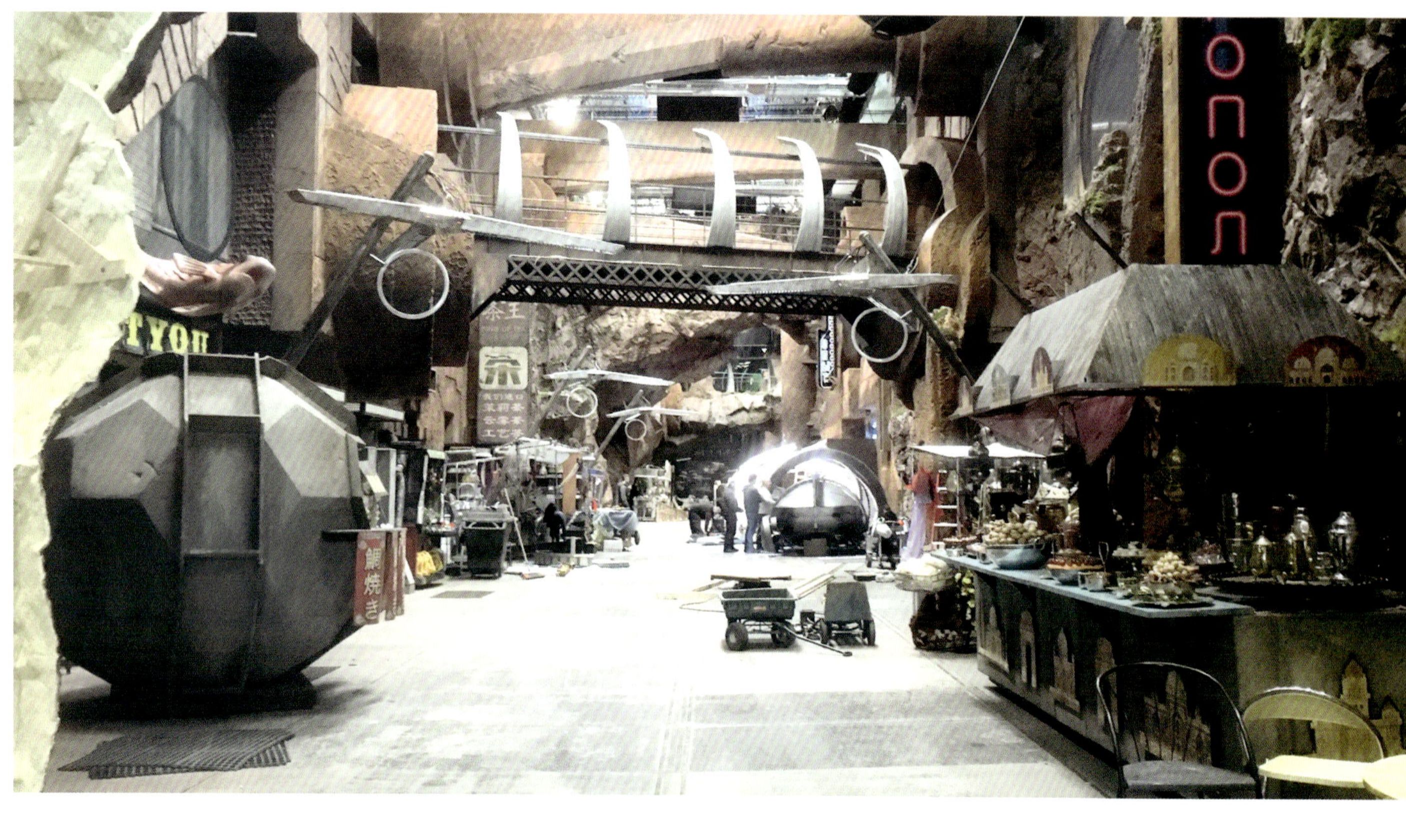

THIS PAGE: The warren of tunnels allow rapid transport around the city by PIL car.

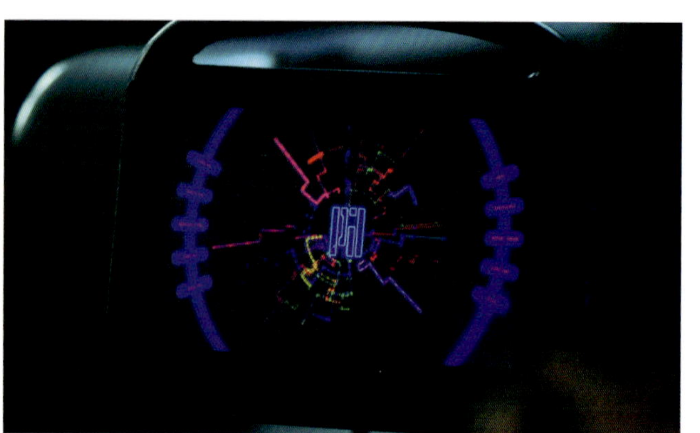

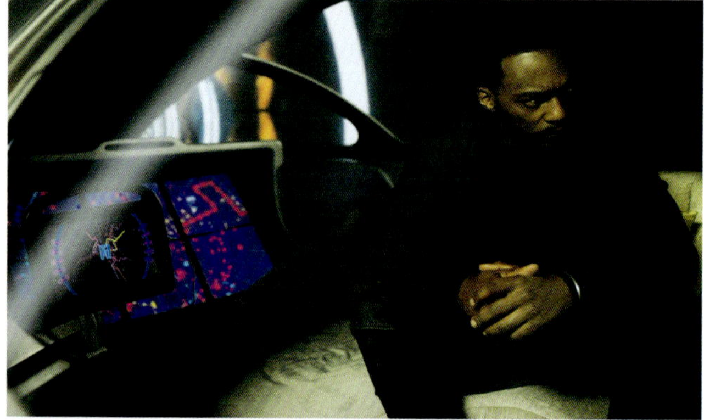

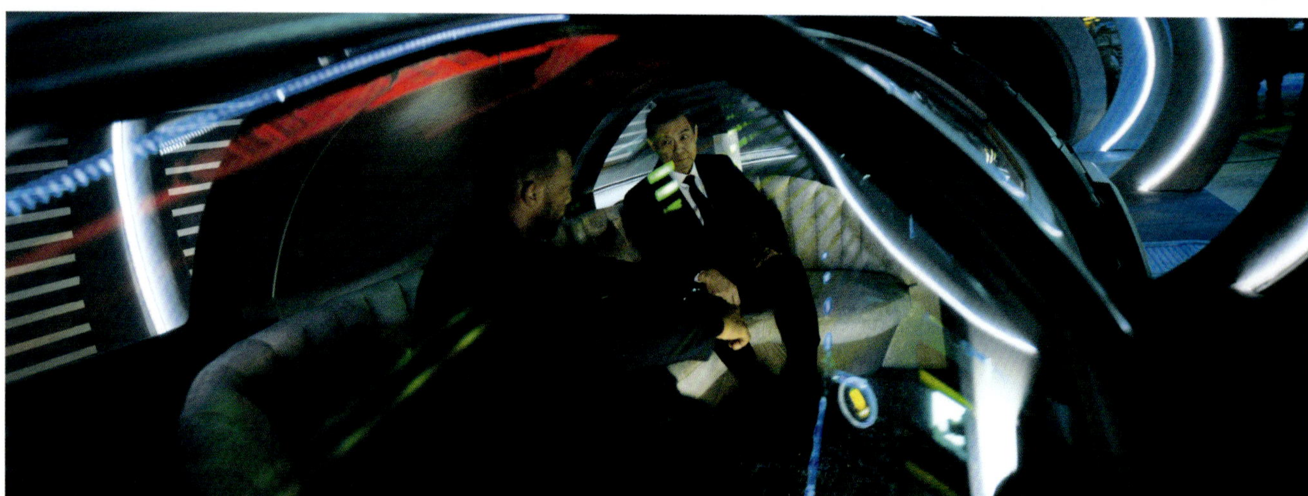

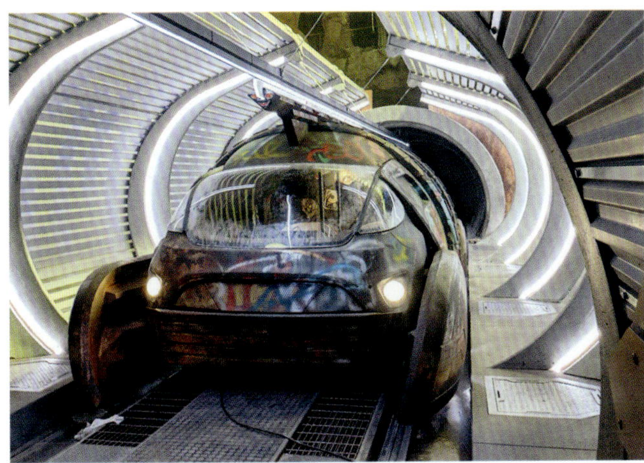

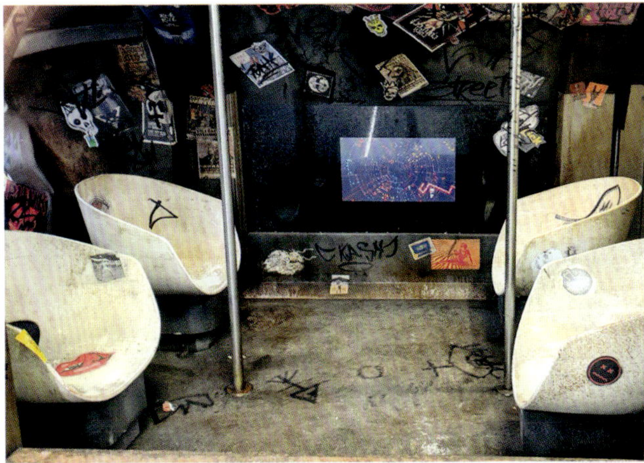

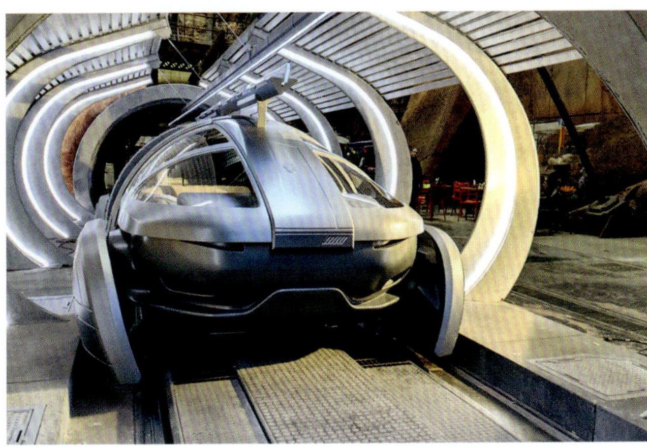

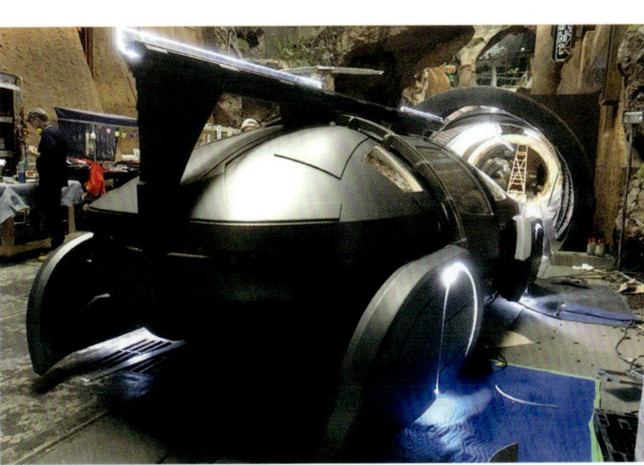

BELOW: Kovacs waits for a PIL car with Poe.

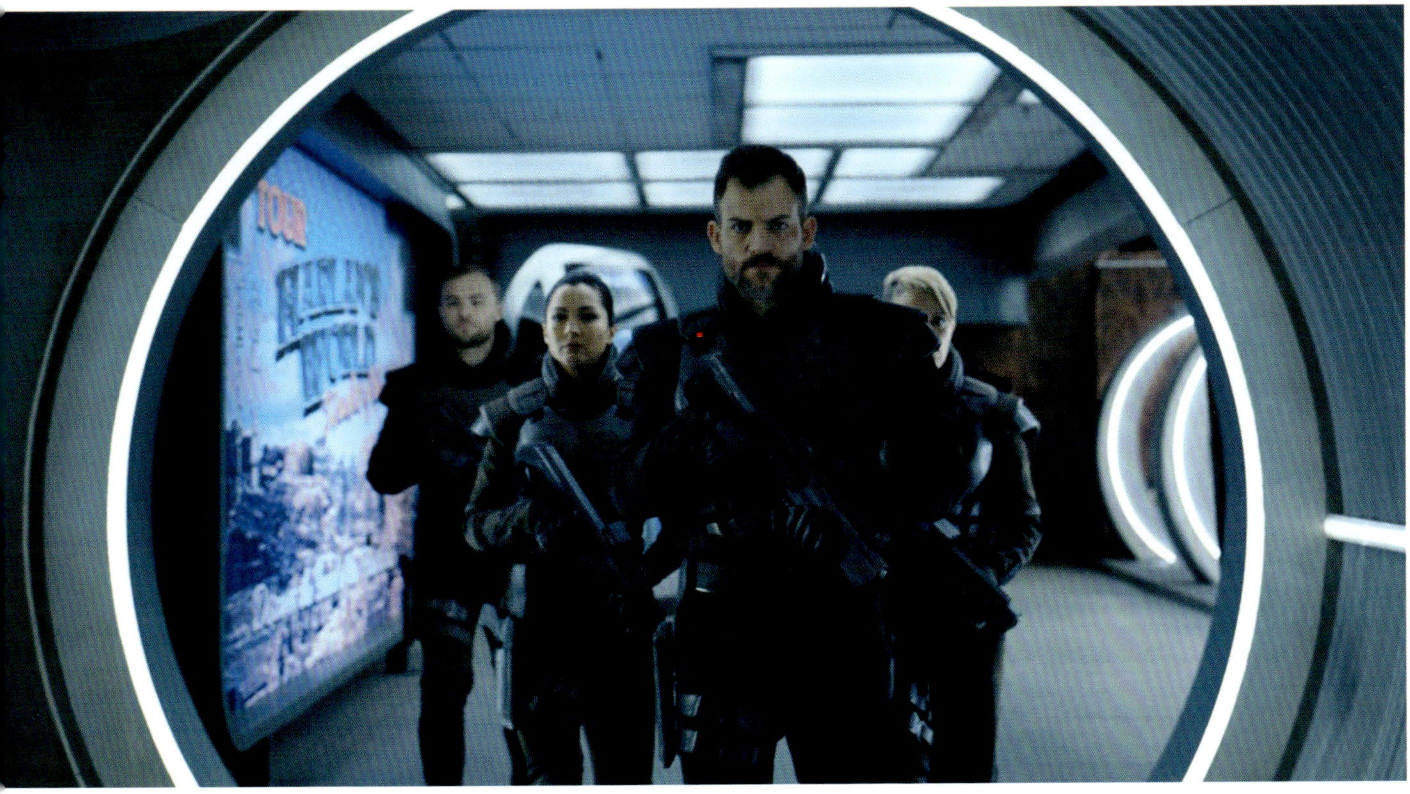

HEAD IN THE CLOUDS

AN IRIDIUM EXPERIENCE

Head in the Clouds is literally the highest of high-end brothels, hovering over Bay City with its name rotating above it in big pink letters. Technically, it qualifies as an aircraft, although it more closely resembles a space station. It is (secretly) owned and operated by Reileen Kawahara, who also uses it as a base of operations. Per Ava Elliot, the whole ship is com-jammed with conventional tech. Reileen's suite has a military-level dark field, which opens every twenty-four hours just long enough for a DHF backup to cast out.

Head in the Clouds caters to extremely wealthy clients whose tastes run to delivering real death to prostitutes – women, men, children – who think they're only signing up for sleeve death (which is bad enough). Reileen has found a way to fake Neo-Catholic coding on the stacks of her employees, which means they cannot be brought back to testify even if they manage to escape real death.

While Kovacs is trying to rescue Ortega and reason with Reileen, the reunited Elliot family agrees that Head in the Clouds needs to be destroyed altogether. They cause the brothel to self-destruct and crash into the bay below.

Series creator Laeta Kalogridis says the reason for the existence of Head in the Clouds is "for people who have experienced so much, lived so much, the only things they want are things that are forbidden. Even if they could murder someone in a virtual construct and it would feel real, that wouldn't be enough for them. They need an actual real person to actually murder, to actually real-death. They need to extinguish human life to feel alive. That's an old idea, but within the framework of our world, where you have so many other options, I think that probably would be the most outrageous thing."

RIGHT: The monolithic floating structure of Head in the Clouds.

BELOW: The brothel is often fraught with violence, but usually only for paying clientele.

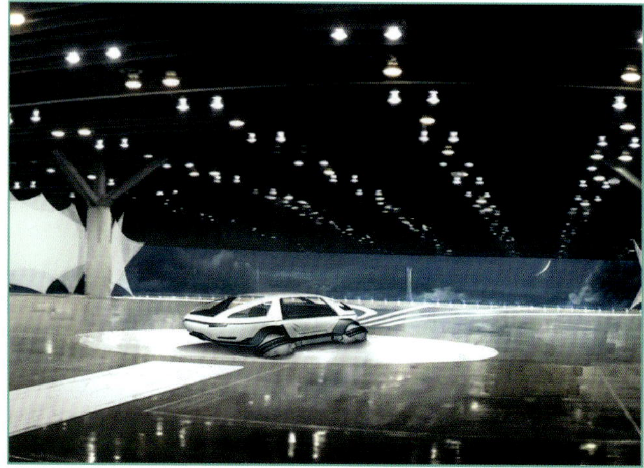

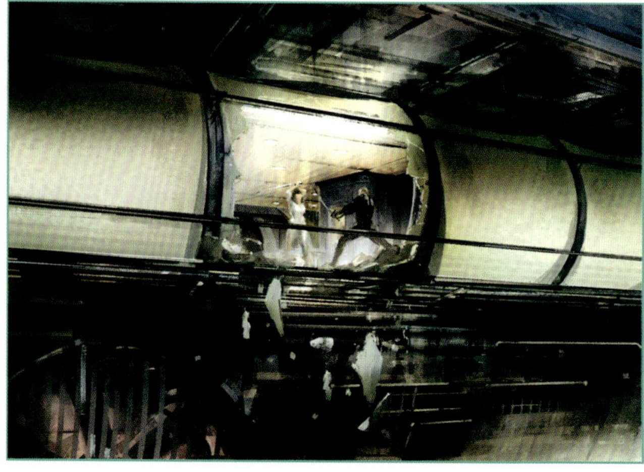

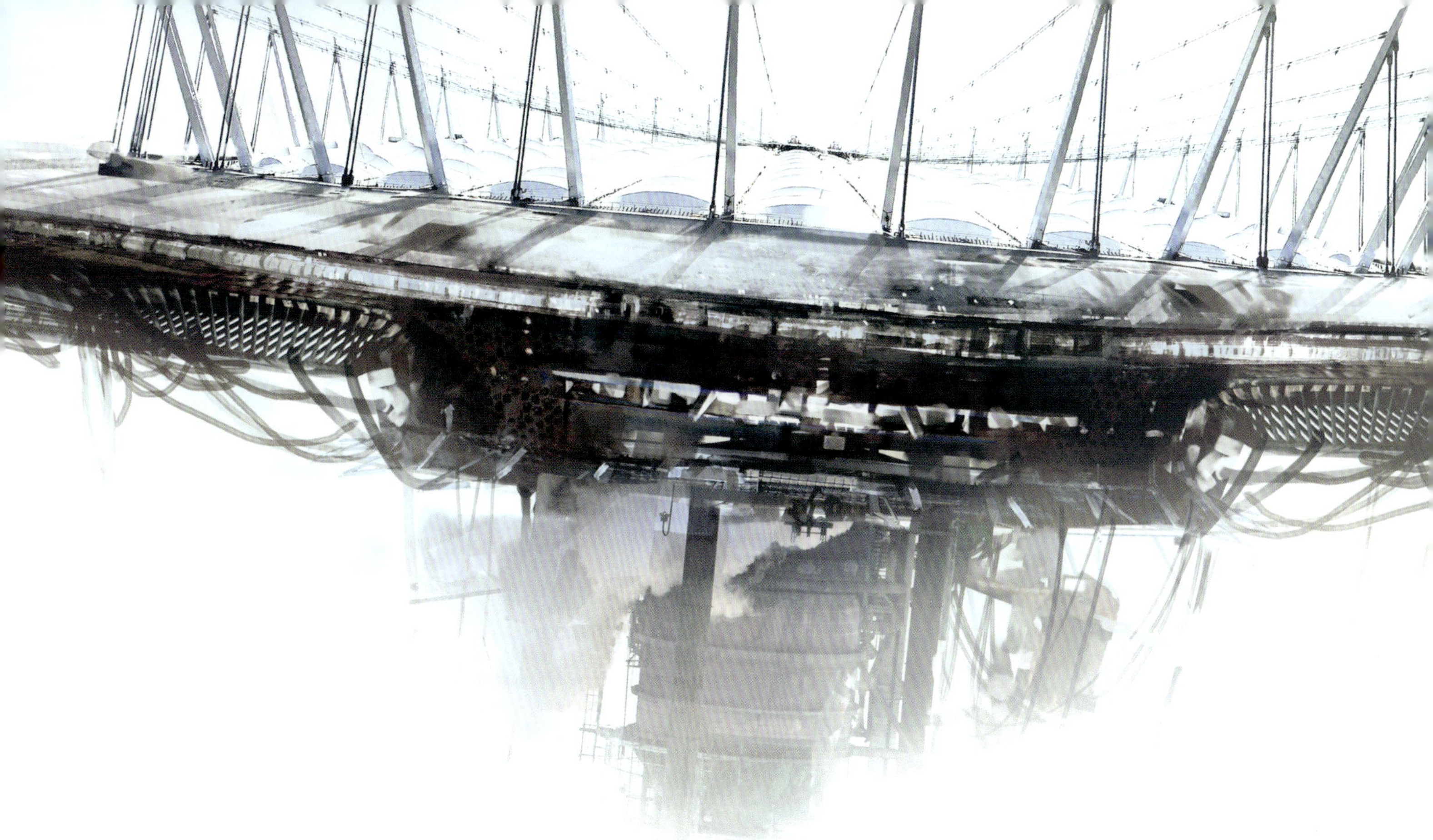

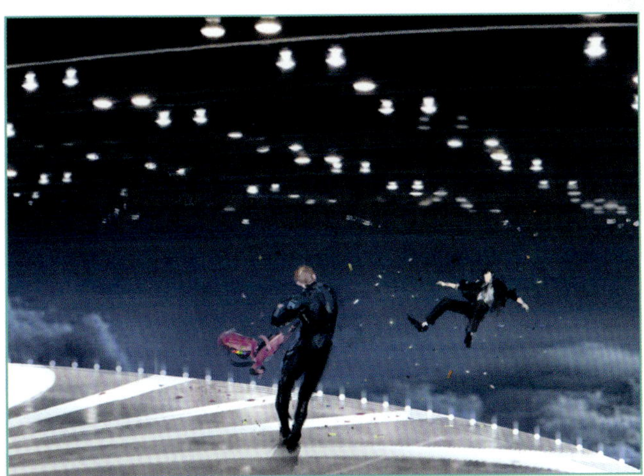

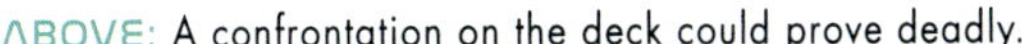
ΛBOVE: A confrontation on the deck could prove deadly.

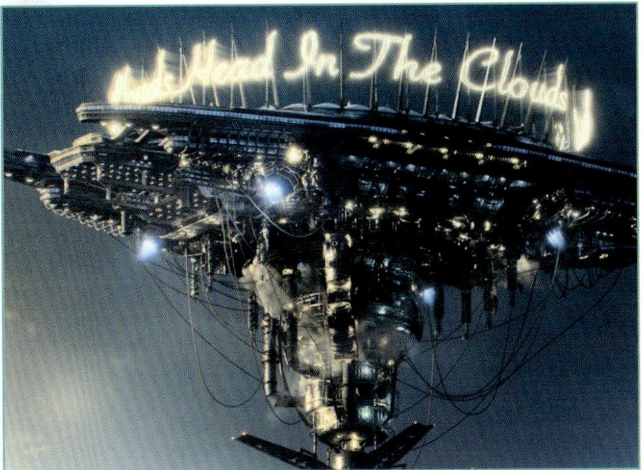

ΛBOVE: Discretion is paramount at the floating brothel.

Executive producer James Middleton adds, "The writers, producers, directors, and cast were always conscious about the level of violence and adult subject matter epitomized by Head in the Clouds. But the point of it all was to illustrate how depraved and dark humanity could become with immortality and limitless wealth accruing to the Meths."

VFX supervisor Everett Burrell explains that the Head in the Clouds exterior "was a very elaborate CG model. Funnily enough, it was actually based on the B.C. Place civic arena, where all the concerts are played in Vancouver. The reason why it is based on that is we were hoping to shoot on top of it, so that's where the design started, and then once we realized we couldn't [shoot on the roof], some of the design elements stuck. We used Lidar to make a 3D digital map of a big chunk of B.C. Place, and we used that as a basis of the model that we built. But it's much more elaborate, with a lot of equipment and venting. The idea [within the story] is that it was some sort of weather station that was bought and turned into a brothel, so that's why it has antennas and is very weather-station-looking."

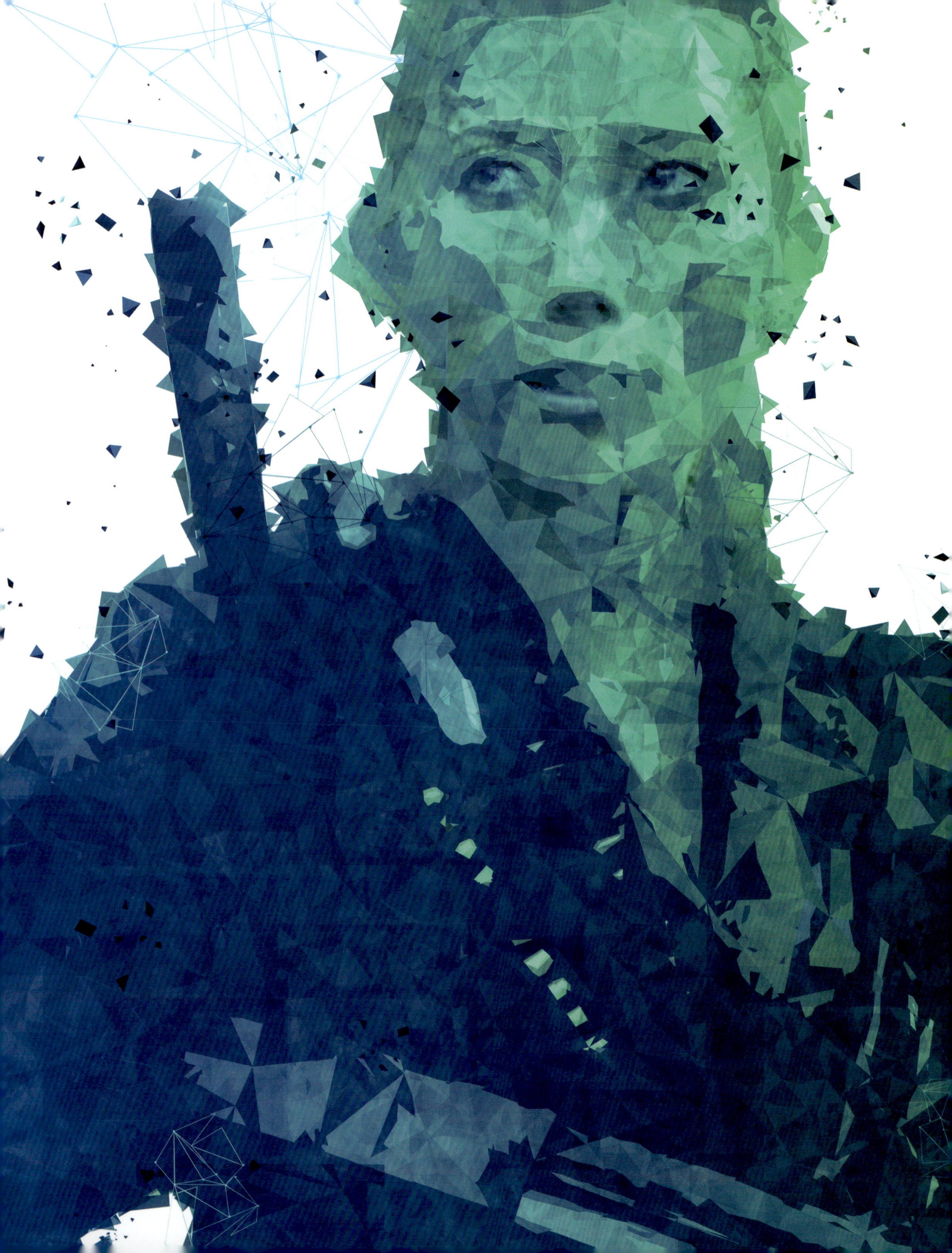

REILEEN KAWAHARA

THE WOMAN WITH MANY FACES

Reileen Kawahara, played as an adult by Dichen Lachman and in childhood flashbacks by Riley Lai Nelet, is Takeshi Kovacs' younger sister. When they are children, they adore each other unconditionally. When they are reunited as adults, Reileen still wants them to be the only people in each other's lives.

Executive producer/director Neil Hurran describes Reileen as "the person Kovacs would do anything for. And she would do anything for Kovacs."

Series creator Laeta Kalogridis explains, "Even though they both join the Envoys, Reileen doesn't really believe in the cause. She's running from something, not to something. So when push comes to shove, she betrays them. She thinks that will result in a better life for her and her brother and, instead, it results in them being separated for two hundred and fifty years. She's been waiting to get him back for all of that time. And in that time, she has become a Meth, and the power of it has corrupted her. So she's not the sister he knew. But even the sister that he knew was embarking on a really dark path because she betrayed the Envoys, because she betrayed the woman that he loved who was their leader. She was already starting down that road.. And when he finally sees her again, she's too far down it to turn back."

THIS PAGE: Reileen is Kovacs' sister, but finds herself begrudgingly opposing him.

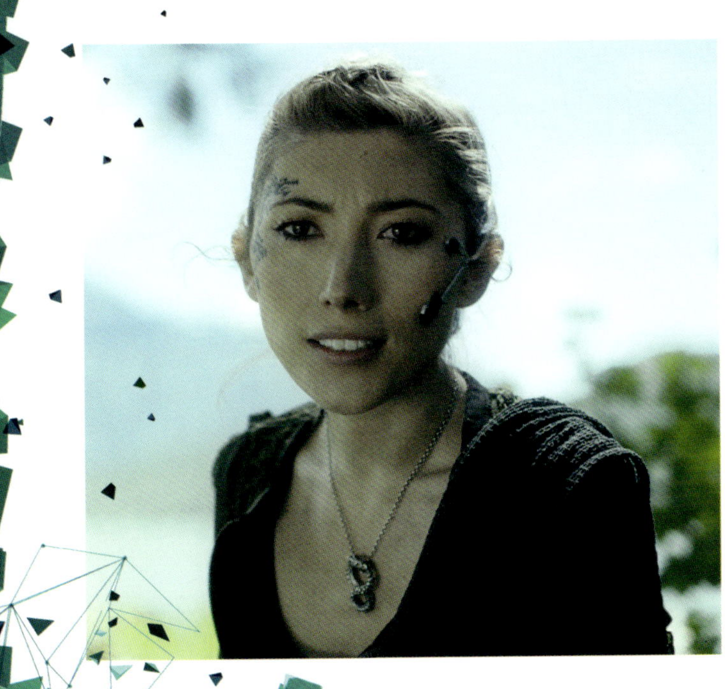

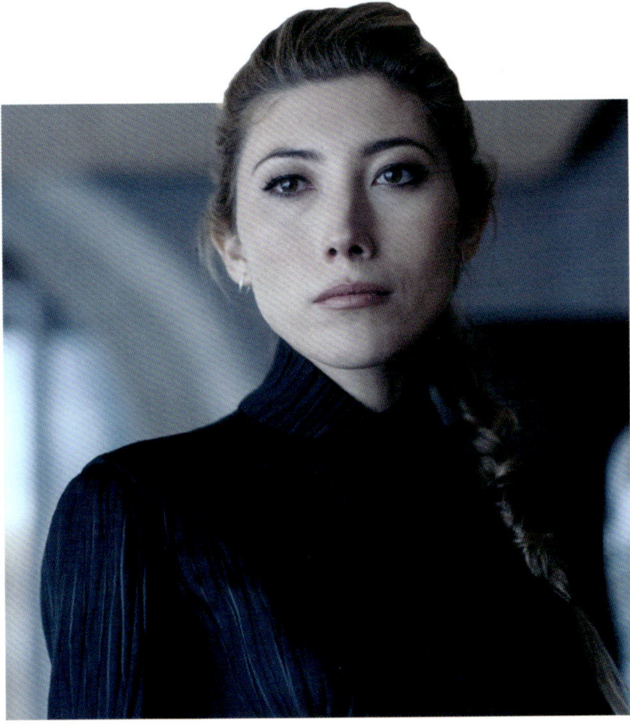

For Reileen's look, costume designer Ann Foley says, "I wanted to show her character arc. We meet [Reileen and Takeshi] as kids on Harlan's World, very green, lush. I wanted to use the color green with her. Her character will follow through with that color all through adulthood. So there's always going to be a subtle touch of green. But she's also a survivor and a warrior, and her clothes reflect that. You want the clothes to be able to move with the actors when they're doing their stunts, but you also want the clothes to look amazing during the fight sequence. So when Reileen falls into Fight Drome, she's got this hooded vest on that has four panels to it. When she comes down, they fly out. When she's doing her sword-fighting, you see them twirling around the sword, and it's pretty spectacular."

Reileen's primary weapons are her sword and her plasma blaster. Property master Nevin Swain credits illustrator Brian Cunningham with the blaster design. "Laeta liked big, powerful guns. Then we ended up building [Reileen] a complete custom sword, from the blade all the way through to the techie handle." This was a completely original creation, Swain adds, not based on any previous designs. "The blades were all custom C and C'ed [a process where a computer guides the actual metal cutting]. Then we anodized the whole blade and cleaned it off to give it a two-tone paint job."

James Middleton praises Lachman's handling of the scene where multiple clones of Reileen, one after another, battle Ortega. "When Ortega kills one of the clones, Reileen's DHF jumps to another clone, ready to attack. This scene was obviously complicated by the fact that Reileen, played courageously by Dichen Lachman, was fully nude. As we neared shooting the scene, the filmmaking team and director, Uta Briesewitz, were concerned about the complications of having Dichen and her stunt doubles nude while doing involved acting and stunt work. Then Dichen came forward and said she wanted to do a full rehearsal with her nude, as she would be on the day of production. Although the set was always closed, she wanted there to be no novelty with her being nude on the day of production for her or the shooting crew. By doing this, we were able to rehearse the whole scene as scripted and went into production with a high level of confidence that we could accomplish it. I can't stress enough that it was Dichen's attitude and leadership that made this scene possible and Uta Briesewitz was the perfect director for this."

BELOW: Though they find themselves in opposition often, it was Reileen who encouraged Bancroft to spin up Kovacs.

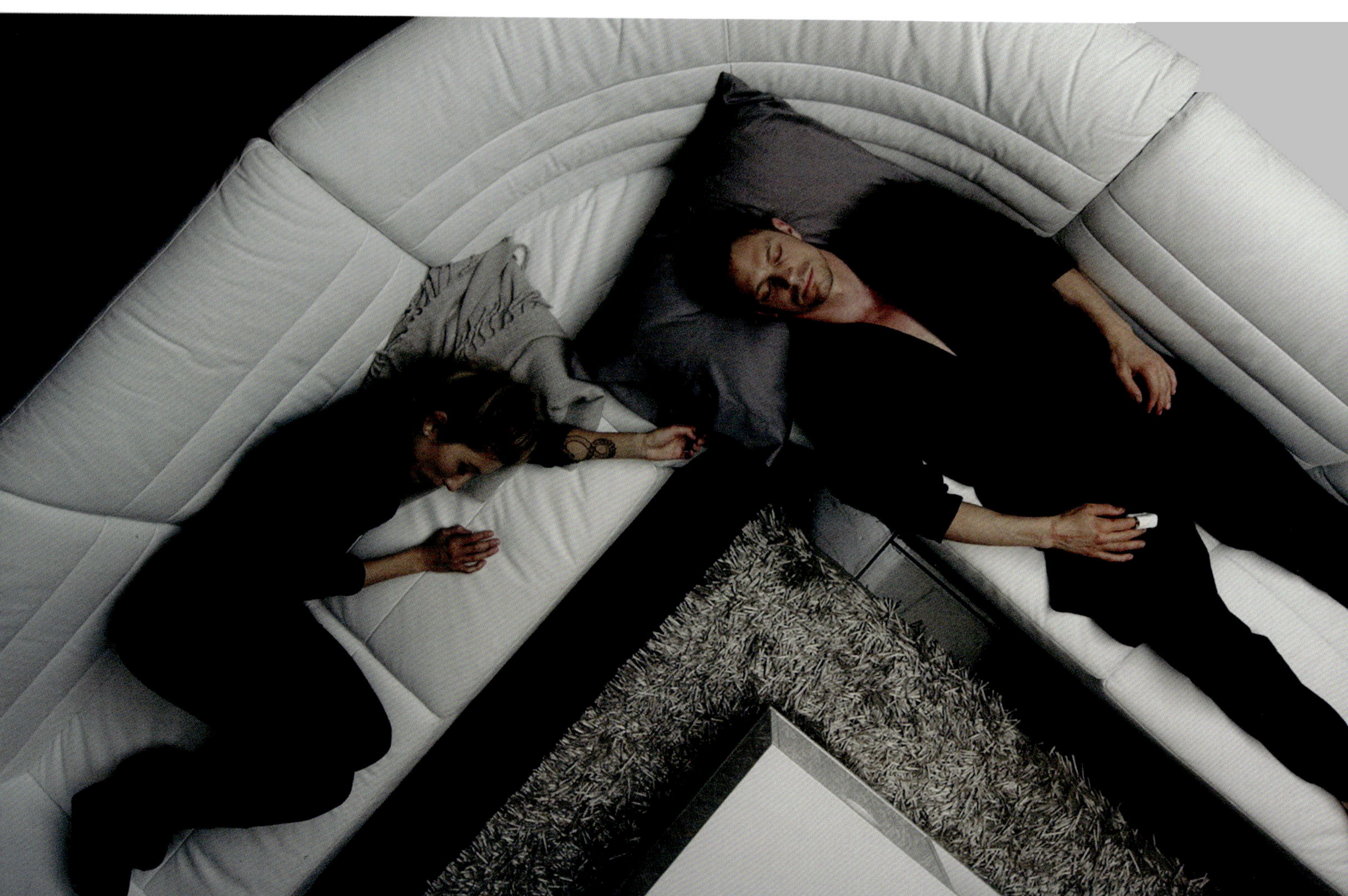

REILEEN'S DISGUISES

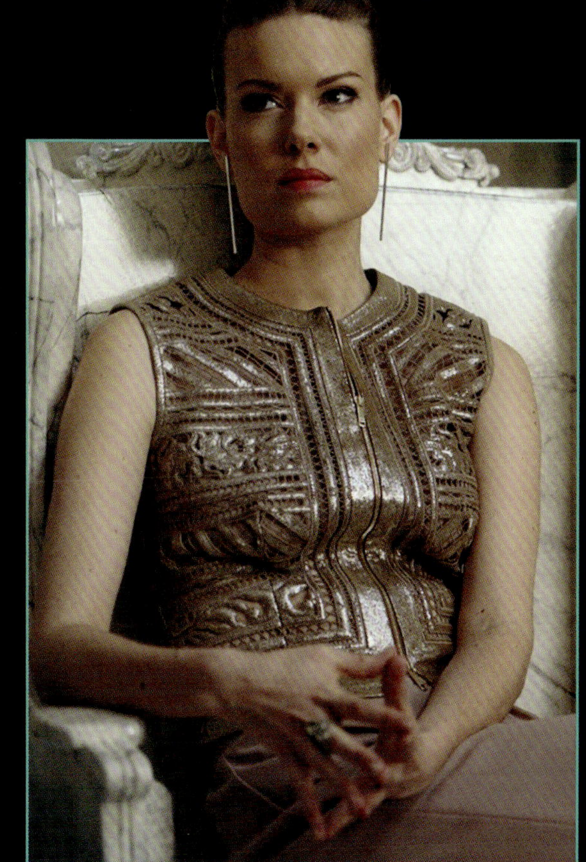

Reileen (Dichen Lachman) uses a number of sleeves throughout season one.

These include the Meth Clarissa Severin (Anna Van Hooft), who advised Bancroft to hire the last Envoy; Hemingway (Arnold Pinnock), who runs the sleeve brokerage Psychasec; and the little girl (Maddie Dixon Poirier) who talks to Kovacs at a museum, and later gets Ortega (Martha Higareda) to lower her guard.

Reileen then sleeves herself as Ortega in an attempt to trick Kovacs into revealing his true feelings. This called for Higareda to play Reileen. Director Peter Hoar says, "Martha came to me with a few suggestions. What was really great is that she got Dichen to record the lines as she would have done them. So Martha studied that, studied Dichen's moves and physicality."

THIS PAGE: Some of the many sleeves that Reileen wears to achieve her goals.

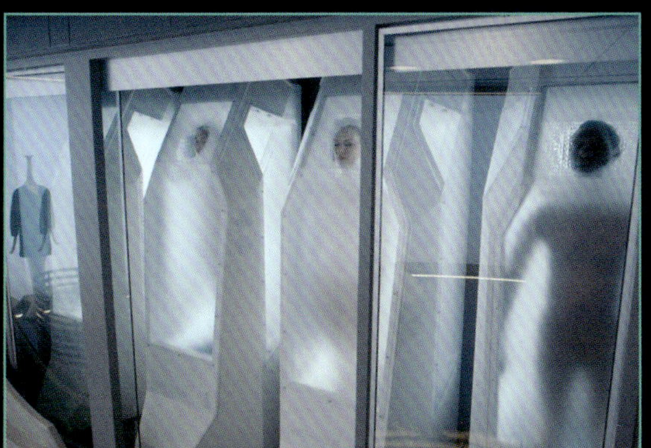

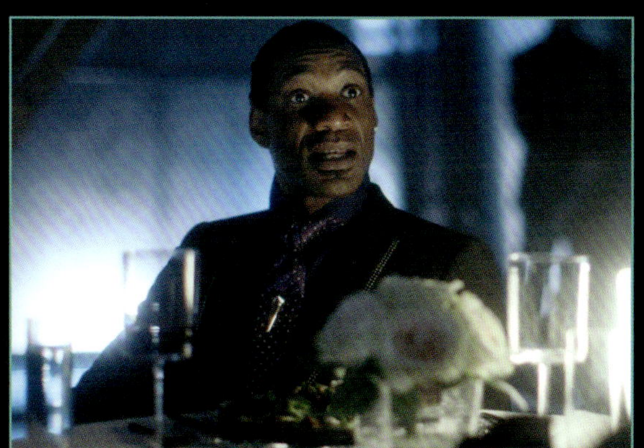

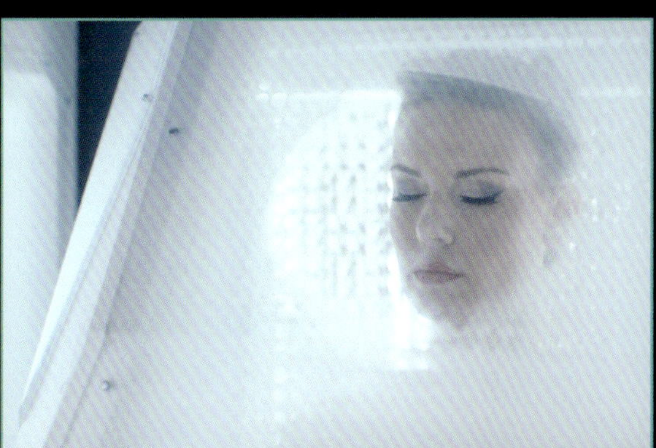

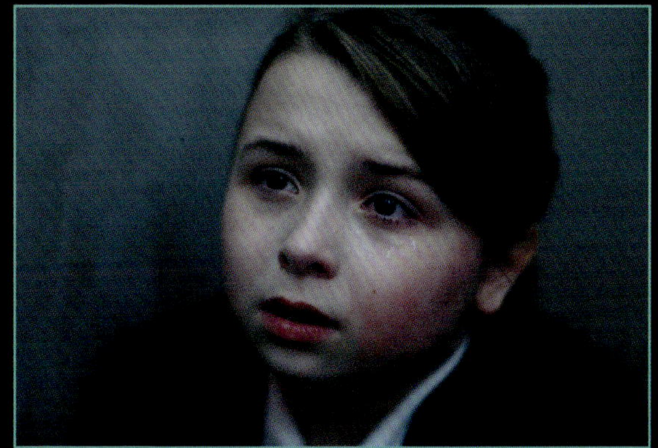

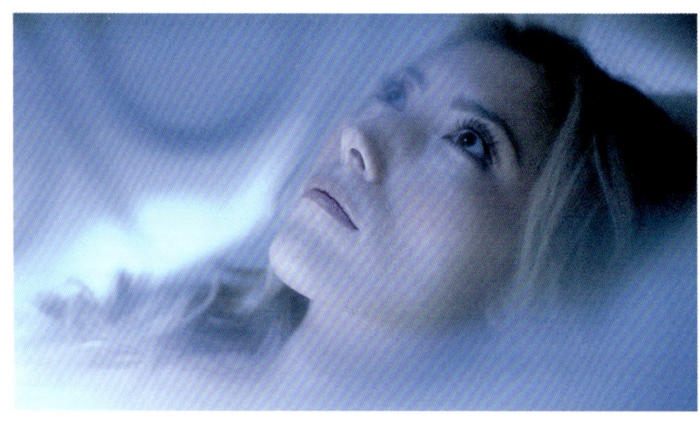

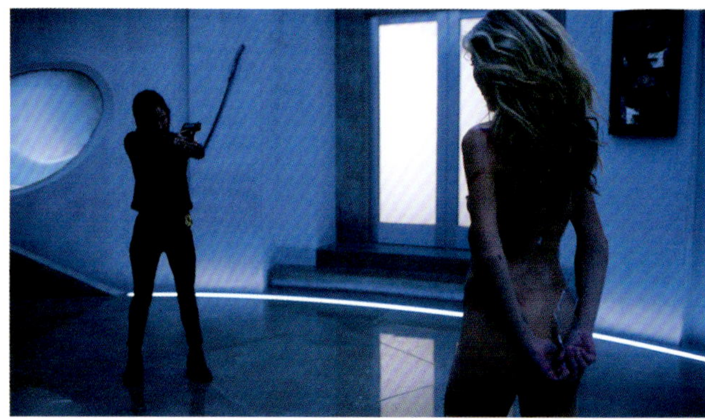

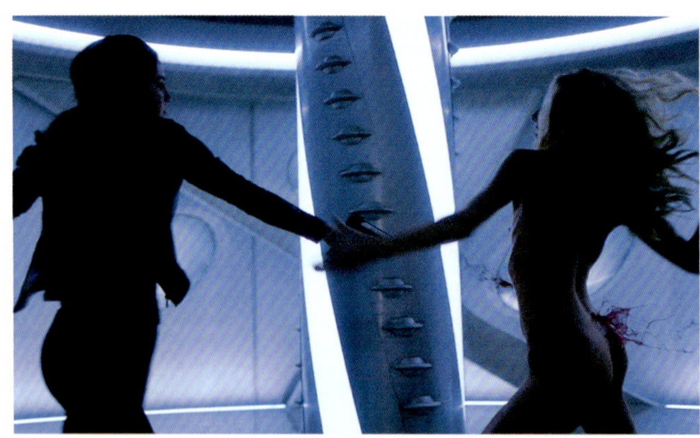

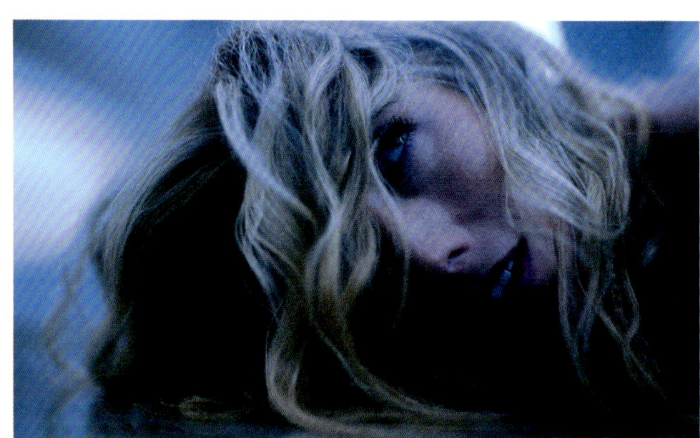

THIS PAGE: Ortega battles off a host of Reileen's clones.

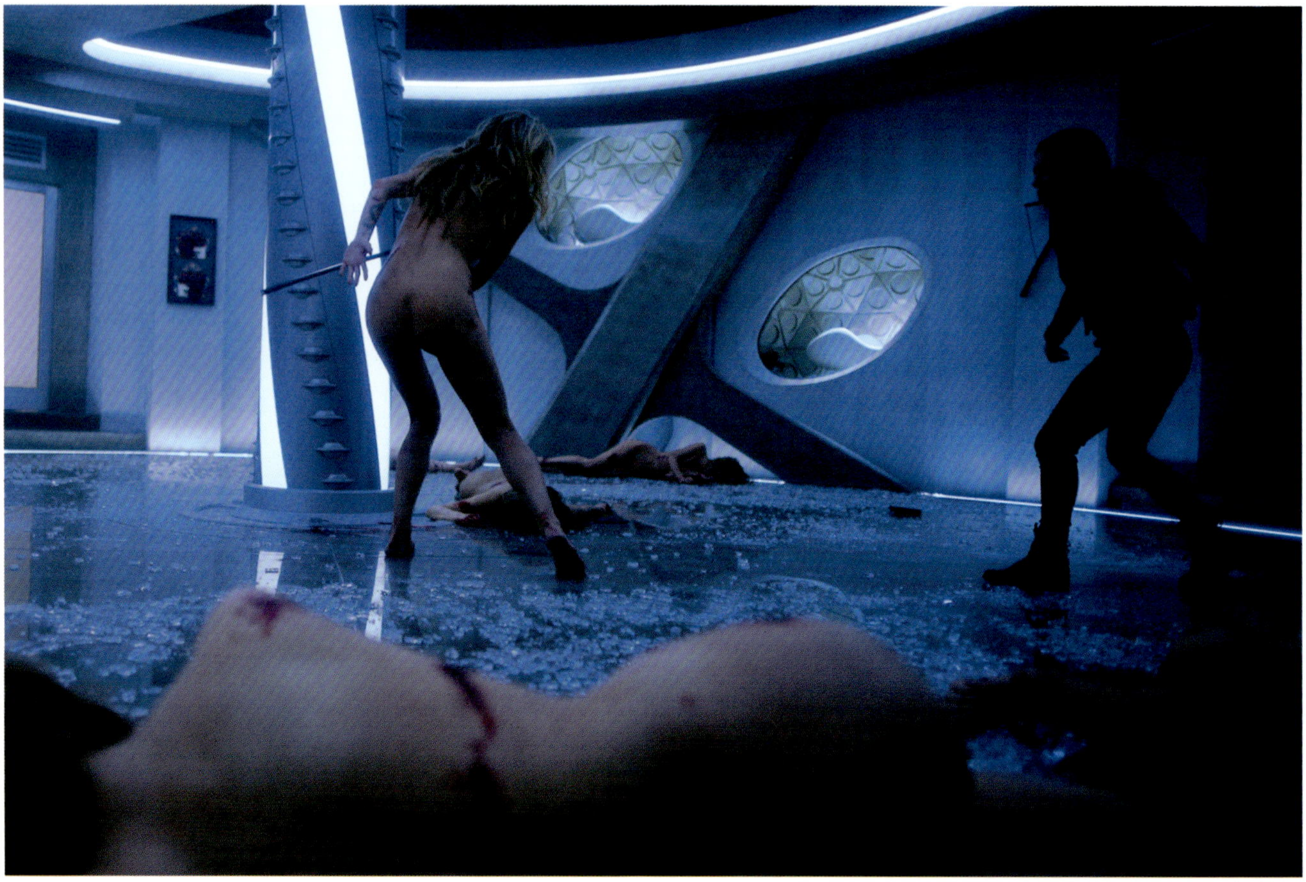

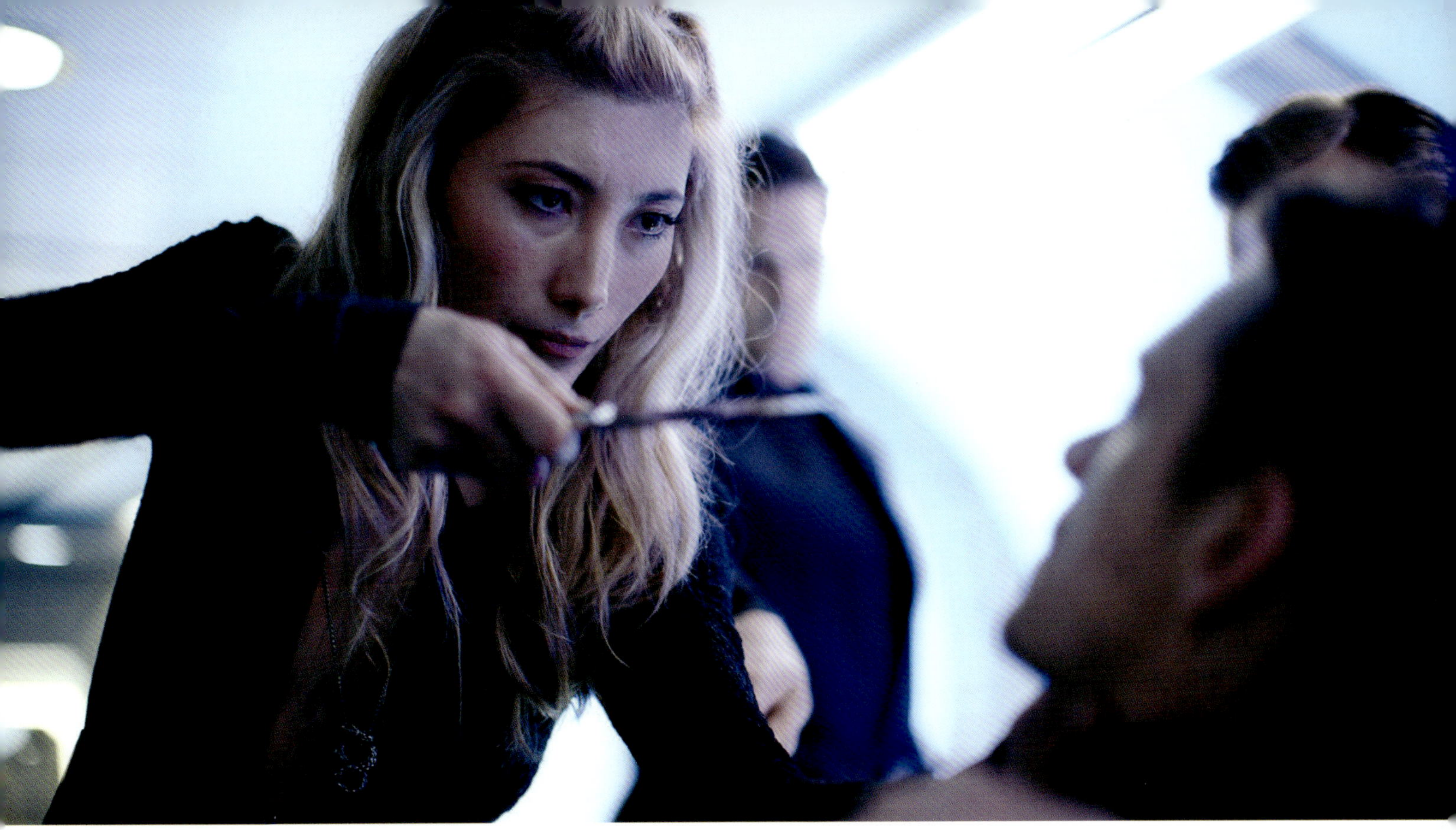

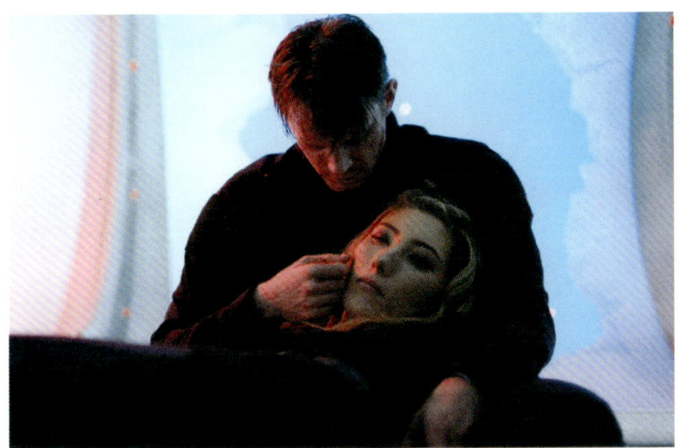

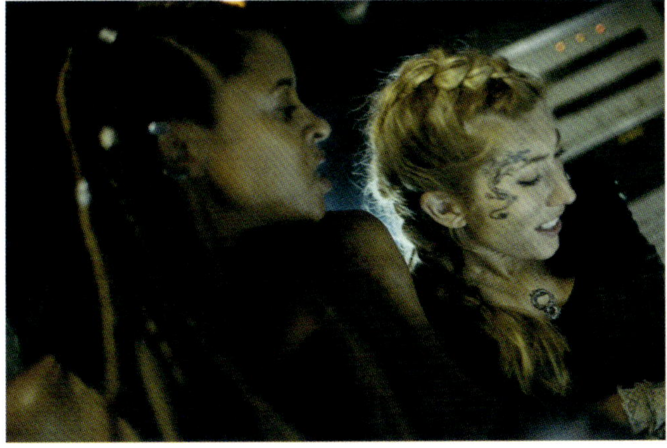

VFX supervisor Everett Burrell says of his department's contributions to the sequence, "We had stunt doubles that we had to do face replacements, we had to do specific motion blur in certain areas for the doubles' modesty, but for the most part, it was the real actress."

Peter Hoar, who directed season one's last two episodes, credits Lachman for being able to dive deep into Reileen's complicated character without a lot of preparation time. Because *Altered Carbon* shoots out of sequence, Hoar believes Lachman's first major Head in the Clouds scene "was the first thing she had shot as Reileen where she was speaking her mind and talking things through. At that point, she was just trying to say to her brother, 'Look, I'm doing the right thing, join me.' She shot that a few days before I shot [Reileen's climactic scenes]. So it really hadn't been long for Dichen to get into her character."

Reileen, immensely wealthy and influential now, is sure that she can get Takeshi to love only her, and make him see that they are the only two people in the universe who mean anything. Their conflict ends with Reileen and Takeshi grievously wounding each other. When Takeshi refuses to run away with her, Reileen tells him to kill her: "I'll never stop." Takeshi shoots her through the stack, then cradles her corpse in his arms as he weeps.

MR LEUNG

THE GHOSTWALKER

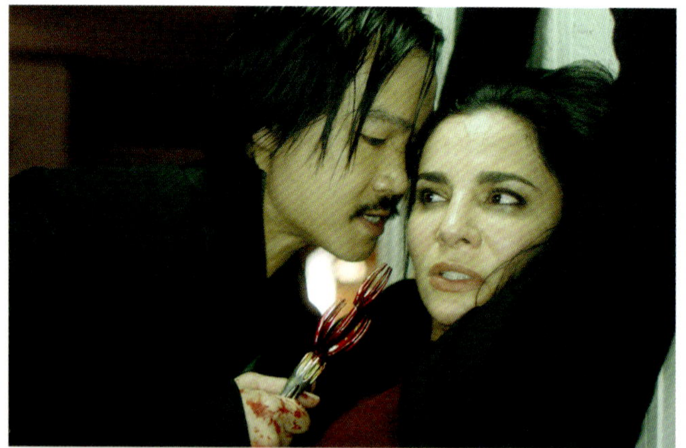

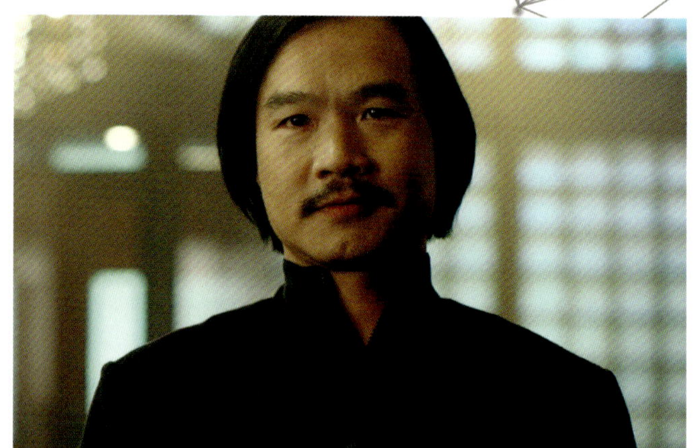

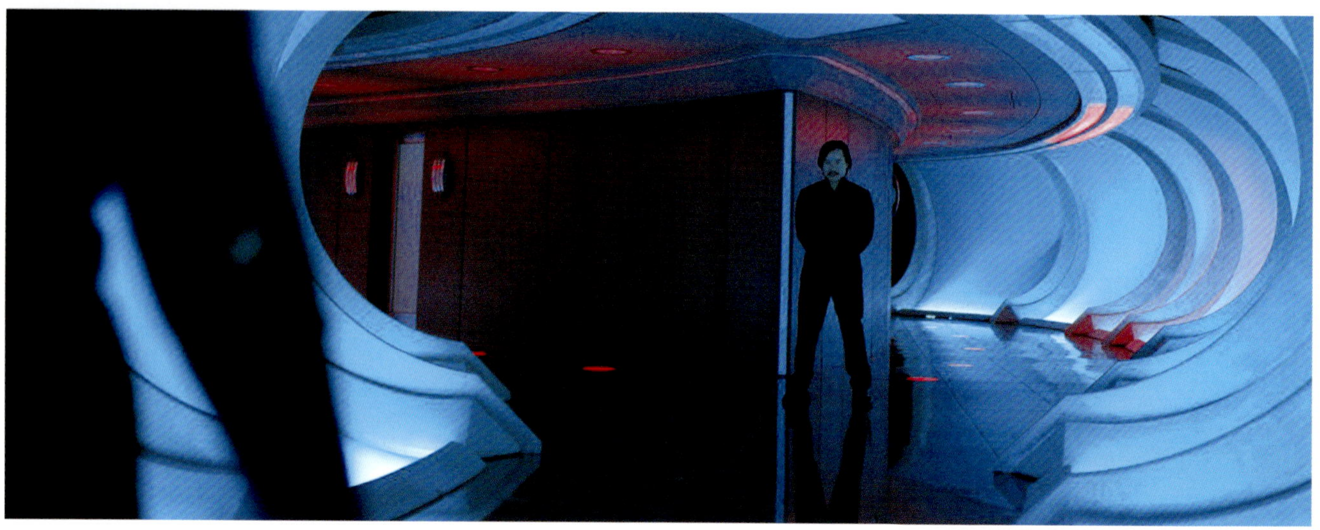

THIS PAGE: Under the direction of Reileen, Leung is a constant thorn in the side of Ortega and Kovacs.

Mr. Leung, played by Trieu Tran, is Reileen Kawahara's top assassin. Kovacs and the team call Leung 'the ghost walker' due to his ability to avoid showing up in digital surveillance.

Leung is an adept torturer, and uses knives, guns, and his hands with proficiency, but his favorite weapon is his stack ripper.

Leung always asks his victims before striking, "Are you a believer?" Leung himself worships Reileen as a living god. He observes that humans formerly worshipped invisible gods who remained silent. Now, for the first time, people can pray to gods, i.e. the Meths, and they answer. When Kovacs opines that the Meths aren't gods, Leung counters, "Their power is absolute, and they never die. What else would you call them?"

Leung finds out too late that Reileen's power is not absolute when he loses a fight to Ortega, who kills him aboard Head in the Clouds.

MR LEUNG'S WEAPON

Reileen's right-hand assassin, Mr. Leung, is terrifying not only because of his remorseless efficiency, but also because of his primary weapon: the stack remover that rips victims' personas from their body.

The prop department made two practical stack removers, one closed and one open. The transition from closed to open was done in CGI.

Property master Nevin Swain says the appearance of the stack remover "came from some African weaponry designs. Laeta shared some images with us, and we gave it a modern twist. Laeta, and Brian Cunningham,– who does amazing illustrations – and myself came up with different variations. We ended up reworking it so that it would have this claw-like effect. It was on a double-ended knife, so you'd be able to stab multiple people."

RIGHT: Concept art of Leung's stack remover weapon.

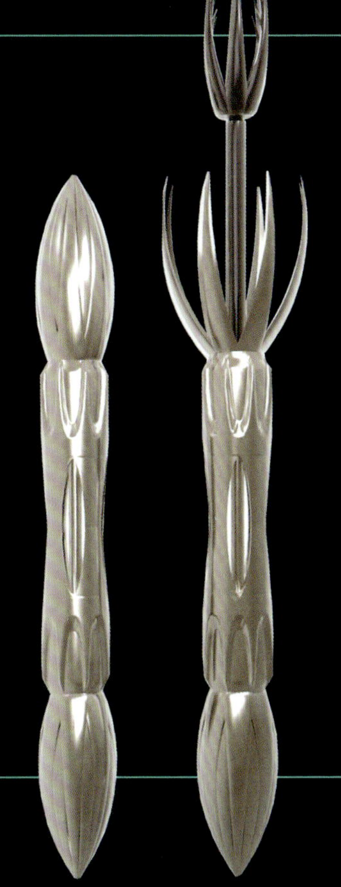

NEO-CATHOLICISM

ONE LIFE, ONE SLEEVE

Series creator Laeta Kalogridis explains that Neo-Catholics are a sect of the Catholic Church who believe "that God has given you one body. If you resleeve, you will automatically be denied access to heaven." Some other religions believe this as well; those who equate resleeving with damnation choose to get 'religious coding' on their DHF. "It's like a Do Not Resuscitate order." This means if someone who is coded dies under suspicious circumstances, they cannot be brought back, even in VR, to say what happened to them.

Resolution 653 would allow coded murder victims to be spun up to testify. Police like Ortega are for it. Reileen deems 653 so dangerous that she blackmails Bancroft into quashing it. Once Bancroft is discredited, resolution 653 passes.

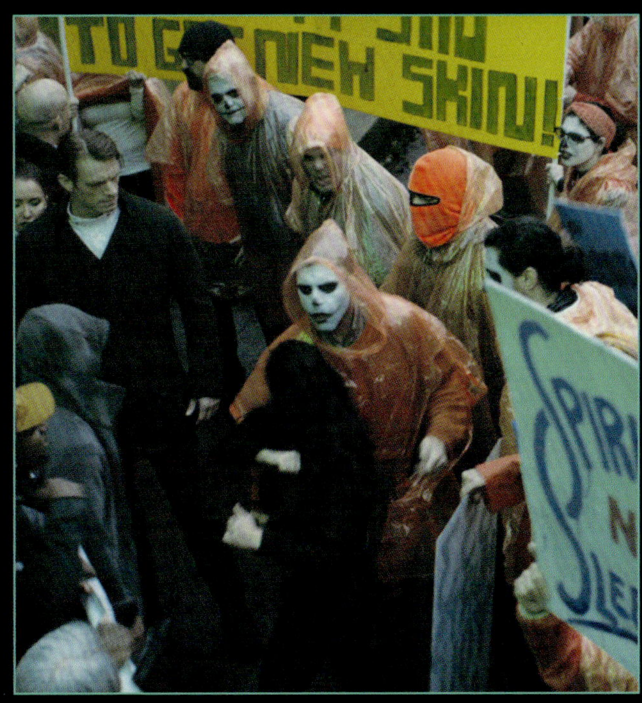

THIS PAGE: Protesters oppose the passing of resolution 653.

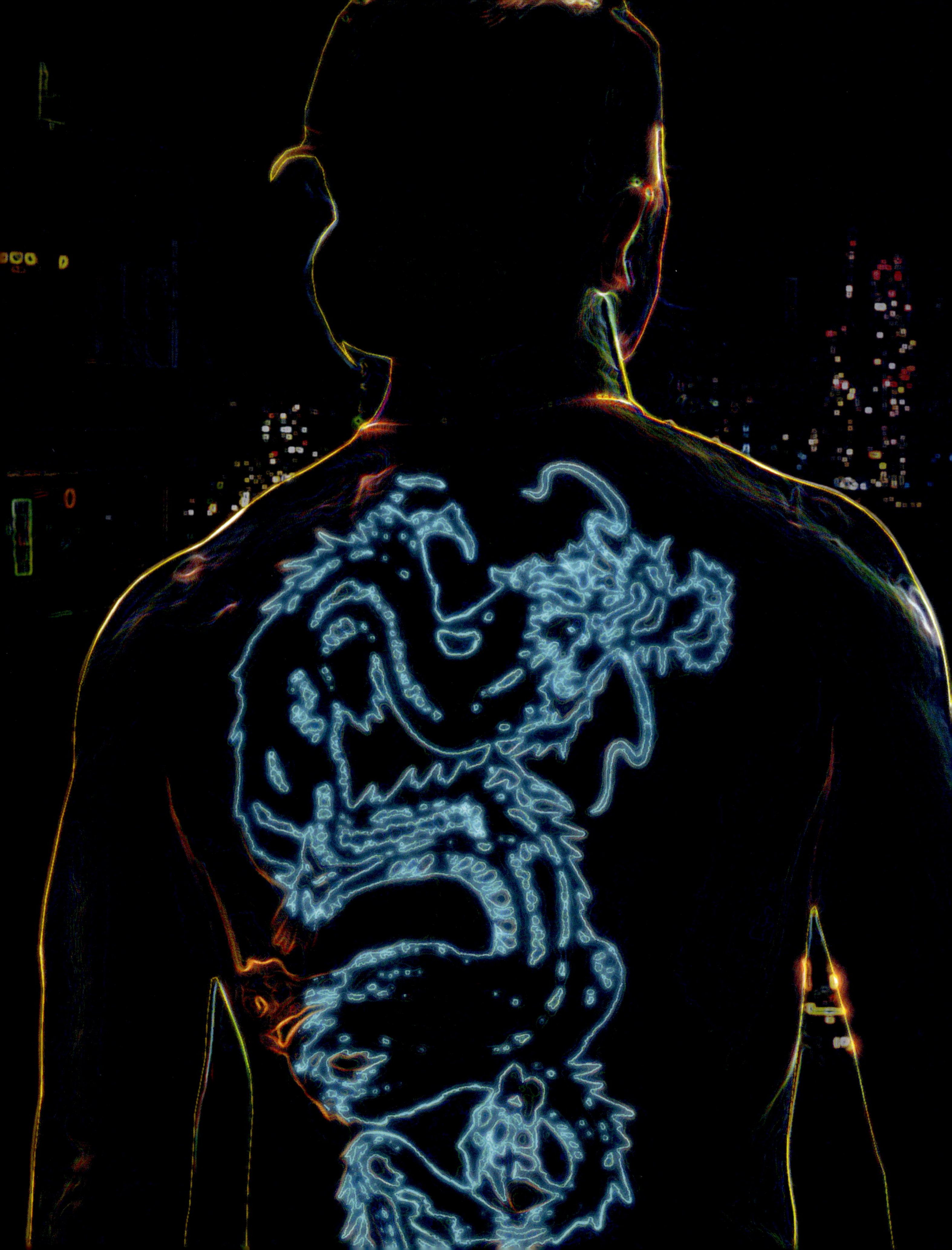

OFF WORLD

世界

HARLAN'S WORLD

THE FOUNDING PLANET

Harlan's World is the original home of Takeshi Kovacs. It is the planet of Songspire trees, and the birthplace of stack technology. It is where Quellcrist Falconer's Envoys gathered in the caves of Stronghold, and where Quellists later defy the Protectorate.

'Founded' by Konrad Harlan (Neil McDonough) and his comrades, Harlan's World supposedly was colonized after the indigenous Elder civilization had died out; in fact, Harlan et al wiped out the Elders in an act of xenocide.

Season one VFX supervisor Everett Burrell explains, "Harlan's World is first revealed in episode one. It's a beautiful planet with two moons, very forest-y and ocean-bound. It's being taken over by the Protectorate and mined for its resources, and being used up. When you see it in episode one, it's a little depressing, because they have stolen the essence from the planet."

Executive producer James Middleton relates, "While we got glimpses of Harlan's World in season one, we fully build out this world in season two. We show the beautiful forests and water bodies, the remnants of the extinct Elder alien civilization and, also, the pernicious effects of human exploitation of the planet's resources."

In season two, Harlan's World is run by Governor Danica Harlan, Konrad's daughter. Despite all the mining, there are still a lot of green places, lakes, and caves.

BELOW: Kovacs looks out over a cityscape on his home planet, Harlan's World.

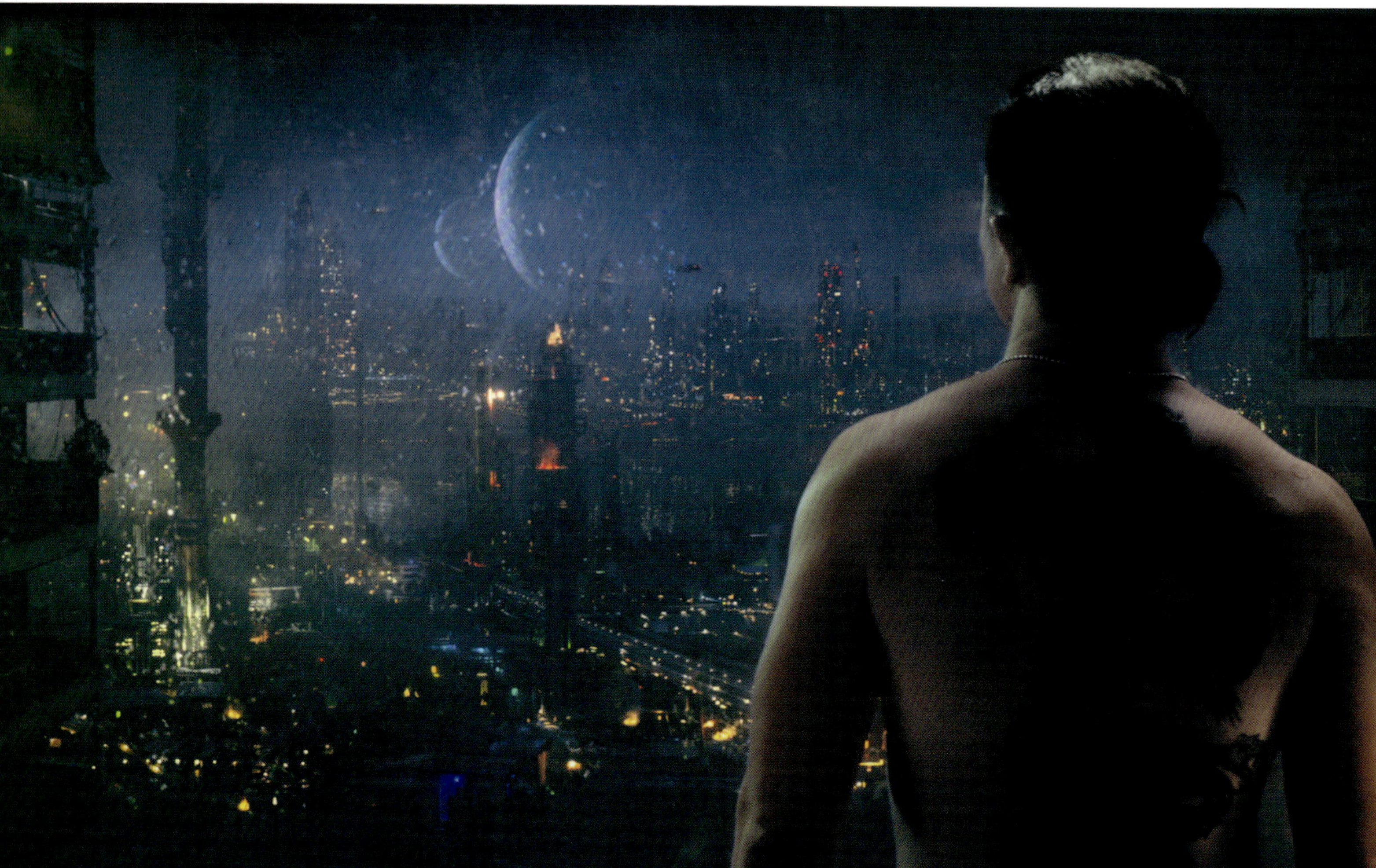

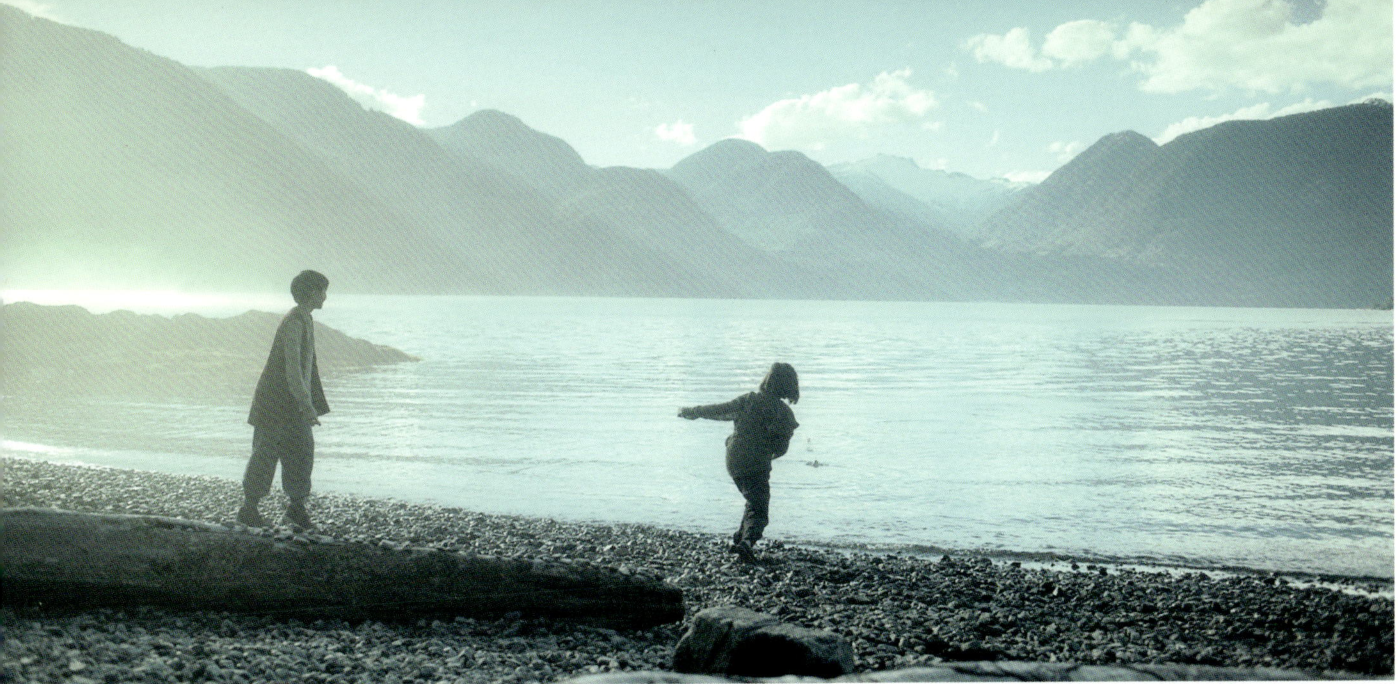

ABOVE: Young Takeshi and Reileen skim stones on a lake.

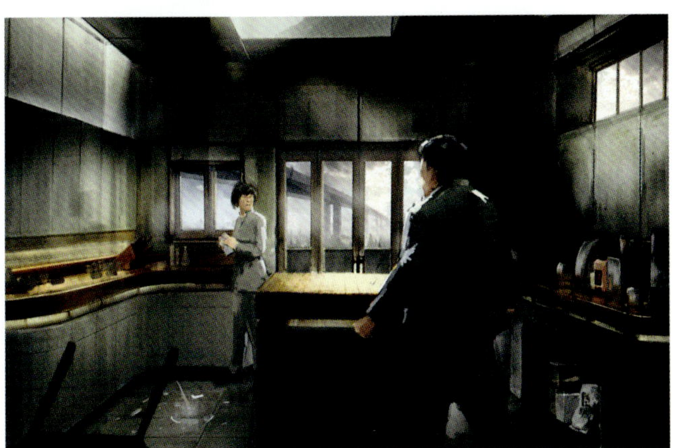

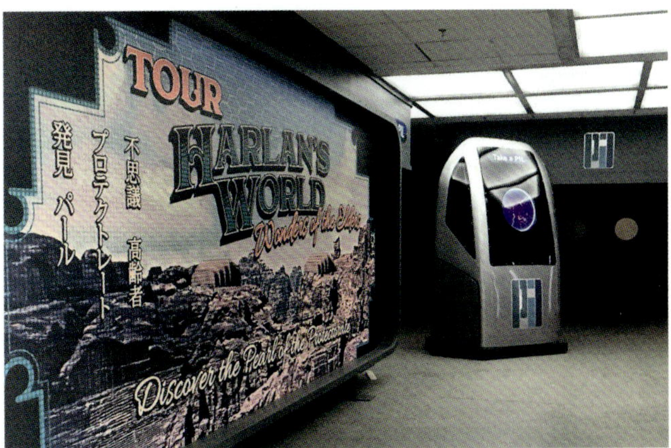

ABOVE: Concept art of the Kovacs' childhood kitchen (left). An on-set still of the PIL station in Harlan's World (right).

And ringing Harlan's World far above, there are orbitals, which are designed to shoot the napalm-like substance angelfire, so-called because it sheds radiant light and falls from above in its murderous arc, on anything unauthorized in the atmosphere or on the ground below.

Season two VFX supervisor Robert Munroe describes how the orbitals look and function. "Imagine a mesh of these things twenty thousand feet above the surface of the planet. They're each only a couple of meters, six feet across, that's kind of small, but there are hundreds of thousands of them all around the planet in a protective shield. Each one can produce a somewhat damaging beam, but when they need them to do something much more destructive, any group of them in close proximity to one another come together and join and create this much larger collective weapon that can just wreak havoc on the planet below in big fashion. They are all identical, and designed to interlock."

The orbitals are completely digital, Munroe adds, designed in CG. "There is no real orbital. The [surface] of the orbitals looks kind of like the panels on a soccer ball. You see how they all fit together, how soccer balls would fit together when they're made into that spherical shape. All the orbitals are either pentagonal or hexagonal, five or six sides, and they all fit together and make a much larger weapon. But they're satellite-looking, nothing fancy about them. They're quite utilitarian."

We never see Harlan's World from the perspective of its placement in the galaxy. There's a good reason for this, per Munroe. "Space is nothing but empty. It would just be ridiculous to try to show Harlan's World's proximity to Earth, because we're talking light years, and lots of empty, cold, dark space.

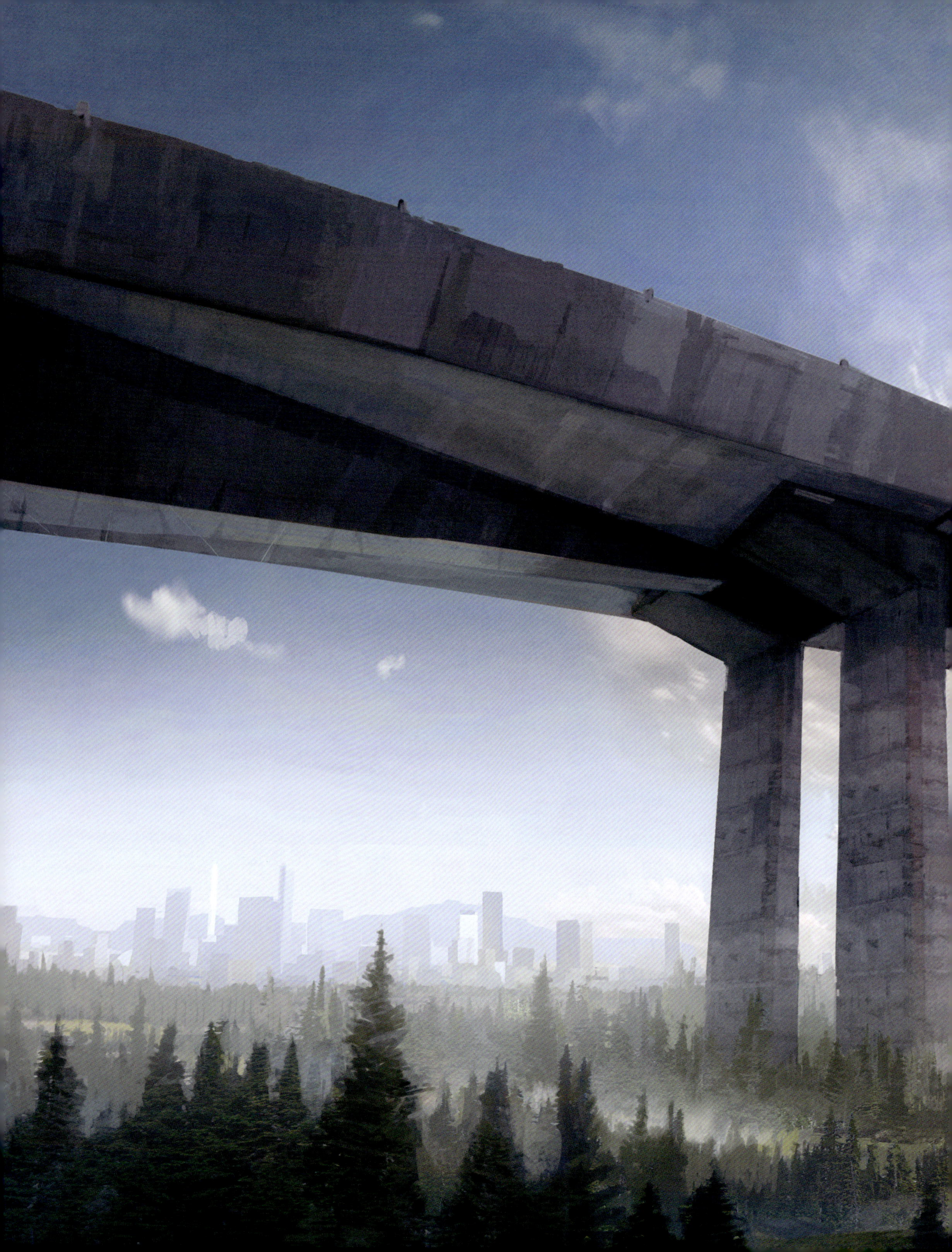

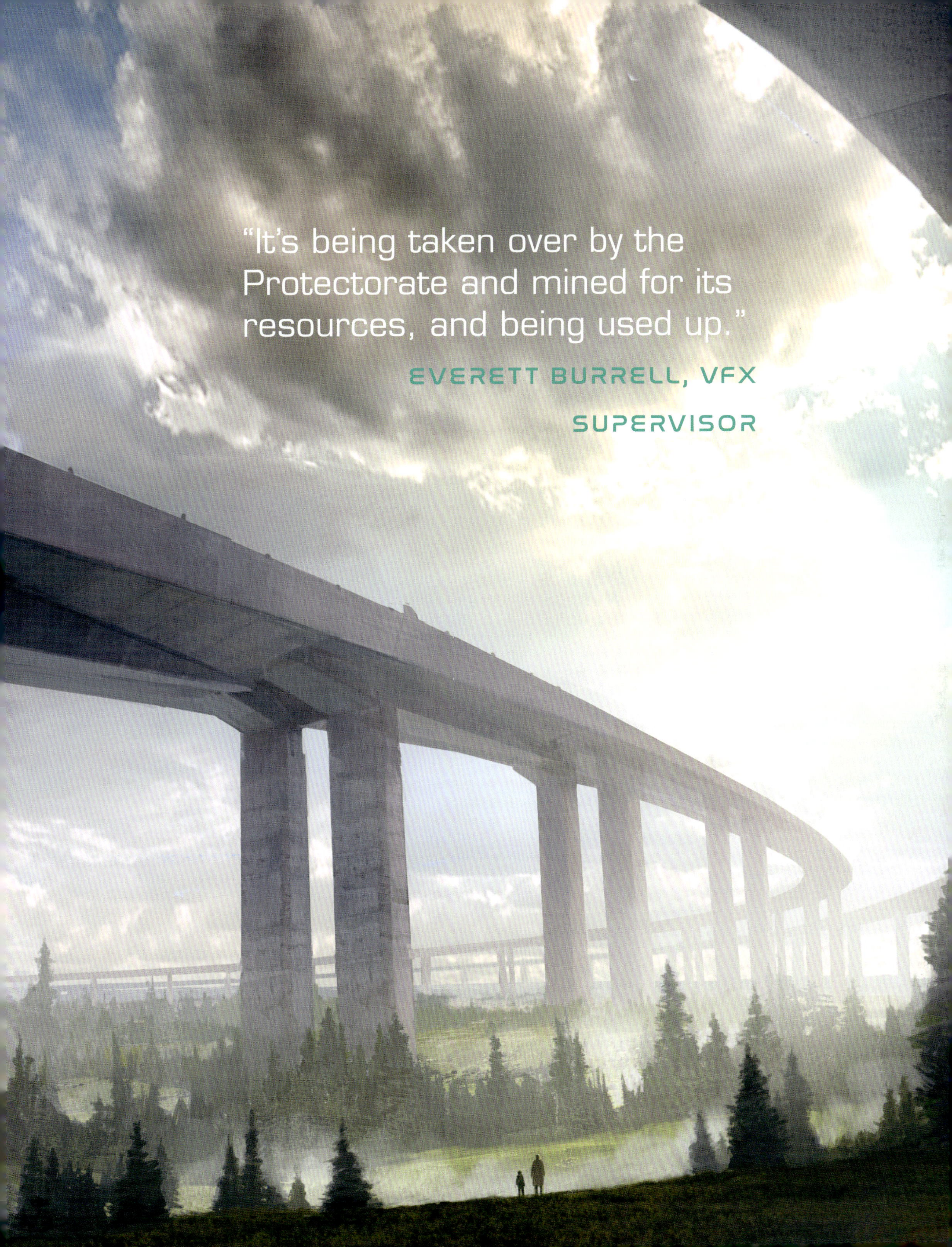

"It's being taken over by the Protectorate and mined for its resources, and being used up."

EVERETT BURRELL, VFX SUPERVISOR

THE PRAETORIANS

COLONIAL TACTICAL ASSAULT CORPS

In ancient Rome, the soldiers of the Praetorian Guard were tasked with protecting the Emperor. In the future of *Altered Carbon*, the CTAC (Colonial Tactical Assault Corps) Praetorians are the foremost fighting force of the Protectorate, charged with keeping order on the inhabited planets. They ruthlessly preserve the status quo.

Kovacs first meets the Praetorians when he's brought in, as a child, by Jaeger. Later, Kovacs is captured by Quellcrist Falconer and her Envoys, who ultimately wins his allegiance and turn him against the Praetorians.

Costume designer Ann Foley says that the look for the Praetorian troopers "was an exciting challenge, to come up with something unique. I worked closely with [series creator] Laeta Kalogridis, and Miguel Sapochnik, who directed the pilot, and [executive producer] David Ellison, about what we wanted these guys to look like. My initial idea was, when they came storming into the Happy Face Motel, I didn't want the audience to know what they were. Are they human? Are they alien? Are they machines? What are these guys? [It's unknown] until one of the guys pulls his helmet off and you see that there's actually a human in there. Iron Head Studios made the armor for us, and they did a fantastic job. My illustrator, Keith Christiansen, was also instrumental in [bringing the look] to life."

VFX supervisor Everett Burrell reveals that the Praetorian helmets had built-in, battery-powered lights. "Sometimes the batteries would go out, so we'd have to [digitally] paint the lights back in. But for the most part, it was practical. They were great suits; we didn't have to enhance them that much."

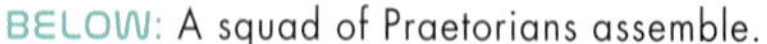

BELOW: A squad of Praetorians assemble.

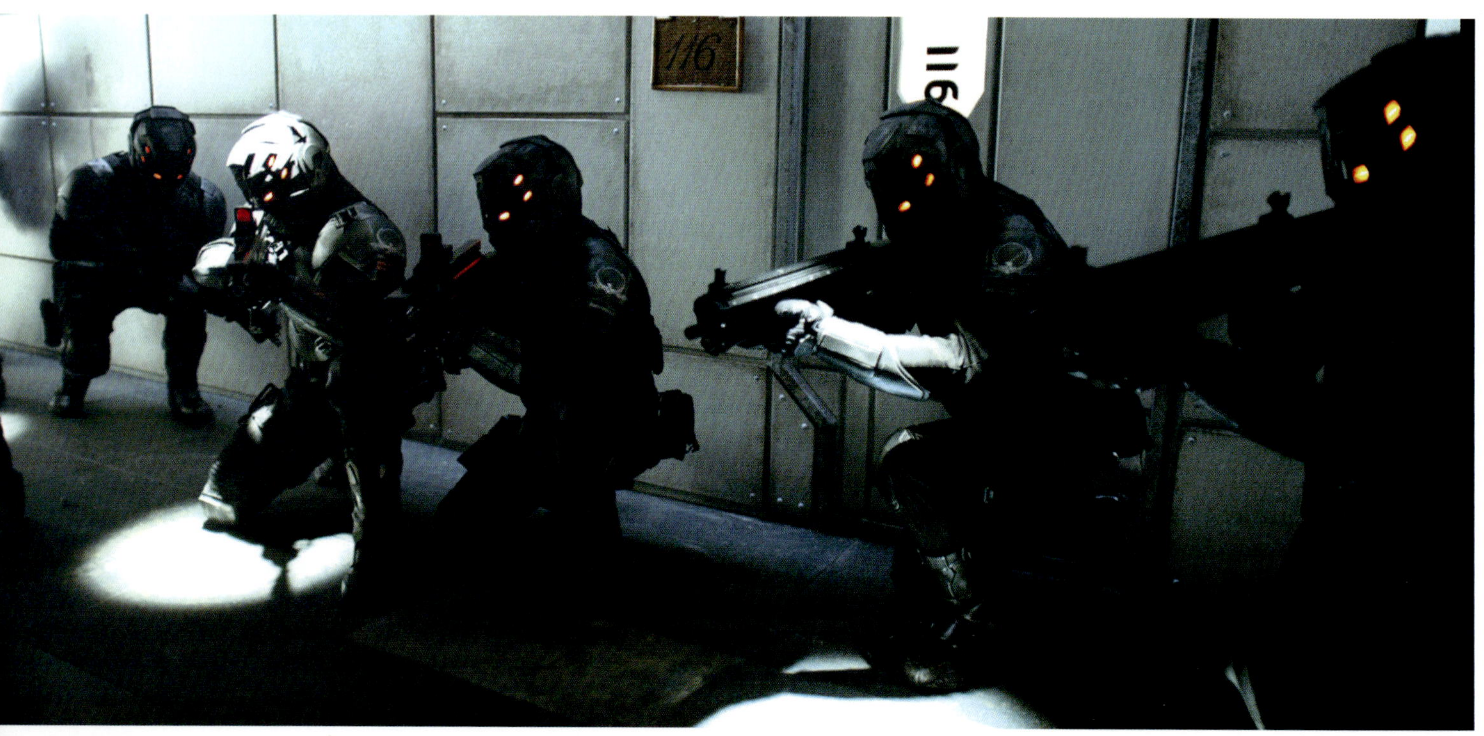

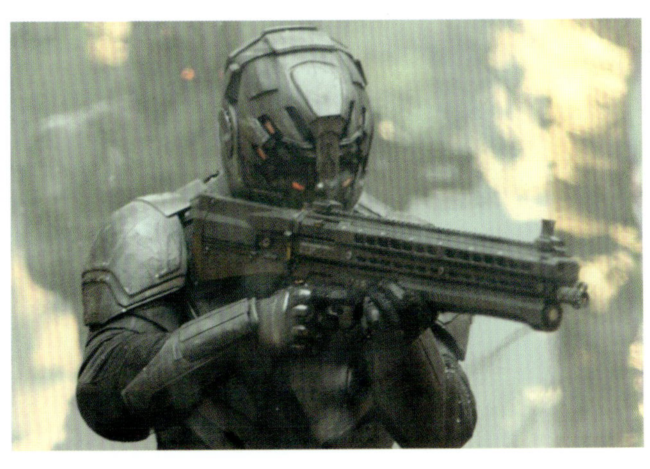

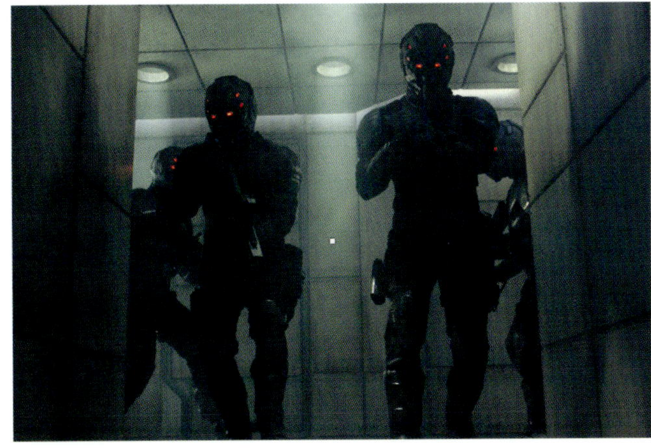

ΛBOVE: Praetorians have special armor around the neck to protect their stack.

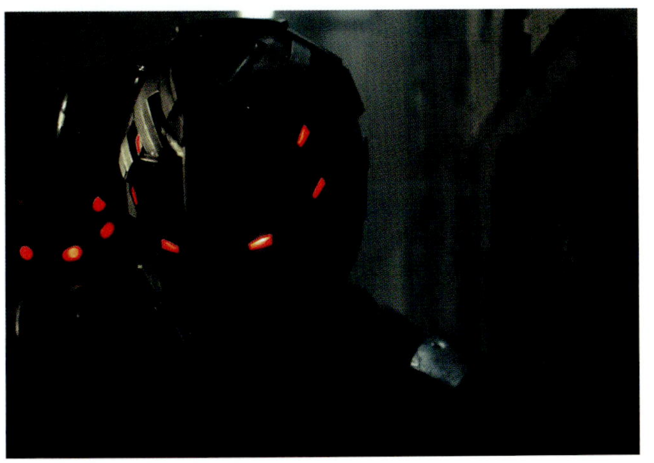

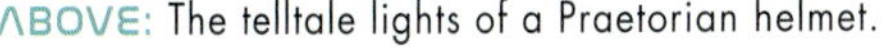

ΛBOVE: The telltale lights of a Praetorian helmet.

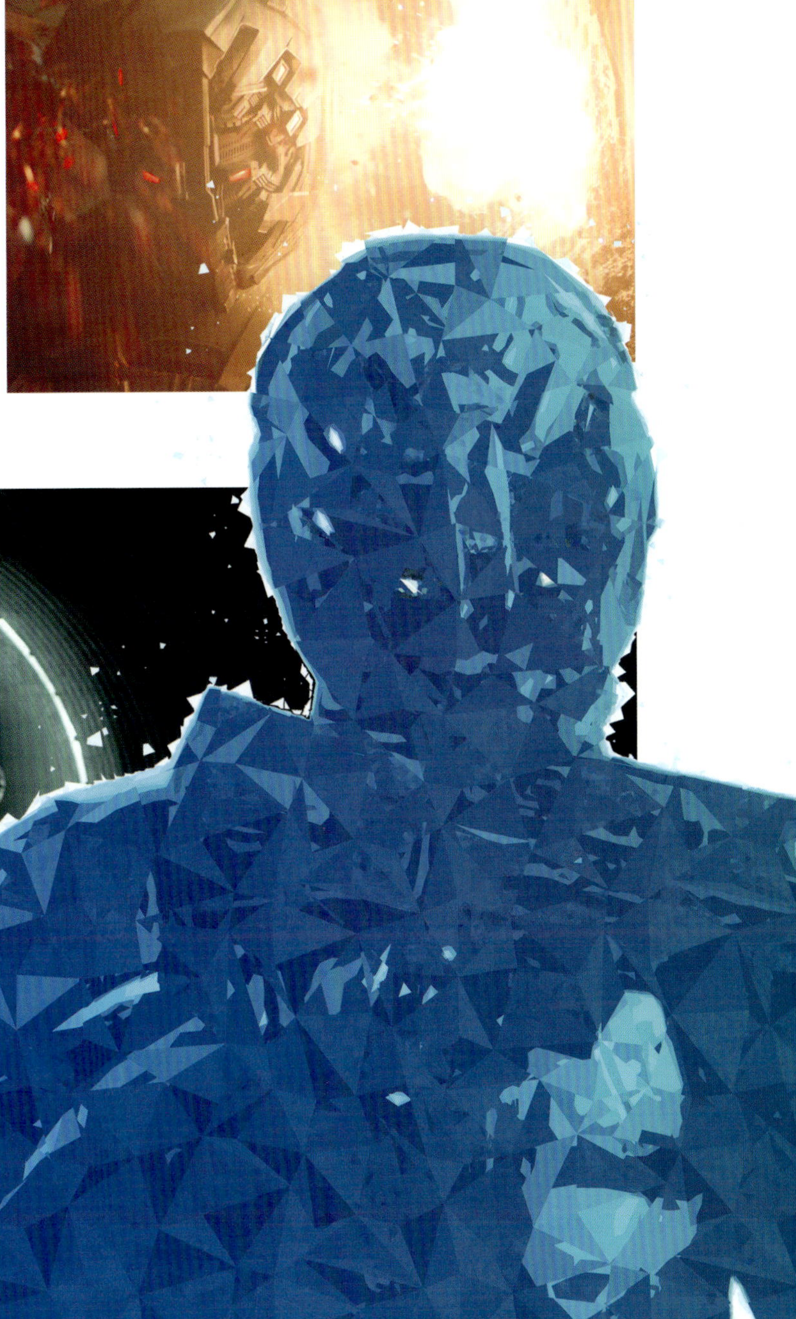

WEAPONS

A WEAPON IS A TOOL

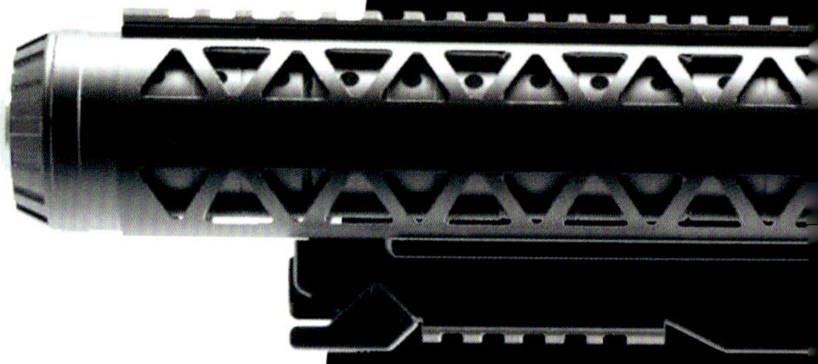

In *Altered Carbon*, there are viruses both organic and digital; explosives; blades of all sizes; and many, many guns.

Property master Nevin Swain relates, "WETA helped design the Praetorian weapons, based off of an AK-74. They were built by Kenney Palkow, of Kenney's Custom Props, who used a C and C to machine them. [In season one], they were blank-firing. [In season two] we're going to more of a caseless ammo look."

The Envoys in season one have weapons "based off of a paintball gun. We changed out the fore-grip, changed out the muzzle brake, changed out the stock on the back, and did a bunch of modifications on the receiver."

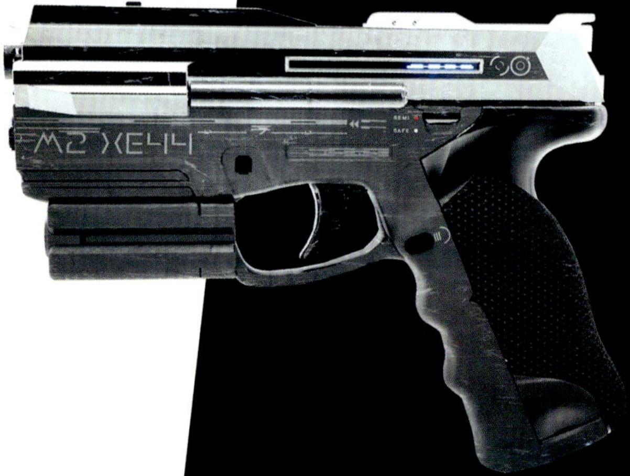

In season one, "Kovacs' gun is based loosely on a Rhino [revolver]. It is a completely scratch build from a C and C. Laeta Kalogridis had a lot of input. She wanted a big, strong cannon, but she also wanted something [unique]. So we ended up doing a custom handle, custom fuel cell, so you're able to pop in and out the fuel cell for the gun. It fires plasma rounds, which are handled by visual effects. He has the fleschett gun as well, which fires these little double-edged projectiles that are able to be recalled back into the gun, so it almost gives the gun infinite rounds. "

In season two, Swain adds, Kovacs has a Wedge tech gun. "It's very futuristic. It falls into that caseless ammo world. It's military, black, simple, efficient, with clean lines."

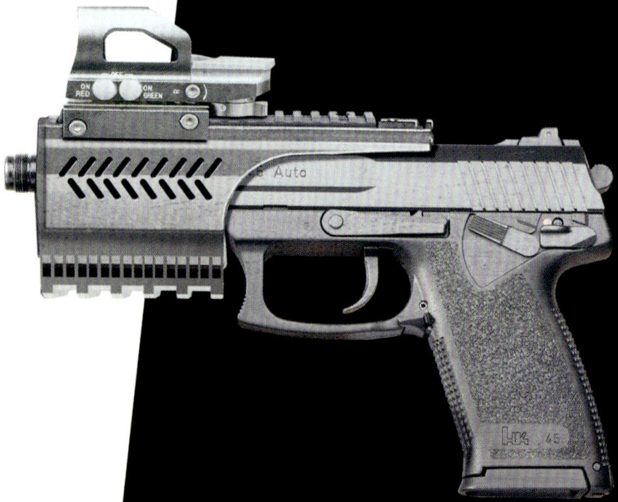

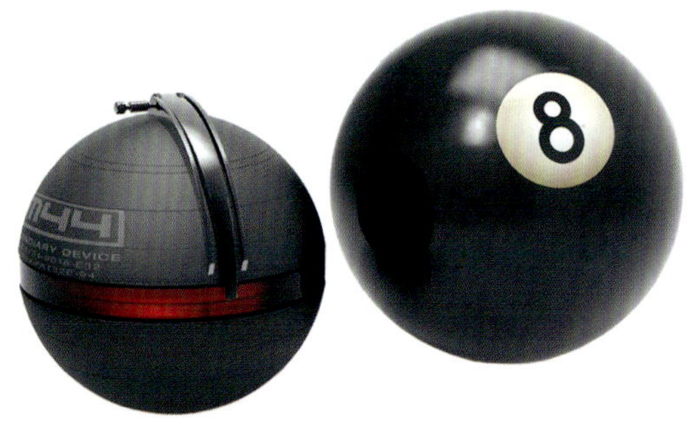

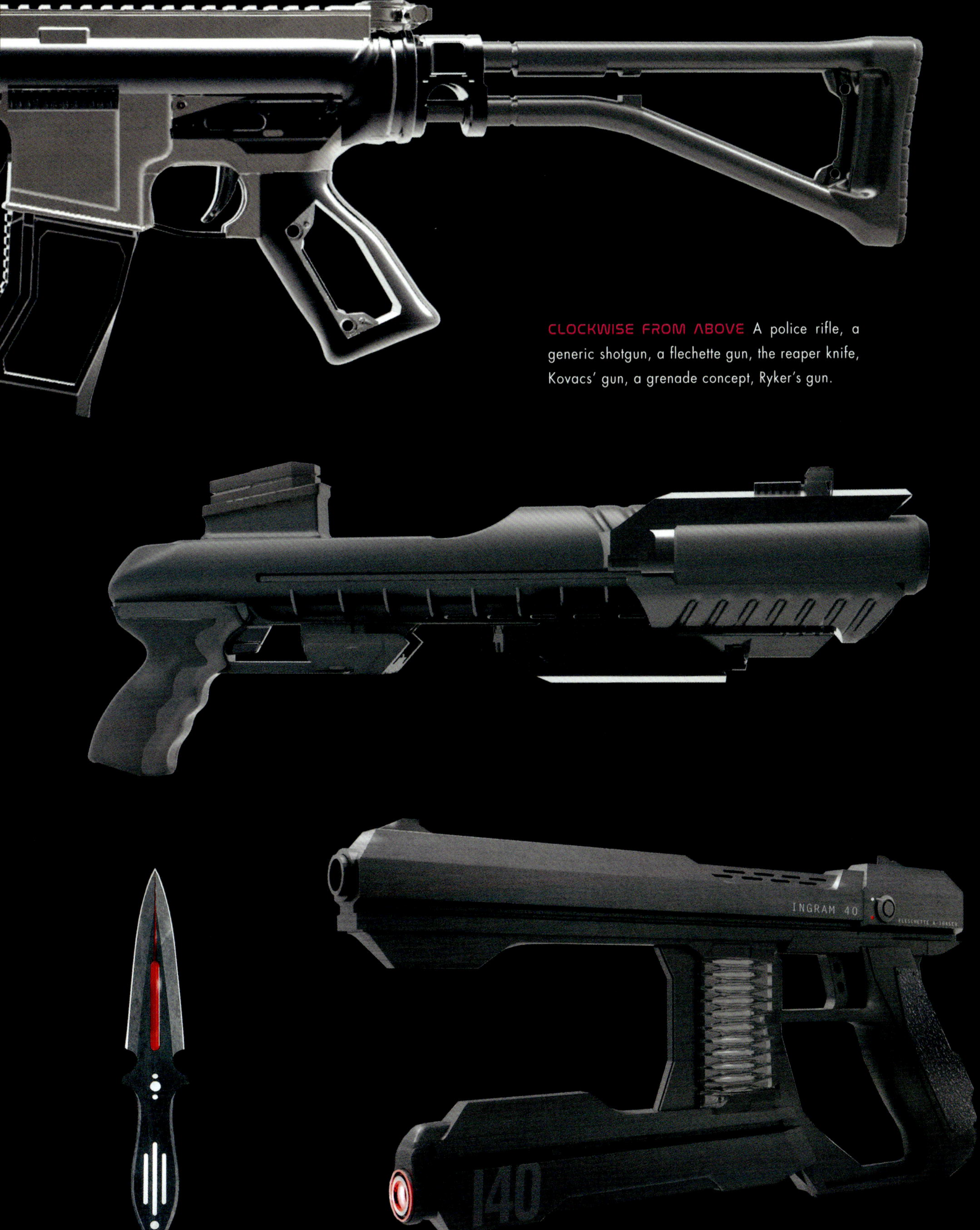

CLOCKWISE FROM ABOVE A police rifle, a generic shotgun, a flechette gun, the reaper knife, Kovacs' gun, a grenade concept, Ryker's gun.

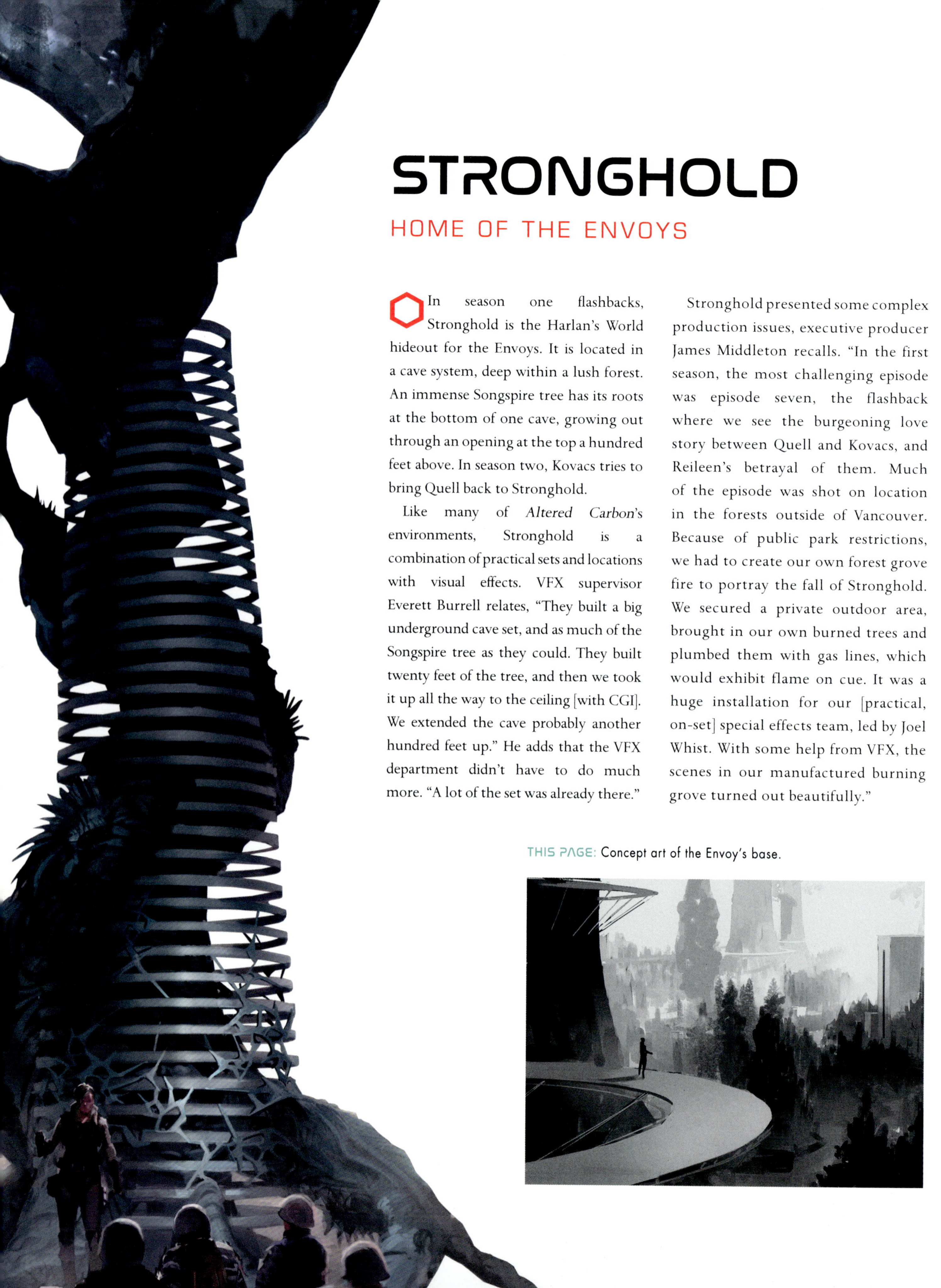

STRONGHOLD

HOME OF THE ENVOYS

In season one flashbacks, Stronghold is the Harlan's World hideout for the Envoys. It is located in a cave system, deep within a lush forest. An immense Songspire tree has its roots at the bottom of one cave, growing out through an opening at the top a hundred feet above. In season two, Kovacs tries to bring Quell back to Stronghold.

Like many of *Altered Carbon*'s environments, Stronghold is a combination of practical sets and locations with visual effects. VFX supervisor Everett Burrell relates, "They built a big underground cave set, and as much of the Songspire tree as they could. They built twenty feet of the tree, and then we took it up all the way to the ceiling [with CGI]. We extended the cave probably another hundred feet up." He adds that the VFX department didn't have to do much more. "A lot of the set was already there."

Stronghold presented some complex production issues, executive producer James Middleton recalls. "In the first season, the most challenging episode was episode seven, the flashback where we see the burgeoning love story between Quell and Kovacs, and Reileen's betrayal of them. Much of the episode was shot on location in the forests outside of Vancouver. Because of public park restrictions, we had to create our own forest grove fire to portray the fall of Stronghold. We secured a private outdoor area, brought in our own burned trees and plumbed them with gas lines, which would exhibit flame on cue. It was a huge installation for our [practical, on-set] special effects team, led by Joel Whist. With some help from VFX, the scenes in our manufactured burning grove turned out beautifully."

THIS PAGE: Concept art of the Envoy's base.

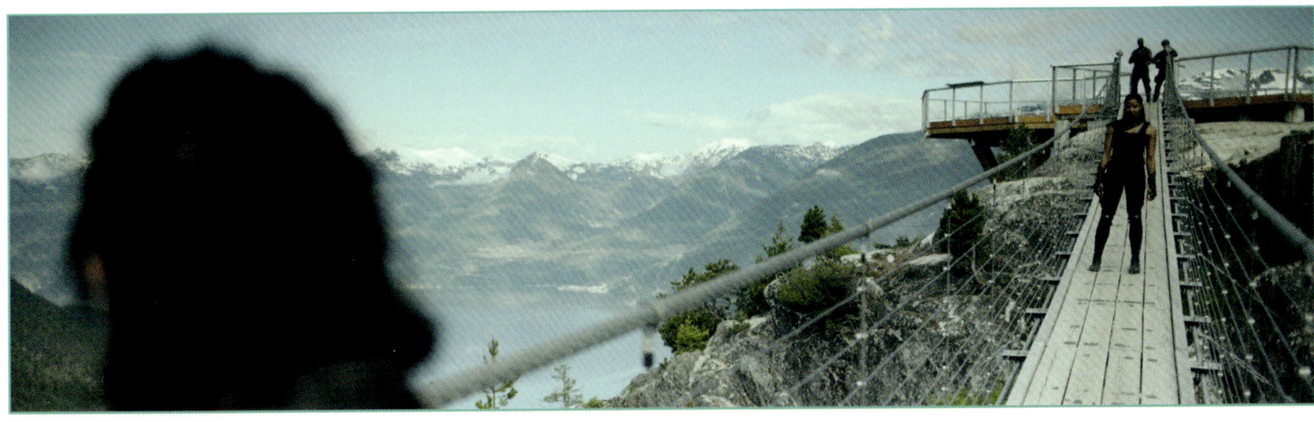

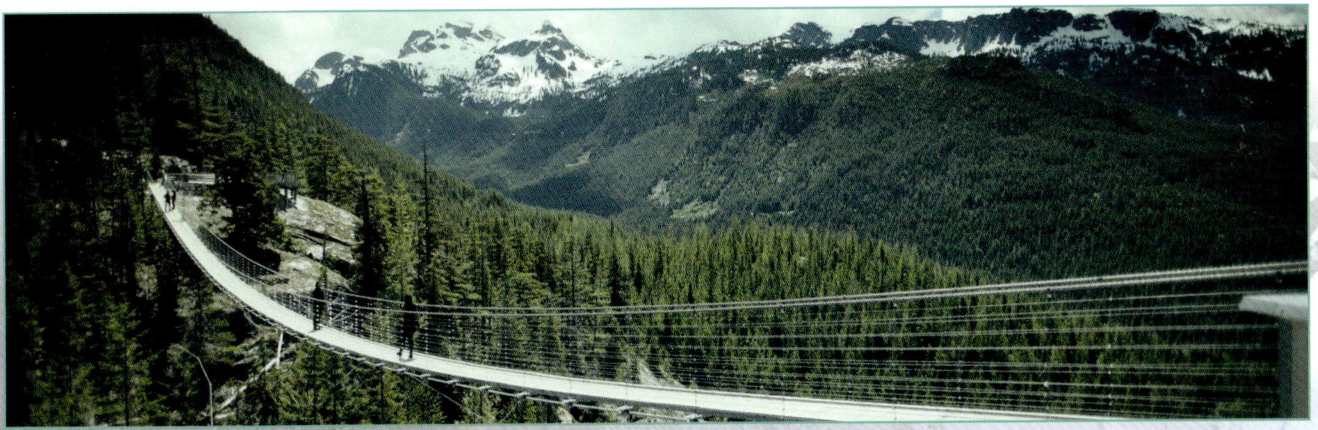

ABOVE: Stronghold's landscape was filmed just outside of Vancouver, Canada.

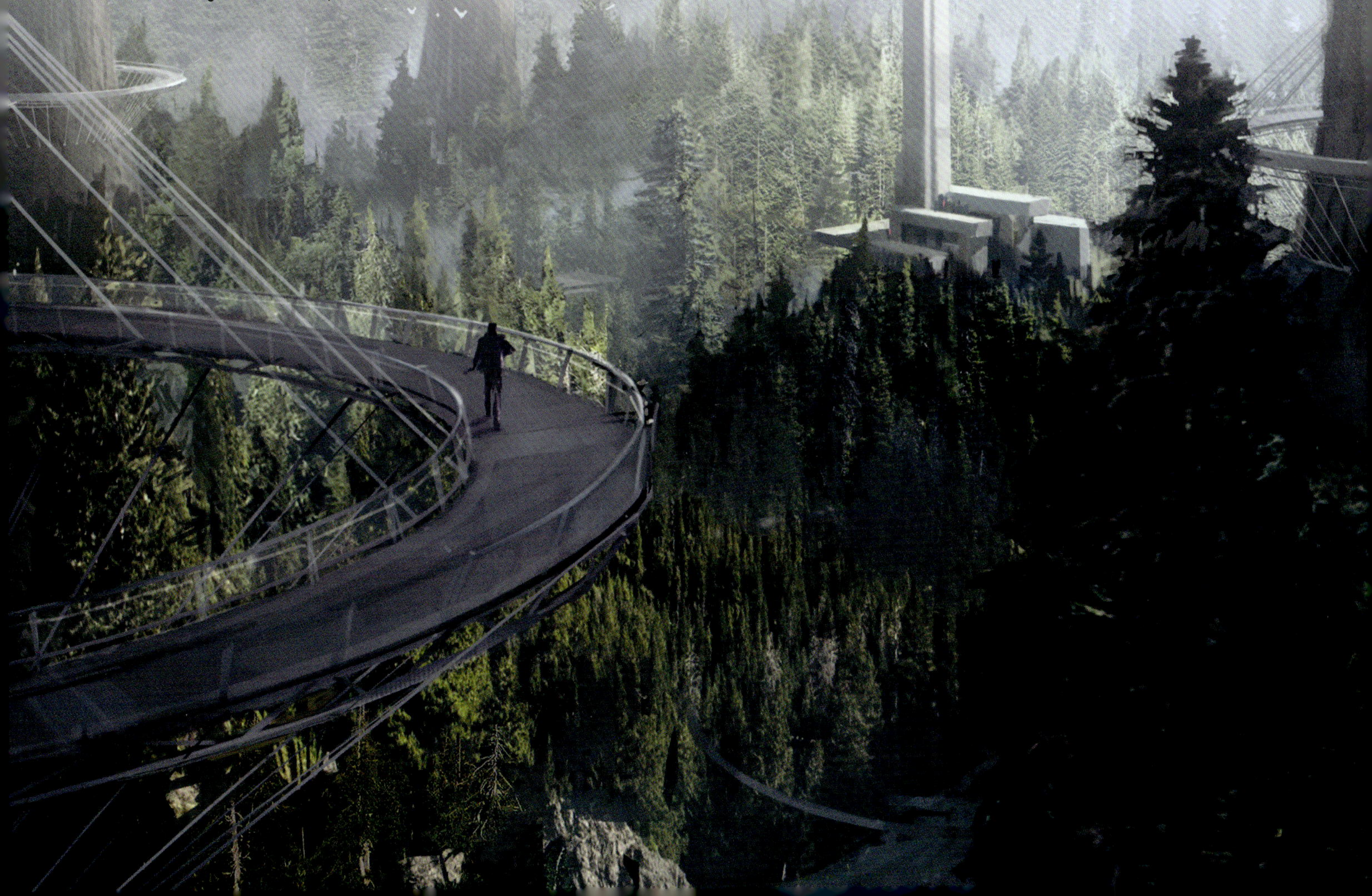

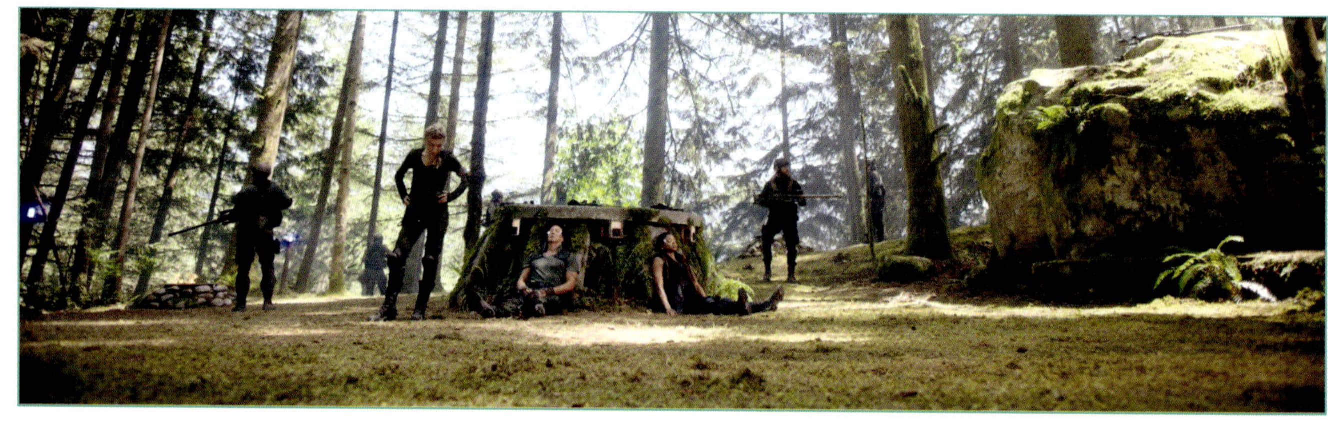

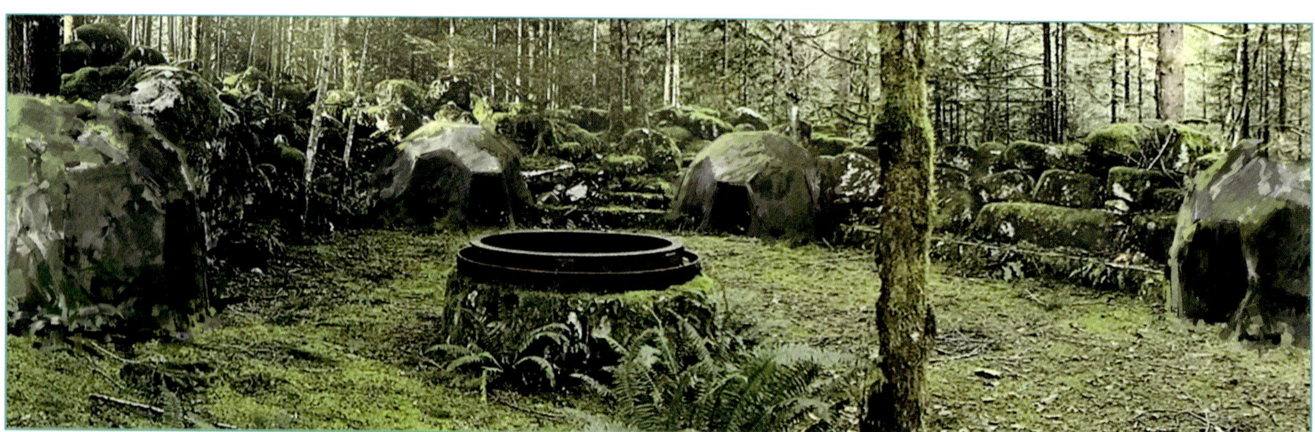

ABOVE: Shots from within the thickets of Vancouver's forests.

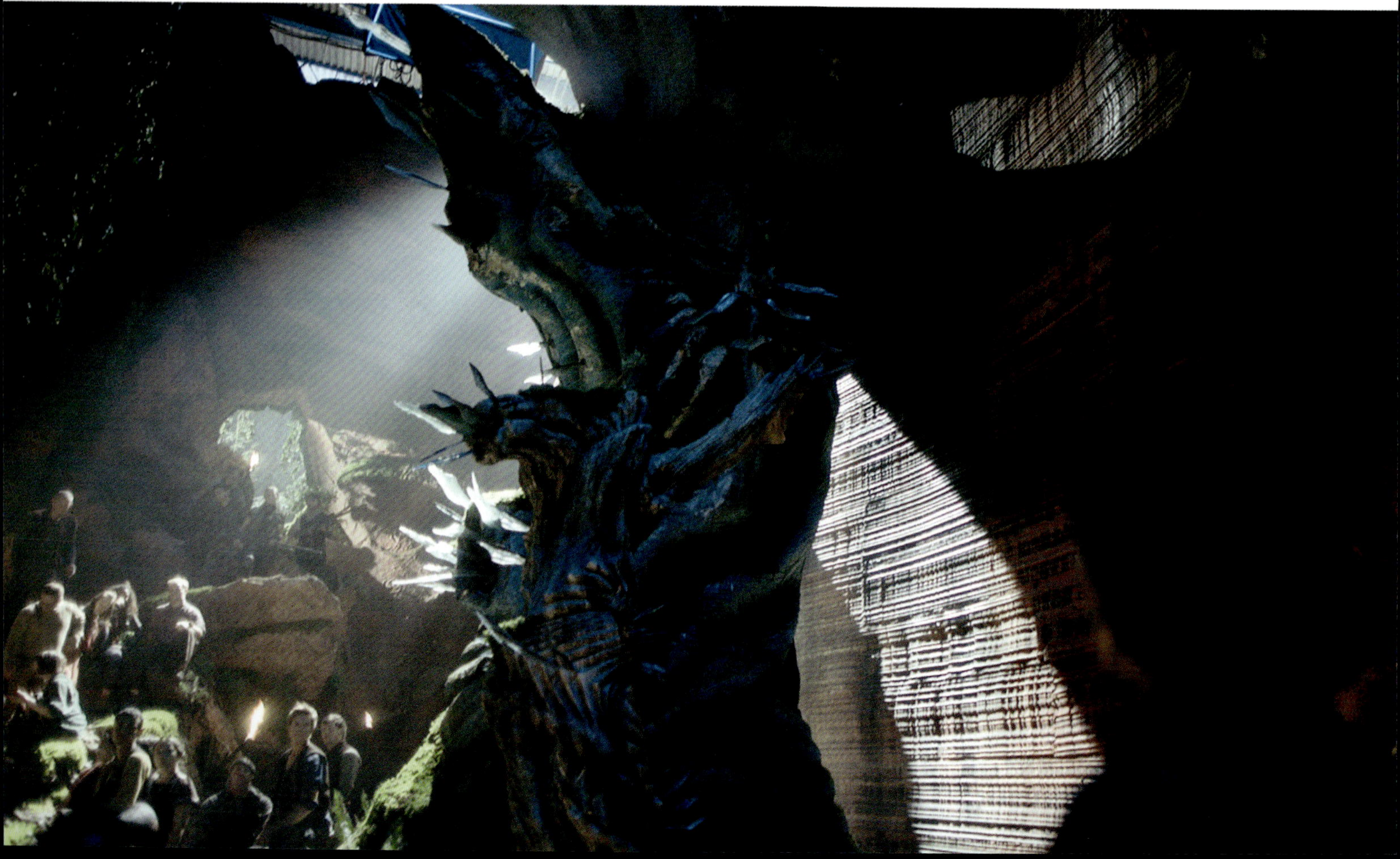

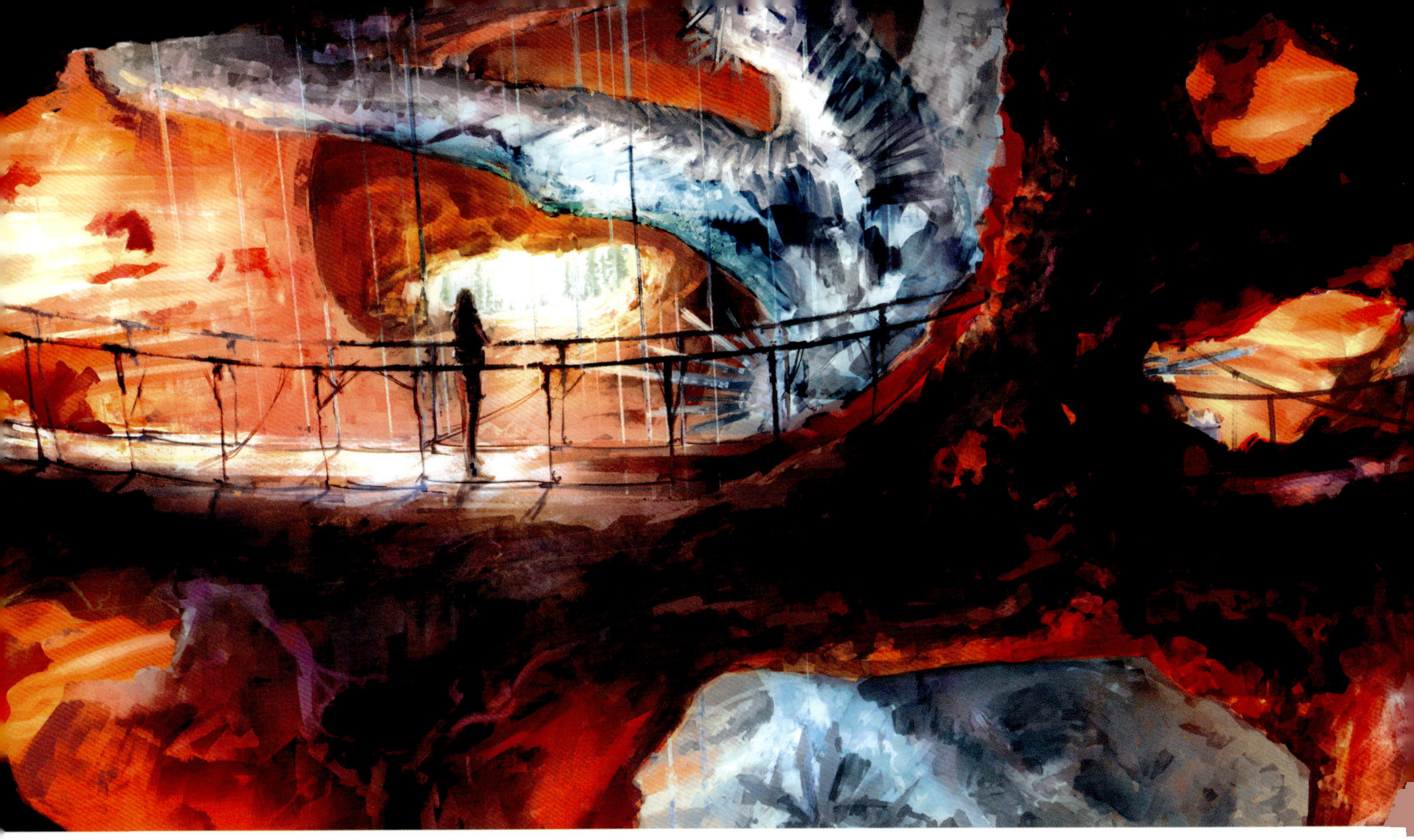

THIS PAGE: The interior of Stronghold is shown as a labyrinthine cave system.

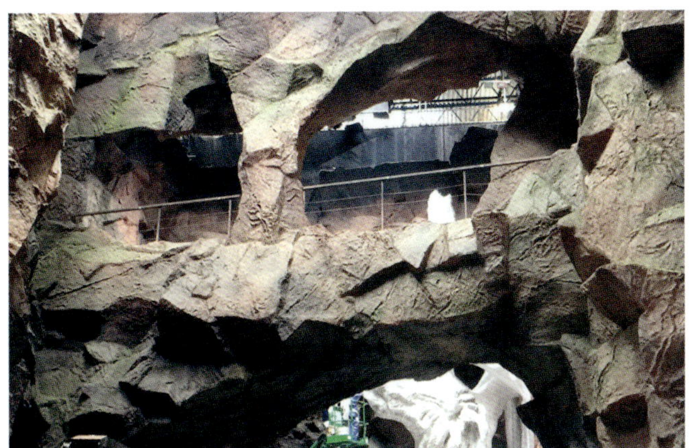

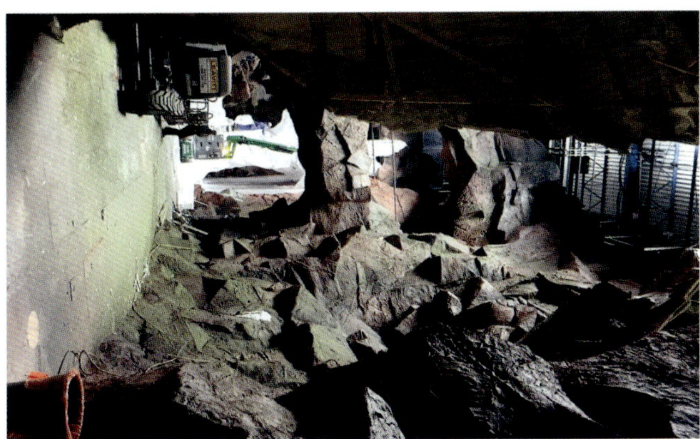

Costume designer Ann Foley wanted the Envoys to be able to blend into their Stronghold surroundings with camouflage garb. "The idea was, like a rebel force from South America, they're mixing different camos from different parts of the world with civilian stuff. So we found existing camo and then we spray-painted over it with a graffiti-like camo pattern, and used the color palette of Harlan's World, which is very forest-y."

Stronghold is also where the Envoys train in fighting techniques. Stunt coordinator Larnell Stovall says that the challenge here was, "When you say you're in the future, you want to make sure you're delivering something that seems futuristic, because the audience nowadays, they're very smart when it comes to action. You've got to think about, what's two-hundred-and-fifty years from now? How does someone attack, how does someone move in a fight scene. You always want to keep that at the forefront that we're not in the now, that we're in the future. So whether it's the way someone kicks, we might change the angle, if it could've been to the neck, we might make it to the inside of the knee. If it could've been to the face, we might make it under the armpit, trying to make it seem like people are a little smarter in how they attack."

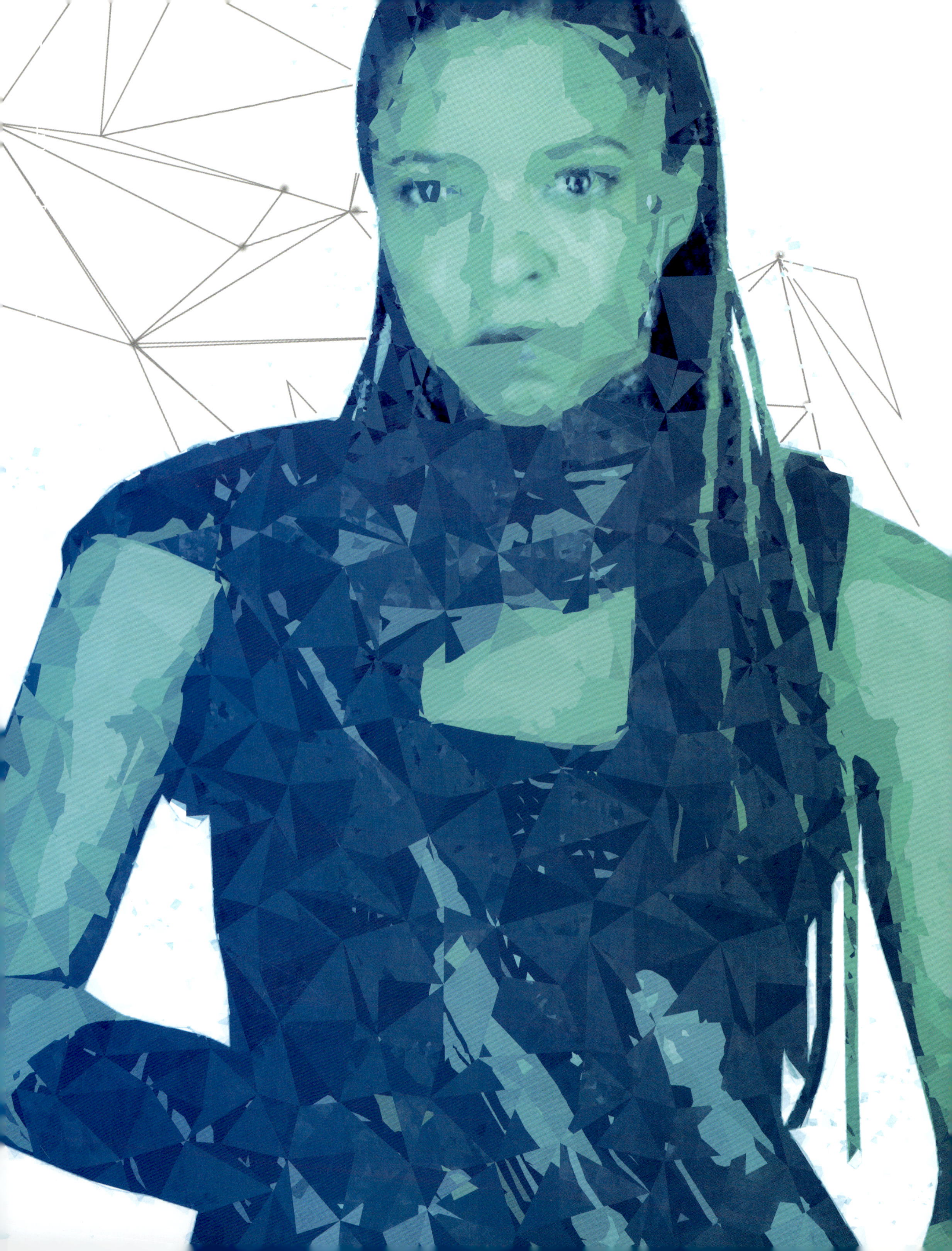

QUELLCRIST FALCONER

LEADER OF THE REBELLION

Quellcrist Falconer, played by Renée Elise Goldsberry, is both the scientist who invented the identity-preserving, society-changing stack technology, and the revolutionary who fights to rid the settled worlds of stacks.

Nadia Mikita wanted to be a galactic explorer. She devises stacks as a way for humans to be able to journey across solar systems without spending a lifetime in doing so. When Meths perverted the stack technology for their own ends, she took responsibility and tried to fix things. She changed her name to Quellcrist, after a type of Harlan's World seaweed, so that no one would know who she really was.

Falconer leads the Envoys, who share her belief that the Meths and their immortality must be brought down. Falconer trains her followers in both fighting techniques and philosophy, telling them not to trust anything, including what they think they remember. She has this to say about why it's important that Envoys know how to physically control a situation: "Rage at injustice is universal; the ability to strike back is not. And at its heart, violence is almost always, in one way or another, personal."

Creator Laeta Kalogridis says that the Falconer of the Netflix series differs in some ways from the character in Richard K. Morgan's novel. "In the book, she's a revolutionary and anarchist. We consolidated her with the inventor of stacks. If we do end up with a third season, the sky's the limit in terms of how much you could explore that back story. She is a young woman whose father was a Protectorate general, whose mother was a scientist."

THIS PAGE: Born Nadia Mikita, Quell is both the pioneer of stack technology, and the would-be architect of its demise.

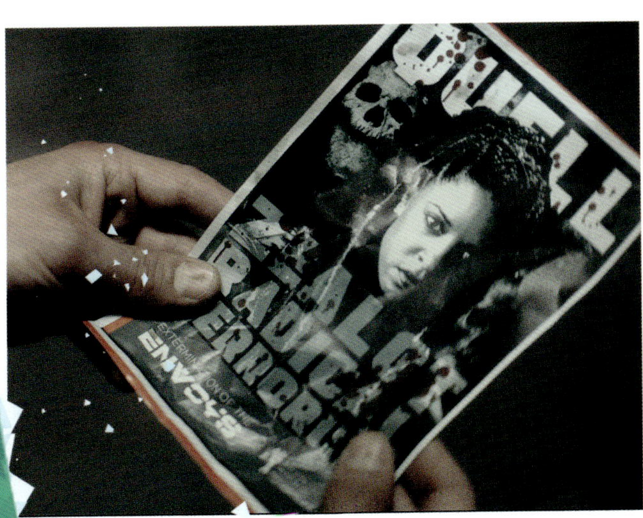

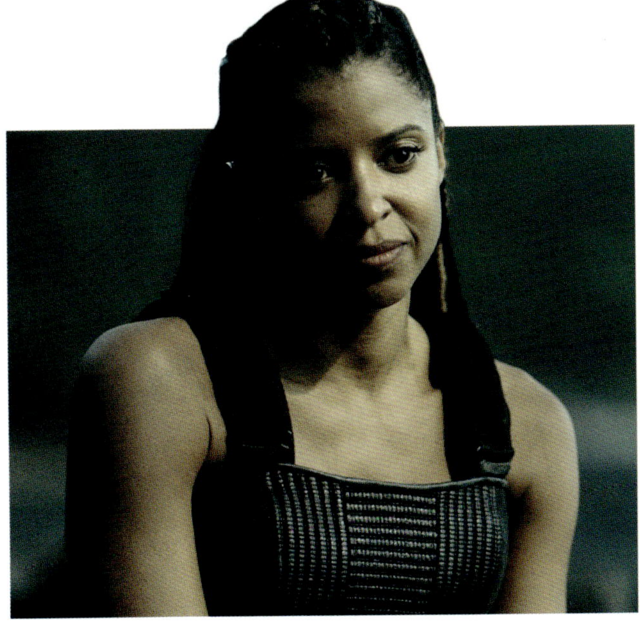

In the *Altered Carbon* universe, there is no such thing as faster-than-light travel, Kalogridis continues. "You leave Earth, it'll take you fifty years to get somewhere. By the time you get there, everybody you ever knew on Earth is dead, and you're isolated from the rest of humanity. And you explore this planet, and then, if you want to go to another one, it's another fifty or a hundred years in cryo-sleep."

When Falconer invents stacks, people can needlecast their consciousness into bodies, aka sleeves, waiting for them on other planets. "So you could go all over the settled worlds," Kalogridis explains. Falconer succeeded with her creation, "but like most scientific breakthroughs, it was almost immediately co-opted by the military." This paved the way for Meths and the swift spread of the Protectorate.

Executive producer James Middleton explains why the makers of *Altered Carbon* felt that Falconer should be the creator of the stacks, as well as their aspiring destroyer. "It gives Quell personal responsibility for how the technology has affected humankind. As brilliant as she is, the unintended consequences of her invention are for her to rectify, which gives her story better dramatic stakes."

Costume designer Ann Foley says that she and Kalogridis worked closely on Falconer's look. "She's a warrior, and a survivor, and she's leading these Envoys. So I wanted her to have sort of armor, but I also wanted there to be a softness to her, because she is Kovacs' true love, she's the heart, and she is sort of his conscience as well. So we created this vest in-house. We printed the fabric. So Falconer's costume was a combination of this printed fabric and leather and cargo pants and a really cool combat boot. All the Envoys have this scarf that has a rebel print on it, whether they wear it around their neck, a band on their arm. In the pilot, Kovacs has it around his wrist. Quell has a piece of the Envoy scarf wrapped around her wrist as her talisman."

Falconer also invented Acheron, which would give everyone one hundred years of life and no more. Her plan was to lead the Envoys to download Acheron into the Central Core, distributing it into all stacks. Because the Envoys were obliterated, the plan was never completed.

Reileen made it look as though she and Quellcrist died in a shuttle explosion during the massacre of the Envoys. At the end of season one, an about-to-die Reileen tells a shocked Kovacs that she backed Quellcrist up right before the explosion.

BELOW: Quell's influence over Kovacs meant he continued to see her, even after her death.

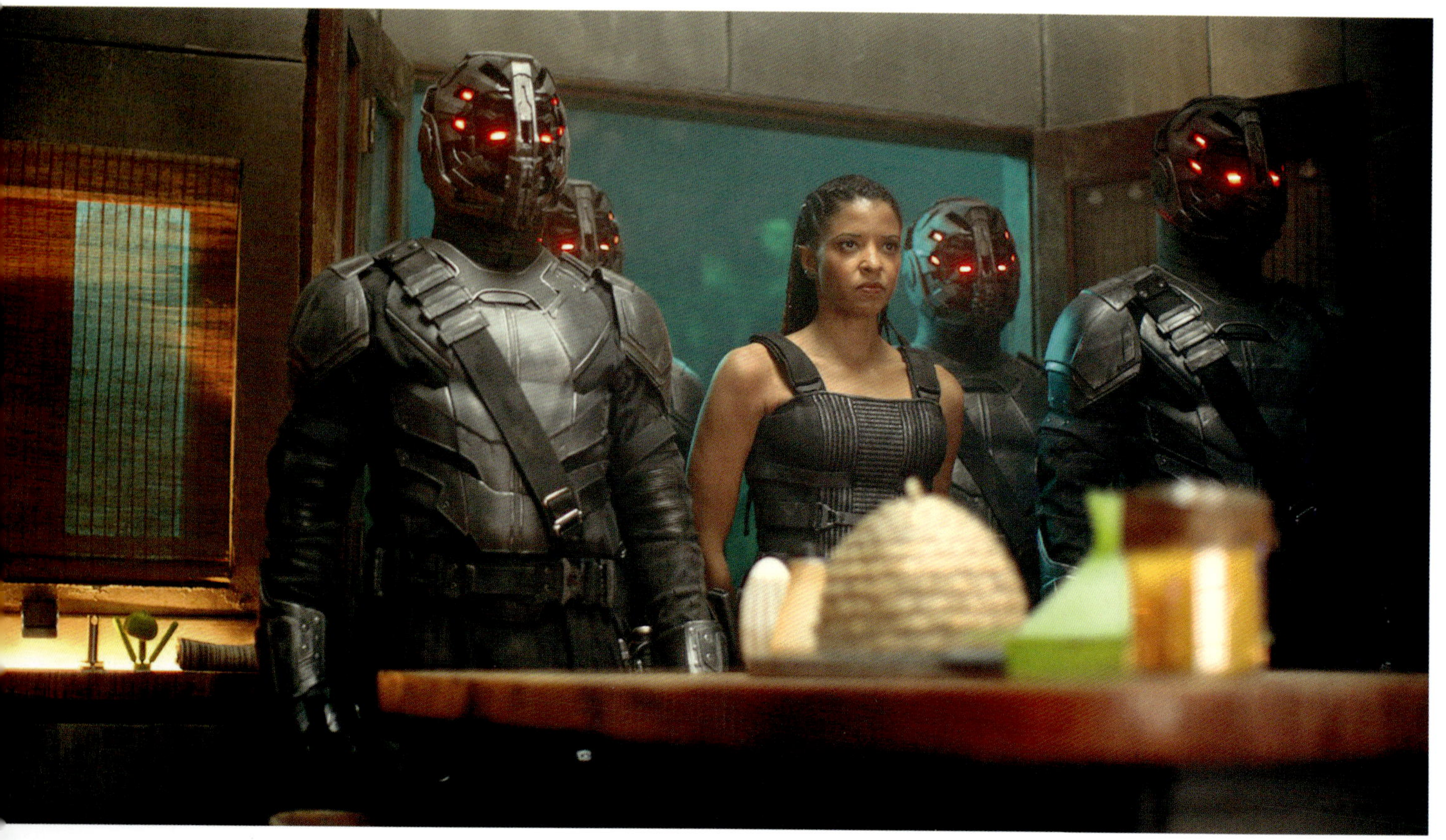

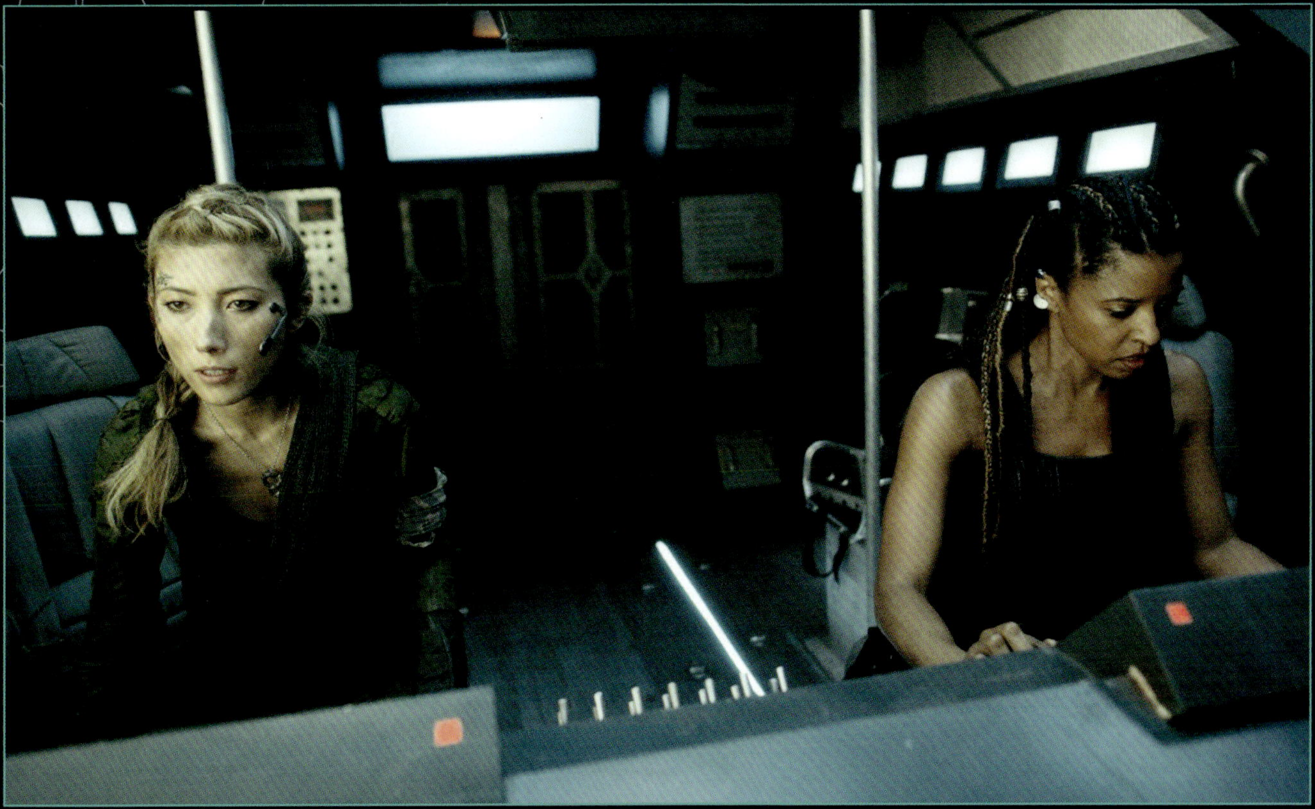

THIS PAGE: Reileen and Quell both survived the Protectorate's slaughter of the Envoys.

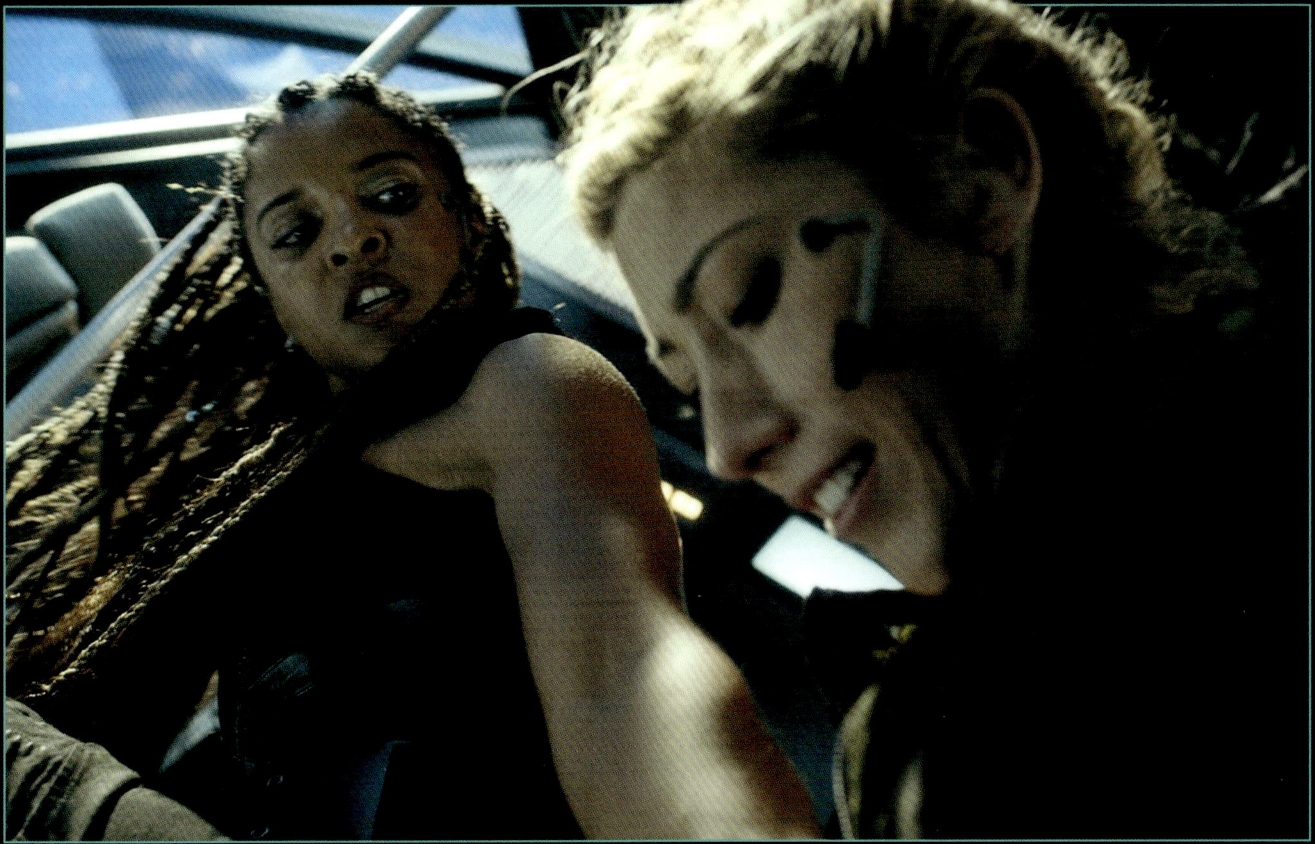

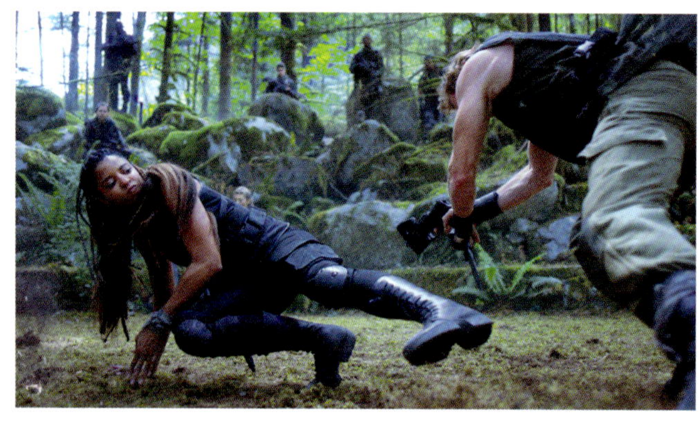

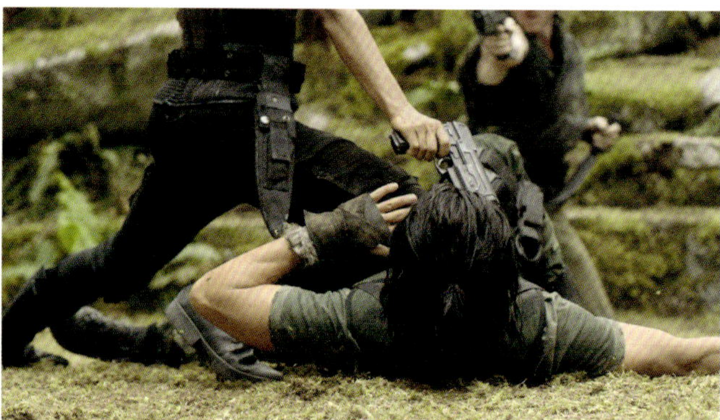

THIS PAGE: Envoy leader Quellcrist tests Kovacs' combat ability.

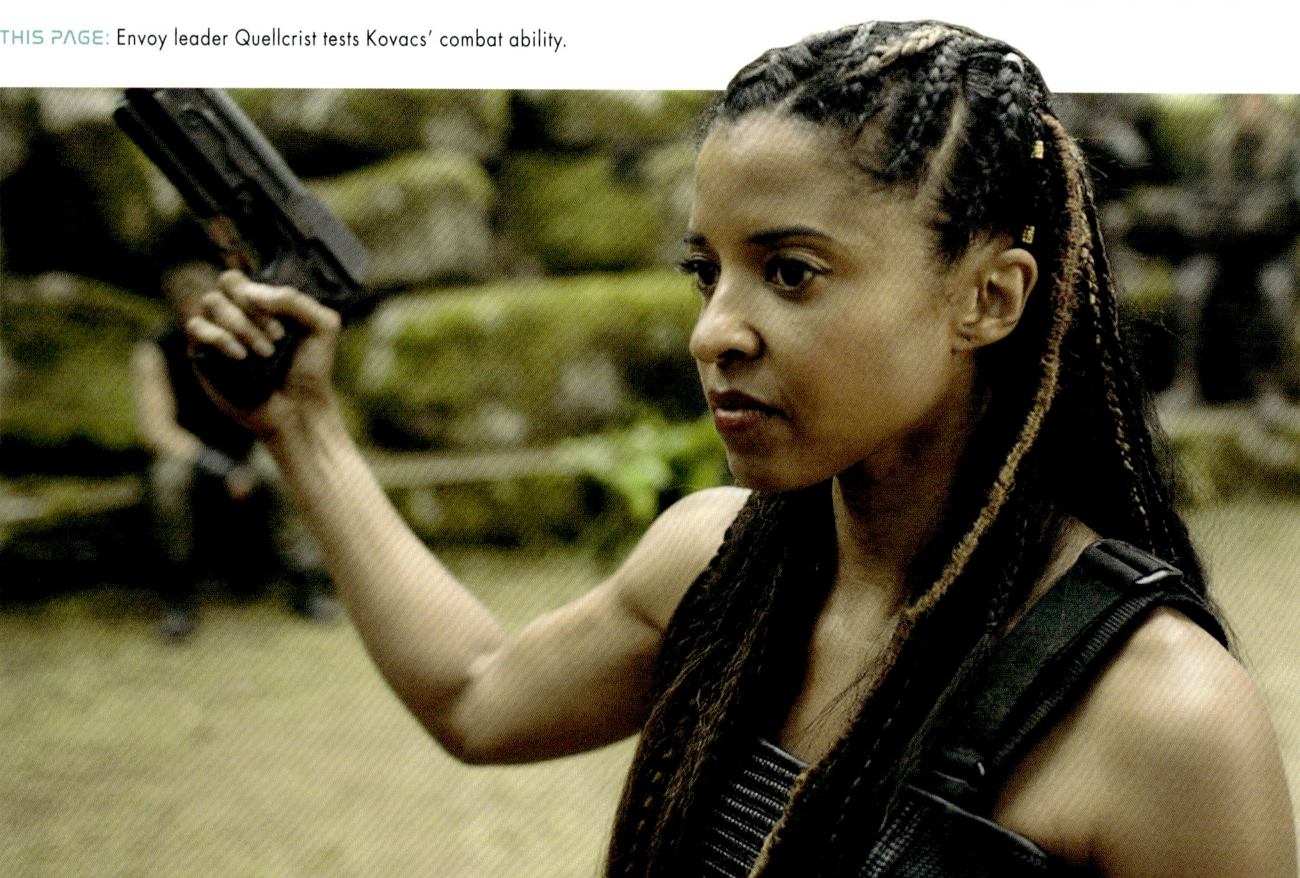

BELOW: Kovacs discovers Quell is still alive at the end of season one and spends decades searching for her.

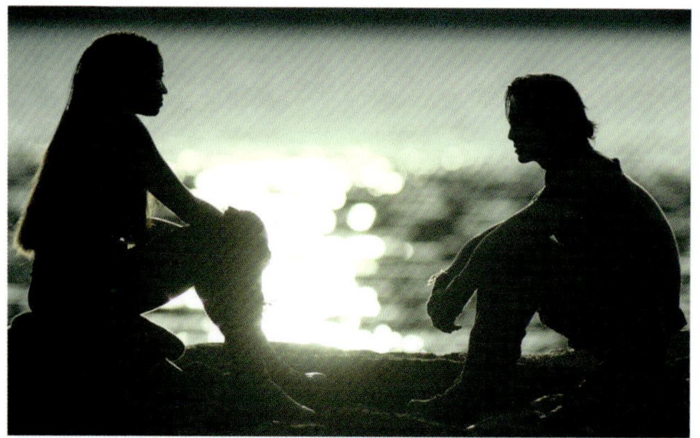

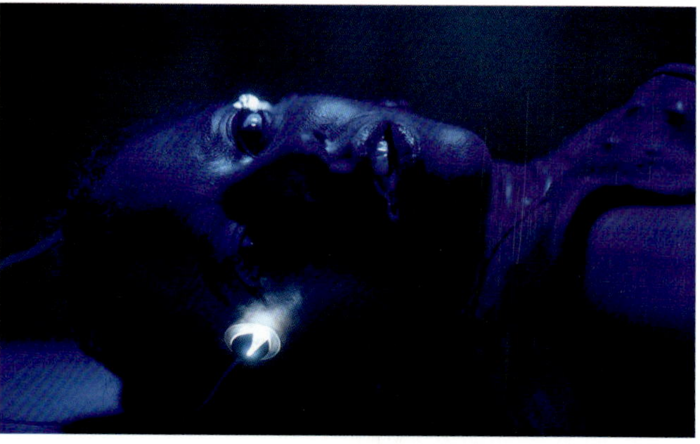

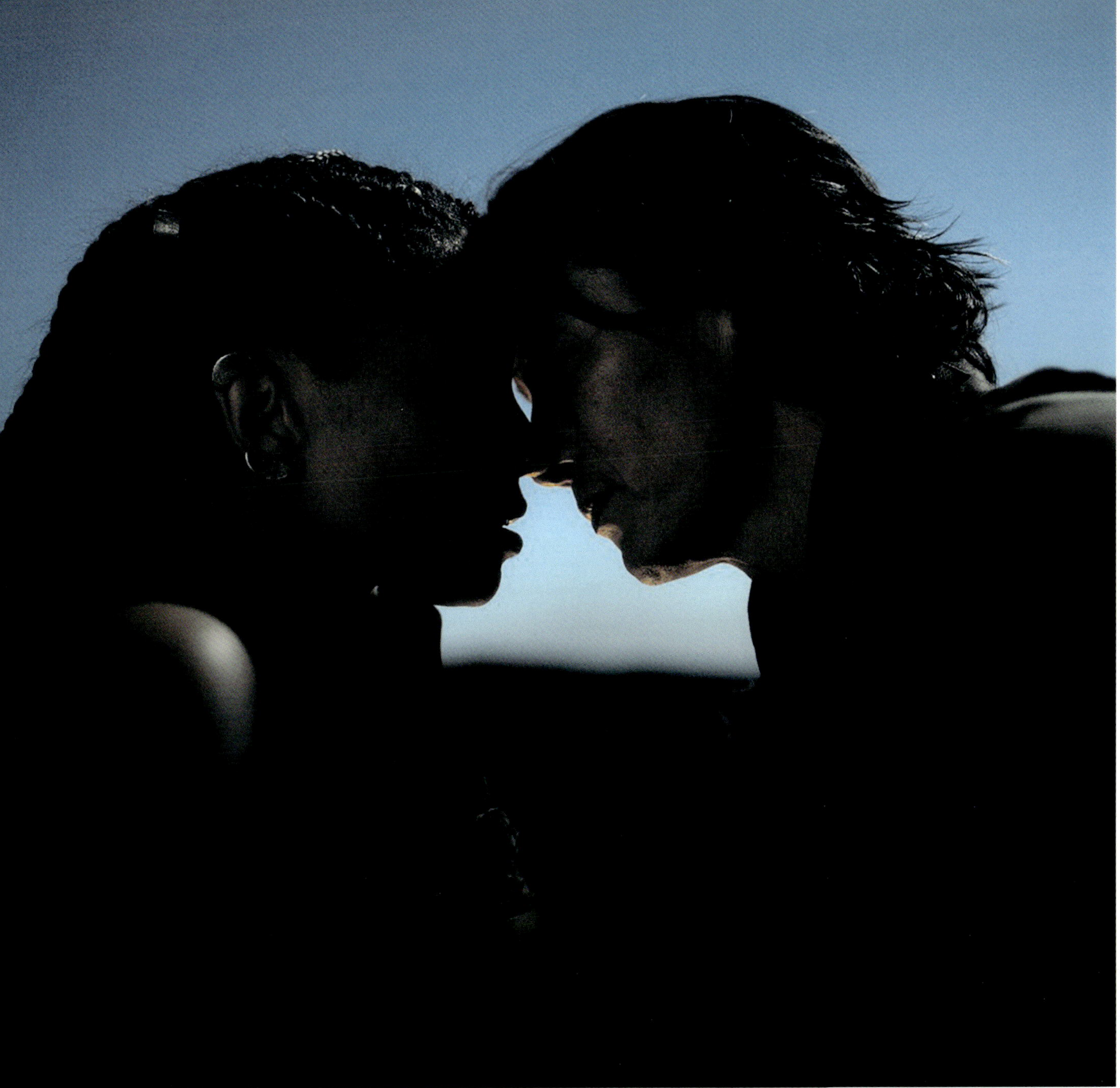

THIS PAGE: Despite his Praetorian past, Kovacs was Quellcrist's true love.

In season two, Quell has mental trauma from her centuries of VR imprisonment. She actually has two personas in her body, one of them bent on vengeance and the other trying to remember who she is and what her purpose is, as well as who Kovacs is. "Season two takes place around thirty years after the events of season one," Middleton relates. "Kovacs has spent those decades looking for Quell to no avail, and wonders if Reileen lied to him about her DHF being saved after the fall of Stronghold. Then, in a twist of fate, Kovacs learns that Quell is alive on his home planet, Harlan's World. But when he finally encounters Quell, it is not clear whose mind is actually in her sleeve. Season two is a mystery story in which Kovacs must discover if the woman he loves still exists and, more importantly, can their love survive centuries and a multitude of sleeves?"

On Kovacs' side, at least, it can. Director/executive producer Nick Hurran observes that it's the power of Falconer's ideas that inspires Kovacs to continue the fight. "One of the reasons he decides to stay [alive], having been brought back into the world, is the inspiration that her thoughts and the love he has for her gives him."

THE ENVOYS

IMMERSION AND TOTAL ABSORPTION

The Envoys, led by Quellcrist Falconer, are a group that existed on Harlan's World three hundred years before season one of *Altered Carbon* begins. The Envoys are dedicated to destroying stack technology, the immortality of the Meths, and the terrible wealth disparity and corruption these have caused.

Falconer teaches the Envoys how to withstand torture, both real and in VR, where they might be mutilated, and murdered over and over. "Control the construct," Falconer advises, meaning that Envoys should be able to mentally manipulate the virtual scenario. "Take what is offered and use it."

When Takeshi Kovacs joins the Envoys, and embraces their philosophy, he brings his sister Reileen with him. Reileen secretly thinks the Envoys are doomed and is jealous of her brother's feelings for Falconer. She infects the Envoys with madness-causing Rawling's virus. This causes them to kill each other and themselves, although their destruction is credited to Konrad Harlan.

The Envoys are widely remembered as terrorists, though in season two, we meet the Quellists, Harlan's World rebels who believe in Falconer's philosophy.

Series creator Laeta Kalogridis relates that one of an Envoy's signature qualities is the ability to swiftly adjust to new situations and even new sleeves. If a normal person were to change bodies too many times, they'd start to go insane. "As an Envoy, Kovacs can download into an almost infinite number of bodies without it affecting his mind."

There is also Envoy intuition, which VFX supervisor Everett Burrell says was hard to convey visually, "because it's an almost chemical activity that happens within an Envoy's head. It's almost like he can see into a parallel universe of organic nerve endings, as if he's in a world that's identical to ours, but skewed in a way that he can identify things. If a bad guy is coming, he can hear that, and that sound triggers his thought process. It builds what that person looks like in his head without his ever seeing [the other person]. He uses his internal way of hearing and feeling and sensing things [to detect what is] on the other side of a wall."

BELOW: Envoys trained their minds to a level of extrasensory perception and resilience.

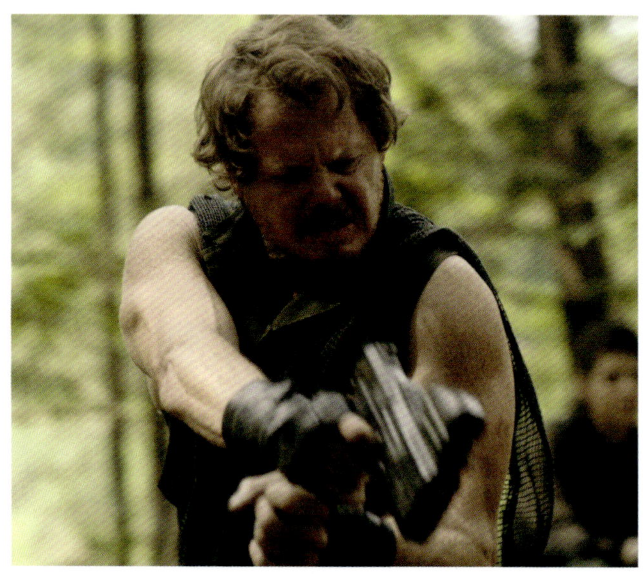

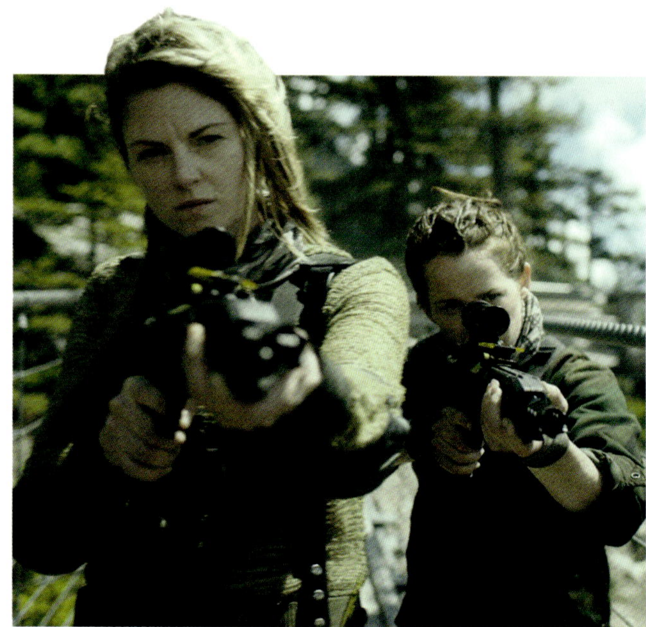

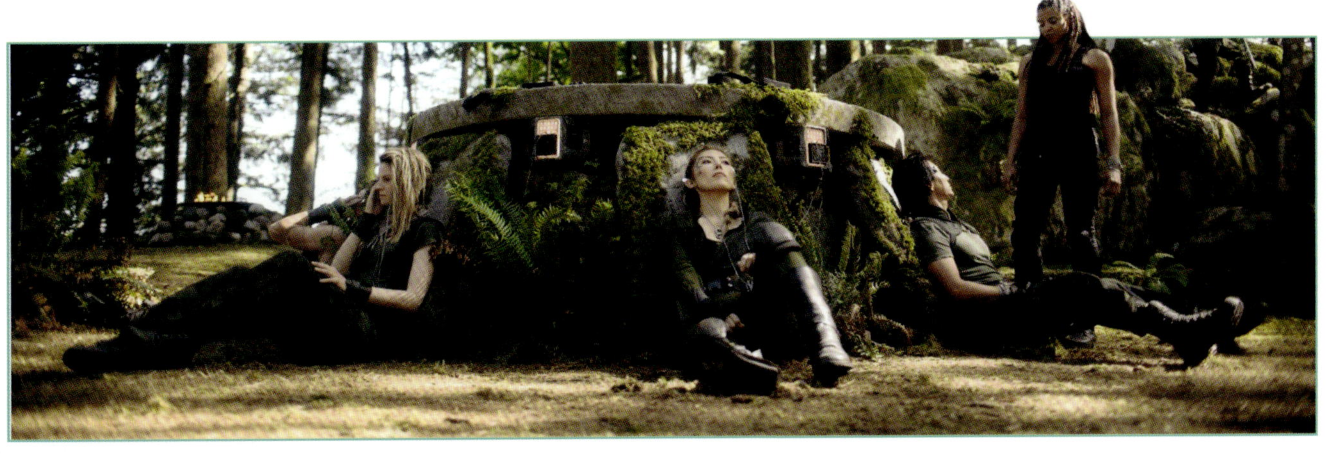

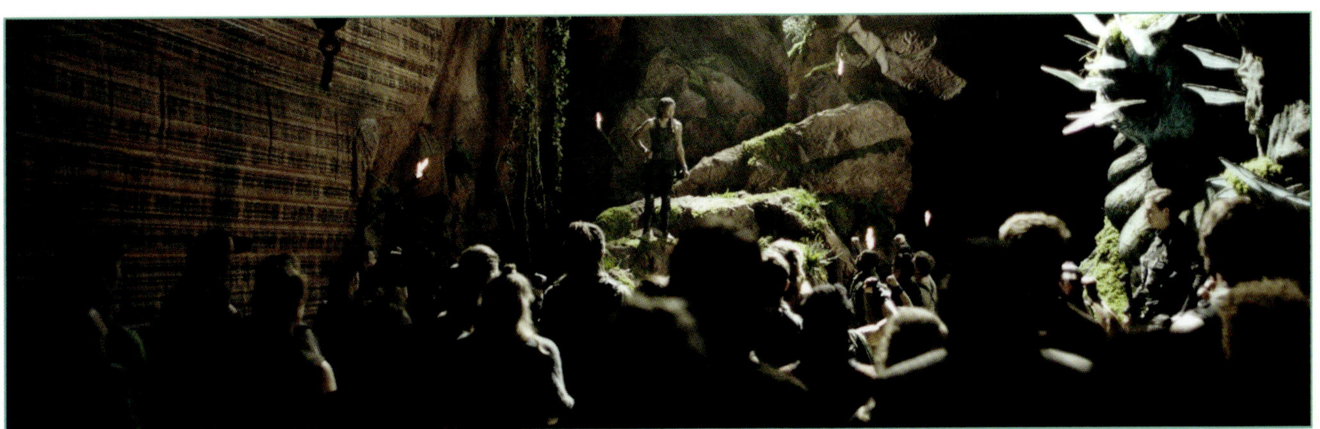

THIS PAGE: Quell trains her Envoy forces to withstand unspeakable tortures.

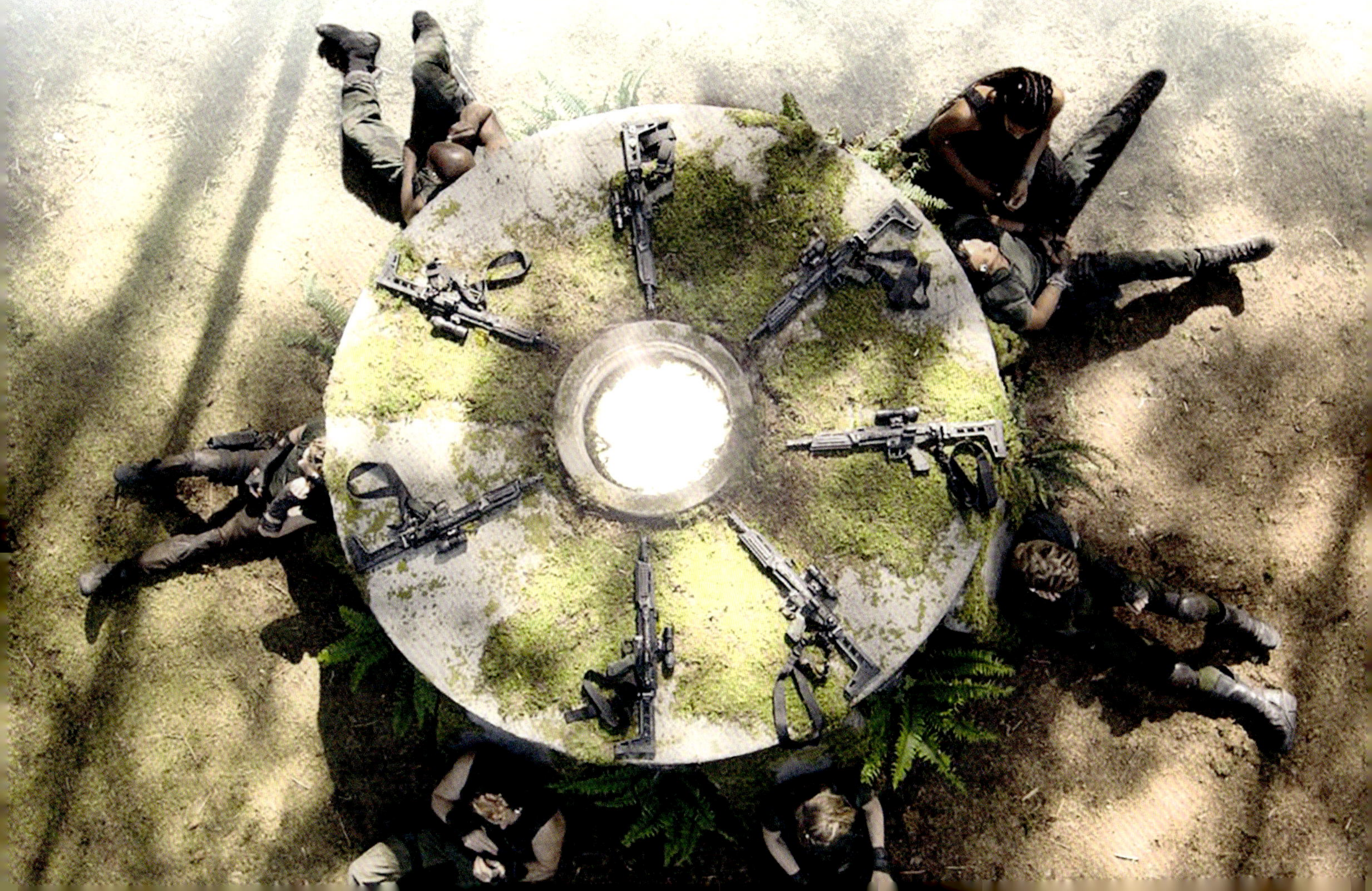

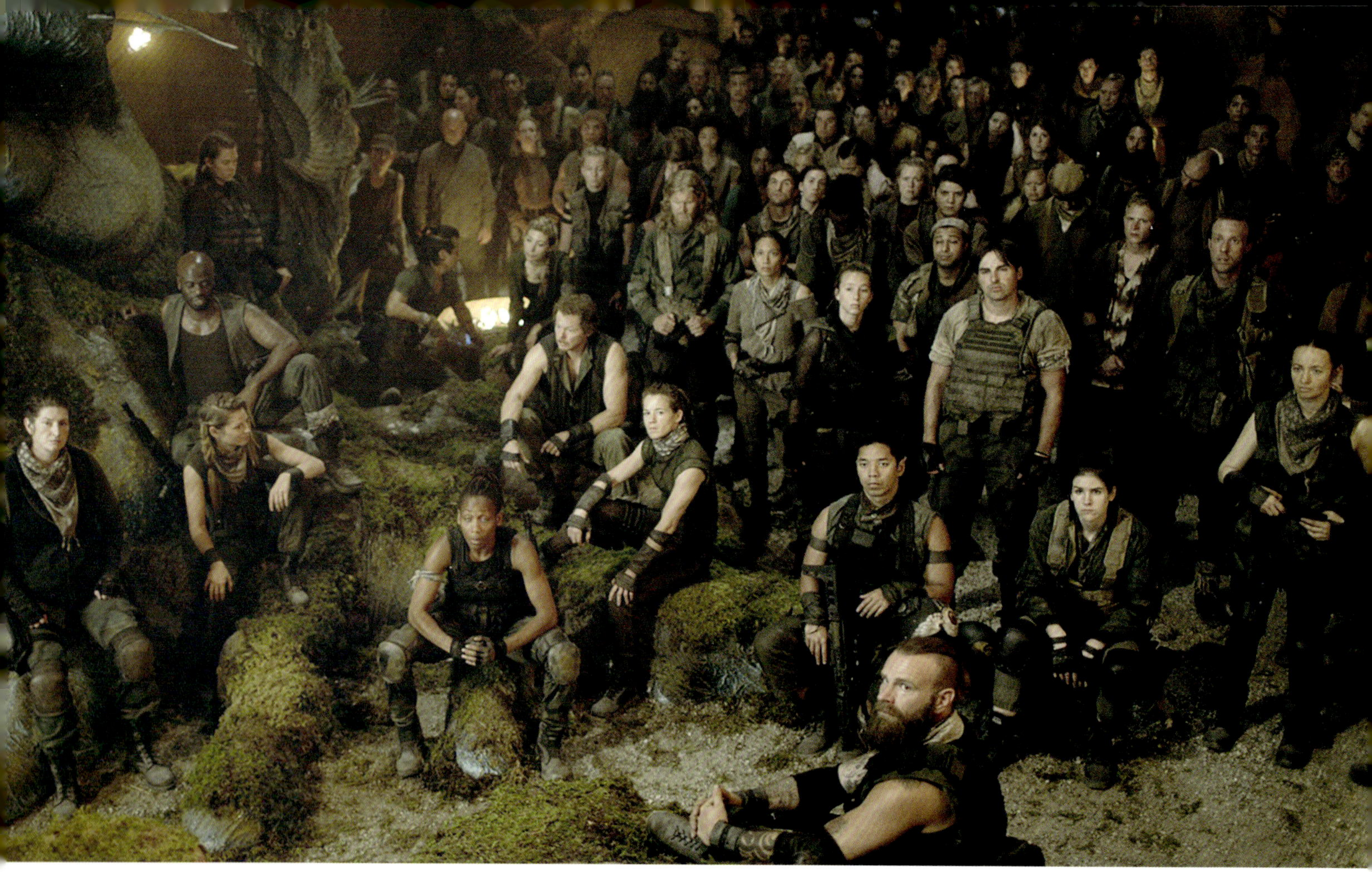

ABOVE: The amassed forces of the Envoy heeding Quell's words.

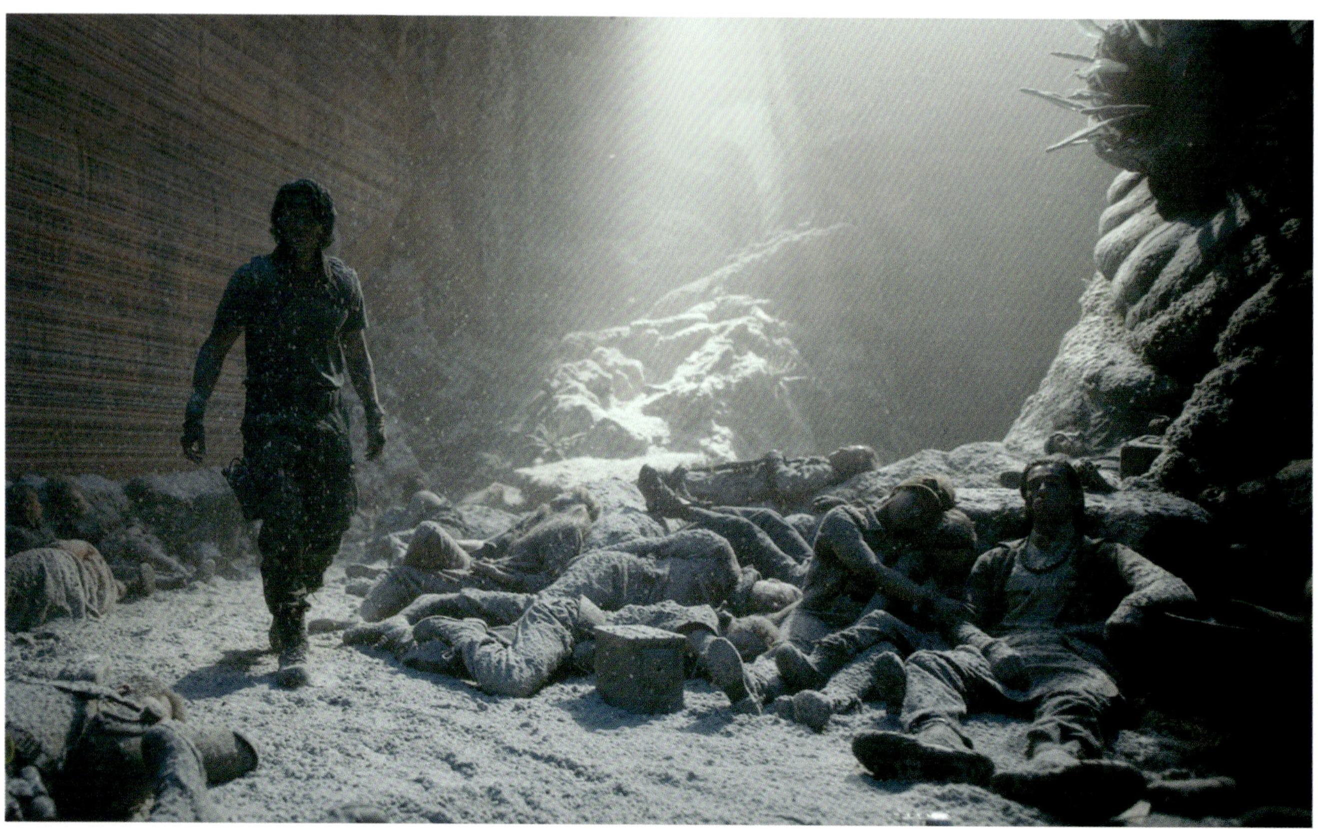

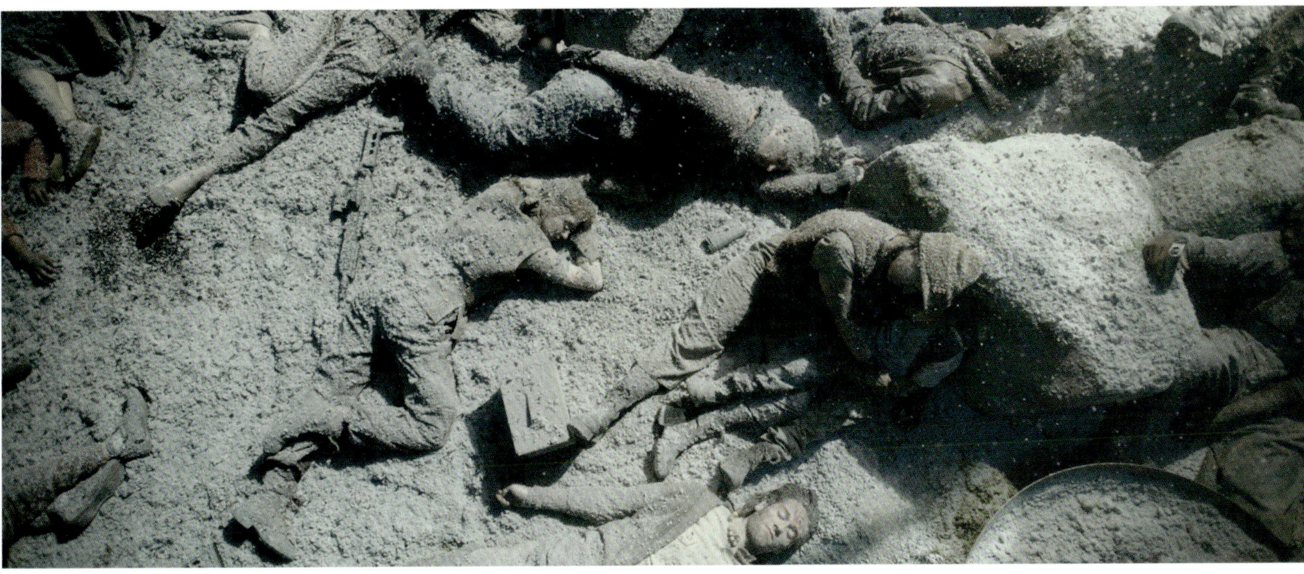

ABOVE: Reileen's jealousy of Kovacs and Quell's romance made her infect Envoys with Rawling's virus.

To convey this, Burrell continues, "We experimented with a lot of different looks, but the one thing that really became very apparent was that that look had to be very organic, almost like a sonogram in a weird way. He's using his brain and all his senses to paint the picture. [Envoy vision] is almost a heartbeat, it has a pulsating feel to it, almost like veins and sinew."

As part of their reference, Burrell and his team used "a great book of babies. [The authors] took photographs of a baby gestating inside a womb. They put a camera in there, and you could see the embryonic fluid, particulates inside the womb, and the way it's lit. That's a very organic feeling."

Burrell shot some test footage, "with an iPhone in my office of one of our production assistants. I had him sit at my desk and stand up and pretend to fire a toy gun. I shot that as one element, and then I closed the door, and shot that as another element, so I could put a person behind the door in Envoy vision."

After compositing the images of the door and the organic map of what would be behind the door, Burrell explains, "I did some experiments in PhotoShop and AfterEffects. I gave those tests to Double Negative in London, and then they did an even more elaborate version of that, and we built upon that."

BELOW: The virus turned Envoys against each other.

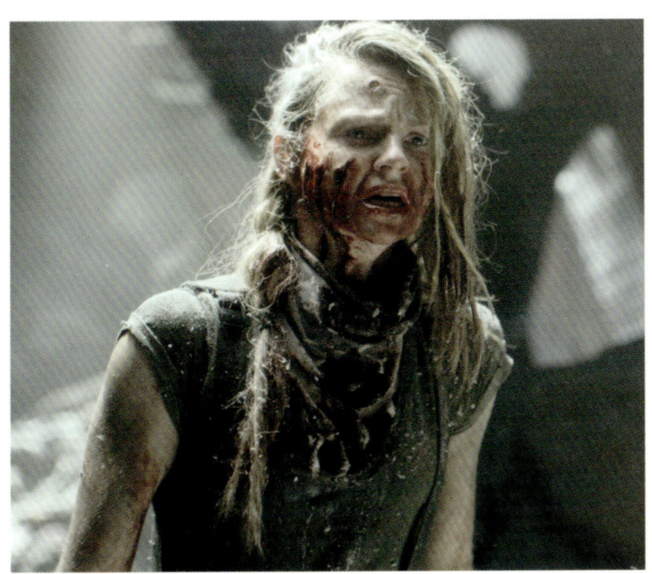

BELOW: Envoys suffering from Rawling's virus.

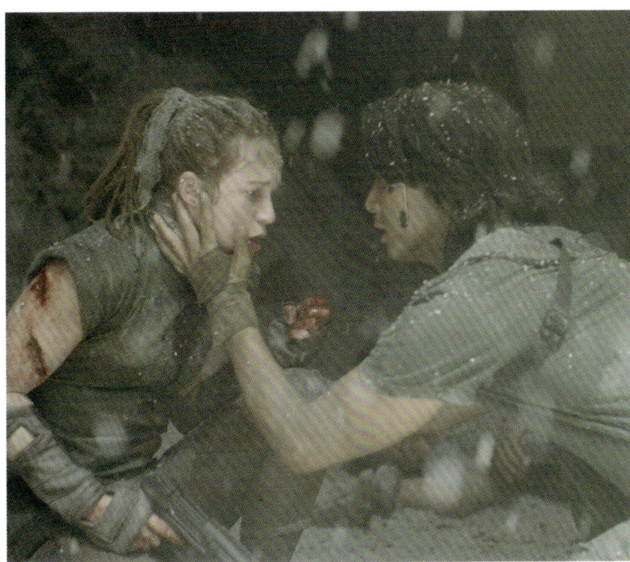

STACKS

FOUNTAIN OF YOUTH

Stack and sleeve technology is what has made the world of *Altered Carbon*. It was originally invented by Nadia Mikita on Harlan's World. When she saw what it was doing to society, Mikita changed her name to Quellcrist Falconer and began her crusade to destroy stacks.

The alloy used to make stacks is made from Elder artifacts found on Harlan's World. Searching for these artifacts and mining for the alloy make up much of Harlan's World's industry, one reason the planet is so important to the Protectorate.

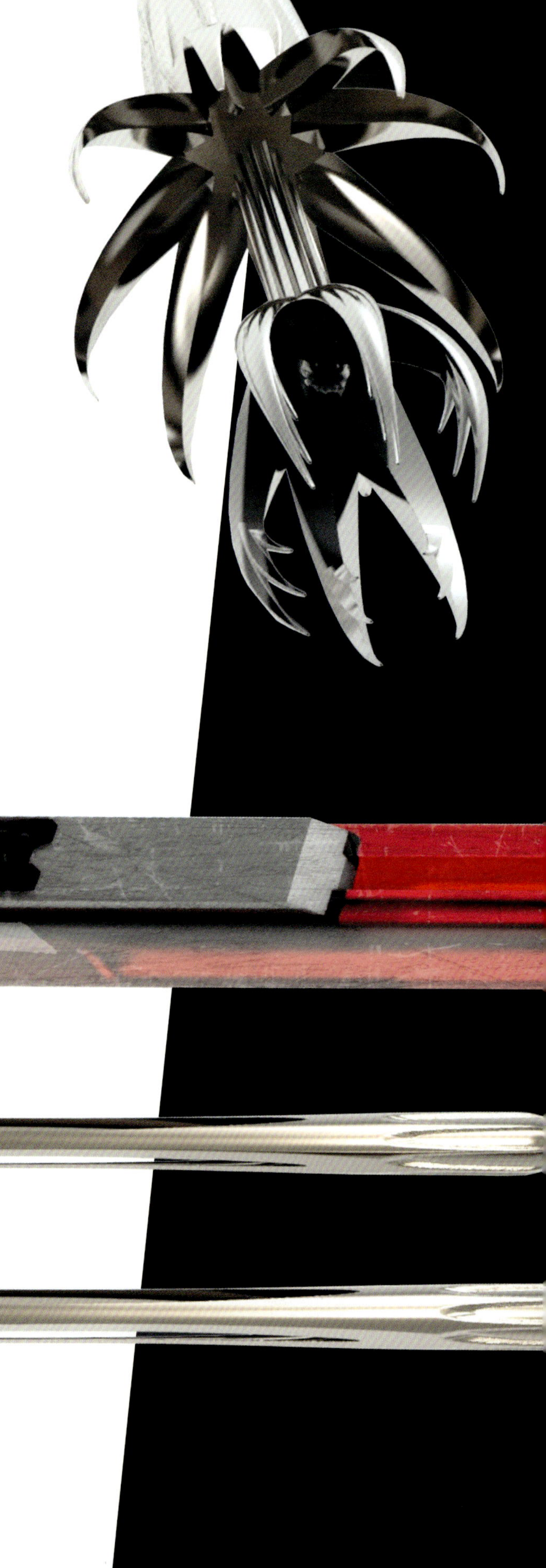

ABOVE: Mr. Leung's weapon used to forcefully remove stacks.

"A stack is a little tiny thing that fits in the back of your neck."

LAETA KALOGRIDIS, SERIES CREATOR

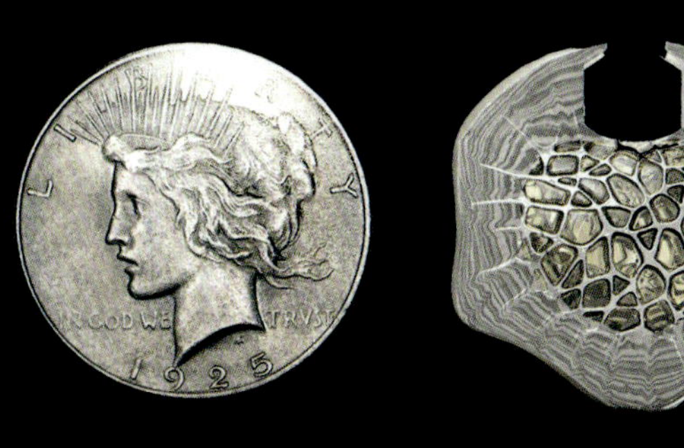

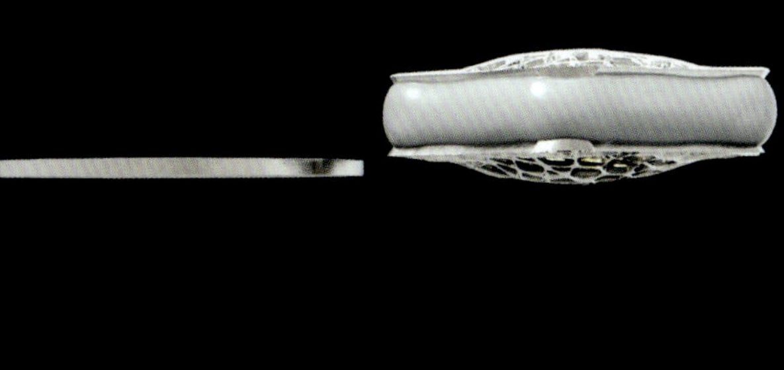

ABOVE: A stack that contains a DHF (Digital Human Freight) and its size in relation to a coin.

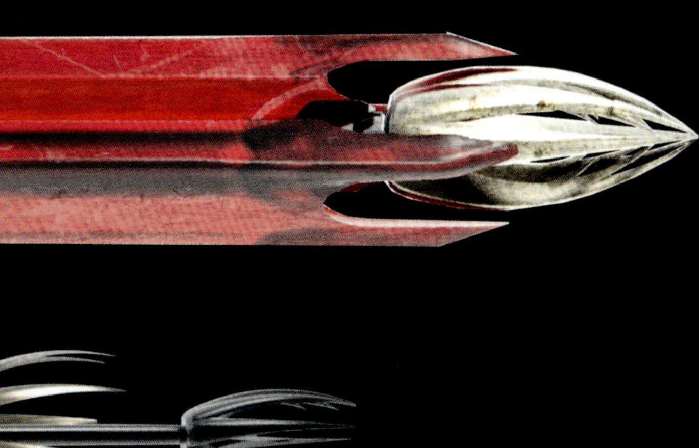

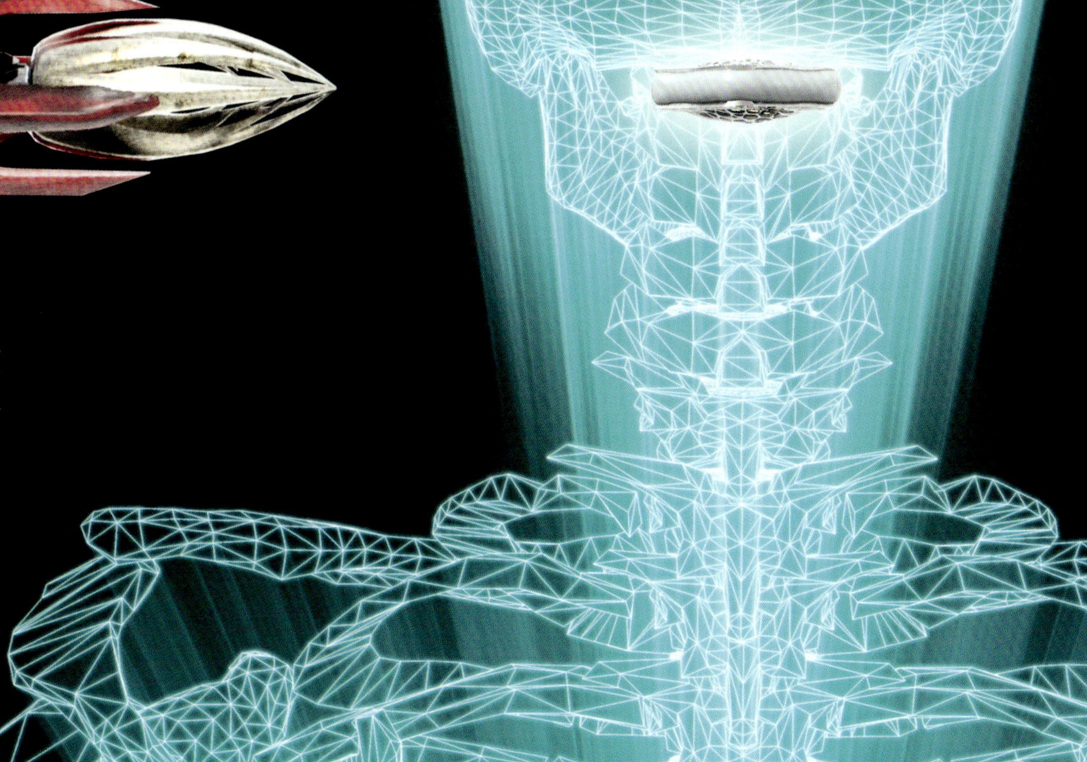

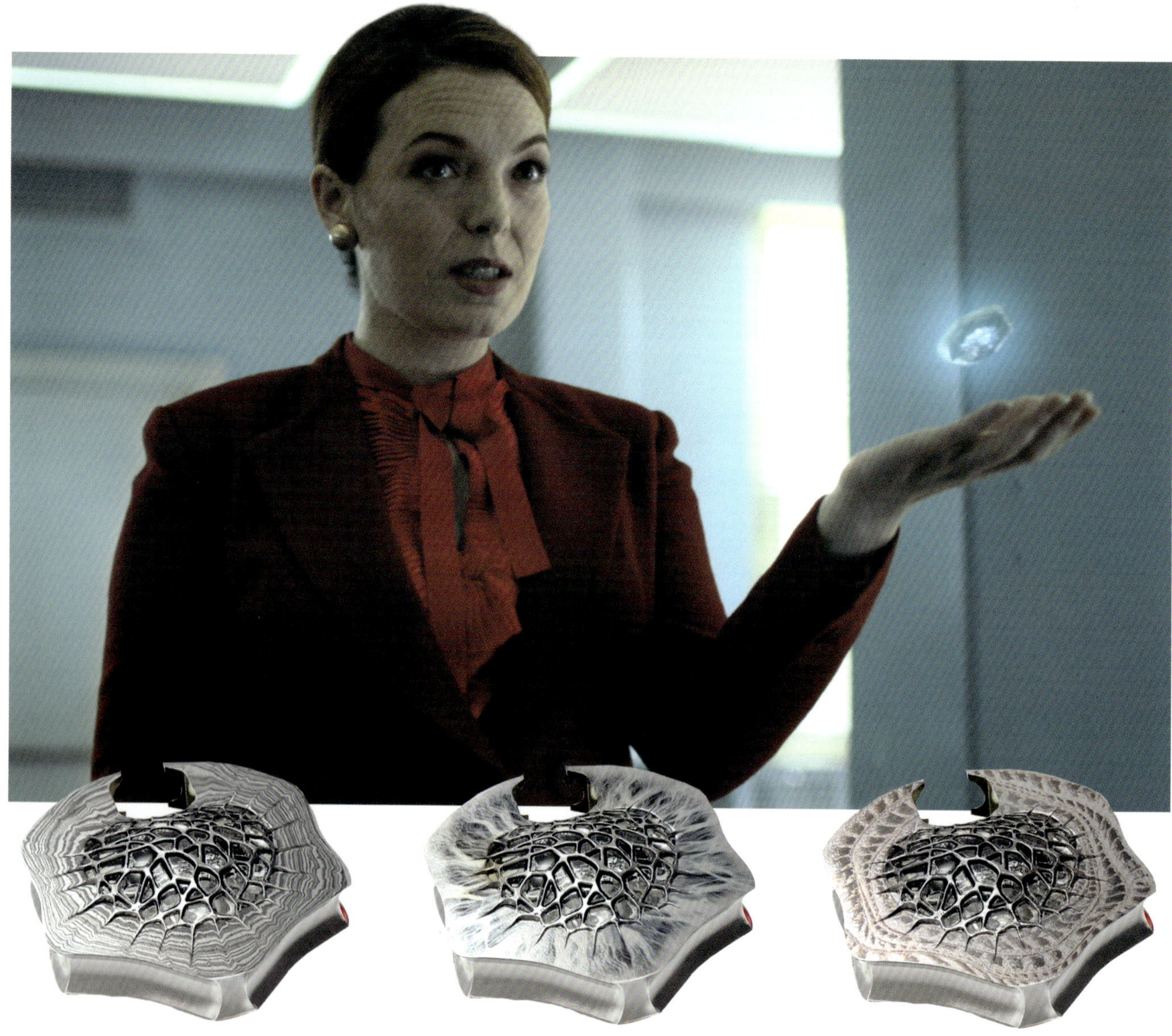

ABOVE: Stacks grow with the spinal column and develop fine rings around them, like trees.

Stacks contain a person's DHF, or digital human freight, i.e. everything that constitutes their identity. Creator Laeta Kalogridis explains, "A stack is a little tiny thing that fits in the back of your neck. Everybody gets one at a year old. Your consciousness is downloaded into it. So the moment that you have a stack, that's what's holding who you are. Your whole personality, your mind, your memories. Everything that makes you you is in the stack. If you're wealthy enough to be able to afford clones, like the Bancrofts are, you can keep downloading yourself into new clones [as the old ones age beyond what the owner wants].

"If you think of the stack as a piece of hardware, the personality and the mind is the software. The mind is contained essentially as electrical impulses inside that stack. If you destroy the hardware and the software at the same time, if the whole thing is destroyed [and there's no software copy], that's real death. You're never coming back from it. [But] if you are backed up as Bancroft was, and there's a satellite copy of him, just the same as a software backup, that can be downloaded into a new blank stack. Then it's not real death, because you can come back, but since your body is destroyed, it's considered organic damage.

"Which is one of the things I love about the book, the way it just so beautifully and casually redefines our relationship to our physicality, because you can exist in any body. Although if you try to hop bodies too many times, there's an expense factor, and also a sanity factor. I've always loved the idea that we evolved over millions and millions of years in tandem with our physical body. Meths can only live forever by downloading into clones [of themselves], because they need to be in the same body."

In *Altered Carbon*, bodies are often called sleeves. It can be the one you're born in, the body of someone who has lost their sleeve for legal reasons (like Elias Ryker, the sleeve Kovacs wears in season one), a clone, or a synthetic sleeve. Executive producer and director Neil Hurran relates, "A synthetic sleeve is very costly to manufacture, whereas they have many bodies from people who die available. How good the sleeve that you can buy really depends on how much you can afford. If you have the money, you can buy almost any sleeve you want. But if you don't have the money, you get put into any sleeve available, a grandma or a small child. It depends on what you can afford."

Property master Nevin Swain relates how stacks work. "The idea is that they are implanted in you at a young age, so an infant's stack would be small, and then they grow with you, within your spinal column. So they actually change in size. If you look closely at them, they've got these rings, almost like a tree, so that they have these rings showing your age. Once you reach adulthood, they stop growing as you do."

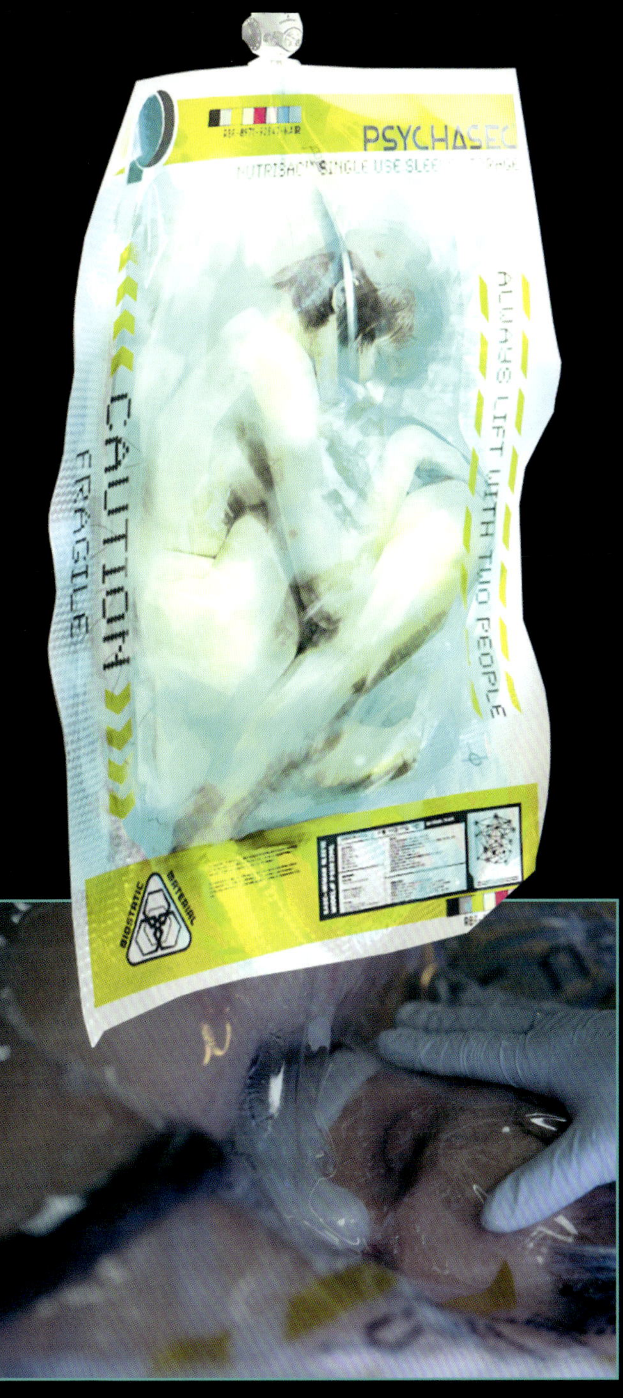

THIS PAGE: Sleeves in storage and the process of spinning up.

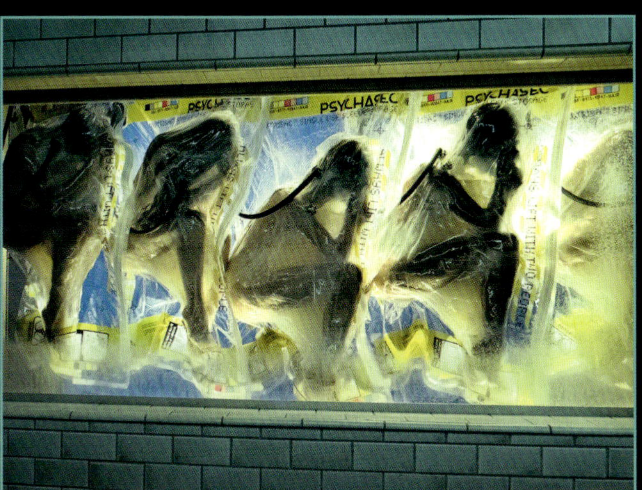

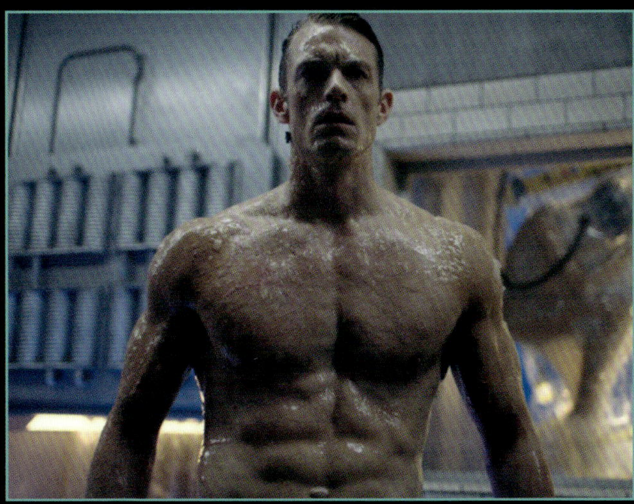

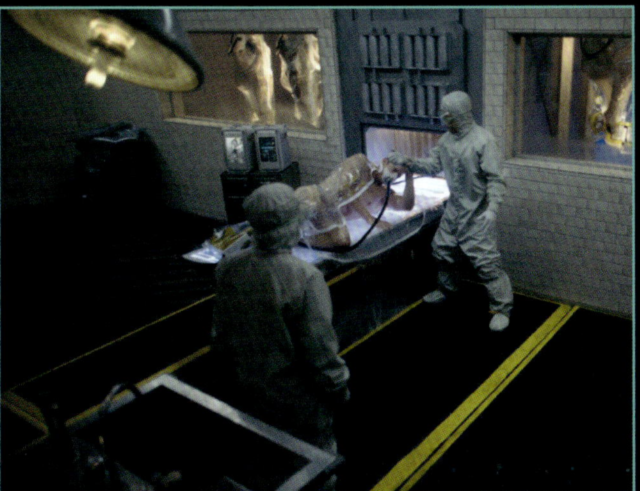

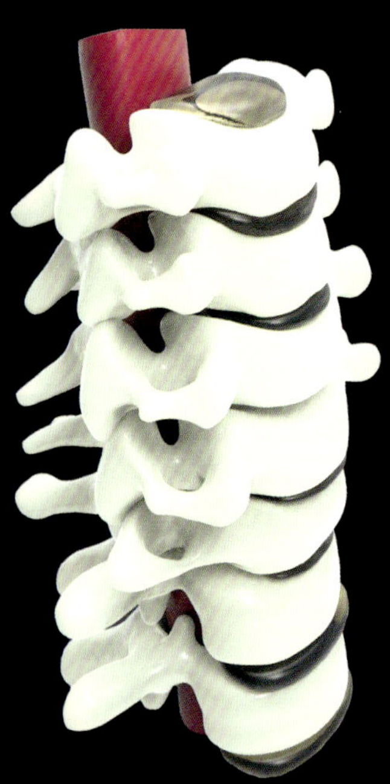

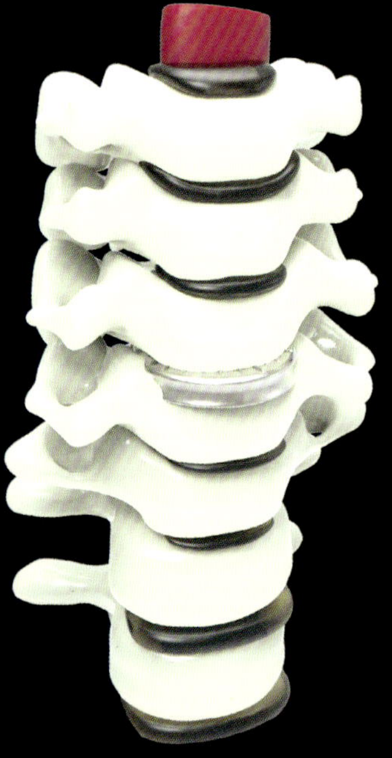

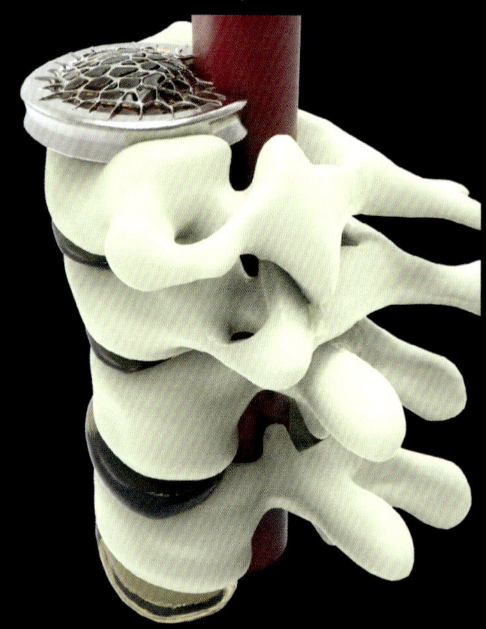

ABOVE: Stacks slot in between the vertebrae of the spinal column.

In reality, Swain relates, "It's got a little plastic 3D-printed center core on the inside, and then the exterior, in two halves, is C-and-C'ed aluminum. The material was selected because they wanted to [make it look like] alien alloy technology. [C and C] is a computerized tooling system. You take a square block of aluminum that holds it for you. Rather than you going in and hand-machining it, it goes down and removes [unwanted] material with various tools, so it's able to change tools, take a solid block and conform it into whatever shape you'd like."

In season one, VFX supervisor Everett Burrell says that the stacks' glow was made by his department. "It was a practical prop, but during post production, we realized it needed to have an inner glow. So we had to add glows to all the stacks, because the practical ones did not glow. We had pretty much a standard very blue glow inside that had life. It was sort of animated inside, and it gave everybody the same glow."

For season two, the glow was built into the prop stacks, Swain relates. Inside the aluminum shell are "a computer board, a resistor, and several small LEDs, two halves that connect together to conform to make the center part glow."

BELOW: Vernon Elliot with his daughter Lizzie's stack.

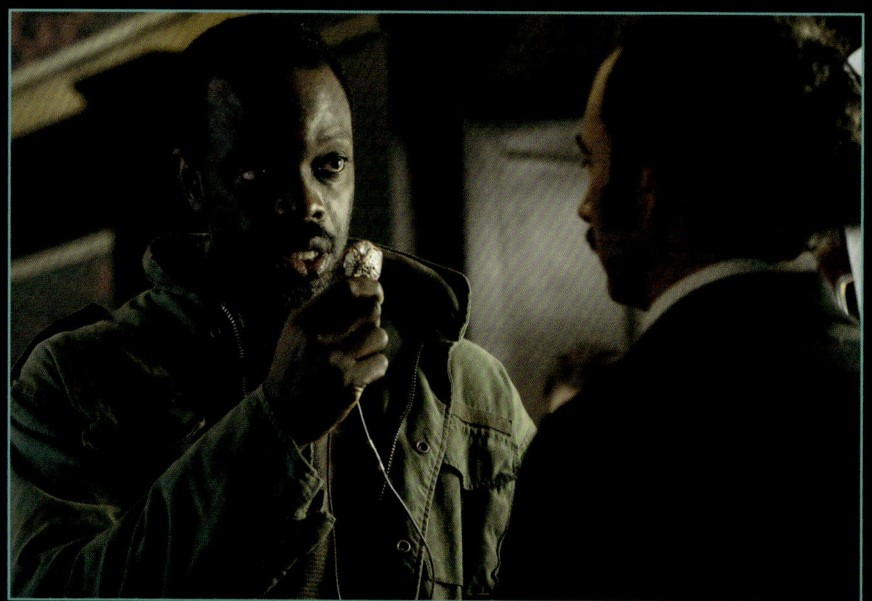

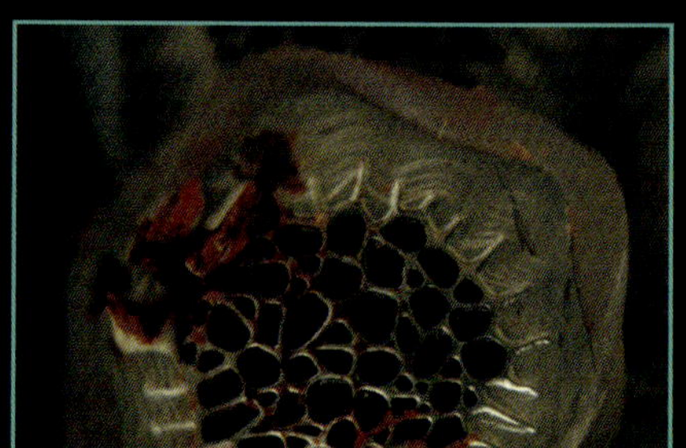

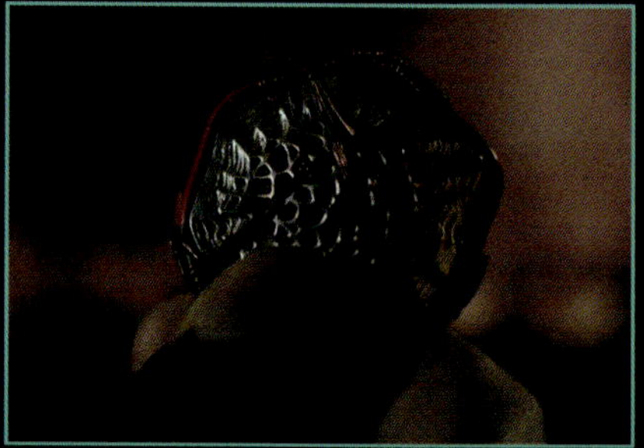

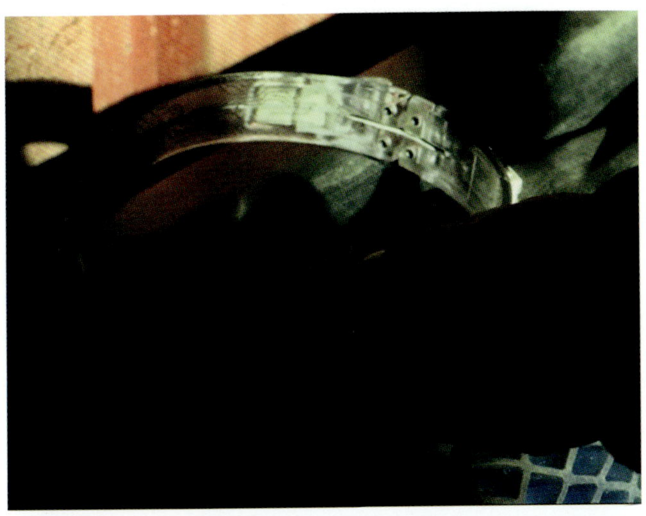

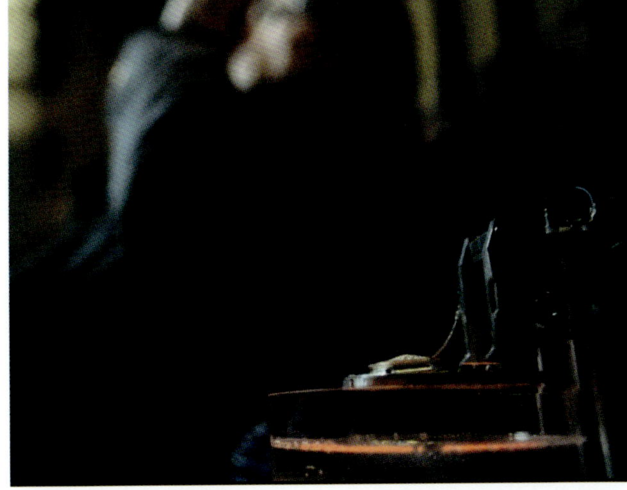

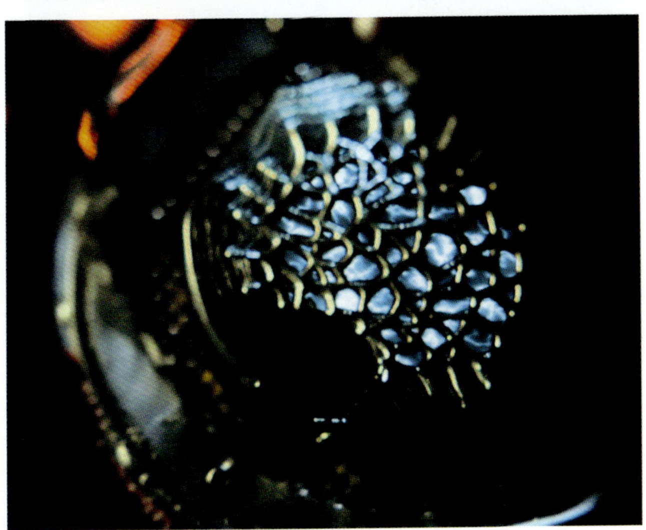

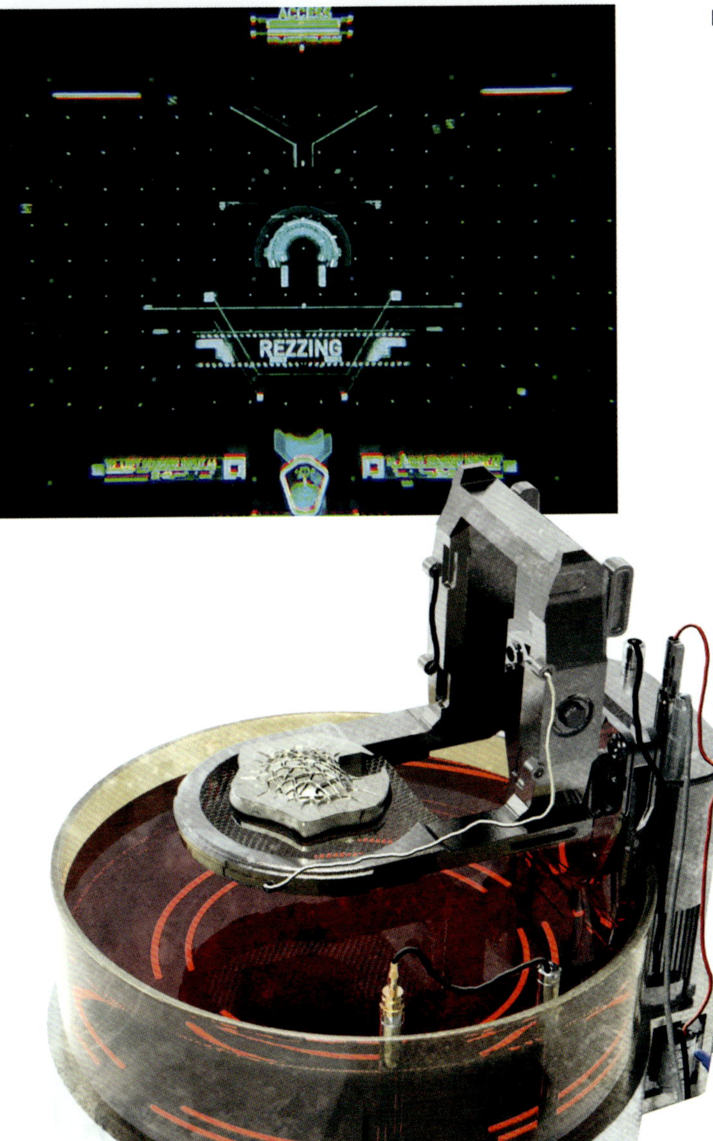

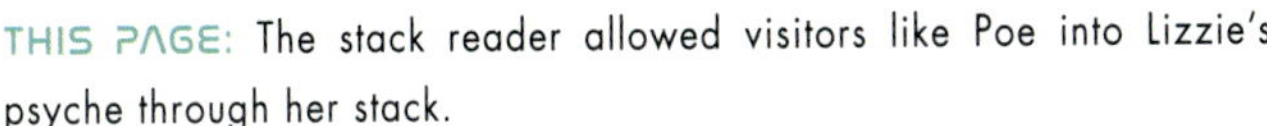

THIS PAGE: The stack reader allowed visitors like Poe into Lizzie's psyche through her stack.

There's also the stack reader, an important element in season one. "Elliott's stack reader was a big prop to the producers," says Swain. "That was his connection to his daughter Lizzie, so that was a very special prop for that character. We were setting the table for how you enter into this virtual reality world. So the stack is suspended and goes into a VR fluid, and allows the user to be transported into that person's stack, and see what their world is like."

In season two, we learn that bounty hunters can collect stacks and turn them in for payment; unscrupulous entrepreneurs can sell individual memories off of stacks to buyers who want to experience moments from the lives of others.

Carey Meyer says he finds the concept of stacks frightening. "I don't want to have a hunk of metal in my neck that's collecting all my thoughts. It's the Fountain of Youth, really, right? That's kind of everybody's dream, but I don't want it."

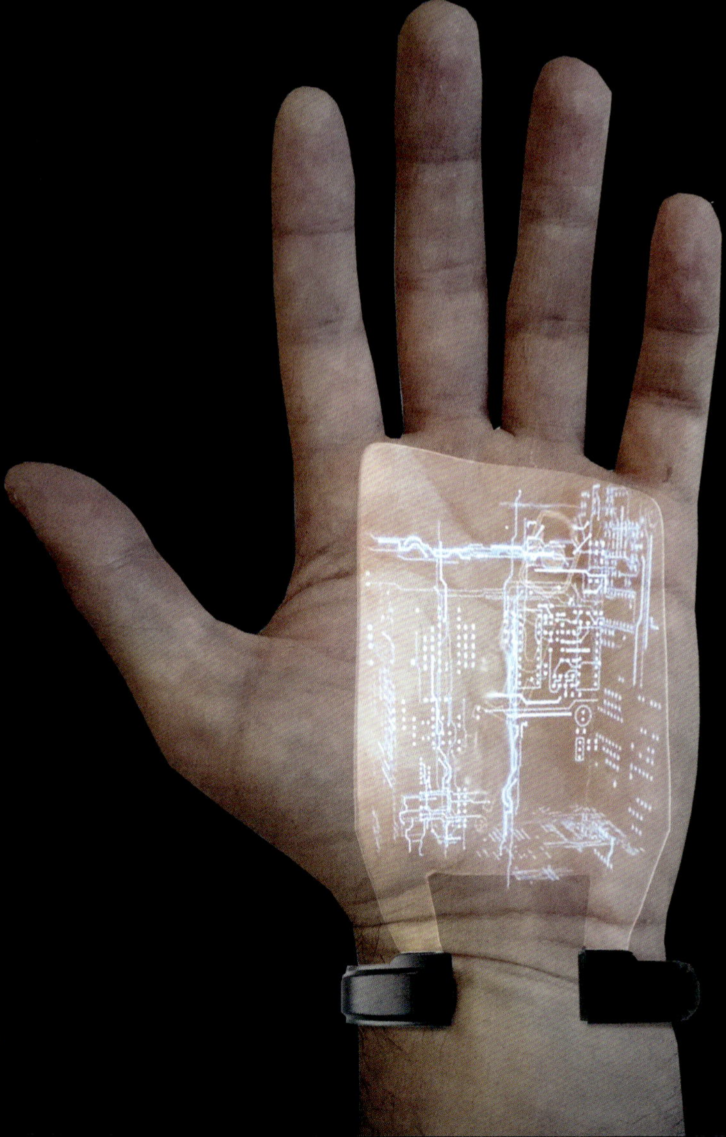

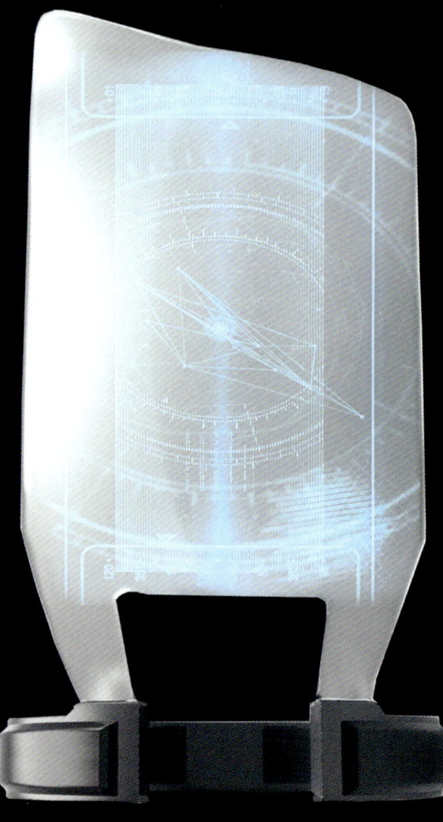

ABOVE: The wrist component of the ONI device.

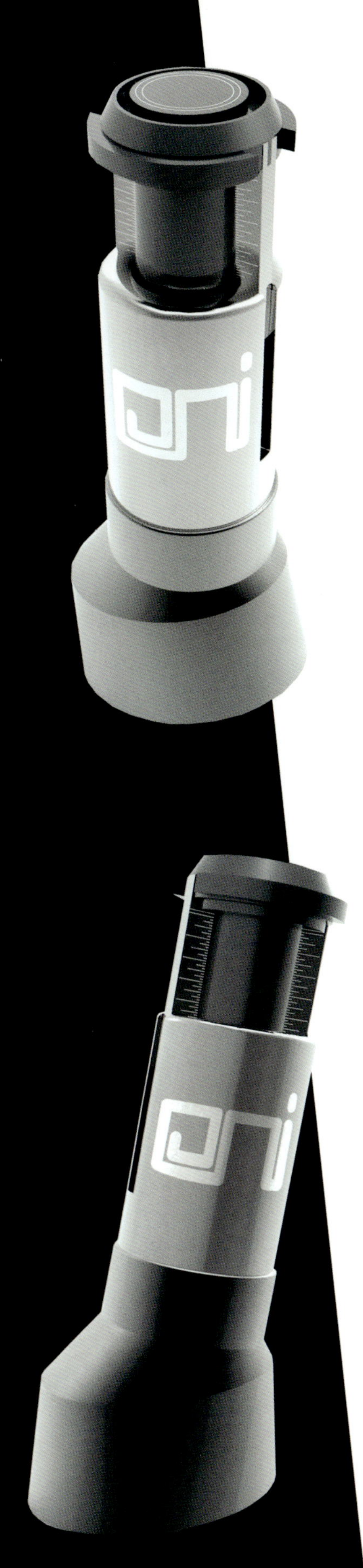

ONI

OCULAR NEURAL INTERFACE

ONI is the acronym for ocular neural interface, a device people wear in one eye that functions much like a smart phone. Probably not accidentally, series creator Laeta Kalogridis notes, ONI "is also a Japanese word for demon. It's [like] a disposable contact lens that you put in every day." The *Altered Carbon* team devised the ONI because, "We were [saying], 'Well, nobody's going to be holding a device to their ear.' So we just came up with the way that we felt people would be communicating with each other that seemed the most natural."

"There was a lot of research and development on that," says VFX supervisor Everett Burrell. "The ONI is personalized to each character, like your iPhone is personalized. You might put stickers or emojis on the back, or put a desktop of your family on there. We built different ONIs for different people. The one that Kovacs is given by Bancroft is a high-end version. Ortega's ONI is a military version. Elliott's is a little more degraded. We tried to give them all a theme, but not make them too crazy/cluttered inside the eye."

The ONI is operated by thought, interfacing with the person's neurons. This aside, Burrell explains, "We based it on the cell phone interface, where you would have access to contacts, and email addresses, and phone numbers, and then you'd have certain buttons that you would use over and over again. So we built it more around a PlayStation interface, and then iPhone."

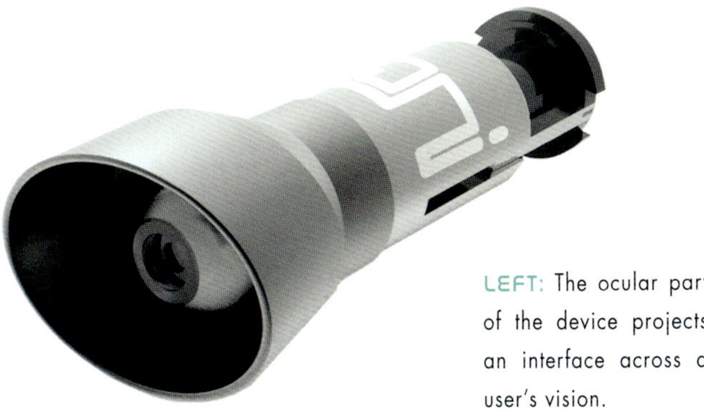

LEFT: The ocular part of the device projects an interface across a user's vision.

HOLOGRAMS

3D ADVERTISEMENTS

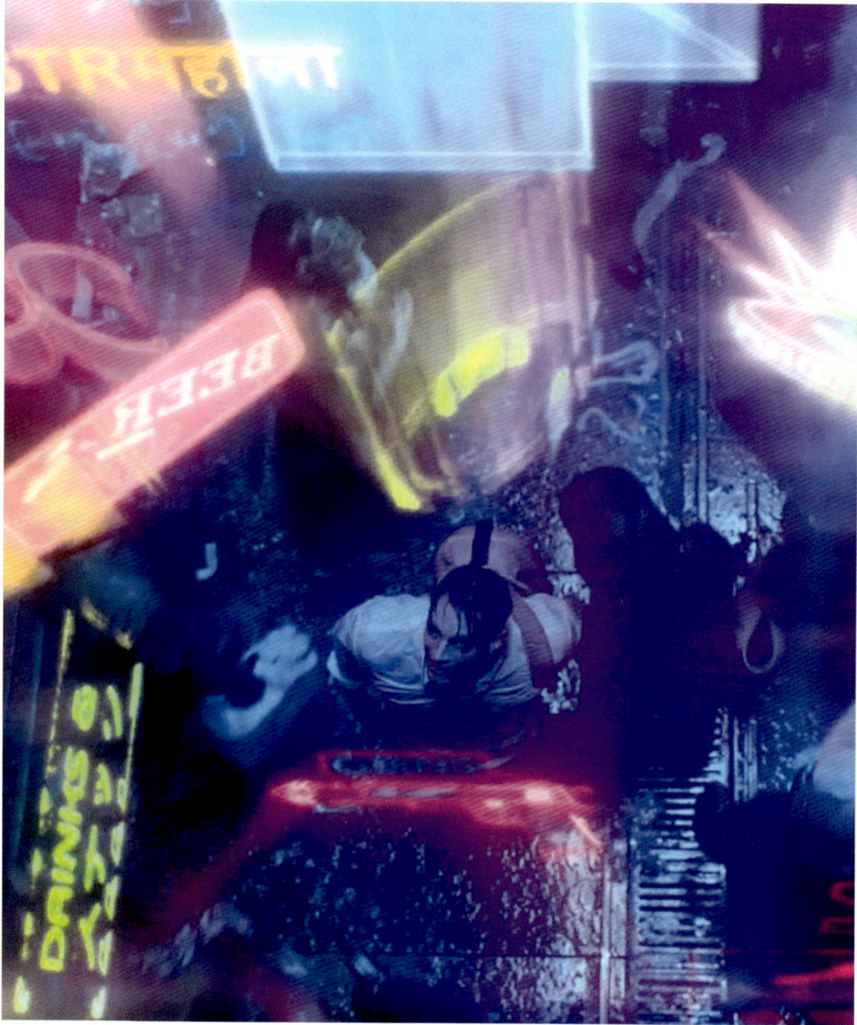

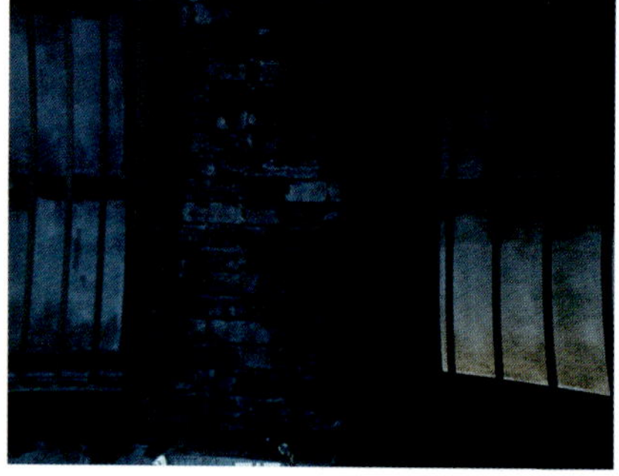

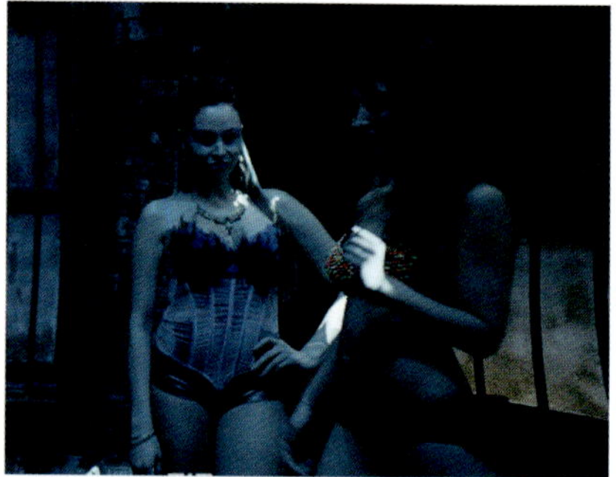

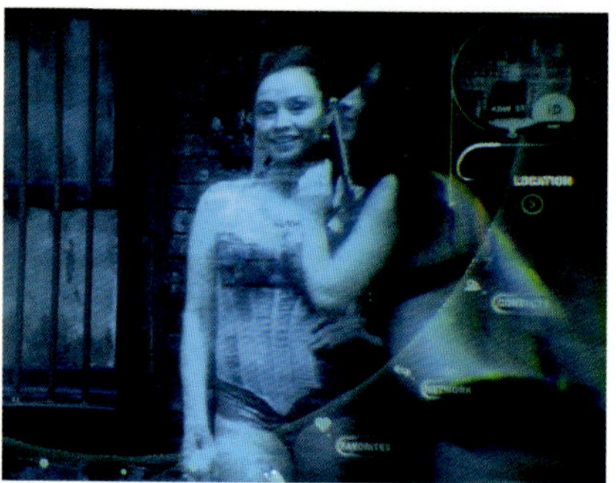

ABOVE: Holograms are projected across the streets of Bay City.

In *Altered Carbon*, there are holograms of many different kinds. VFX supervisor Everett Burrell explains, "There are holograms that everyone can see without an ONI that are standard advertisements. But if you put your ONI in, if you don't have an ad blocker, you get even more advertisements. We had designs that Double Negative had done, that production design had done. We shot actors as a lawyer doing a lawyer ad, kids spinning hula hoops, dancers, all these holograms that we used throughout the season."

The actual holograms are added in post production. "The key to it is that we had interactive light on set that would simulate the glow from a hologram, and then we put our hologram on top. It would look more integrated."

SONGSPIRE TREES

A LIVING ARTIFACT

Indigenous to Harlan's World, Songspire trees can grow hundreds of feet high. They glow with a blue light from within, and make a sound that gives them their name. They are in some way connected with that planet's indigenous species, the Elders, though no human knows exactly how. There was one in the Stronghold base, Laurens Bancroft has a Songspire tree in his mansion, supposedly the only one on Earth, and Tanaseda Hideki grows miniature bonsai versions in his Harlan's World garden.

For the Songspire in Bancroft's home, director Peter Hoar reveals that much of what we see is VFX. "There was a practical base of a tree." He estimates that only the bottom fifth was practical. "Because this set was so huge, with the Alexa 65 camera, you can use a certain size lens, and it looks bigger."

For Tanaseda's bonsai trees, property master Nevin Swain says, "Lisa Godwin, one of our in-house sculptors, along with build supervisor Don Matlo, came up with the bonsai Songspires. They were carved out of foam, and then treated with rubber, and then we made little Songspire buds on them. They're in this huge glass tank that set decoration has built, and they have roots. VFX is going to make them light up, as though the information is traveling through them."

VFX supervisor Robert Munroe says that the full-size season two Songspire trees are similarly an amalgamation of a practical build and digital effects. "We have the Stronghold cavern, where [production designer] Carey Meyer and his team in the art department have built a Songspire root that is probably forty feet tall. It's carved out of Styrofoam and painted, and looks fantastic, and we will be making components of that come alive with both movement and color. And then there are other areas of the show where the roots of the Songspire tree literally come alive and are very threatening and do some things to people, and those will all be completely digital Songspire roots."

These roots move faster than, for example, movie squid tentacles. Munroe observes, "I'm not a fan of nondescript, floaty animation. I want things to attack, hard and fast. And that's what they're doing. They are like angry tentacles, but they're extremely violent, rather than underwater floating."

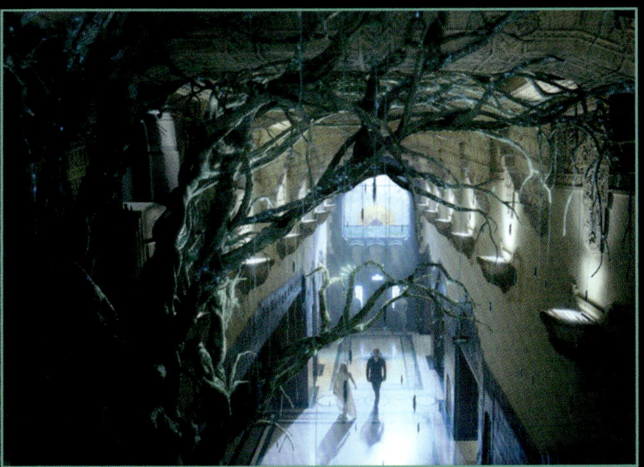

ABOVE: The Songspire tree in Suntouch House.

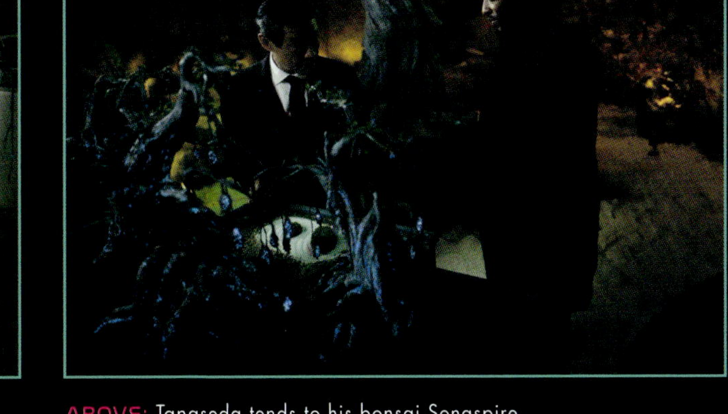

ABOVE: Tanaseda tends to his bonsai Songspire.

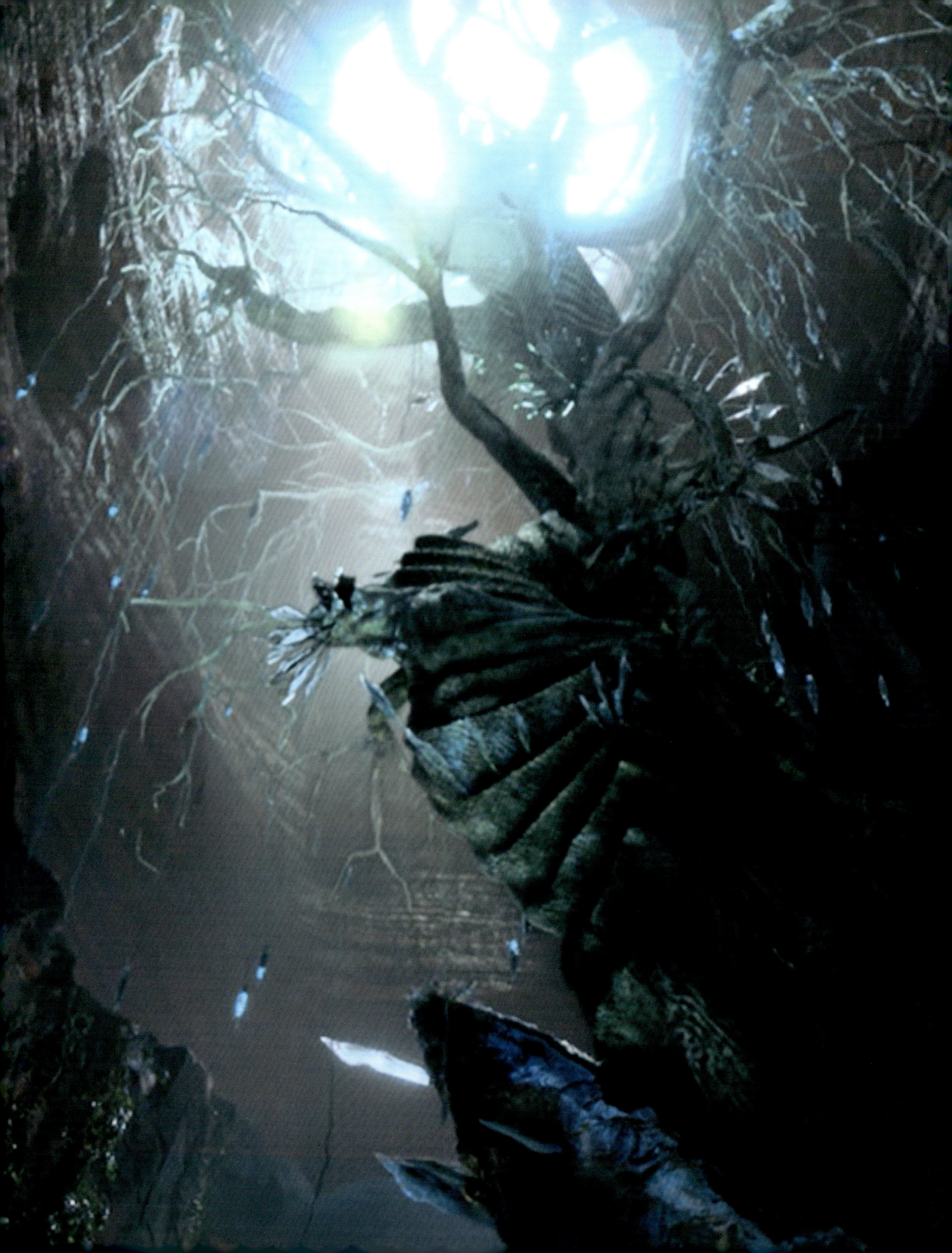

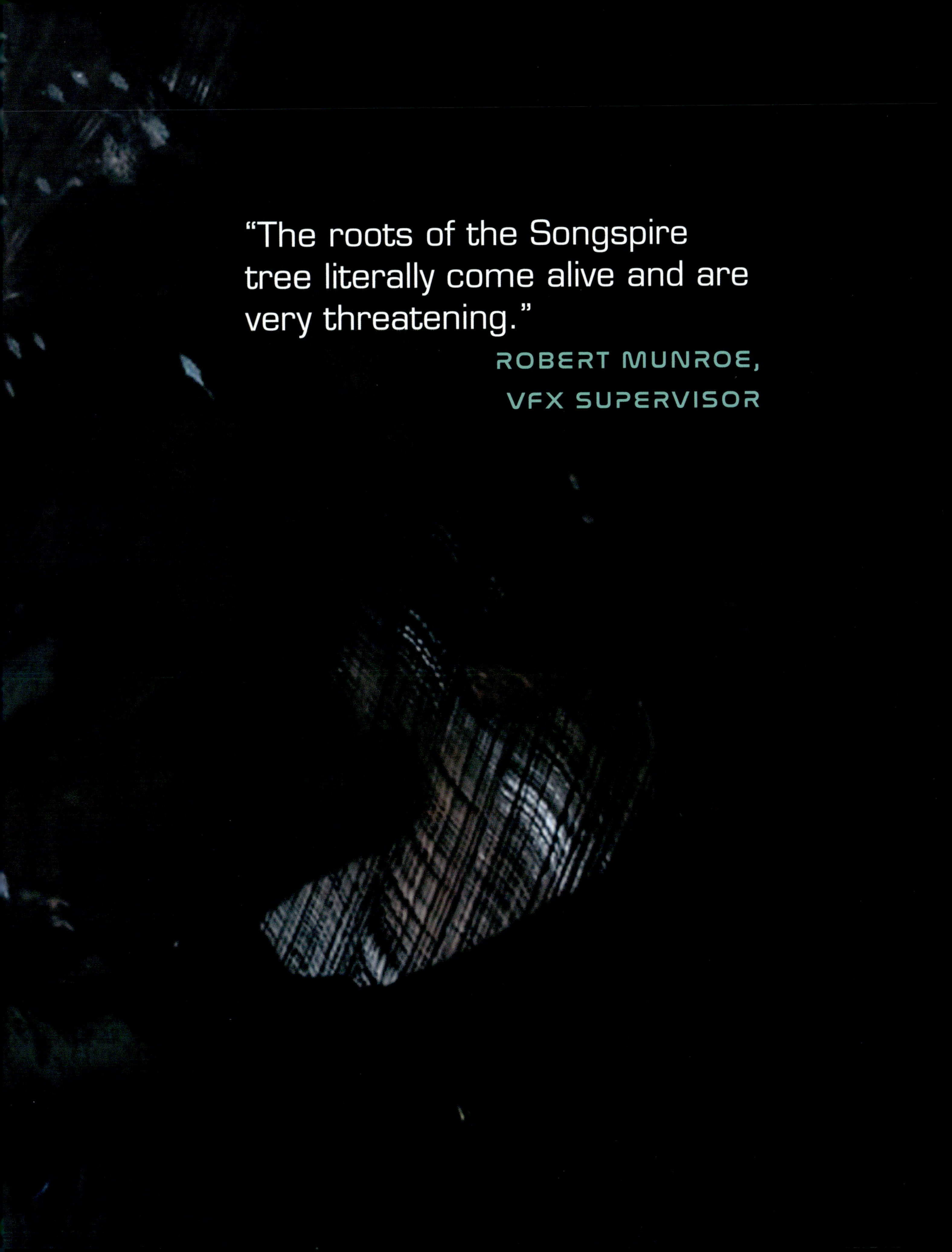

"The roots of the Songspire tree literally come alive and are very threatening."

ROBERT MUNROE,
VFX SUPERVISOR

VISUAL EFFECTS

CREATING THE WORLD OF ALTERED CARBON

O*Altered Carbon* the series could not exist without its expert visual effects. These are found everywhere from full cityscapes, to flying cars, to the slightly manufactured sheen on the faces of clones, all courtesy of the VFX teams, supervised in season one by Everett Burrell and in season two by Robert Munroe.

In season one, Kovacs, as played by Joel Kinnaman, creates a clone of his Ryker sleeve with a copy of his DHF so that his adversaries can be fooled as to his whereabouts. Several of the more complex VFX sequences involve the two identical Kovacses interacting with each other.

Peter Hoar, who directed the two episodes that contain these, describes a scene where the Kovacses are plotting together. "It's the first one that I had ever done the motion-control camera, where you get a big camera on a crane, and you plan out the move with the camera, and it's all programmed in, and you do it with Joel and his double [whose face is replaced in post production with Kinnaman's]. Joel maps out the double's moves as he wants to play them, because he's going to be playing those moves when he plays the clone. So it was mostly mapping it all out, and programming the camera so that it reshoots exactly the same shots, frame for frame." The camera repeated each move exactly when Kinnaman was playing the original Kovacs and his photo double was playing the clone, and then the other way around. In post production, Kinnaman's face was placed over that of the double. Hoar adds that the camera movements were tailored to follow exactly what Kinnaman wanted to do in both roles. "I talked with Joel about how he wanted to see it. He had planned it out, and so he brought everything he needed on the day, which went really well."

THIS SPREAD: Kinnaman shot this scene twice along with his body double.

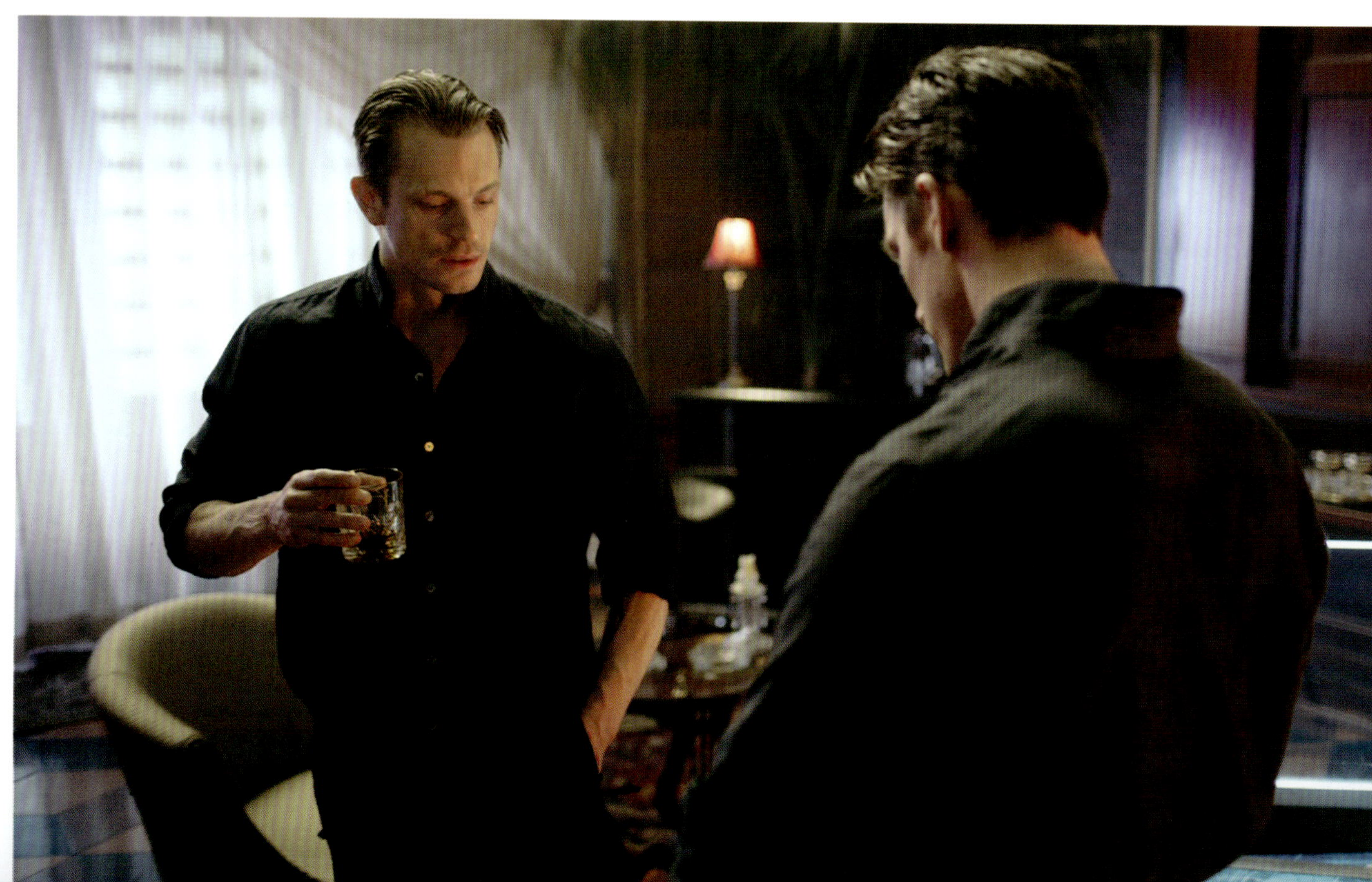

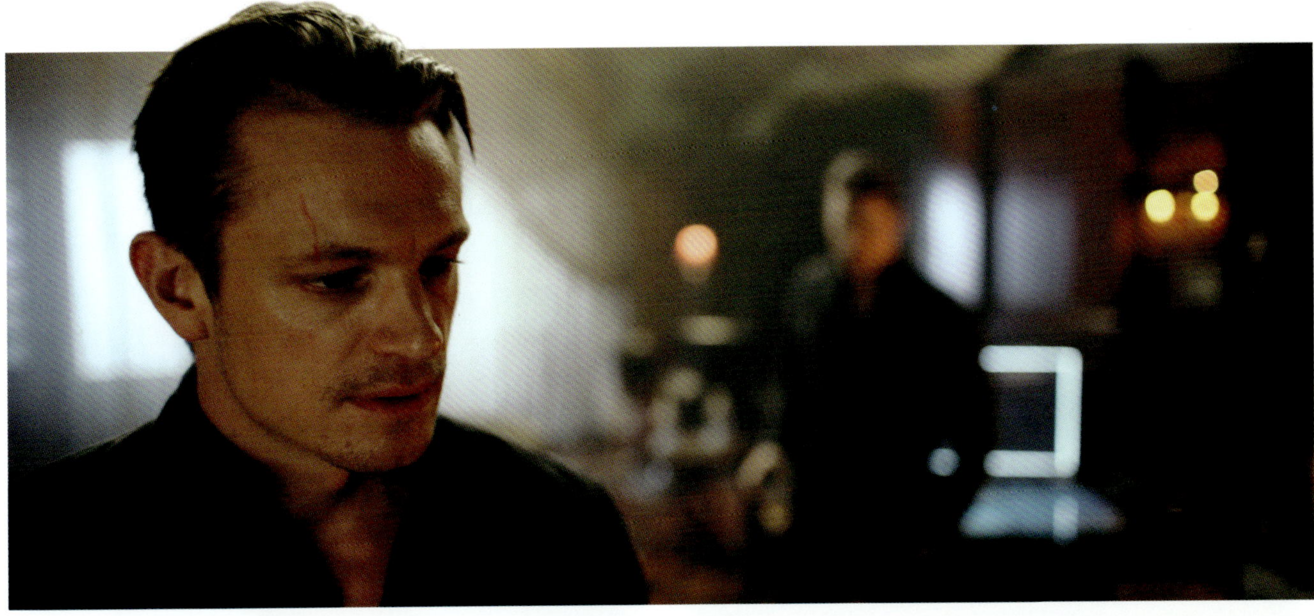

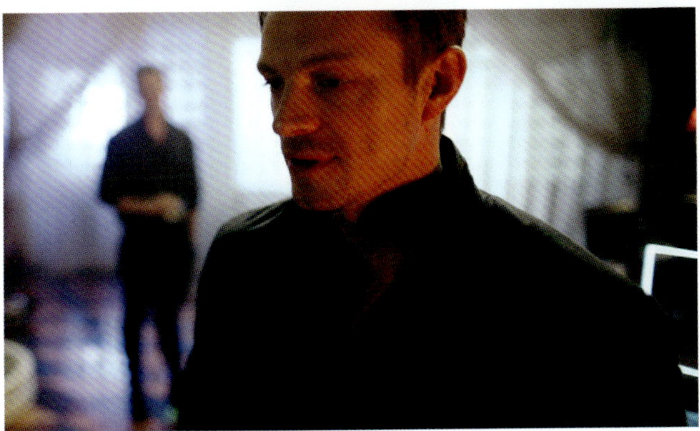

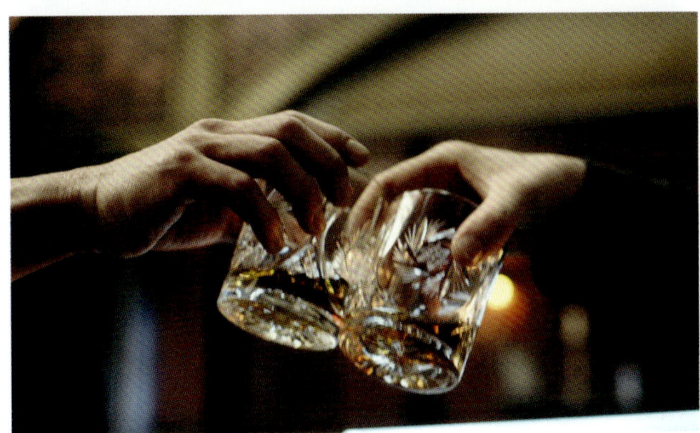

There turned out to be a few technical issues in post production, Hoar adds. "We had to shoot the shots bigger than they would normally be, fifty-percent larger frames, so that we could then track within that frame and line up the shots, in case there was a little misalignment, but my experiences were good. I came out of that thinking, 'Yeah, let's do that,'" he laughs.

Another scene where the two Kovacses clink glasses was challenging, Hoar reports. "When you see these scenes where one actor plays two people, you're always looking for the bit where you go, 'Oh, that's clever.' Because it's just two people moving around the different sides of the room. That's not a complicated shot. It's where they're handing each other a drink, and clinking glasses, that's the tricky bit, because you've got to line all of that up, with both Joels, and the double again [making exactly the same movements]. You can't get it wrong, because the camera is going to do the same thing, exactly, programmed. But we got it to work."

VFX supervisor Munroe says there are some equally complicated shots with Anthony Mackie's Kovacs, who has been tortured to find out which people matter to him. "You have Ortega from season one, Elliott from season one, his sister Reileen. [Kovacs' captors] use synth technology to recreate them to walk out into this Colosseum-like arena, they have weapons and he doesn't. It disorients him when he sees [a killer in a synth sleeve of] Ortega walk up. He's like, 'Oh, my God…?' And then she starts to try to kill him."

VFX comes into this, Munroe explains, because "There's a lot of digital technology in there – digital weapons, digital blood, there's a big bullet-time sequence, where everything is completely frozen for thirty seconds, and the camera flies around and through everyone, and then it all goes back to real time again."

Munroe relates, "I'm not quite sure if The Matrix invented bullet time or were early adopters of it but there was a rig where they would have a rail with a hundred 35-millimeter cameras, all designed to trigger at the exact same moment. When you took those frames with each one of those cameras, it looks like a motion picture camera was moving through

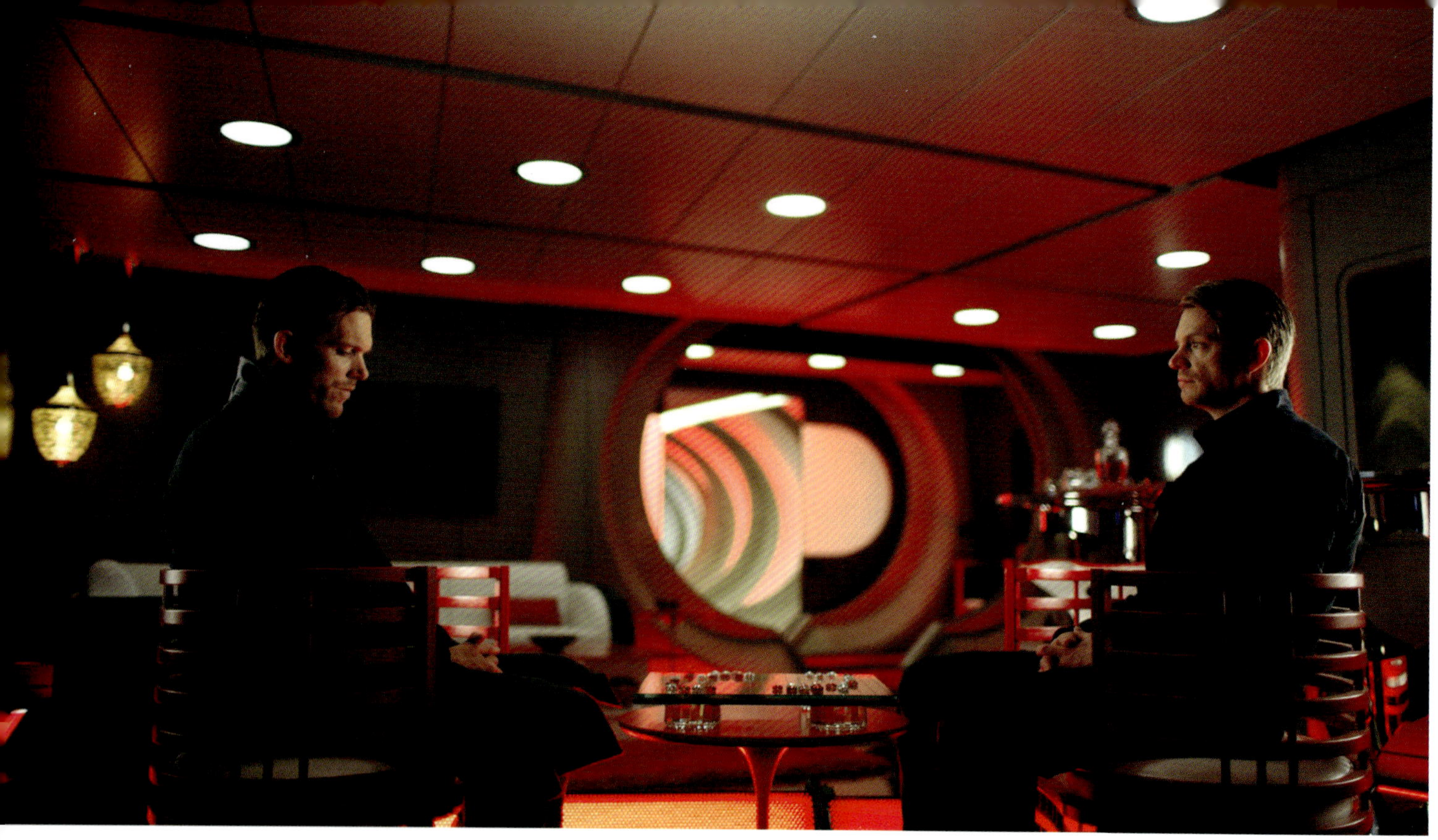

THIS PAGE: A technique called motion control allows a camera to capture the same shots repeatedly.

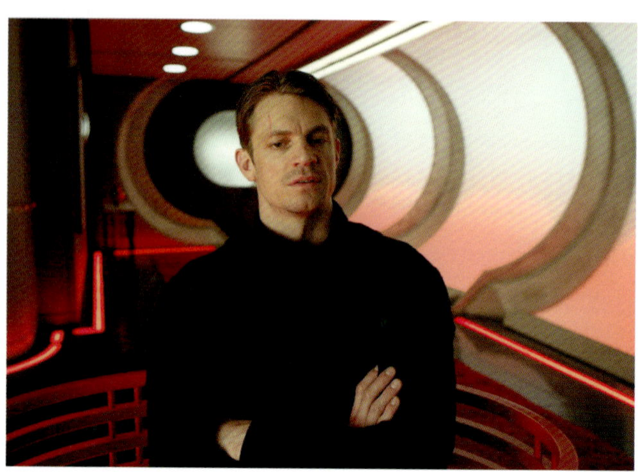

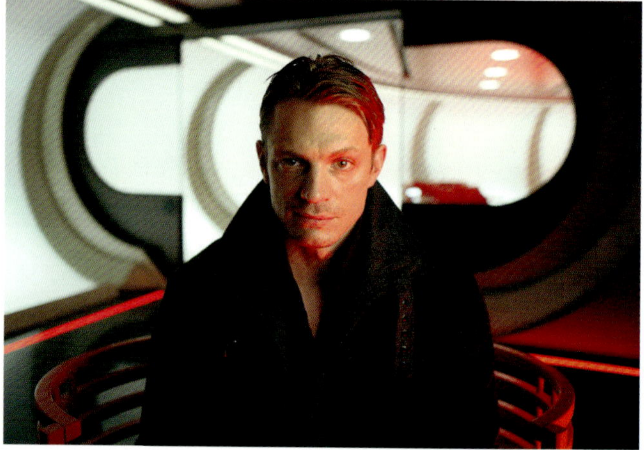

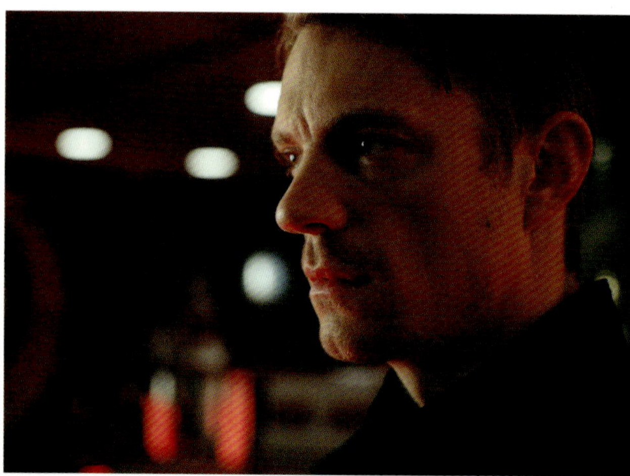

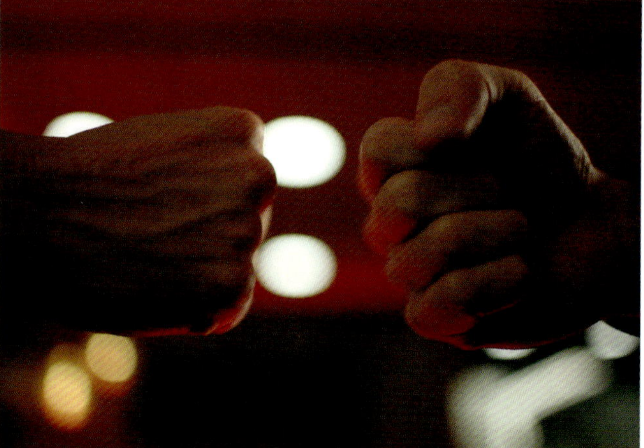

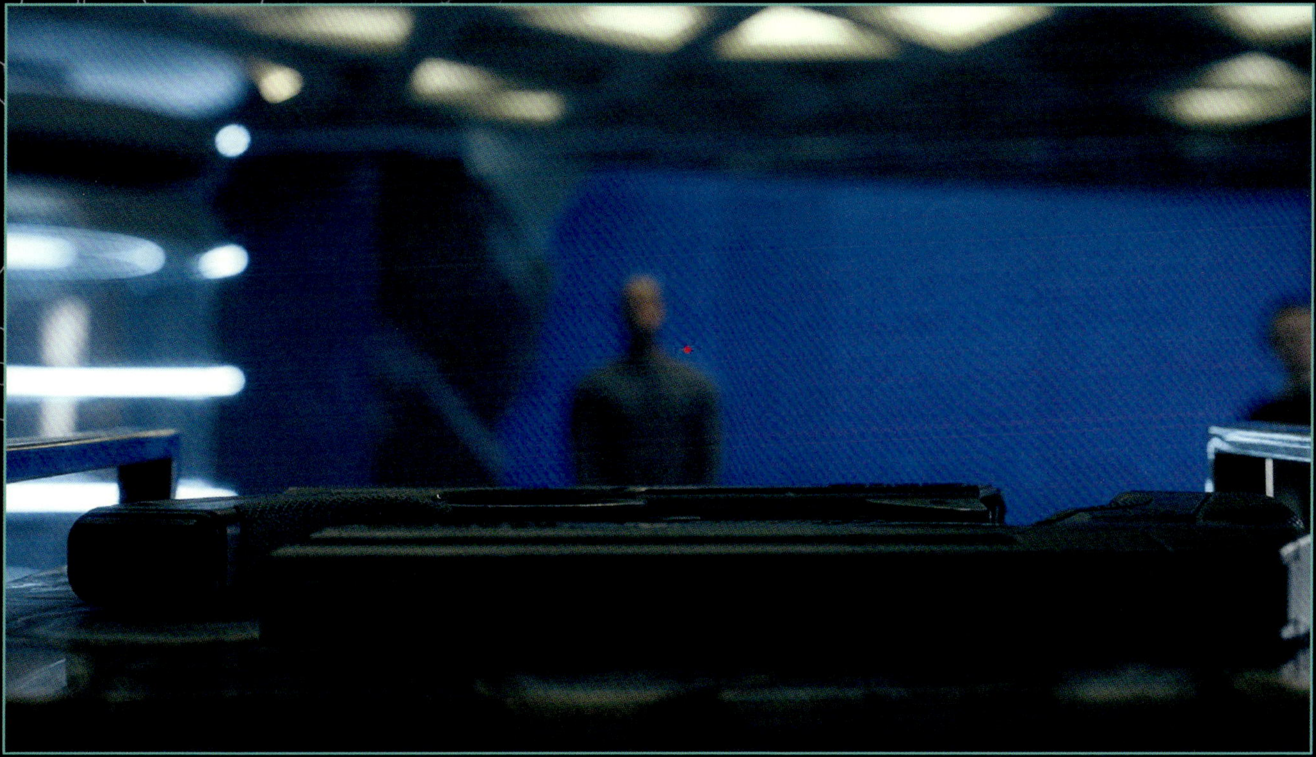

THIS PAGE: Anthony Mackie as Kovacs, shooting a scene against a blue screen.

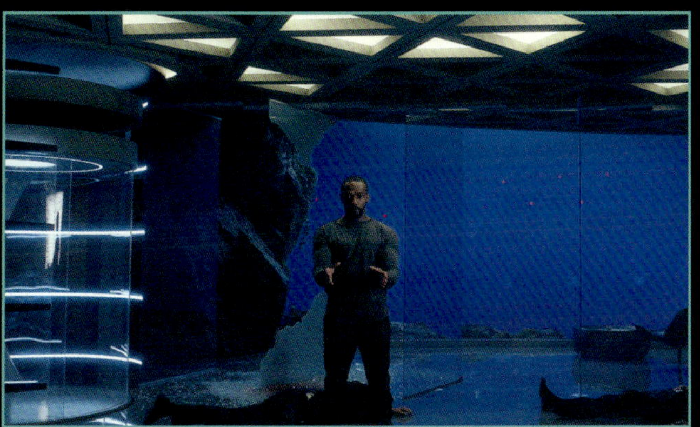

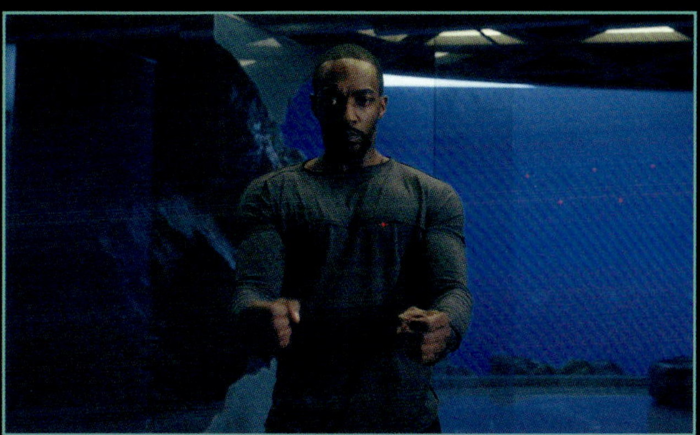

the set, but everybody was frozen in that moment. So that's where bullet time technology comes from."

However, even a high-end TV series like *Altered Carbon* cannot afford one hundred 35-millimeter cameras. Munroe says he discussed the sequence with its director M.J. Bassett and cinematographer Bernard Couture. Munroe referenced a commercial known as 'Philips Carousel.' "It was a two-minute-long shot. You could never have done that with 35-millimeter cameras on rails. They yelled, 'Action!' and everybody just froze in position, and with the camera operator, they walked through the whole environment, filming the whole time, and things like broken glass were added in visual effects. If a person was frozen and their arms were moving slightly, they would stabilize it. Some people were hung on wires, and the wires were removed. Anything in terms of a blood hit: that was all digital also. But the foundation of the shot was just a bunch of people staying very still for a two-minute period. We did the same thing, and it worked out great."

Later, Munroe continues, "We're doing a really large battle between [Mackie's] Kovacs and [Will Yun Lee's] Kovacs Prime. They have a major battle on the edge of a cliff. So there's this large battle, where people are on this precipice of a big cliff with a thousand-foot drop, and there's both practical and digital stunt work, and a large environment, set extensions there, and all that kind of stuff. So there's a wide variety of things that are unique to this season."

MILLSPORT

HARLAN'S CAPITAL

Millsport is the capital city of Harlan's World, built directly into the rock all around it. VFX supervisor Robert Munroe relates, "It's like, if you were to take an Aztec or a Mayan ruin, and spread it across the ground plain to a city size, and then have only twenty to twenty-four skyscrapers, not densely packed like Bay City was in season one, but more sparsely populated. Some of the skyscrapers are futuristic-looking, and others look like they're stalagmites, growing out of the ground, like tall, pointed rock structures. everything else around it feels like a Mayan ruin. The streets have been cut into the canyons, thirty/forty meters [or] a hundred/two hundred feet deep. It's a very rock-driven environment. So it looks a little more ancient, with modernism that has been tacked on top of it."

Executive producer James Middleton describes Millsport's Harlan Square as "The narrative location of the planet's main needlecast station and the offices of the Meth cartel. The location is fully realized through a combination of a practical location in Surrey, British Columbia, and full digital model of the square by DNEG. Practical footage of the square and its hundreds of background extras are married with digital backgrounds and set extensions to create a seamless photo-real futuristic city."

"There are market streets," Munroe elaborates, "where there are scratchers, the people who eke out a day-to-day existence in the city. We built one of those streets on set, and [VFX] fill in the green screen at the end of it."

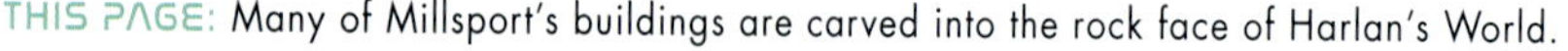

THIS PAGE: Many of Millsport's buildings are carved into the rock face of Harlan's World.

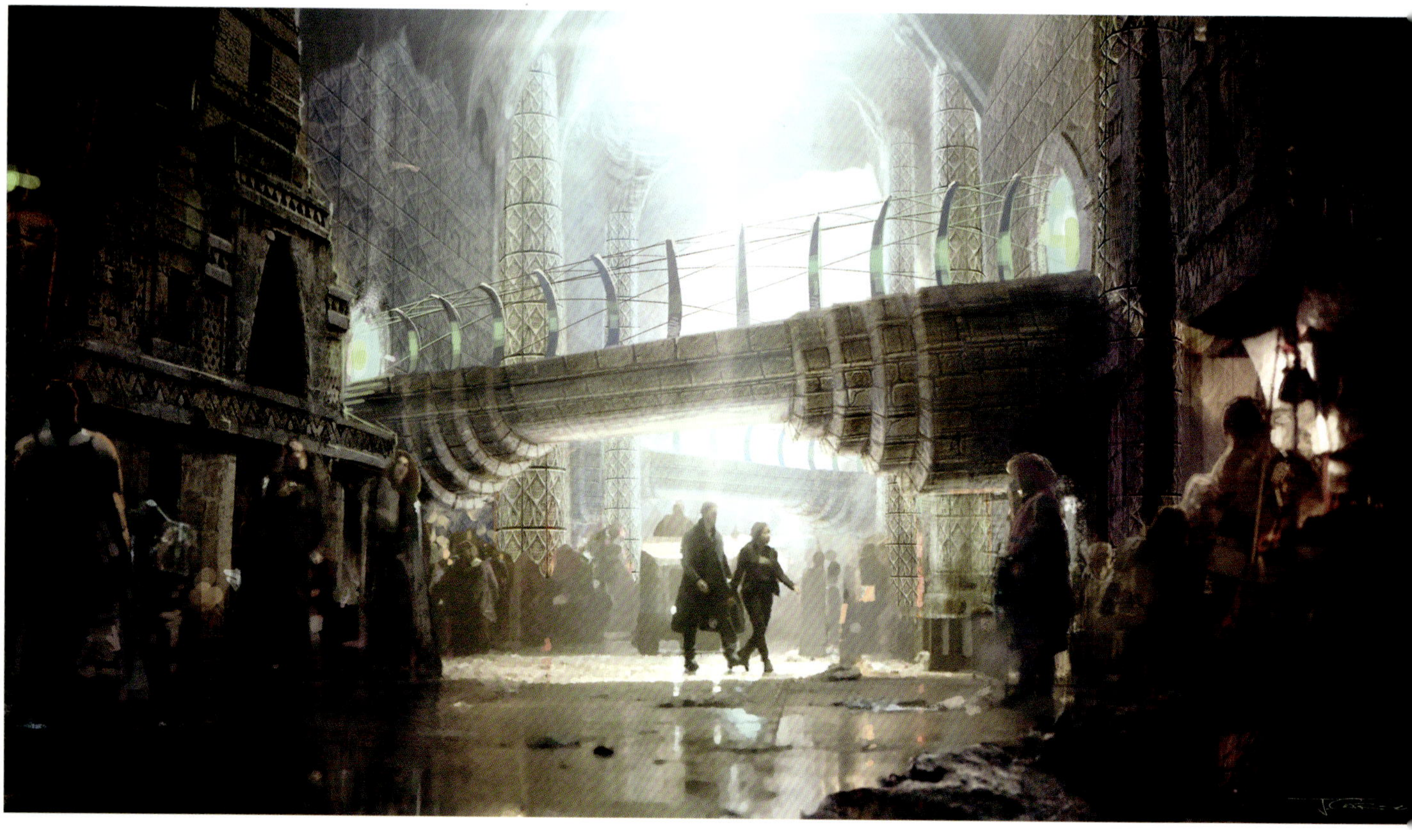

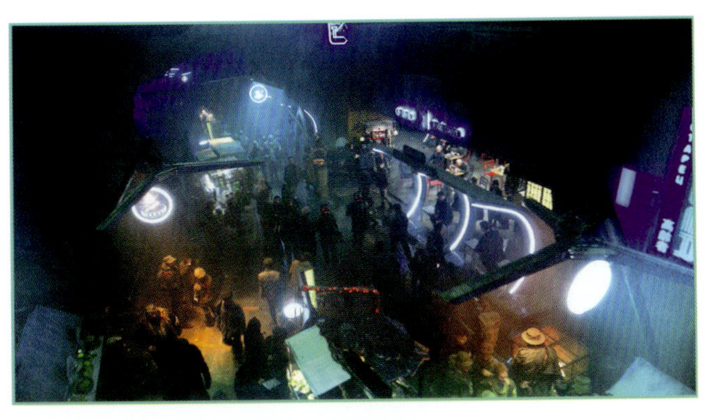

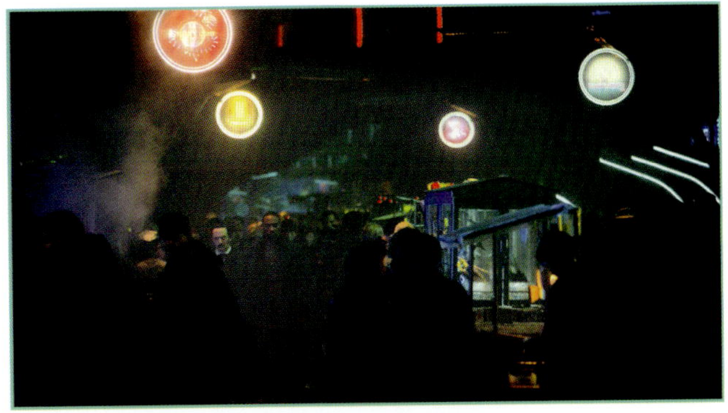

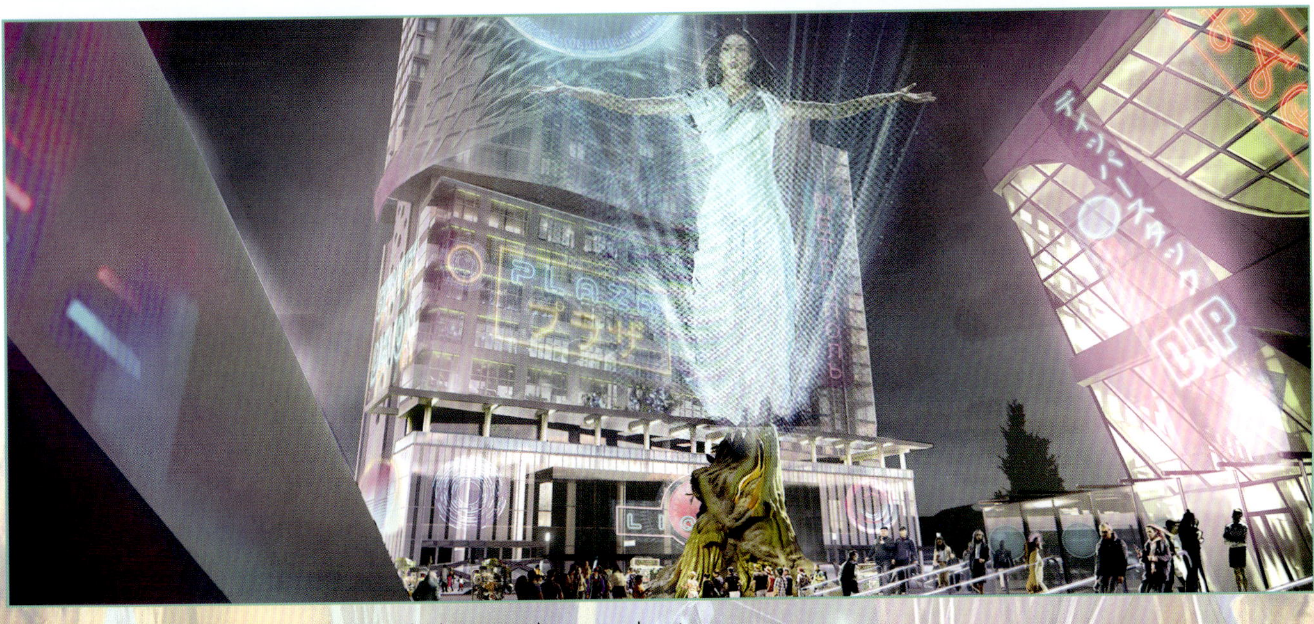

THIS PAGE: Millsport combines technological advances with its natural setting.

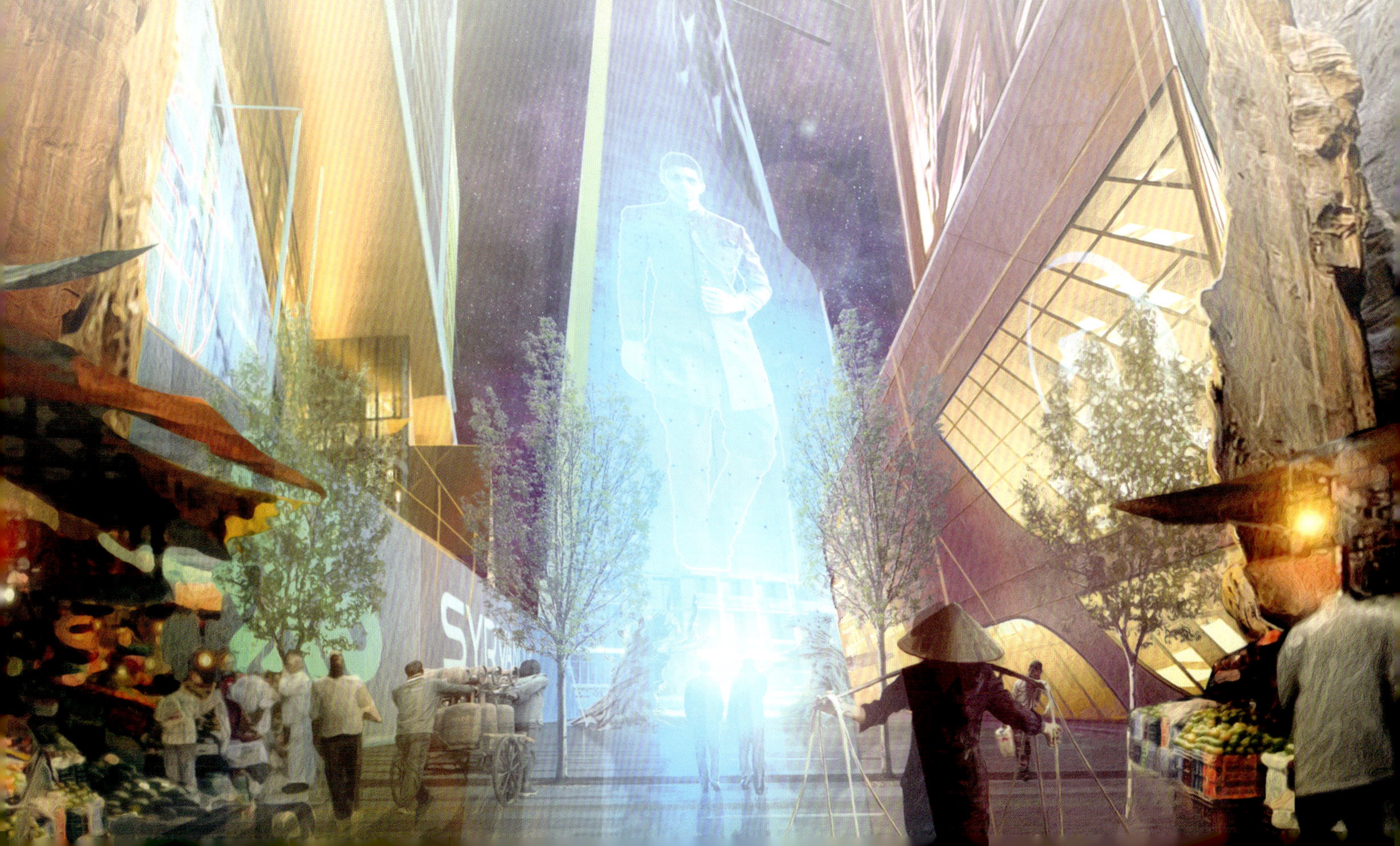

TREPP

LOOKING FOR A BOUNTY

Trepp, played by Simone Missick, is a Harlan's World bounty hunter, with a wife, a young son, and a missing brother. Despite mistrusting Kovacs, Trepp teams up with him so that they can help one another find their respective loved ones.

"Trepp does not prioritize one relationship over the other when it comes to those that she loves," Missick says. "Her wife is just as important as her son, who is just as important as her brother. For better or worse, she's not willing to put any one of them ahead of the other, and if any one of them is in danger, that person is the most important at that moment."

To prepare for playing Trepp, whom she describes as "a very powerful woman," Missick observed women police officers, security guards, and probation officers. "I did a lot of research on female bounty hunters specifically, in the way that they enter rooms and drive, simple things that their body language does that's completely different from ordinary citizens."

Trepp has data processing coils that go from her hair into her brain. According to property master Nevin Swain, the coils are "like having a supercomputer inside of her body." Swain's department laser-etched a pattern into the coils that reflects their Elder tech origins. "They have a little port that runs into her temple. Bill Terazakis, our fabulous makeup effects person, built a piece that looks as though the coils are embedded into [Missick's] scalp. And we've wired that coil up, so that it's able to light [up] as data is being transmitted."

The coils called for a lot of preparation time, Missick notes. "They put a bald cap on part of my scalp, and then they put

BELOW: Trepp is a bounty hunter searching for her missing brother.

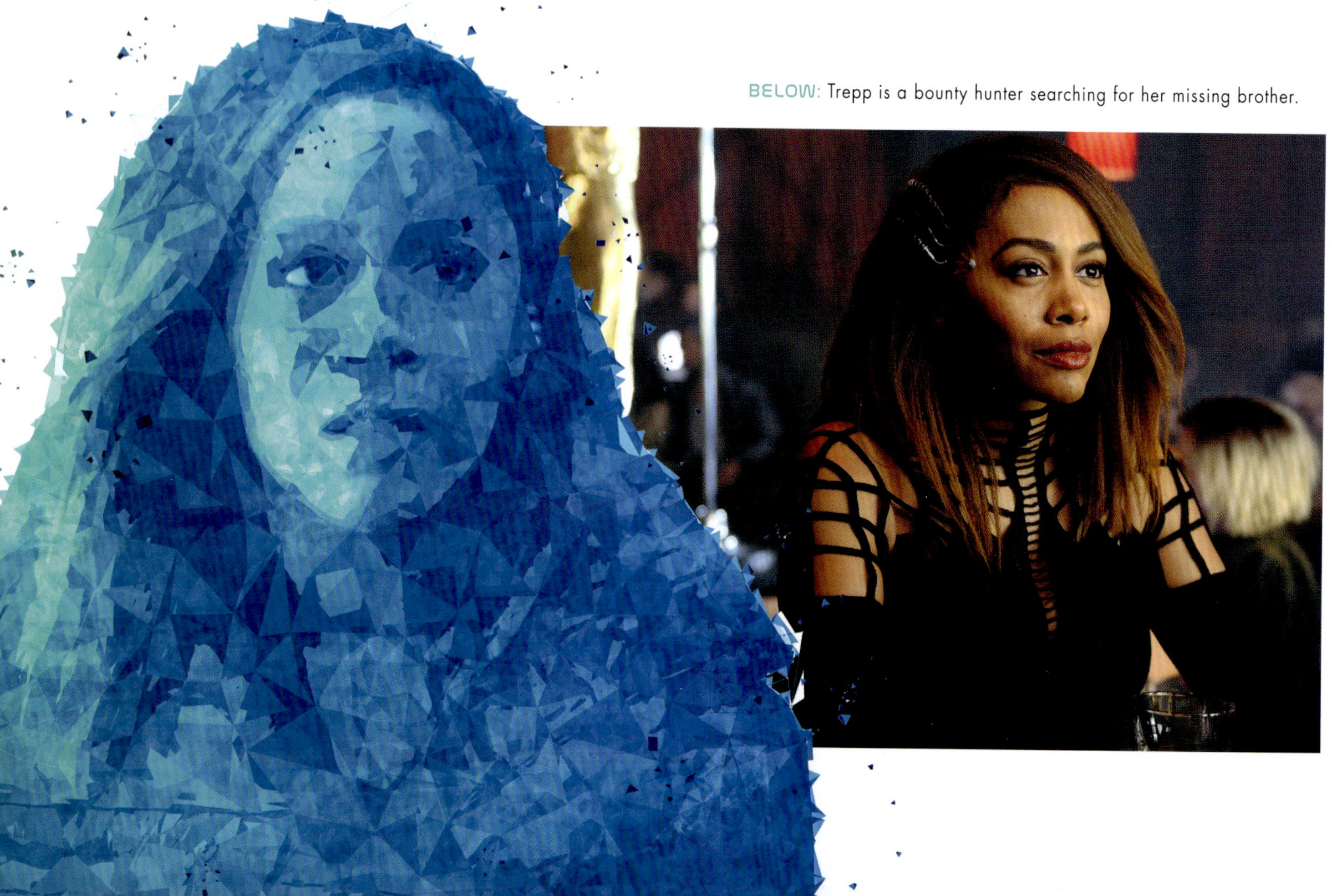

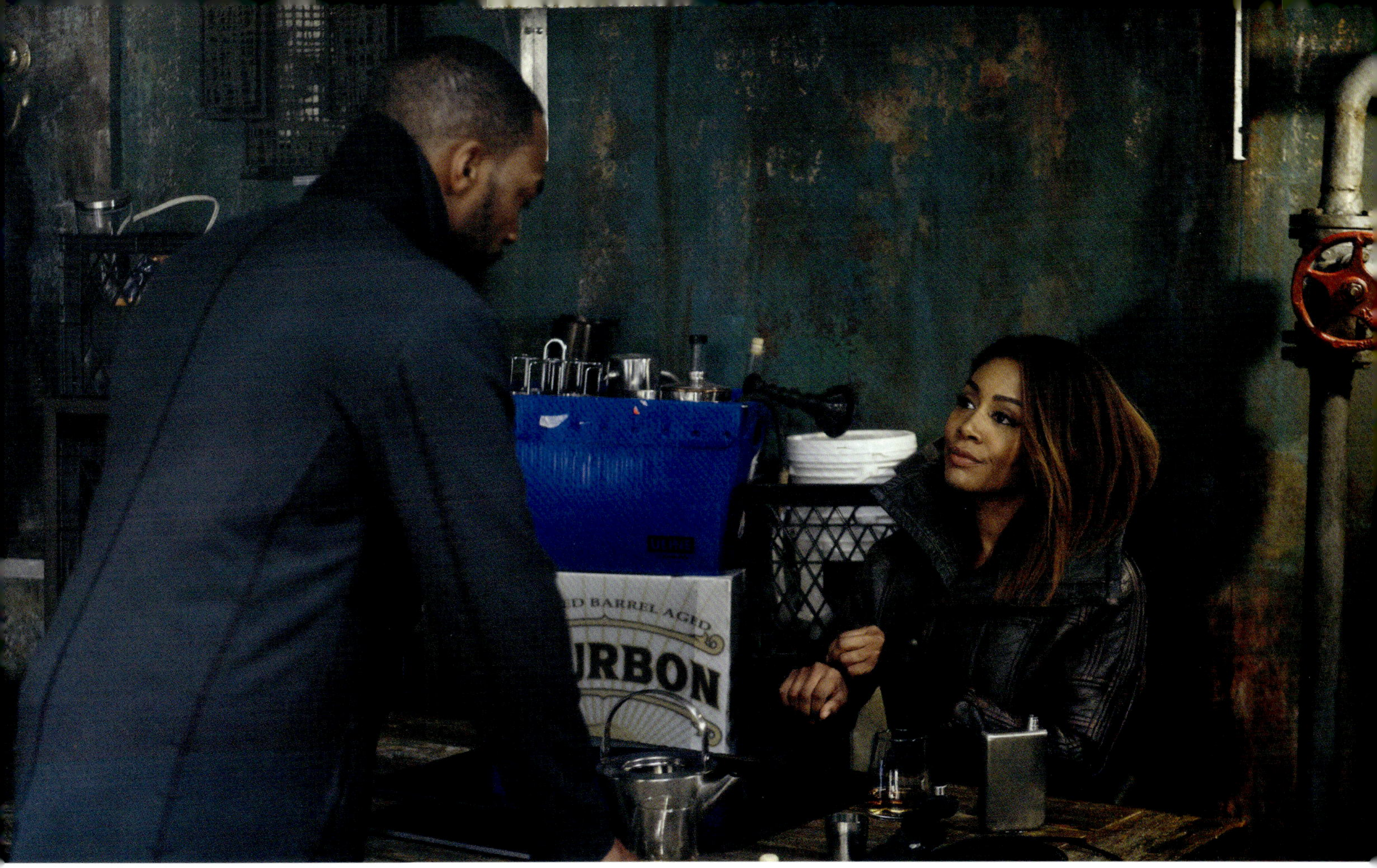

THIS PAGE: Trepp reluctantly partners up with Kovacs when he arrives on Harlan's World.

the coils in, and then they put the wig on top, and integrate the coils into that, and then another thing is makeup to make it all look seamless. Every morning, there was a three-hour-long experience in our makeup and hair and makeup effects trailers. I [would feel] like a ping-pong ball, bouncing from one department to the next," she laughs.

The most difficult stunt sequence involving Trepp, per Missick, is her rescue of Kovacs when he's hanging from a cliff edge by his fingertips. The actors, protected by concealed harnesses, worked on a real cliff. "That required more rehearsal than I've had for anything else. We had a rehearsal with the stunt department and the rigging department to make sure everything felt safe. Then we shot a version of it in the forest on solid ground, with the blue screen, as a backup, in case anything was out of our control on the day. Then we had another day of rehearsal to get comfortable with the rigging, and then we shot that scene [at the cliff] over the course of two days. We both worked really hard, and our stunt department, and our rigging department, all of our doubles, were on the top of their game in order to make sure that it looked realistic."

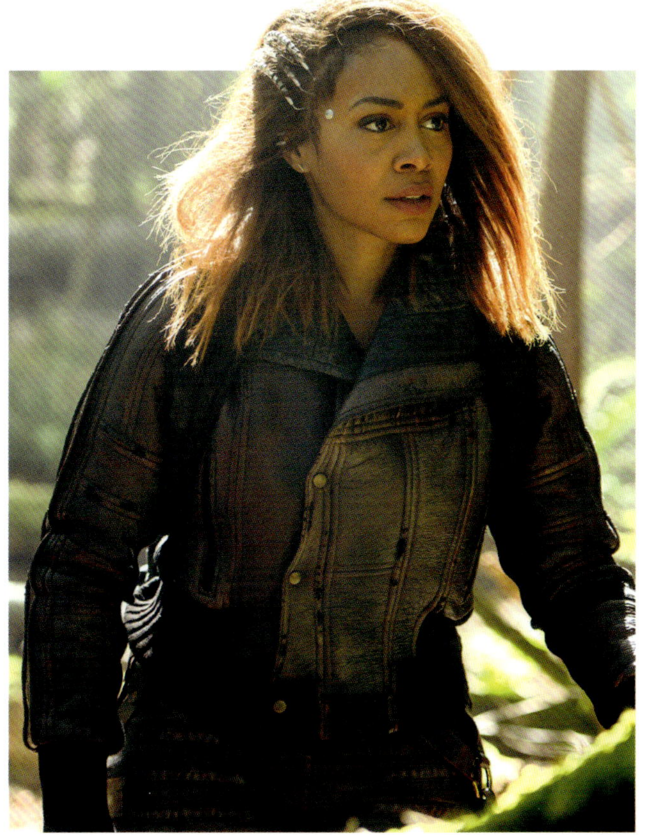

AXLEY TOWER

A FORTRESS IN SPACE

Axley Tower is the property and residence of Meth Horace Axley, played by Michael Shanks, who is one of the Founders of Harlan's World. Axley meets in VR with Kovacs, who is currently sleeved as a lounge singer, played by JiHae. The clearly terrified Axley gets Kovacs to agree to protect him by offering to lead him to the living Quellcrist Falconer.

Axley says he is older than stack tech – he crossed the stars in a colony ship before stack tech was invented (a clue that he was involved in the Founders' murderous actions).

Axley Tower's resleeving room has its own needlecast bay, a very expensive accessory that only a Meth could afford. Kovacs, newly resleeved in the military body played by Anthony Mackie, is still in the room's dream tank when he is awakened by gunfire. He has to break his way out of the tank.

In the tower's study Kovacs finds Axley, who is dying of injuries, with rupturing blood vessels in his face. There are a few Elder artifacts on display here. The room is furnished in minimalist luxury.

Kovacs steps out on the balcony, which gives him a view of the two moons of Harlan's World as well as the Millsport cityscape below, sprawling and industrial, carved out of the primal rock. It is futuristic and yet ancient-looking.

Axley Tower has a glass elevator that ascends and descends through the rockface that holds the tower. At the base, it lets passengers out directly into the PIL station.

BOTTOM: The city of Millsport orbits around Axley Tower, the highest point.

RIGHT: Axley resleeves Kovacs in a new body on Harlan's World in order to enlist his help.

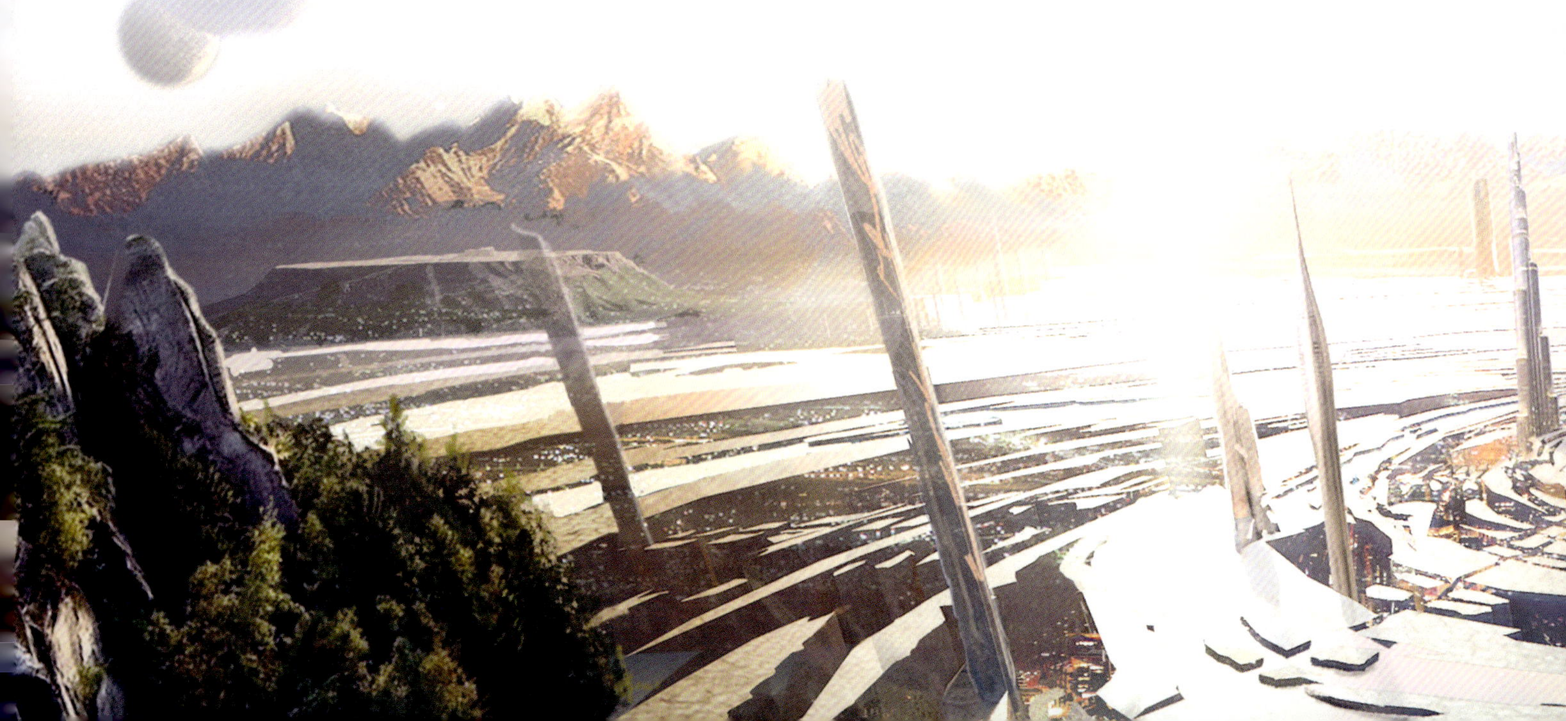

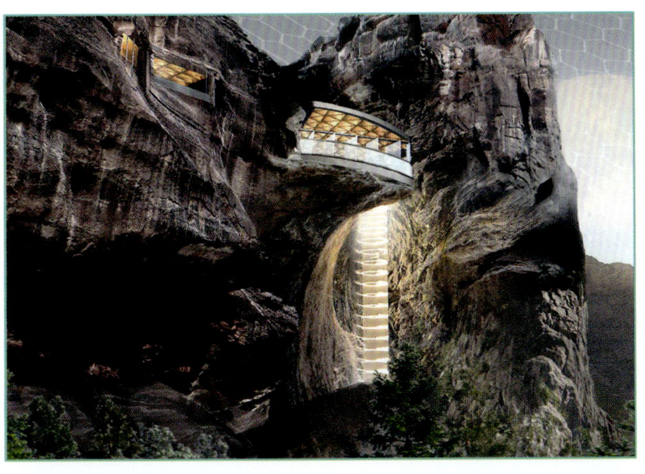

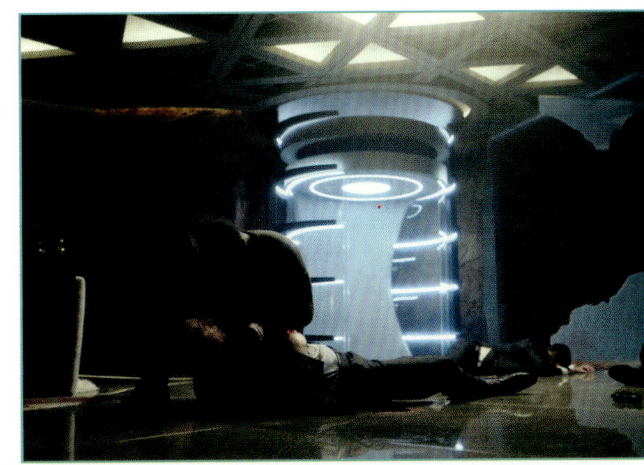

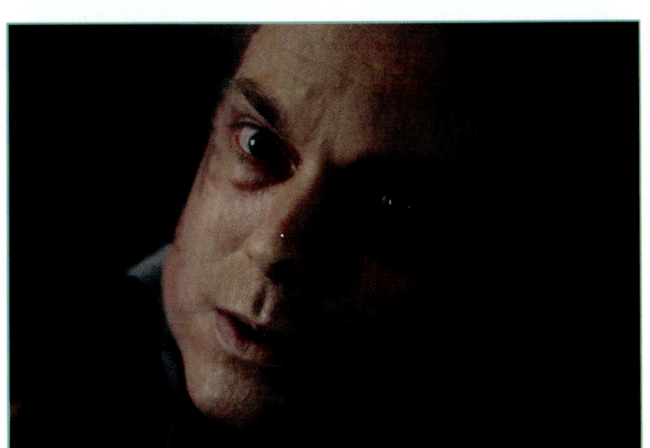

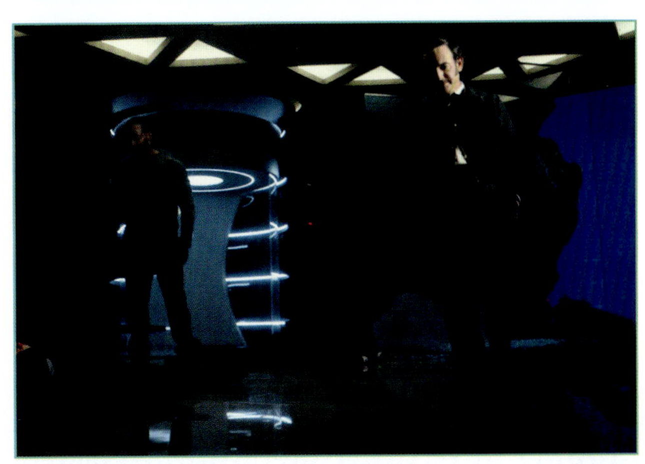

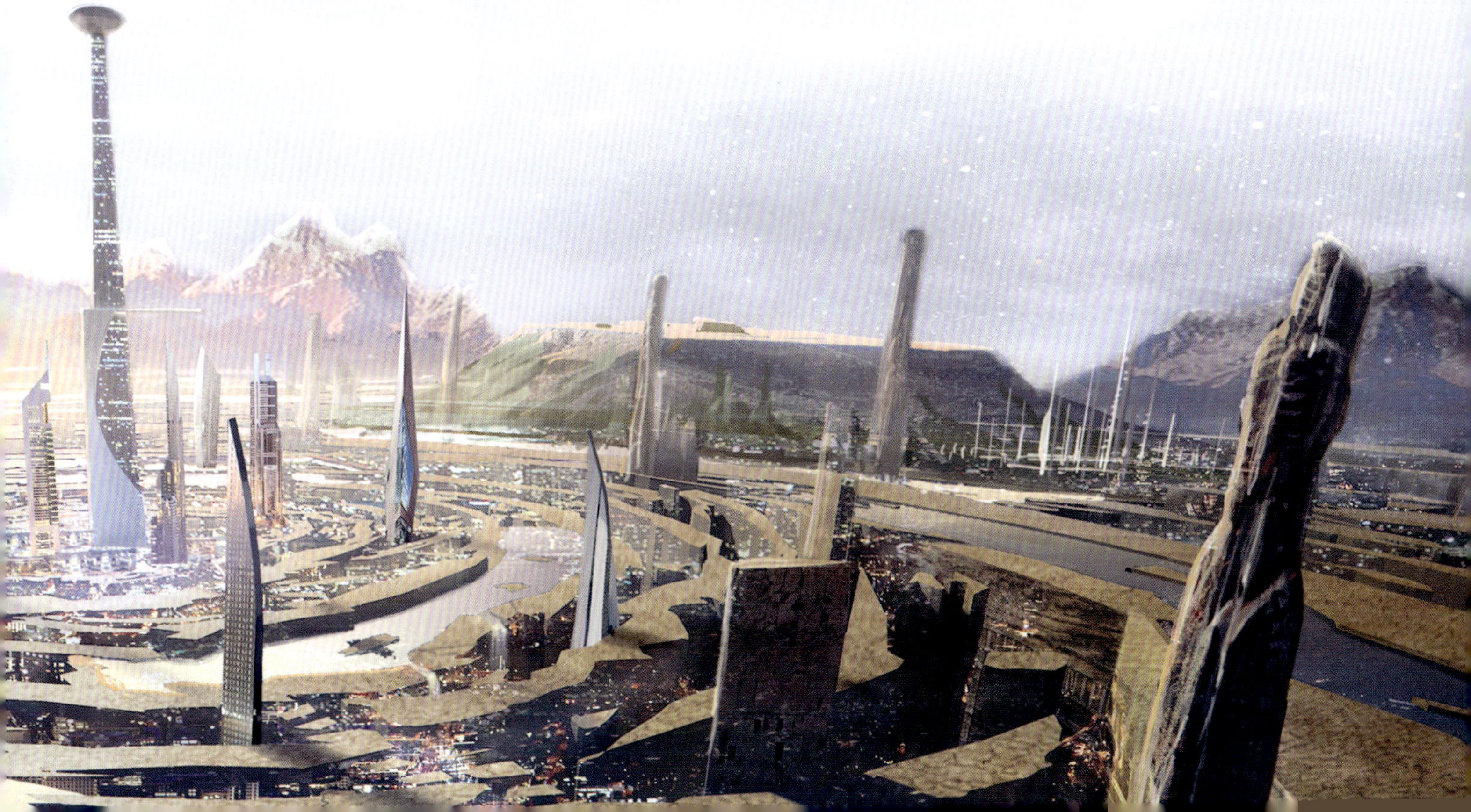

NEVERMORE HOTEL

HOME AWAY FROM HOME

The Nevermore Hotel on Harlan's World was once the rundown Happy Face Hotel, where Jaeger and the Praetorians captured O.G. Kovacs. In season two, Tanaseda gifts it to Kovacs. When Kovacs revives Poe, the AI renames their new hideout the Nevermore.

There's a lot of VFX extension in and around the Nevermore, VFX supervisor Robert Munroe relates. The onscreen transformation of the abandoned Happy Face into the Nevermore required research and development into swarming simulation, plus a full scan of Poe actor Chris Conner. "We have a scene that I designed and storyboarded and pitched. Inside the Happy Face, there are nanobots. They look like big piles of sand everywhere. Kovacs is able to reactivate them, and these piles start to stream and swarm together. They create Poe, in his physical form, as well as the interior of the Nevermore Hotel, which is very reminiscent of the Raven."

Actor Conner loves both the Raven and Nevermore sets. "[Production designer] Carey Meyer gave me two wonderful playgrounds, vast and detailed at the same time."

The nanobots are represented by sand that is both practical and digital, Munroe adds. "We had [practical] silt piles that we could just toss in anywhere that looked good, and then for the construction shots, we're also putting in digital piles, because we have to animate that, and make that come alive, and start to take on Poe's form, Poe's shape, the color of his shoes, his pants, his eyes, everything. He forms out of these both real and digital piles."

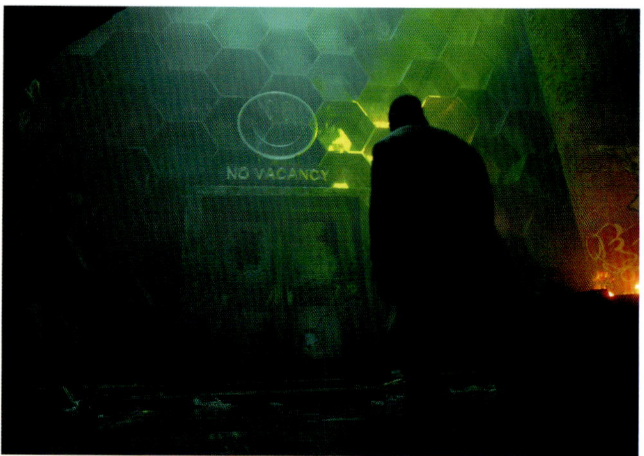

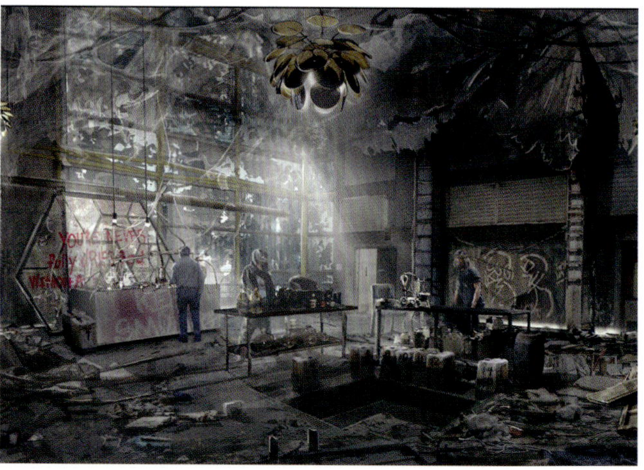

TOP: The dilapidated exterior of the former Happy Face Hotel.

RIGHT: A concept of the Nevermore lobby.

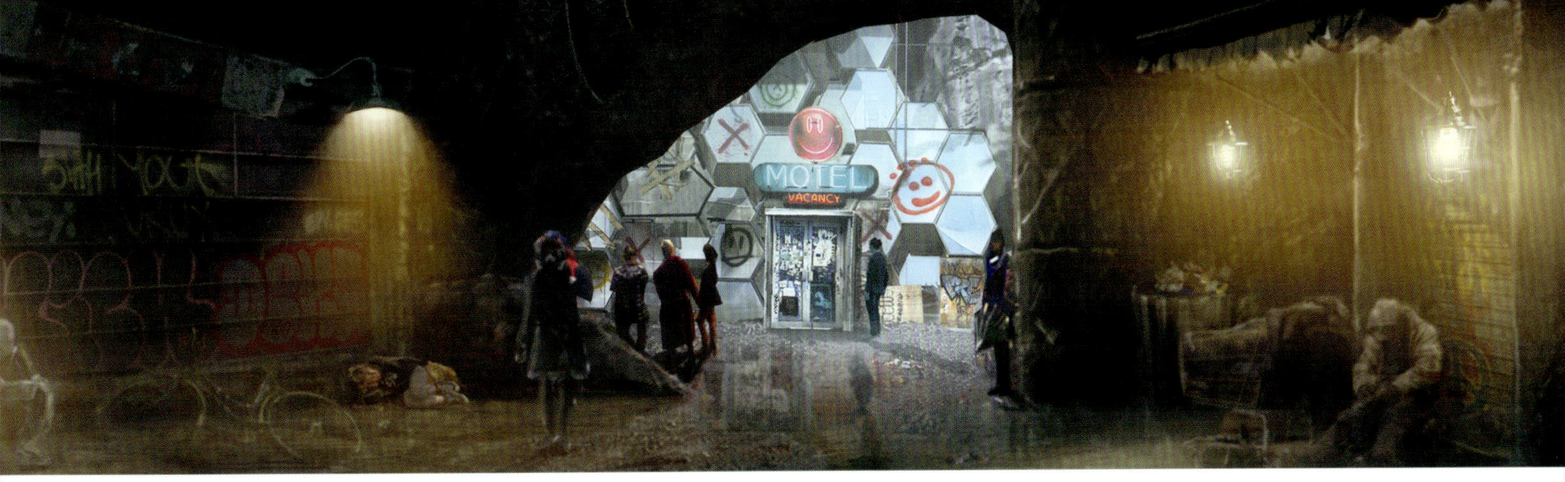

THIS PAGE: Views of the hotels exterior and some of its underwhelming residences.

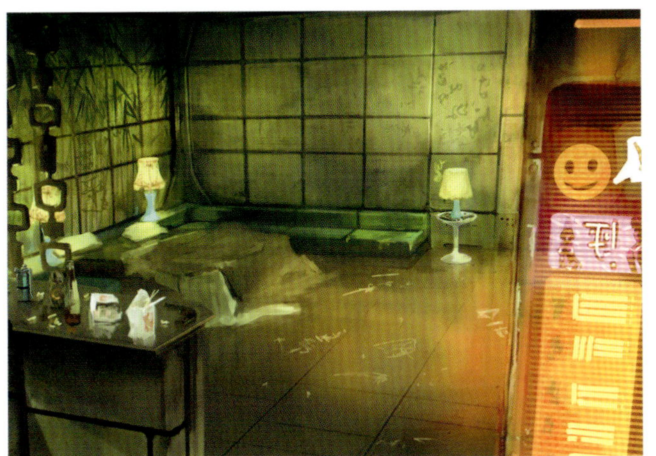

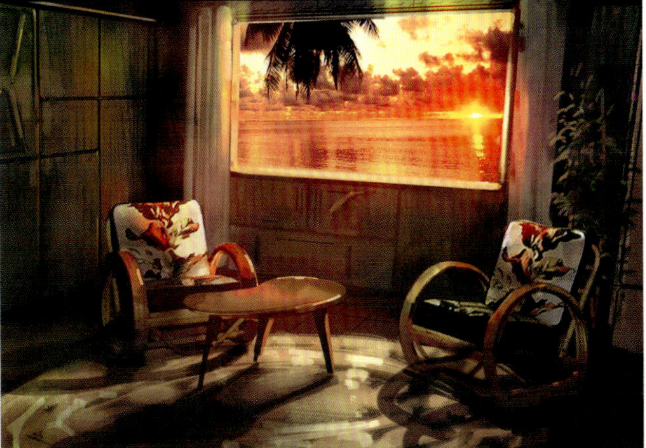

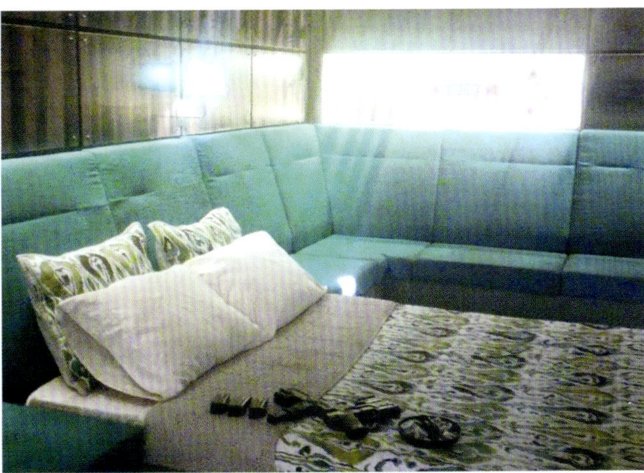

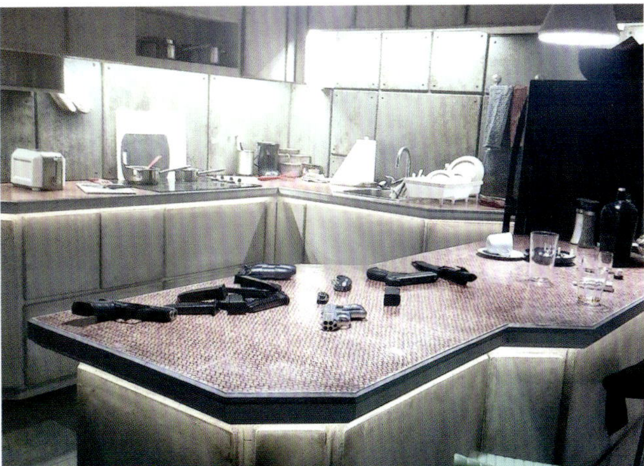

DIG 301

ARCHEOLOGICAL AI

Dig 301 is an AI designed to assist archeologists on Harlan's World dig sites. Unfortunately, there are no more archeologists.

Dina Shihabi, who plays Dig 301, explains that when we meet her, she's "in a world where she has no purpose. And then she connects to Poe, and that changes the course of her life."

Poe and Dig 301 develop a unique relationship, Shihabi continues. "There's a love between us, but it's unclear as to whether it's romantic or not. It feels like a soul connection of two people that understand what it's like to be the other person. They develop this beautiful bond, where Dig helps save Poe, and ultimately, Poe does the same for her. The writers and some directors have said there's something more human about the AIs than there are about the other characters in the show, that there's a simple humanness to them that is really special."

For Dig 301's costume and overall look, Shihabi says, "They took inspiration from Amelia Earhart and *Raiders of the Lost Ark*. They wanted that classic, on-the-field working woman, with a period feel to it. So I have a cargo jacket and a shirt, and high-waisted pants and boots, and my hair is done in a wave, very 50s Hollywood, so there's a masculine and feminine energy to the costume."

To play an AI, Shihabi got guidance from Poe actor Chris Conner. "He taught me how to do little AI personality ticks. There are all of these subtle things that AIs do when they're bringing up a screen in front of them, or looking at something in the database of their minds."

Dig 301 spends a lot of time with Poe and Kovacs in the

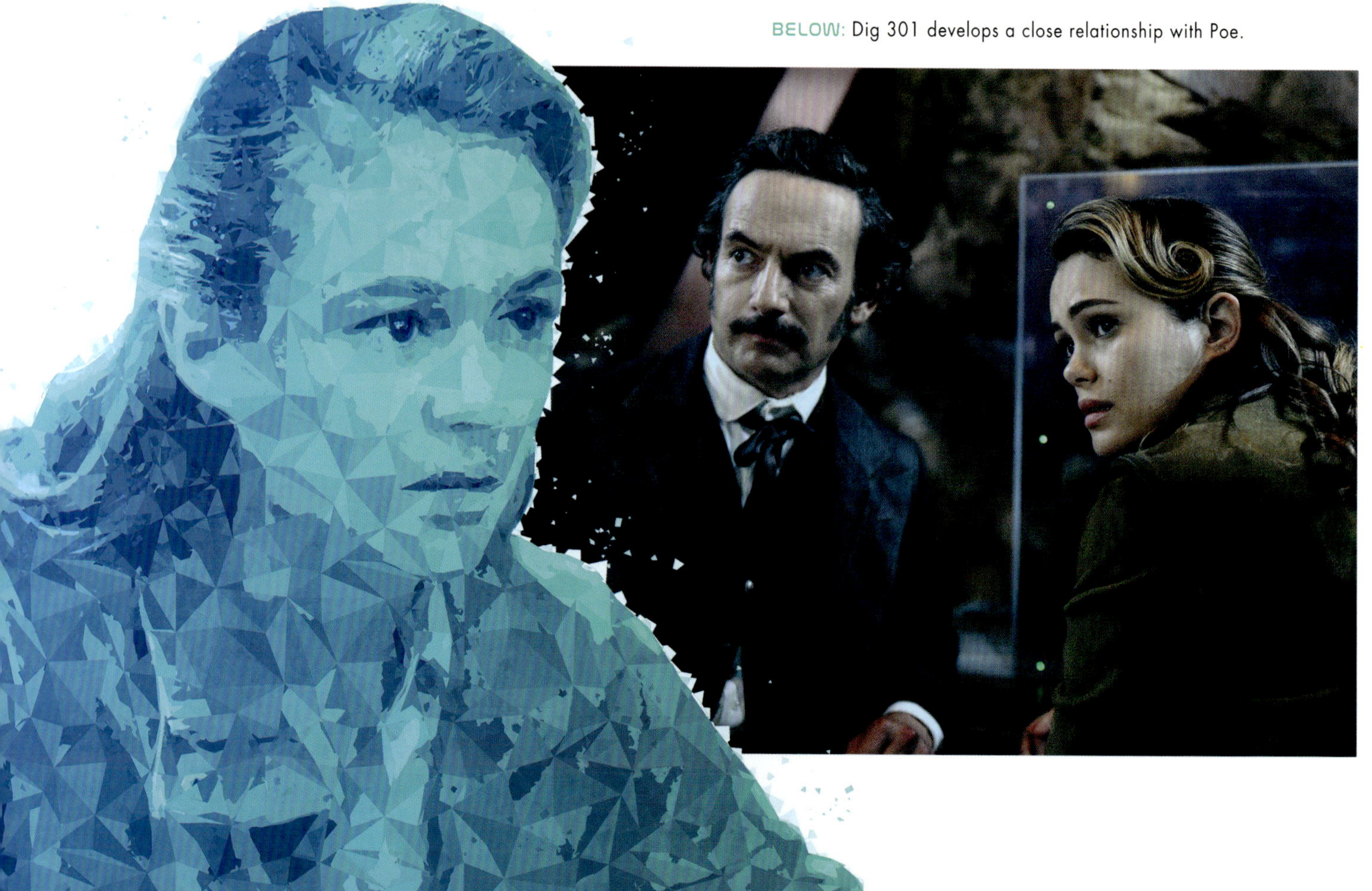

BELOW: Dig 301 develops a close relationship with Poe.

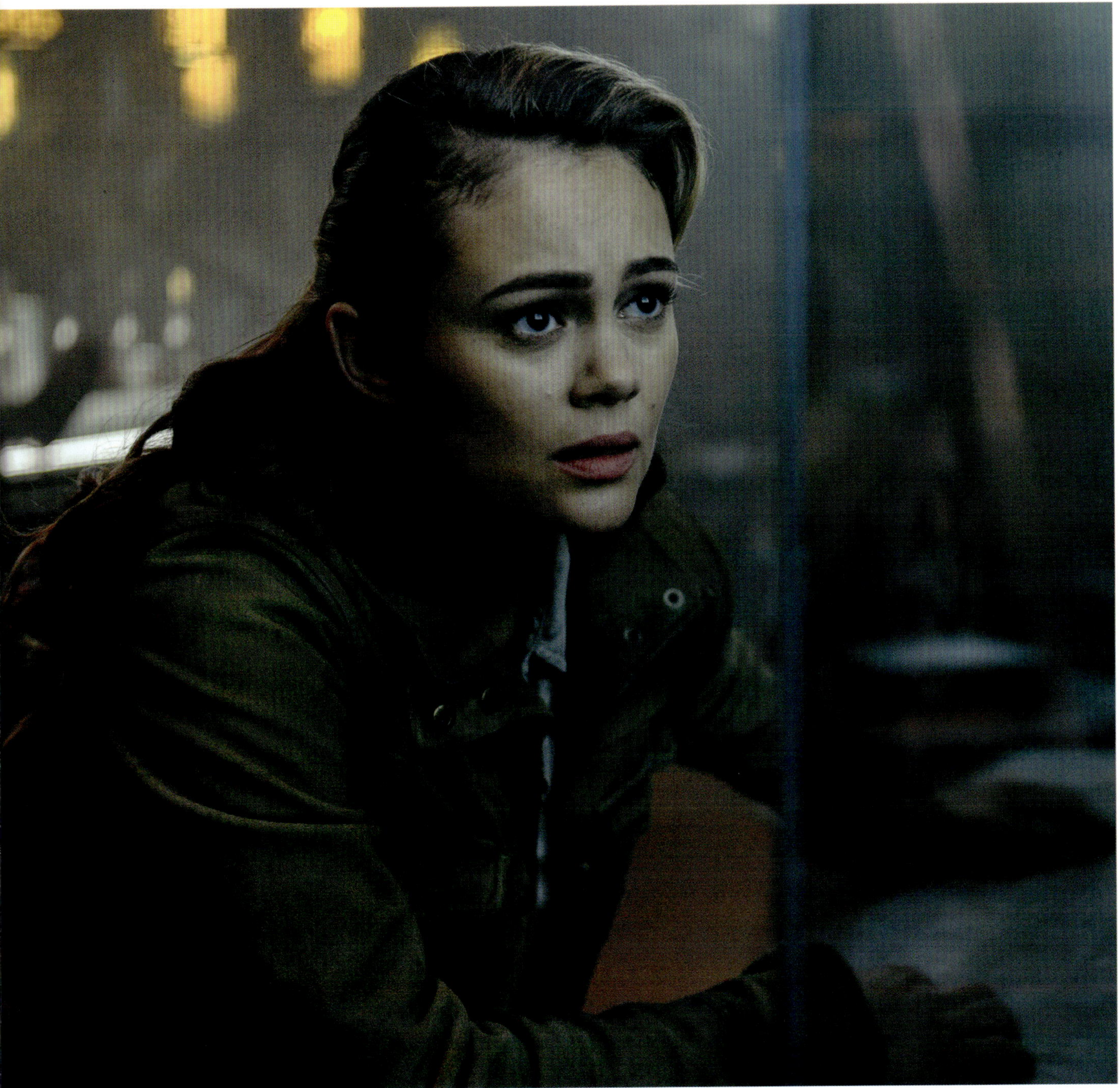

ABOVE: Her history as an acheological AI makes Dig 301 an excellent companion on Kovacs' mission.

Nevermore Hotel, which Shihabi describes as "stunning. What's cool about the set is, you go into a corner where there's a bookshelf, and the books are specifically chosen. I love details like that, that are almost secret, to create the energy of the space."

As for Dig 301's story arc, Shihabi relates, "She comes in to help Poe, but Poe has a lot of problems since last season. He's breaking apart and making mistakes, and so Kovacs decides to give Poe's job to me. So I take over for the Nevermore, and as Kovacs' right hand. That's hard on [the Dig 301/Poe] relationship, because I've just taken away Poe's purpose. It's a story about what you will do for the people you love. It has a lot of action, but I think what makes sci-fi really special is that, in that heightened space, you get to connect to deeply human themes in a way that allows you to experience them without a boundary."

COLONEL IVAN CARRERA

MANY FACES MANY NAMES

In season two, we meet Colonel Ivan Carrera, played by Torben Liebrecht. Then it turns out we already know him.

Executive producer James Middleton explains, "Carrera is a military and tactical genius who is not allowed to keep his name or sleeve after his victories. He is spun down after engagements until he is needed for the next war. However, in season two it is revealed that Carrera is actually Jaeger [played by Daniel Bernhardt] from season one."

Jaeger was young Kovacs' Praetorian recruiter and mentor, who brought down the Envoys during the original rebellion. Now, as Carrera, he's the leader of the Protectorate Special Forces Team, aka the Wedge, the military's ultimate weapon. When Carrera learns that his erstwhile protégé Kovacs is on Harlan's World, once more fighting for Quellcrist Falconer, the colonel attempts to set a trap by bringing back Kovacs Prime.

Liebrecht admires Bernhardt's performance as Jaeger, but didn't try to imitate it. "I was very aware of what Daniel did, and there are certain details that you will be able to find if you look for them, but in general, it's new sleeve, new rules."

For Carrera's combat sequences, Liebrecht's background in martial arts was helpful. "I was happy that I could use those skills, but I had to master how to make things look more dramatic, more specific. I learned from so many talented, patient stunt performers. Getting to spend time with them, and pick their brains, was one of the great perks of being in *Altered Carbon*."

BELOW: Jaeger recruited Kovacs to the Praetorians centuries before.

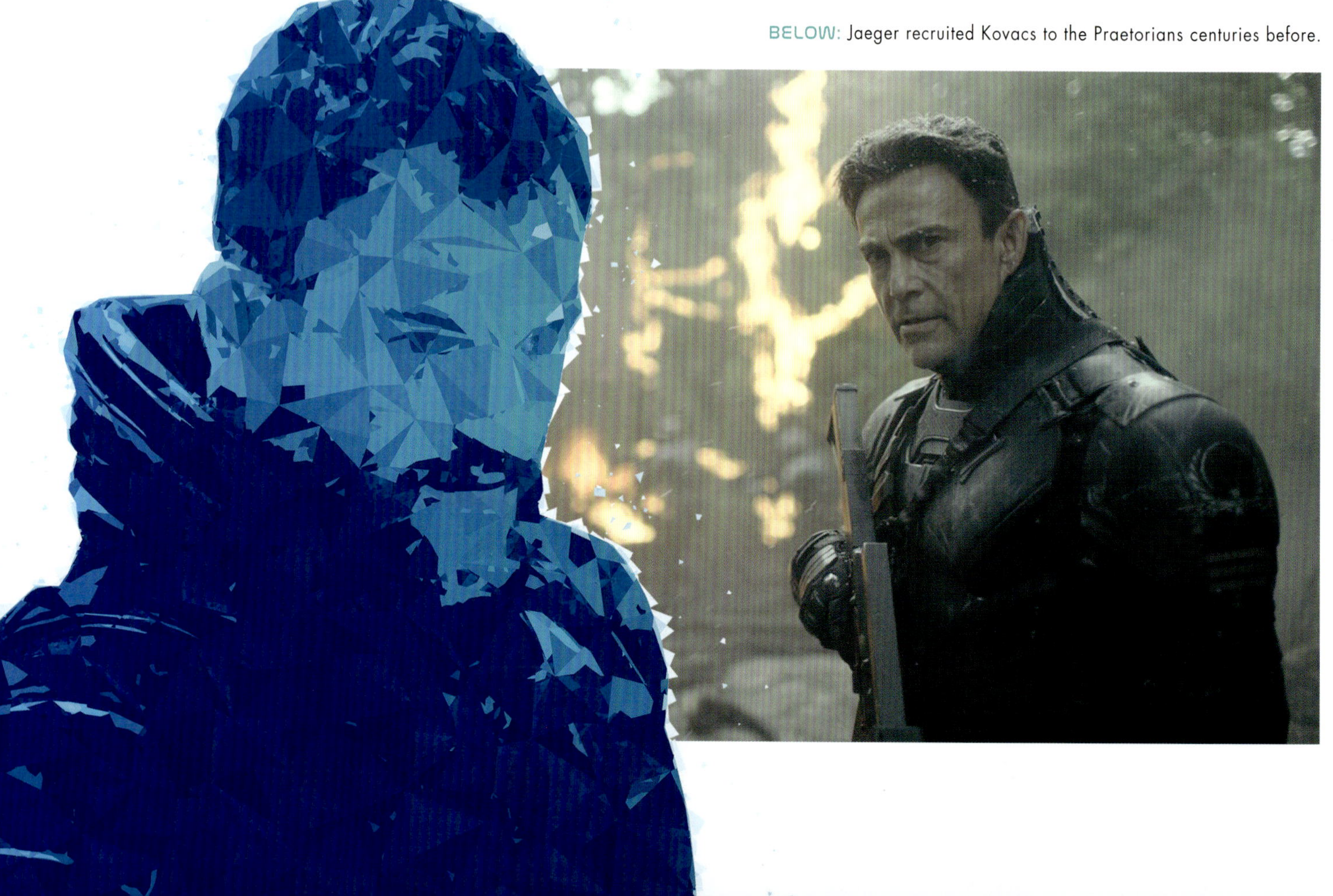

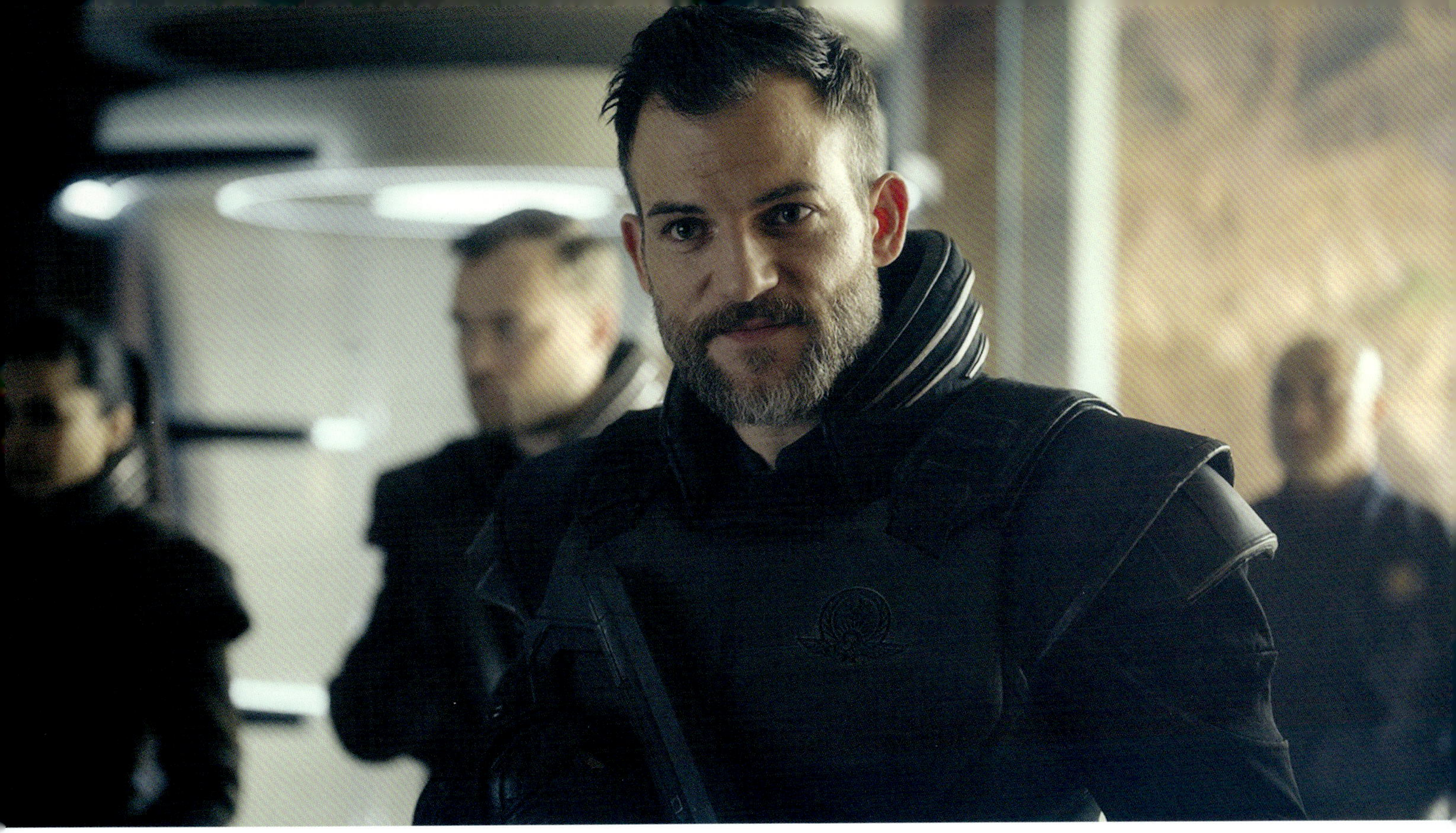

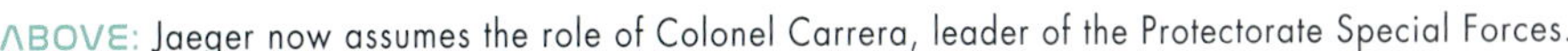

ABOVE: Jaeger now assumes the role of Colonel Carrera, leader of the Protectorate Special Forces.

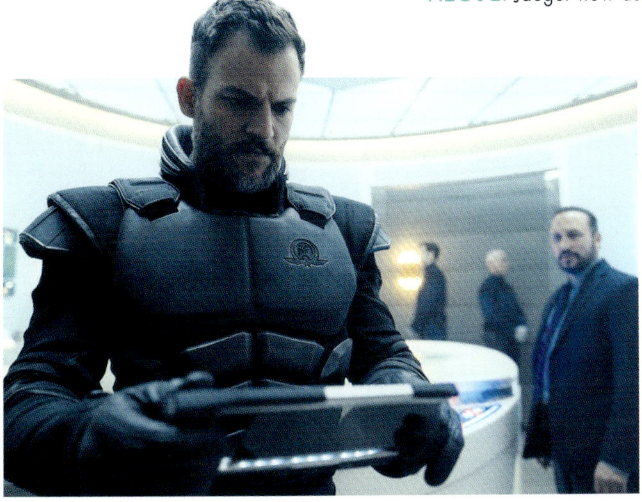

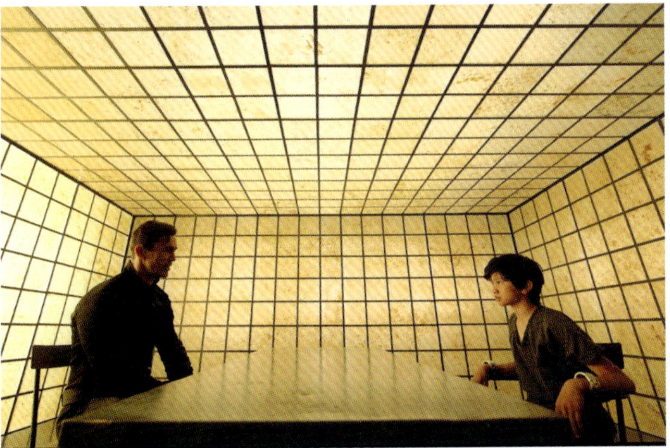

Liebrecht continues, "I love the opportunity to explore the vulnerability of a character that seems to be bulletproof. Carrera's constantly being put on ice and brought back up again. He sees that as an honor, and he's willing to pay the price. But on the other hand, there is something that he sees in Kovacs that he just can't let go of. That obsession is foremost a fatherly love. That's rewarding fodder for me as an actor. It's about finding purpose in your life."

"[Carrera] is not a cut and dried villain," points out show runner Alison Schapker. "From his point of view, he rescued Kovacs when Kovacs was a lost and abused kid. He took Kovacs under his wing and mentored him. He took pride in the soldier Kovacs became. And then Kovacs betrayed him. [Carrera] wants revenge, but underneath his anger, he is driven by a longing to reconnect to the man he once thought of as a son. As writers, we were interested in what would happen if [they] crossed paths again."

Liebrecht saw *Altered Carbon* season one before he was involved with the series. "It was unlike anything I had ever seen in a TV show. Sometimes I felt like I was being pulled into a fever dream, because of the complexity and the unity of this universe, and the conflicts the show is dealing with. There is so much philosophy underneath that. It's a show that constantly discusses the terms of what humanity is."

TANASEDA HIDEKI

AN OLD FRIEND

Tanaseda Hideki, played by James Saito, is a powerful Yakuza warlord, who is secretly one of the Founders of Harlan's World. He favors tailored suits, and is described in the script as having a voice like iron in velvet. In his courtyard garden, Tanaseda grows bonsai (miniature) Songspire trees, the first to be successfully cultivated in captivity. Like their full-sized kin, the bonsais glow and 'sing.'

Yukito, Tanaseda's great-grandson, wants to be like him, but where Tanaseda is restrained and lethal, Yukito is impulsive and error-prone. Kovacs pretends to be Tanaseda in a military sleeve when he's accosted by Yukito. Kovacs doesn't yet know of Yukito's family connection, but he's aware that all Yakuza venerate Tanaseda.

Tanaseda feels that he still owes Kovacs from a time after Stronghold fell. Kovacs had done a job for Tanaseda and was tortured for information by the Protectorate, but never talked. Tanaseda gives Kovacs the Happy Face Hotel in compensation and agrees to help Kovacs and Quell get off-world. The older man confides to Kovacs his growing doubts about resleeving. Perhaps the spirit degrades if it is moved too many times from body to body.

Tanaseda goes to Danica Harlan's Harlan's Day party. When fellow Founder Dugan tells Tanaseda he shouldn't be there, Tanaseda responds, "After what we've done, none of us should be here."

Tanaseda knows that Quell will kill him because he is a Founder. He leaves a message for Kovacs, telling him to forgive her. Quell respects Tanaseda enough to make his death painless.

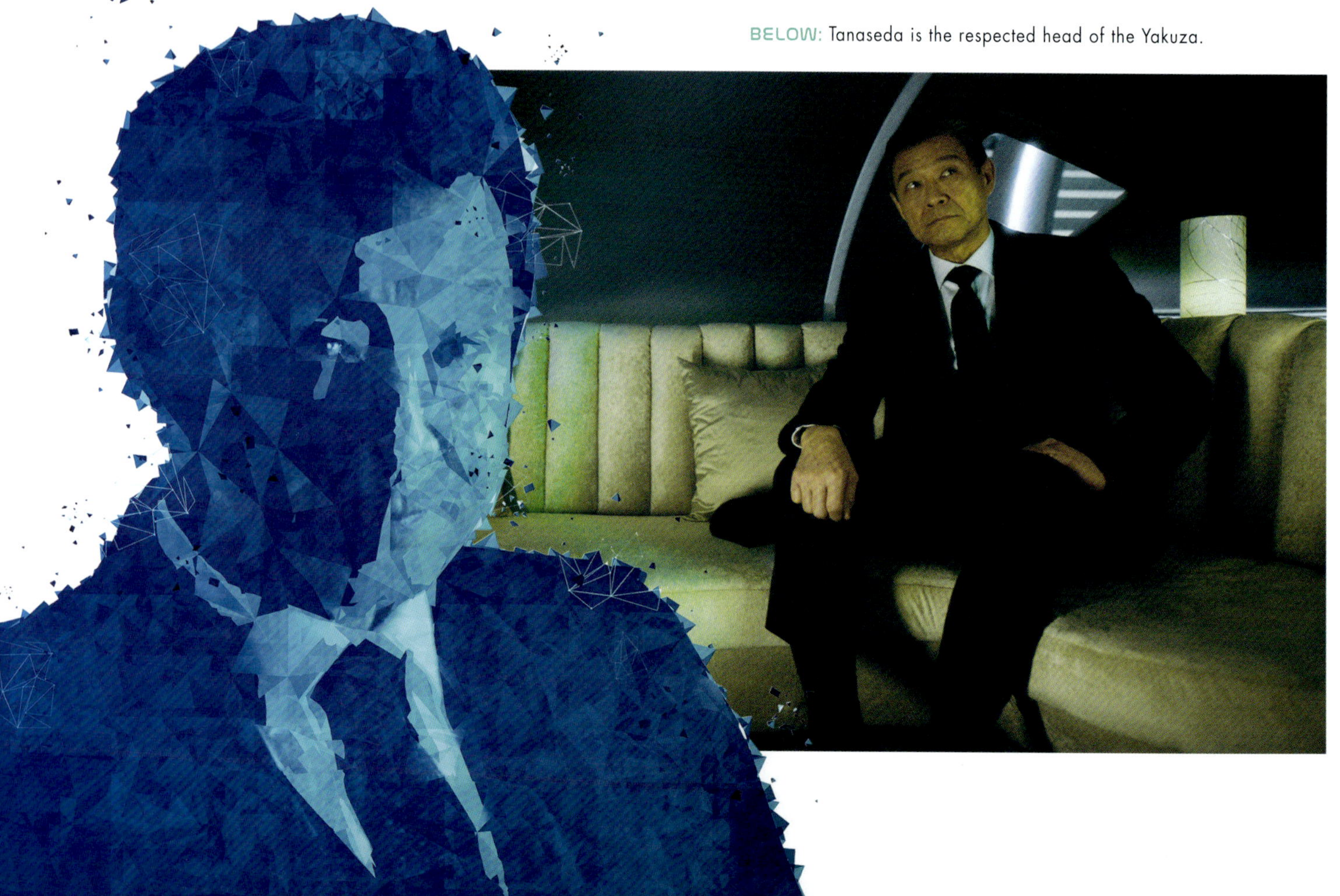

BELOW: Tanaseda is the respected head of the Yakuza.

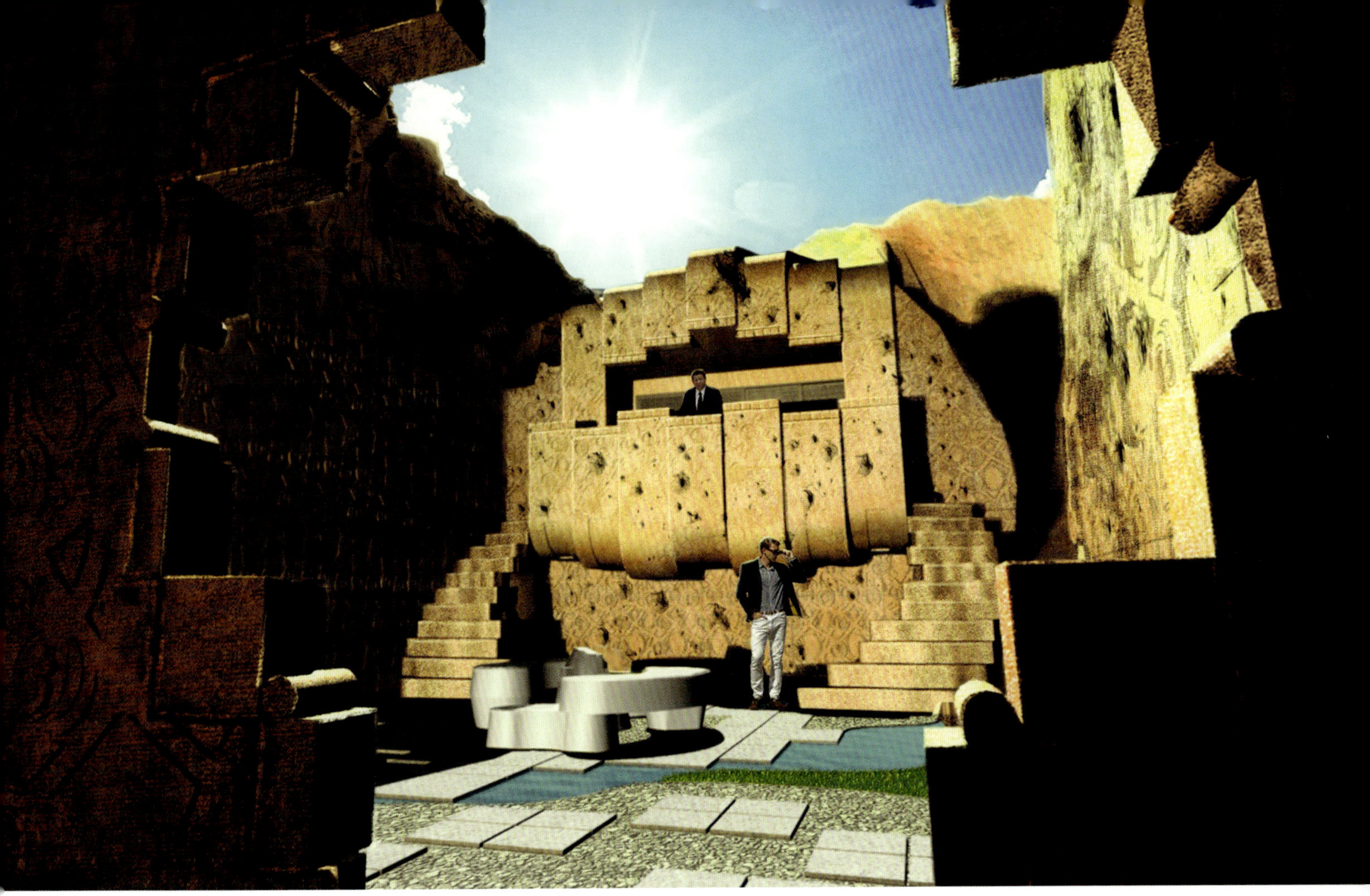

BELOW: Tanaseda owes a debt to Kovacs for Stronghold's fall.

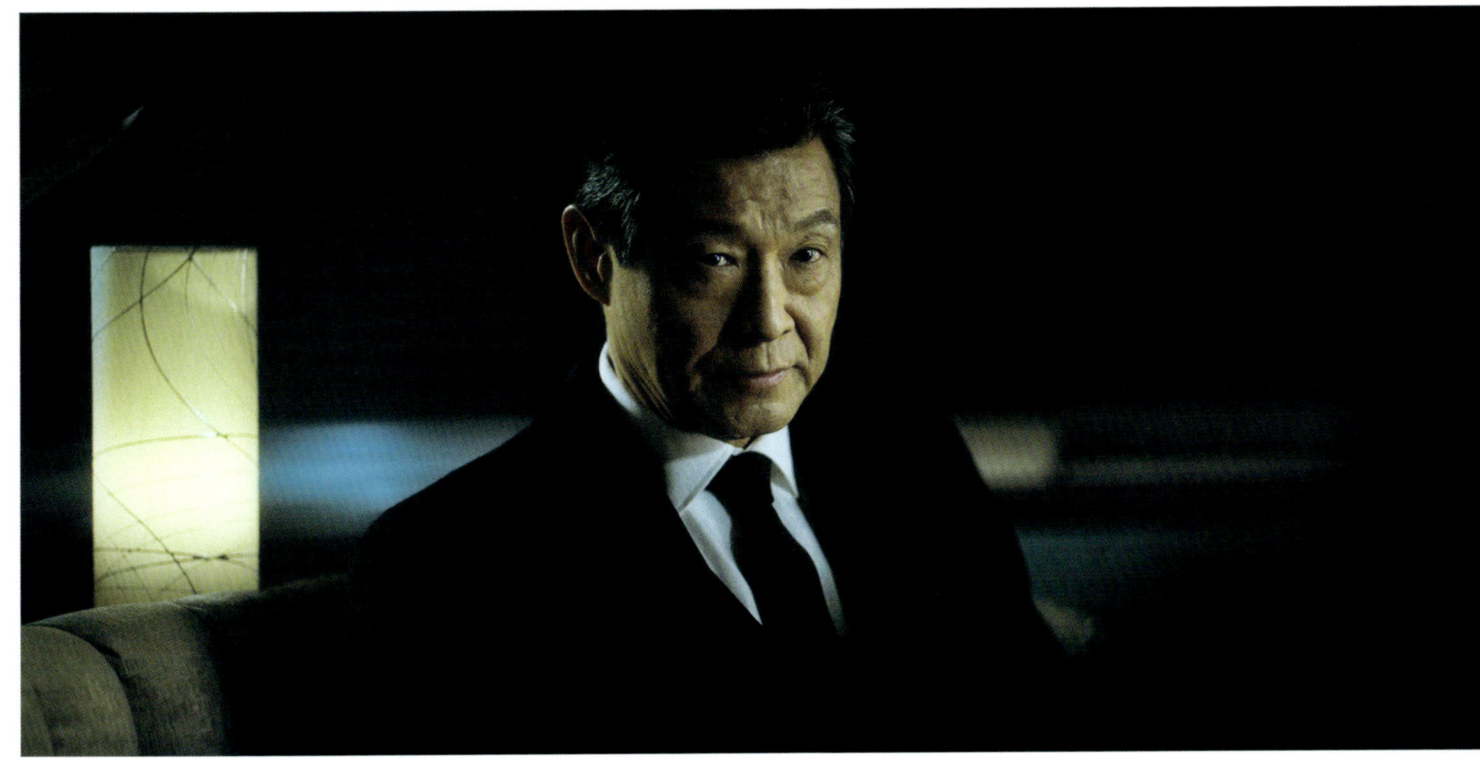

THE ELDERS

WHAT CAME BEFORE US

The Elders were the original sentient inhabitants on Harlan's World. The Founders claim that the Elders were gone before humans arrived, but in fact, the Founders exterminated them in an act of planet-wide xenocide then appropriated the Elders' technology.

Executive producer James Middleton says, "The Elders, or what is left of them, shows the limitations of human understanding. They illustrate how little human civilization knows about the universe and how we exploit resources and technology we don't fully understand. Richard Morgan describes the Elders as winged creatures in his books. We took that basic information and fully developed the Elder anatomy with WETA Workshop in New Zealand. We wanted the Elders to exhibit a beauty of their own, but not to make them anthropomorphic. The design was also informed by what we devised to be the Elders' methods of communication and written language. A lot of thought by our entire team was put into the Elder design and that, in turn, influenced the set design, architecture, topography, and hieroglyphs of Harlan's World."

THIS PAGE: Early concept art of the Elders, ancient winged creatures that originally inhabited Harlan's World.

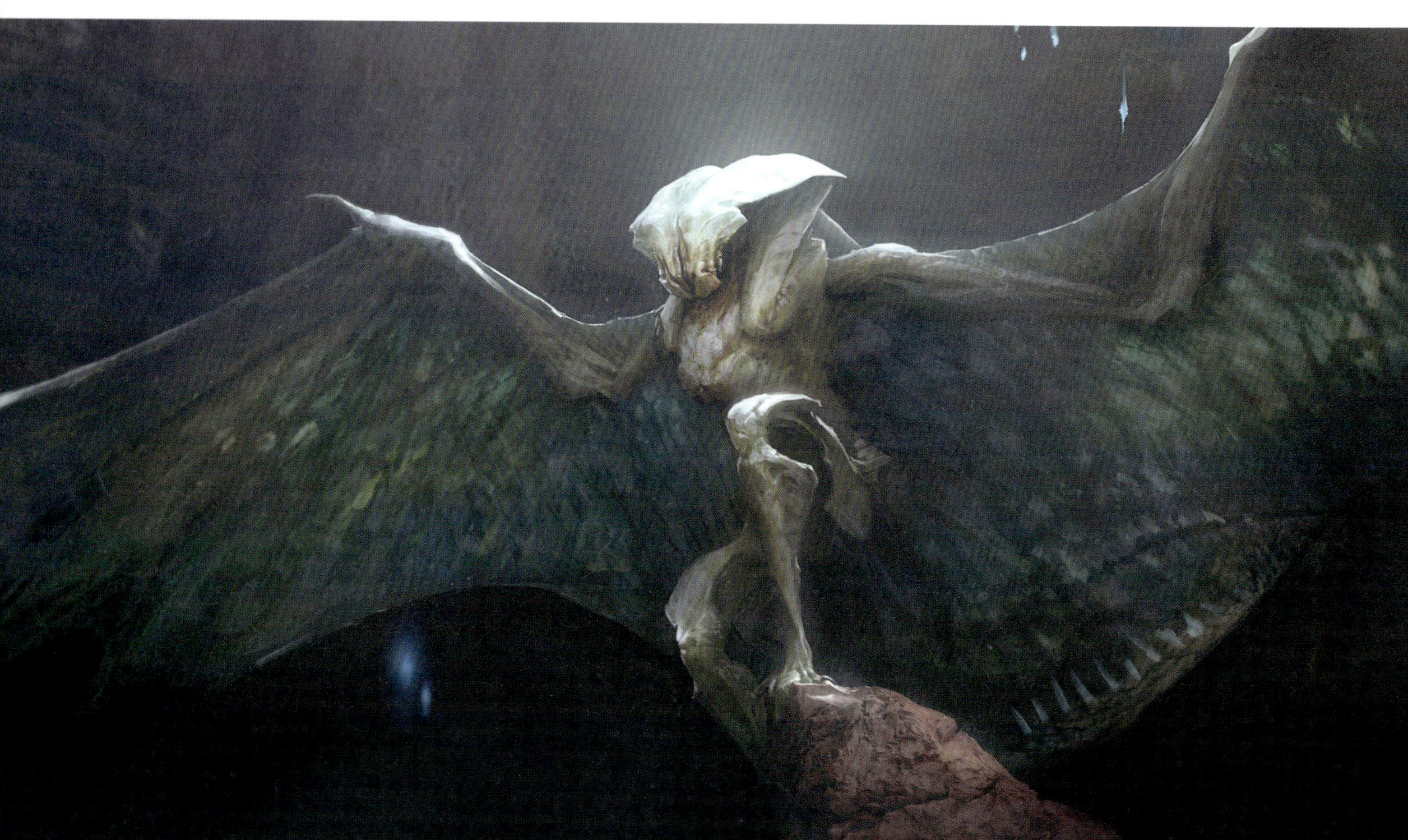

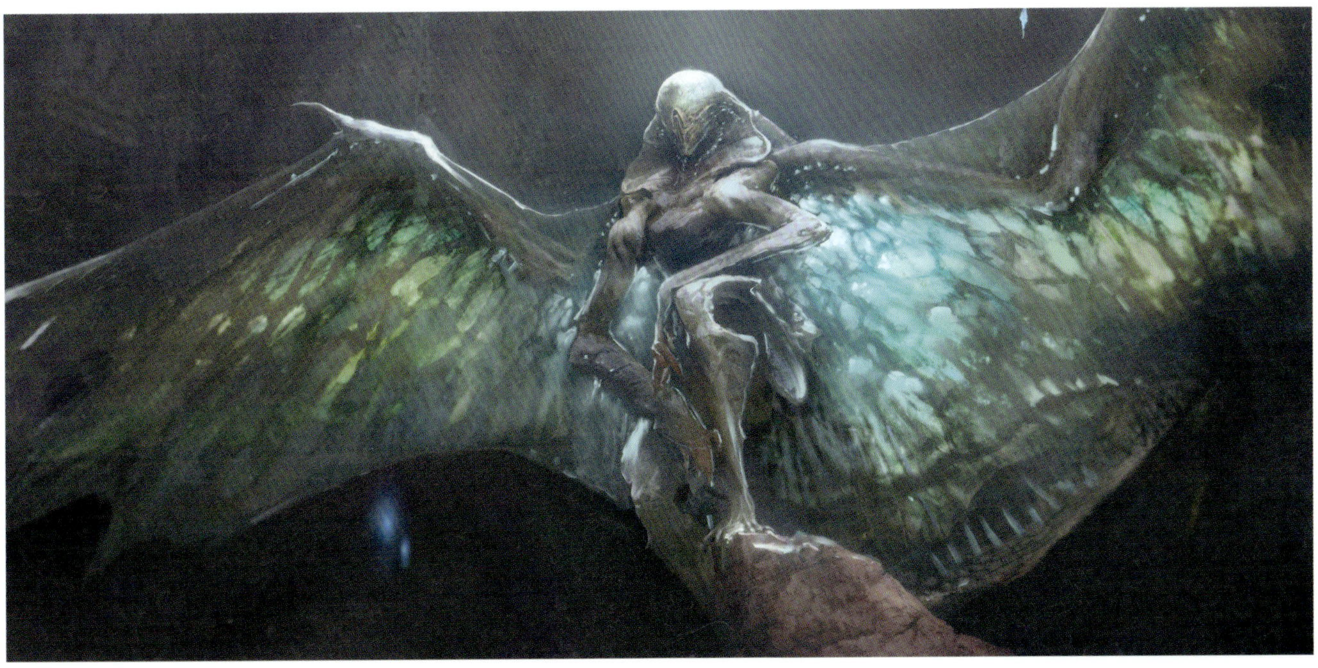

THIS PAGE: Different variations on the early concept art of the Elders, who had some intrinsic relation to the Songspire trees.

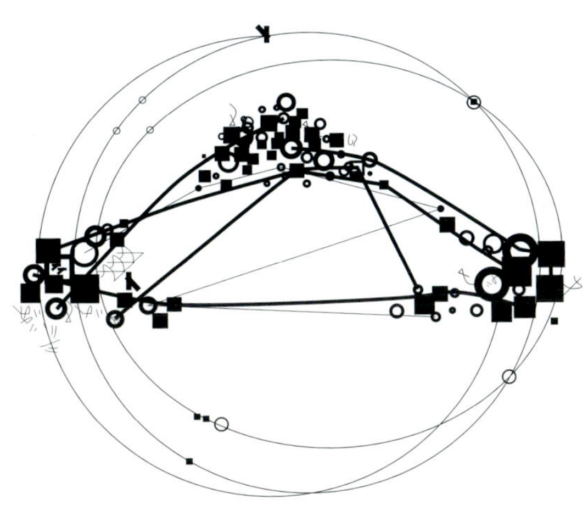

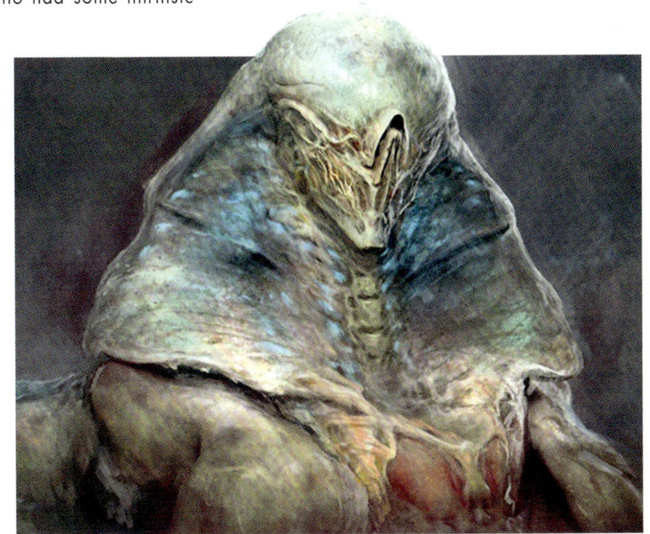

BELOW: While developing the design of the Elders, the concept artists also created a language.

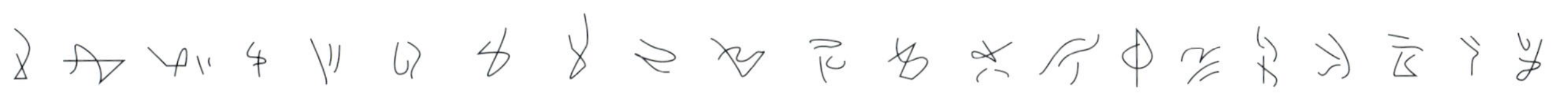

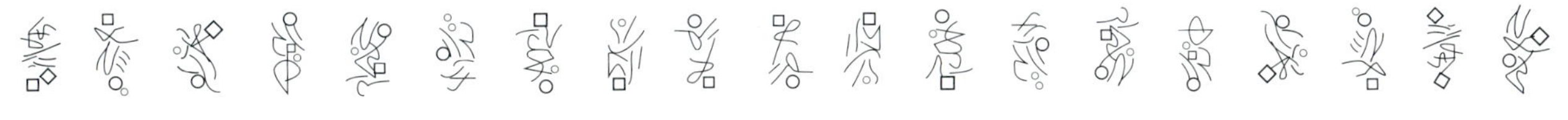

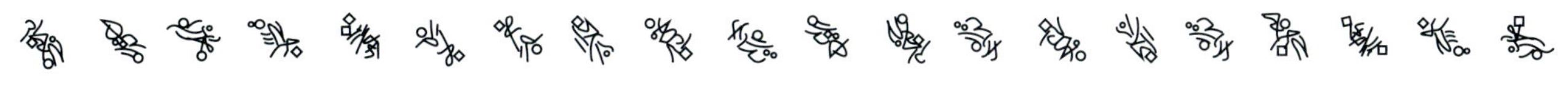

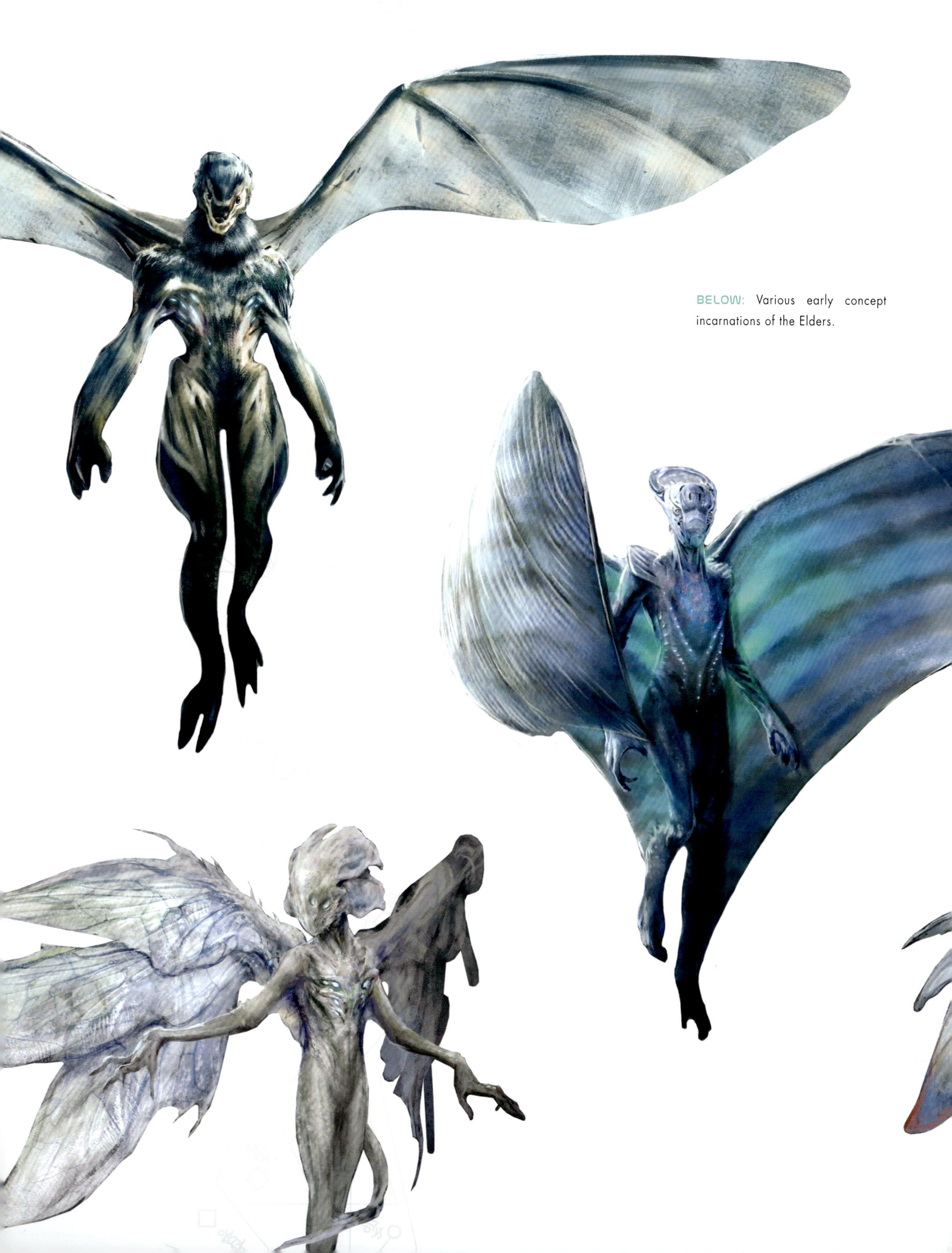

BELOW: Various early concept incarnations of the Elders.

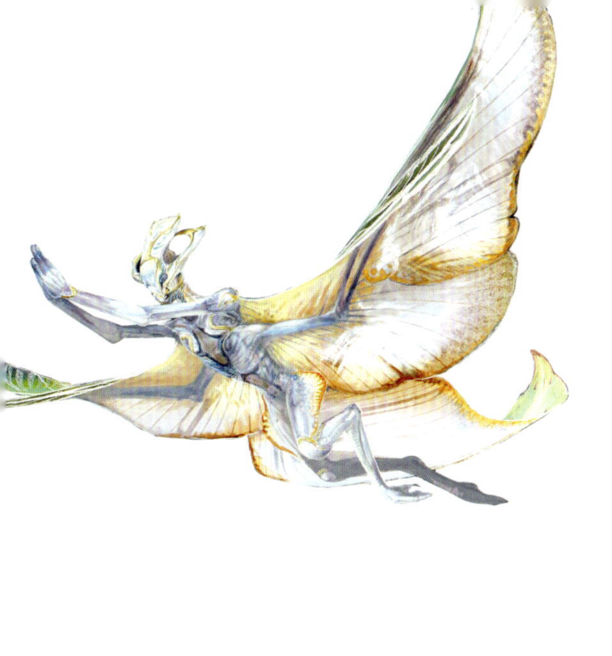

Season two VFX supervisor Robert Munroe expands on this. "They're nine-foot-tall, terrifying-looking creatures. There's a combination of human quality, some insect quality, and some birdlike quality to them. When you see them, and they move, they look very threatening, but the other thing about them that is quite remarkable is that they're highly intelligent. This is the species that effectively discovered and evolved the technology that made stack technology possible, and they're very protective of society and family. We don't necessarily see a lot of that. We do see one VR scene at Tanaseda's, where you've got a family of Elders that's been completely burned to ash, but still maintain their huddled shape as they're covering over the atrocity that's been exacted upon them. So that's a little bit of back story. It's not shown a lot during the show, but we will see the Elders, and we will understand a bit more about their history. It's quite sad when you realize that humans have arrived and decimated the planet, and decimated the species."

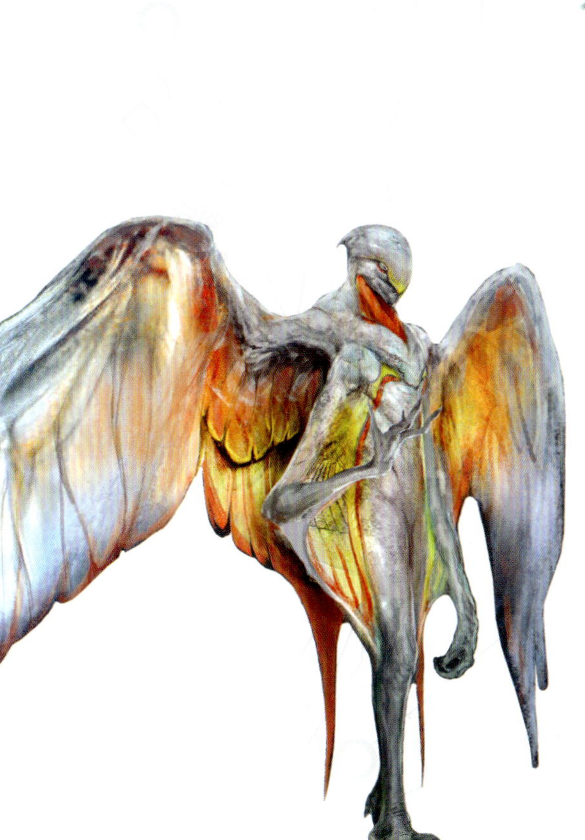

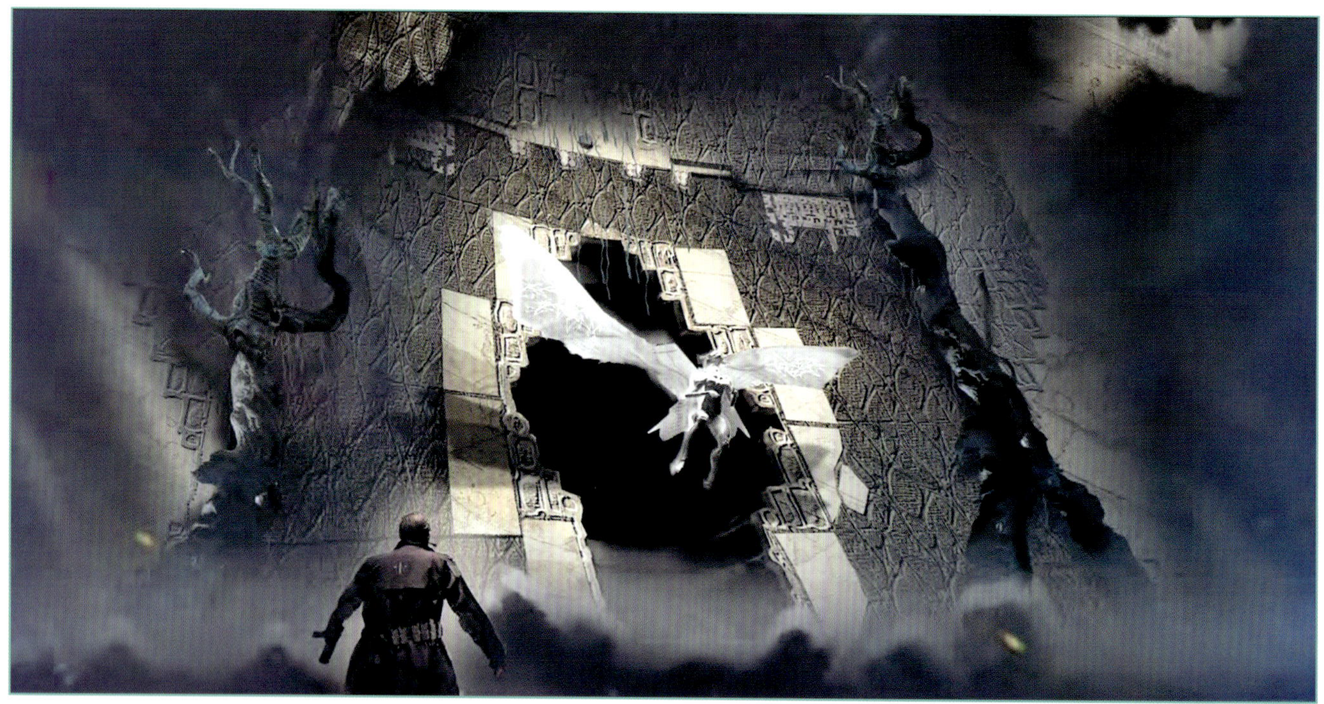

ABOVE: Sketch of a human encounter with an Elder. BELOW: A close-up early concept of the aliens.

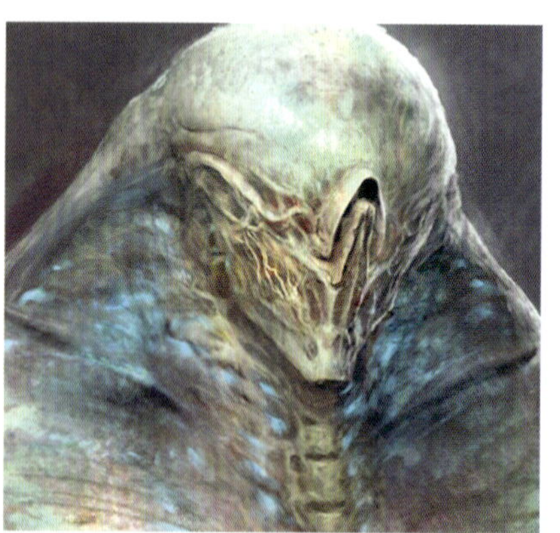

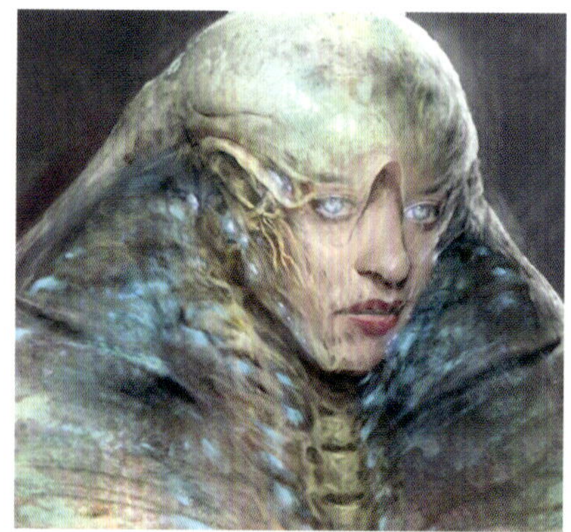

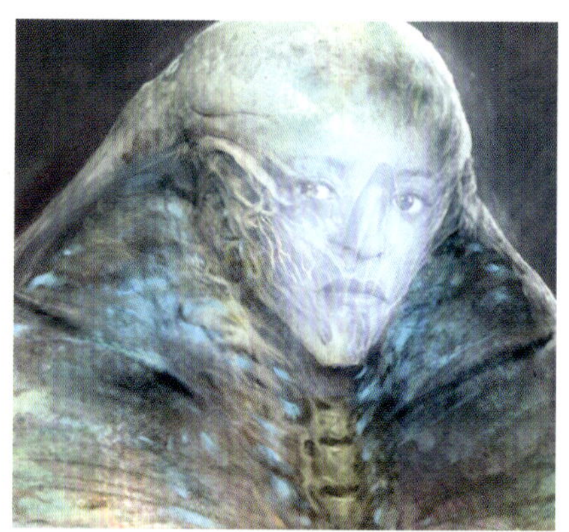

BELOW: 3D render of one of the early concept designs.

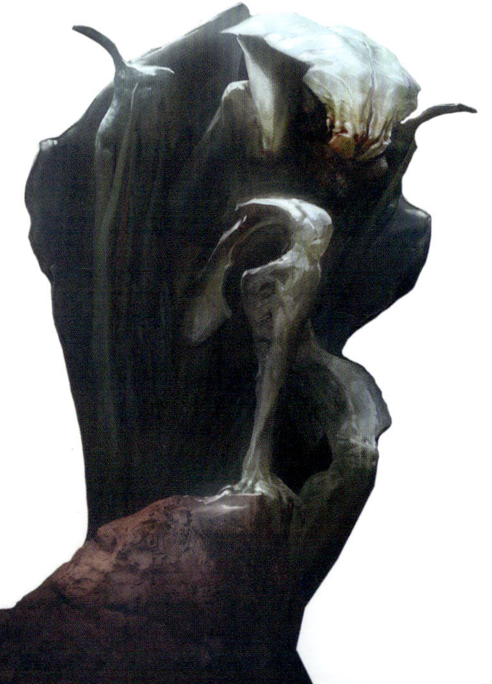

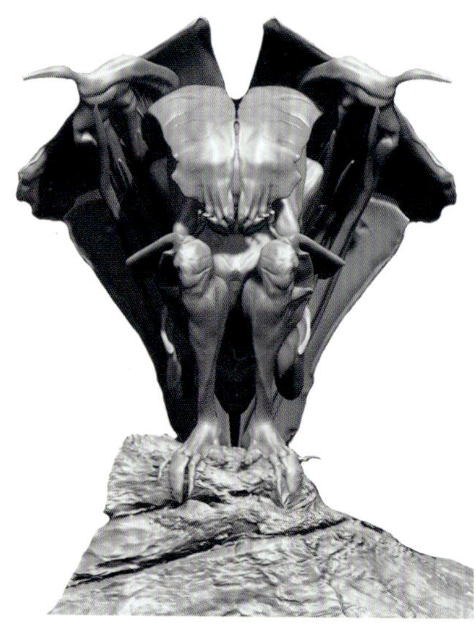

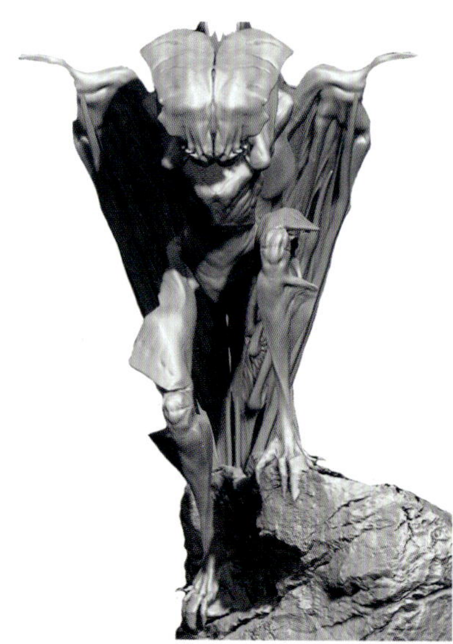

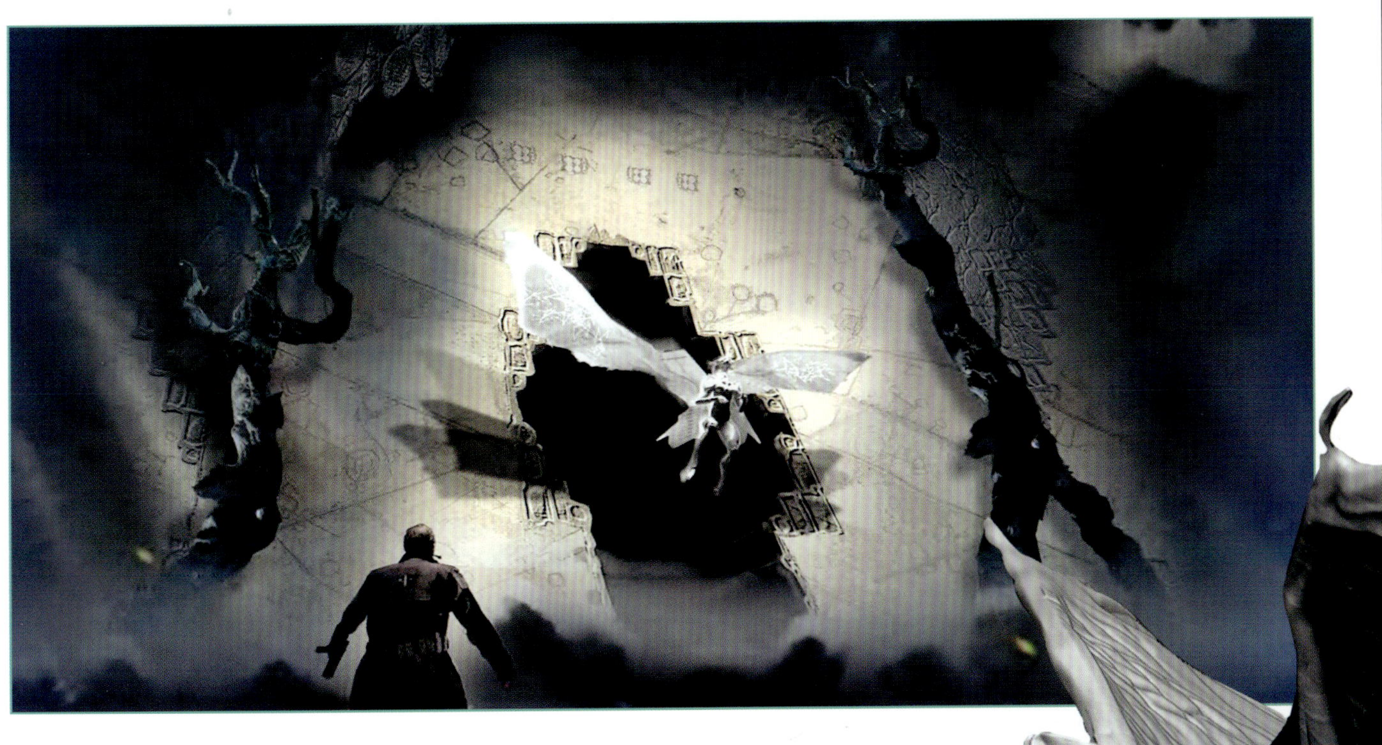

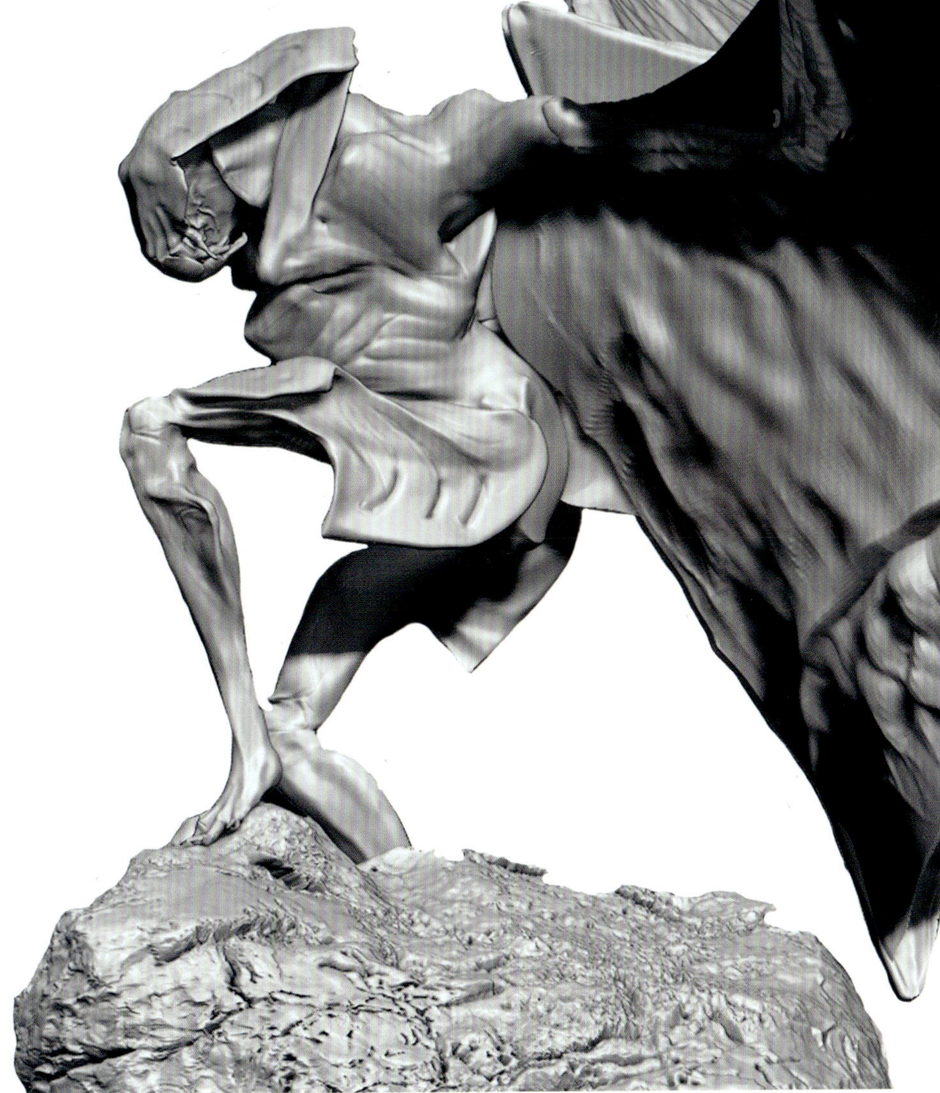

At the time of this interview, Munroe's team is still working on the Elders, so it's too early for him to know certain specifics. "They'll be completely CG-modeled. In terms of how we animate them, it might be key-frame animation, although I am making a push for motion capture."

Middleton adds that the Elders are clearly connected to the Songspire trees still found on Harlan's World. "[The trees] appear in Richard Morgan's novels. They are beautiful and mysterious, and their function is not completely known. While humans call them 'trees' and perceive them as being alive, they are also a technology that the Elders employed in architecture and other ways. In season two, it will be revealed that the Songspire trees have an important function as vessels containing the emotion and spirits of those who are close to them. They are essentially the original 'stack' system used by the Elders."

RIGHT: An early 3D render of an Elder.

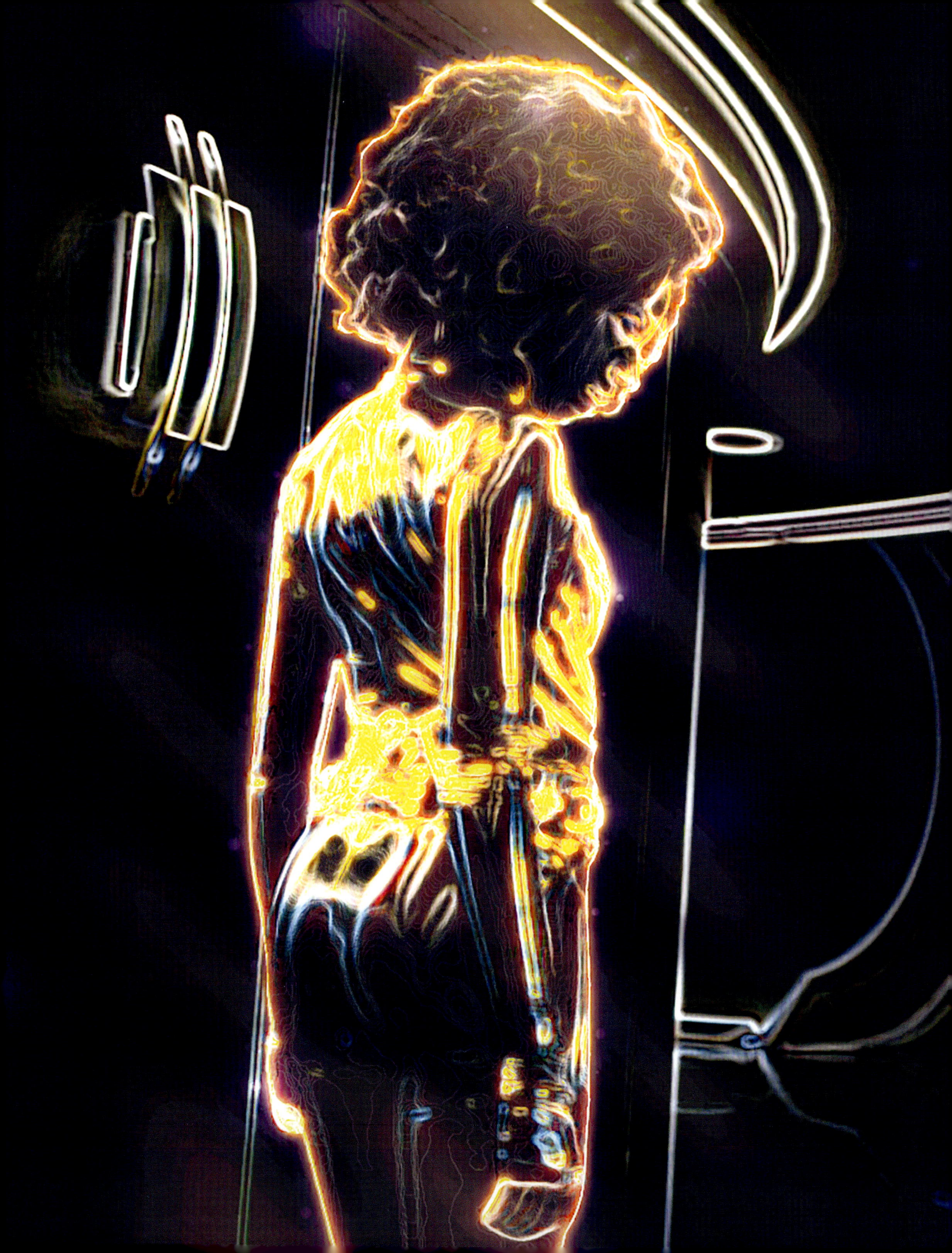

物語 STORYBOARDS

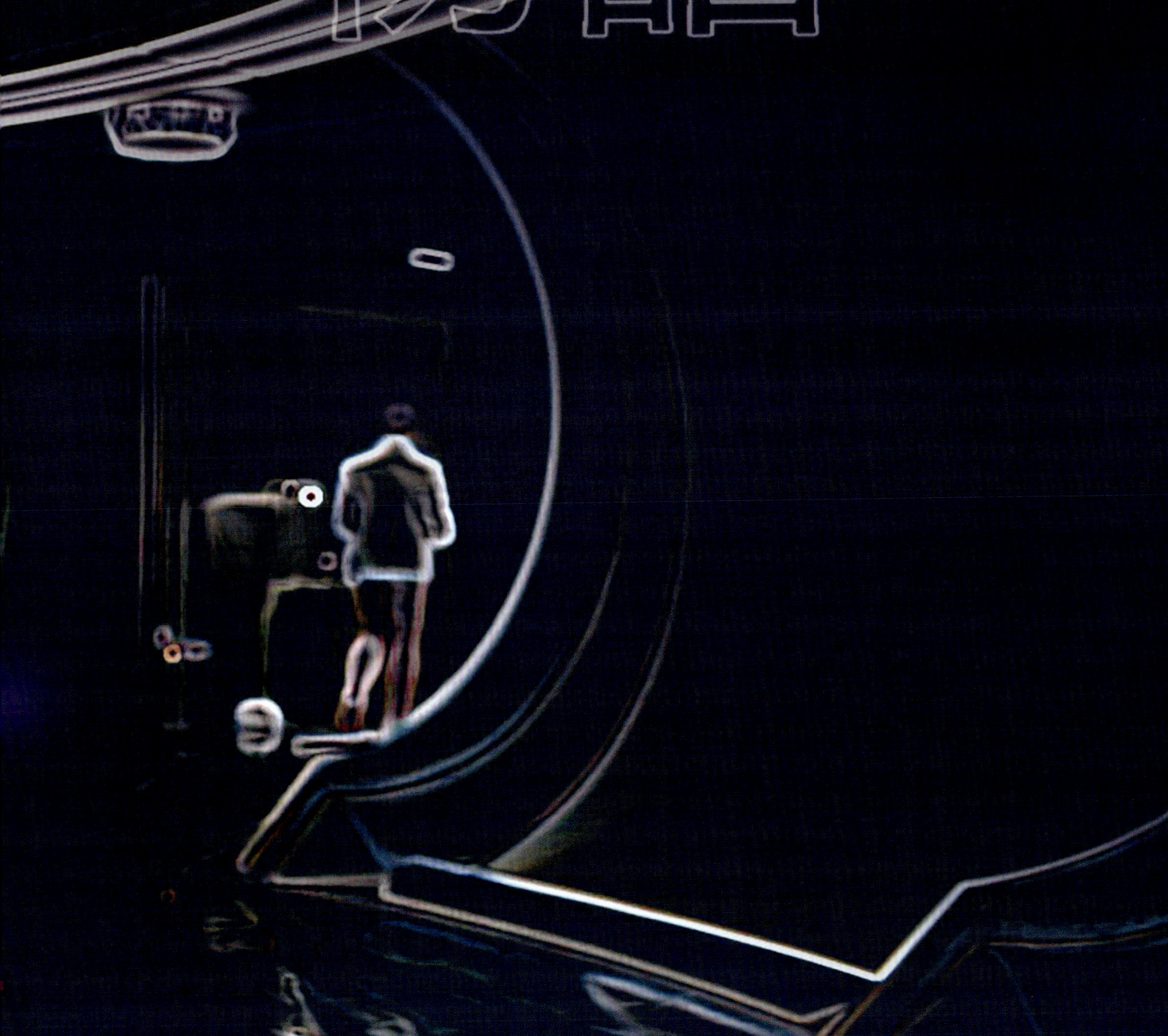

SEASON ONE EPISODE SEVEN SCENE THIRTEEN

Storyboards are shot-by-shot illustrations of sequences that help the director and production team plan everything from camera placement to stunts to props. In this flashback sequence, we see the surprise reunion of siblings Kovacs (Will Yun Lee) and Reileen (Dichen Lachman), who have not seen one another since childhood. Kovacs is now a CTAC Praetorian, part of a task force assigned to bring down a Yakuza clan that employs/owns Reileen. Kovacs recognizes Reileen because she's wearing their mother's necklace. When Kovacs removes his helmet, Reileen realizes he's her brother. The two go within an instant from strangers trying to kill one another to blood kindred protecting each other, fighting back to back against CTAC and Yakuza soldiers who were only moments ago their comrades-in-arms.

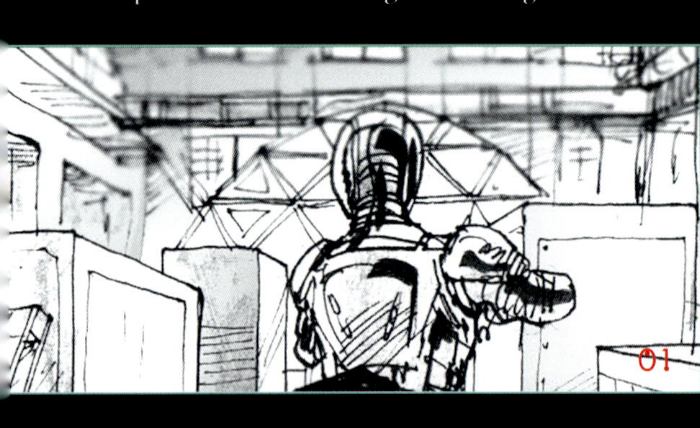

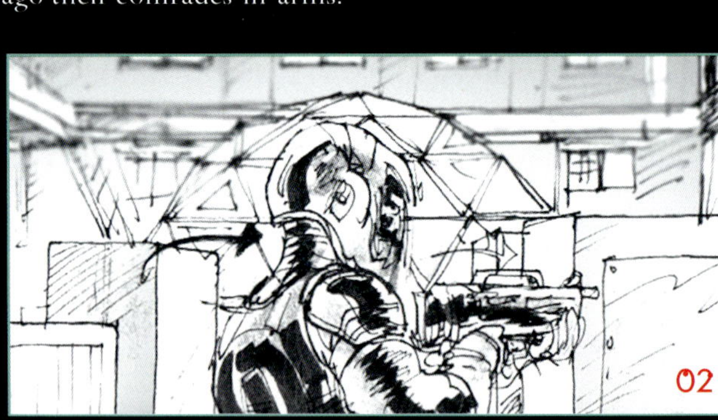

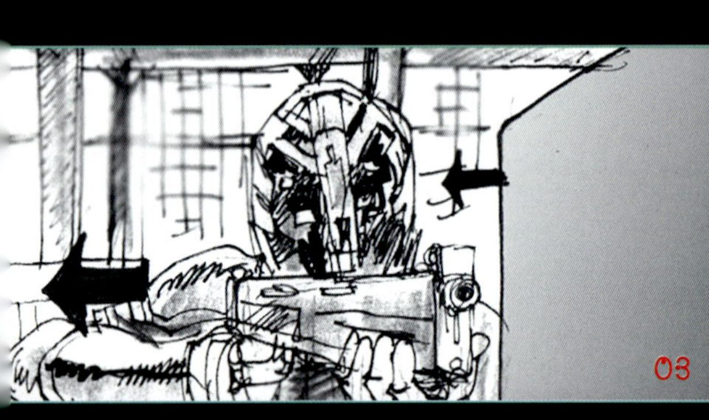

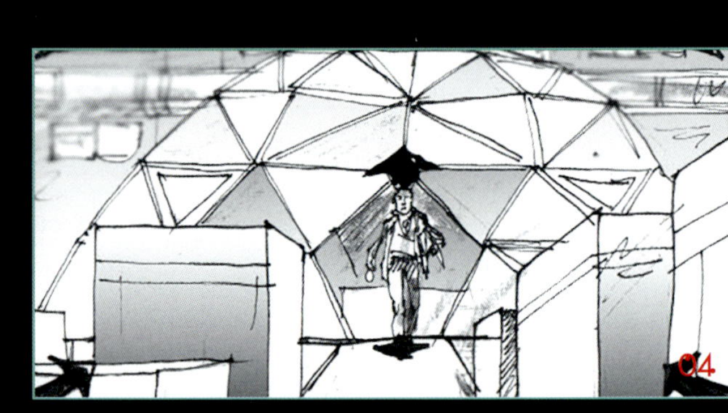

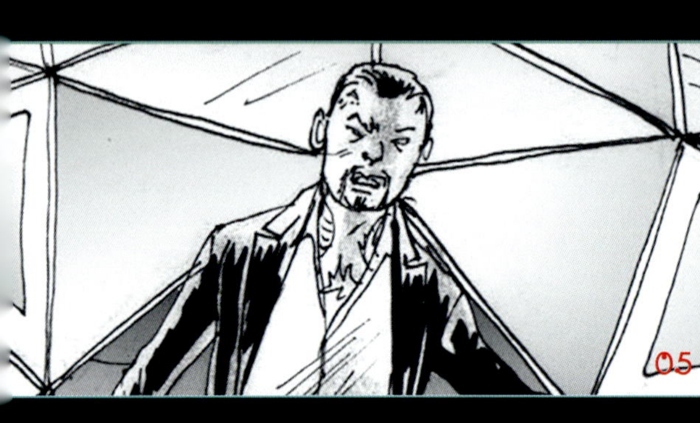

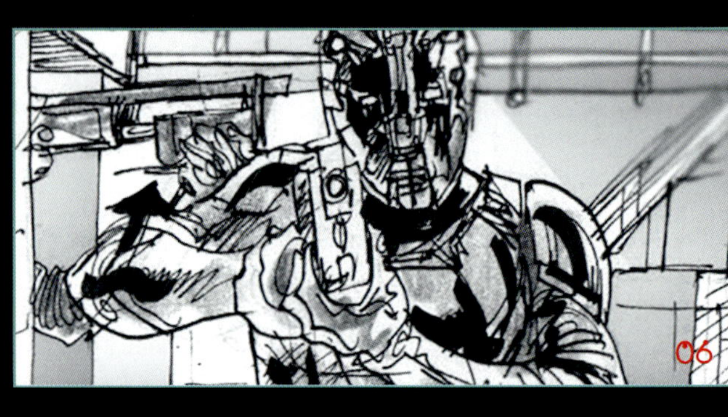

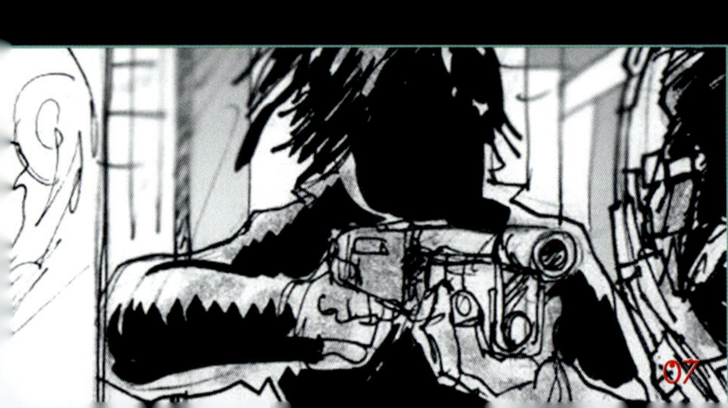

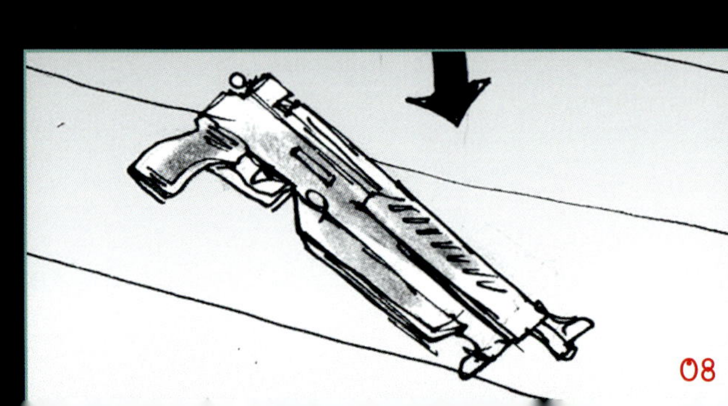

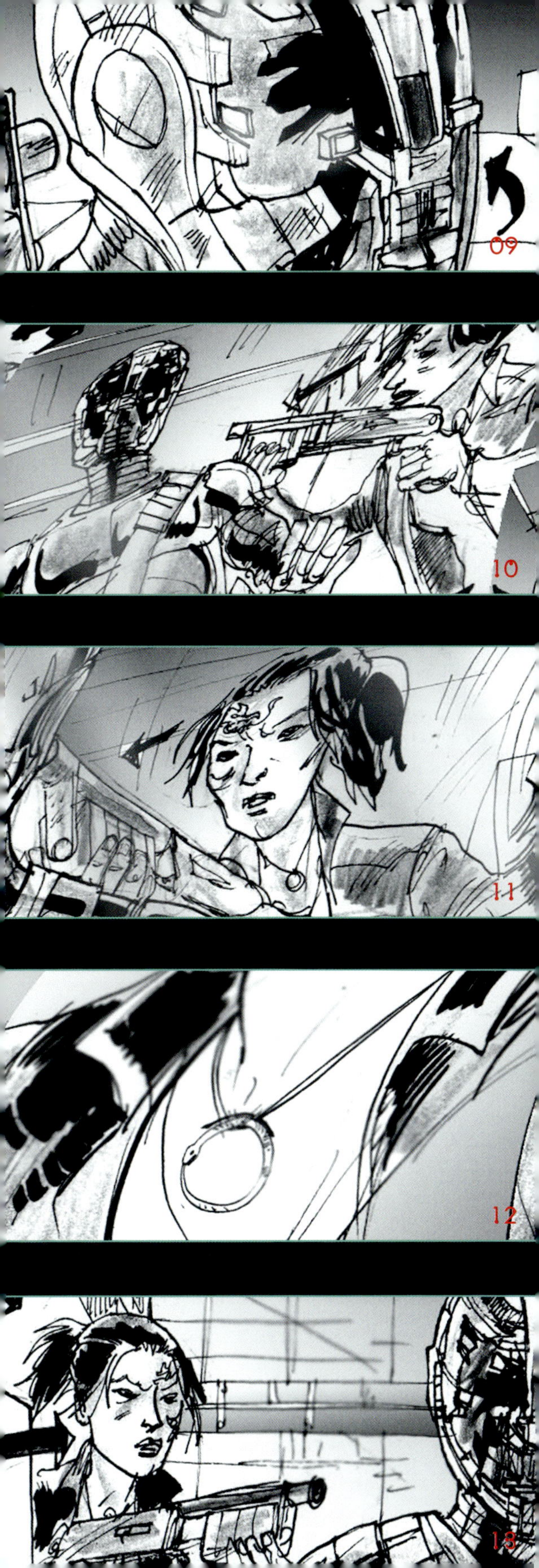

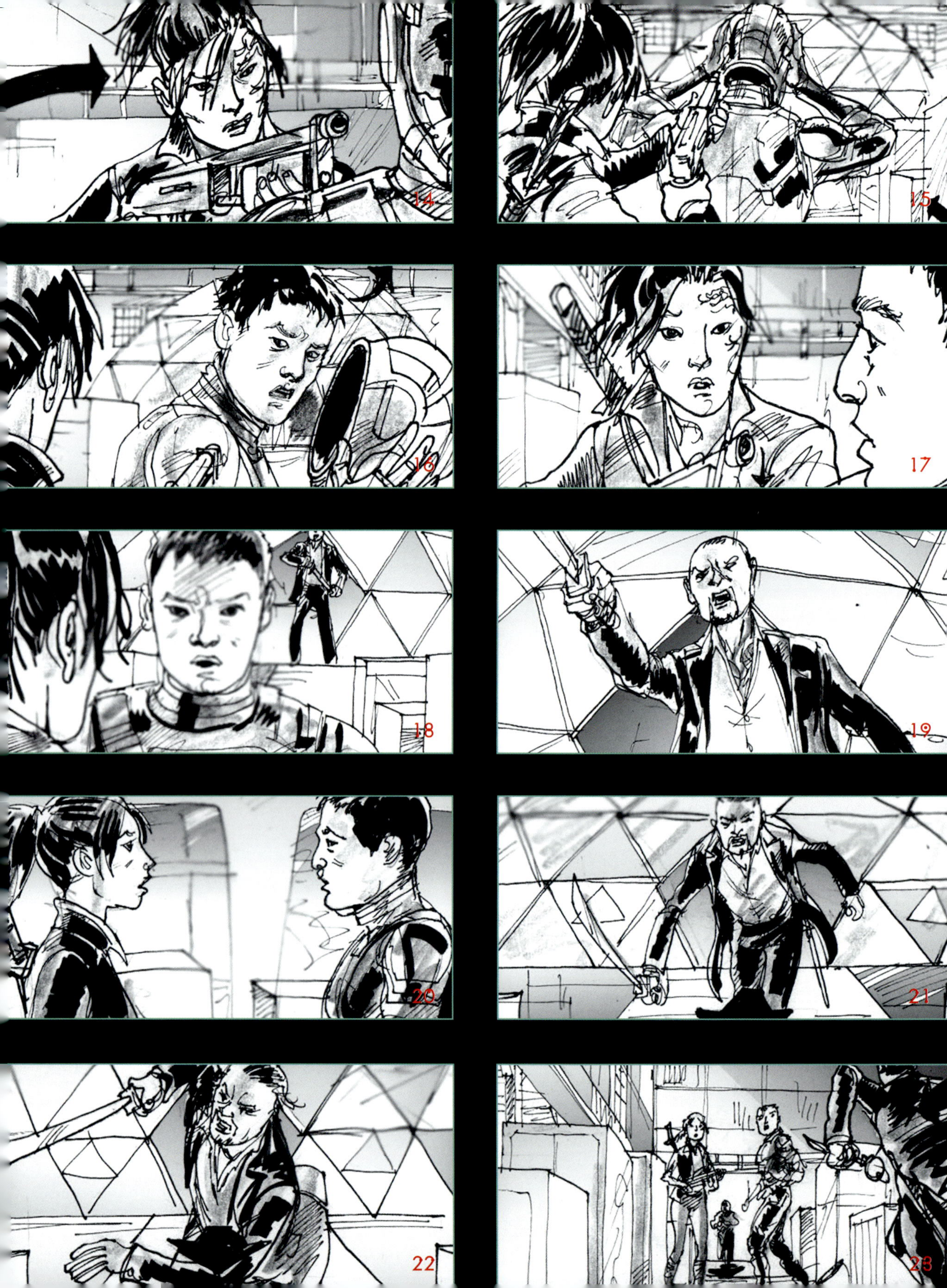
14
15
16
17
18
19
20
21
22
23

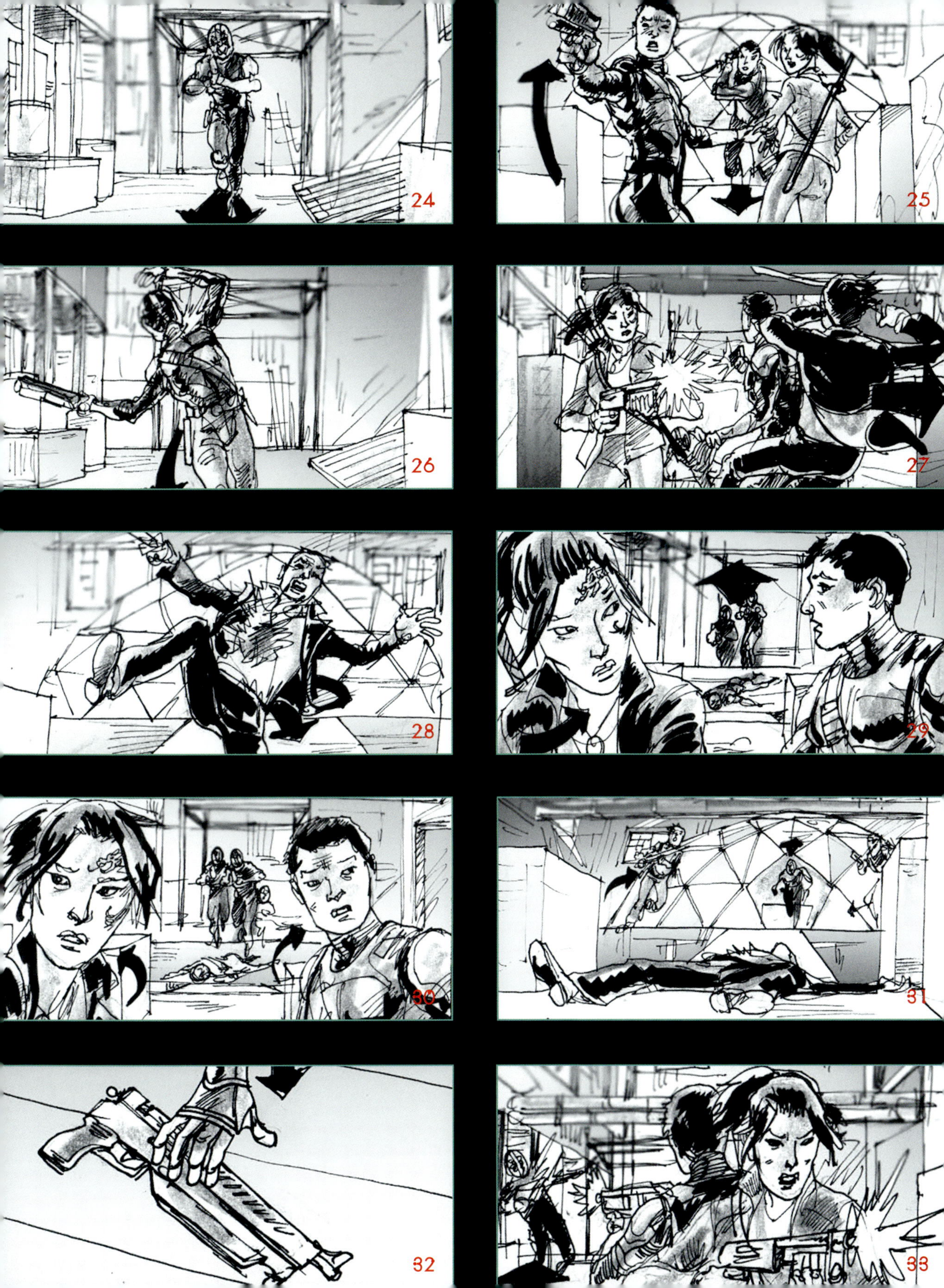
24
25
26
27
28
29
30
31
32
33

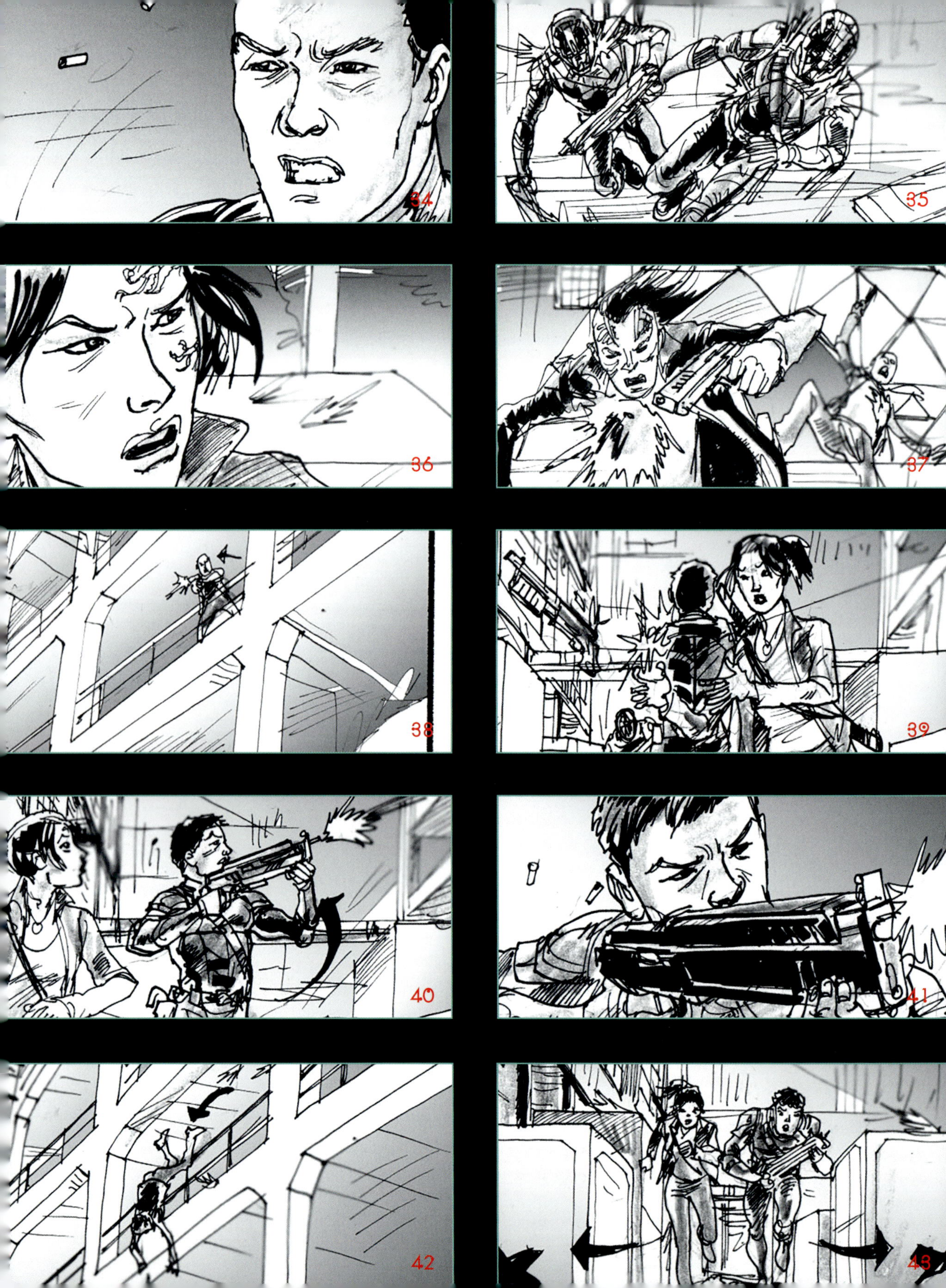
34
35
36
37
38
39
40
41
42
43

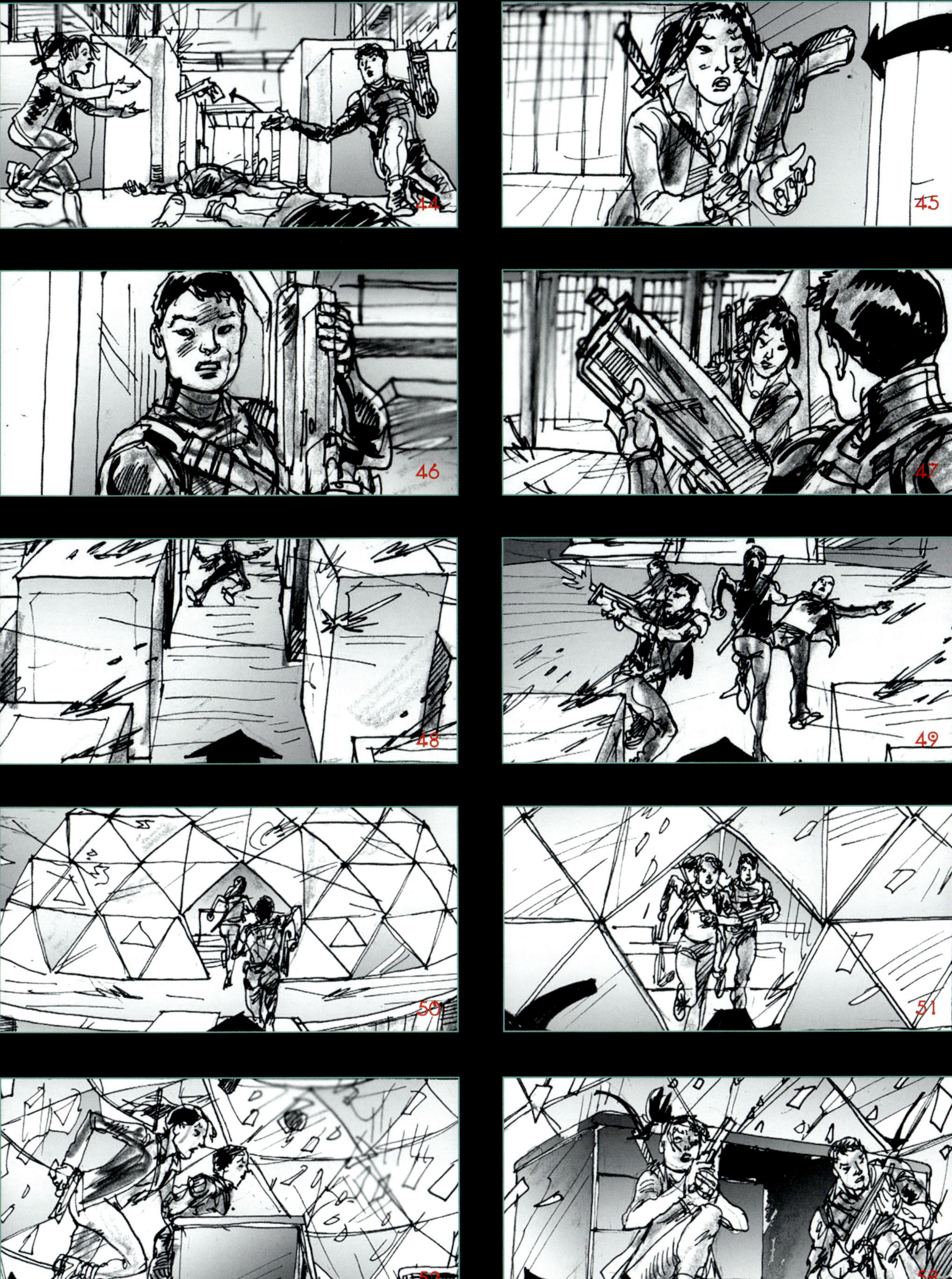
44
45
46
47
48
49
50
51
52
53

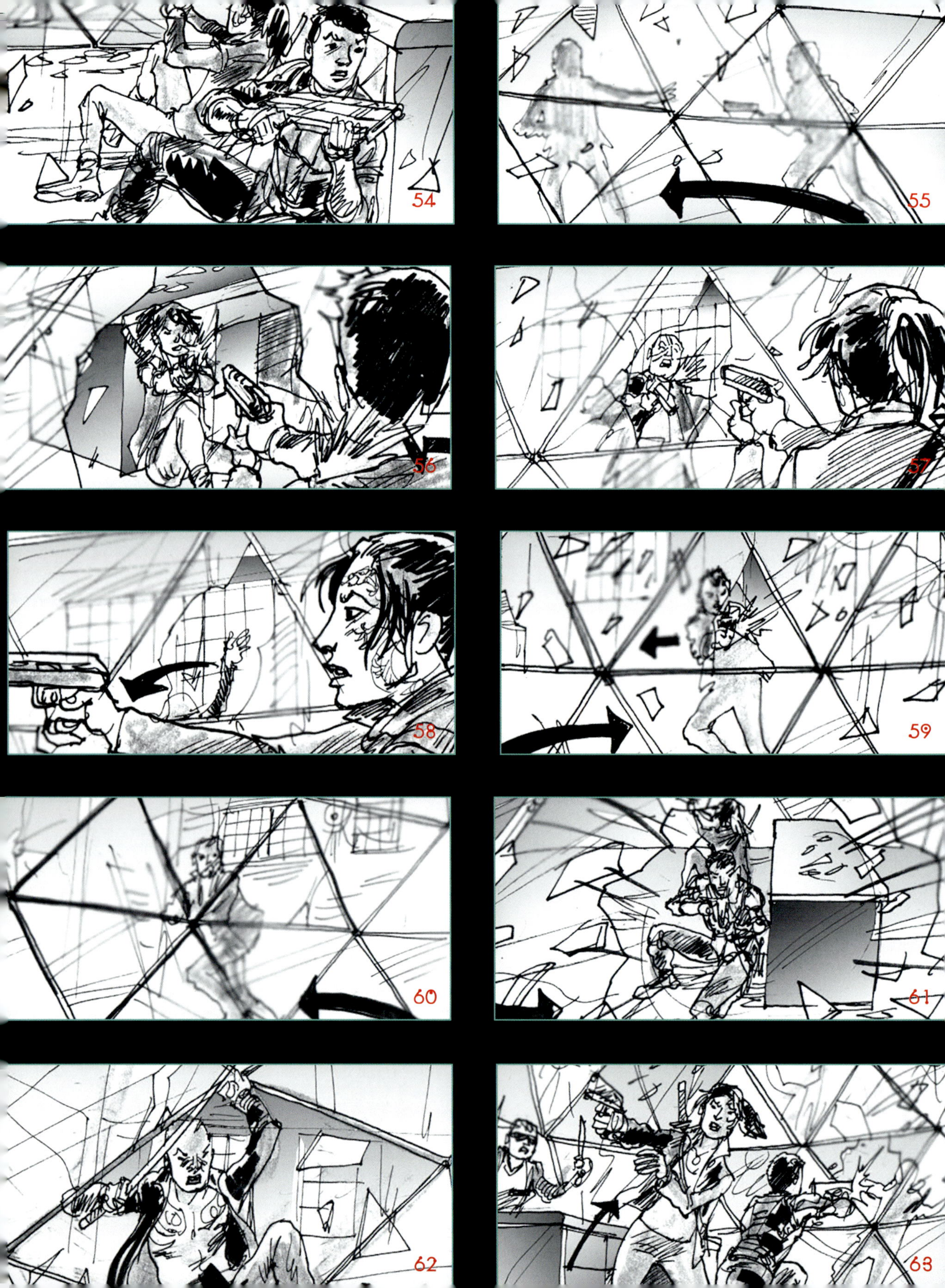
54
55
56
57
58
59
60
61
62
63

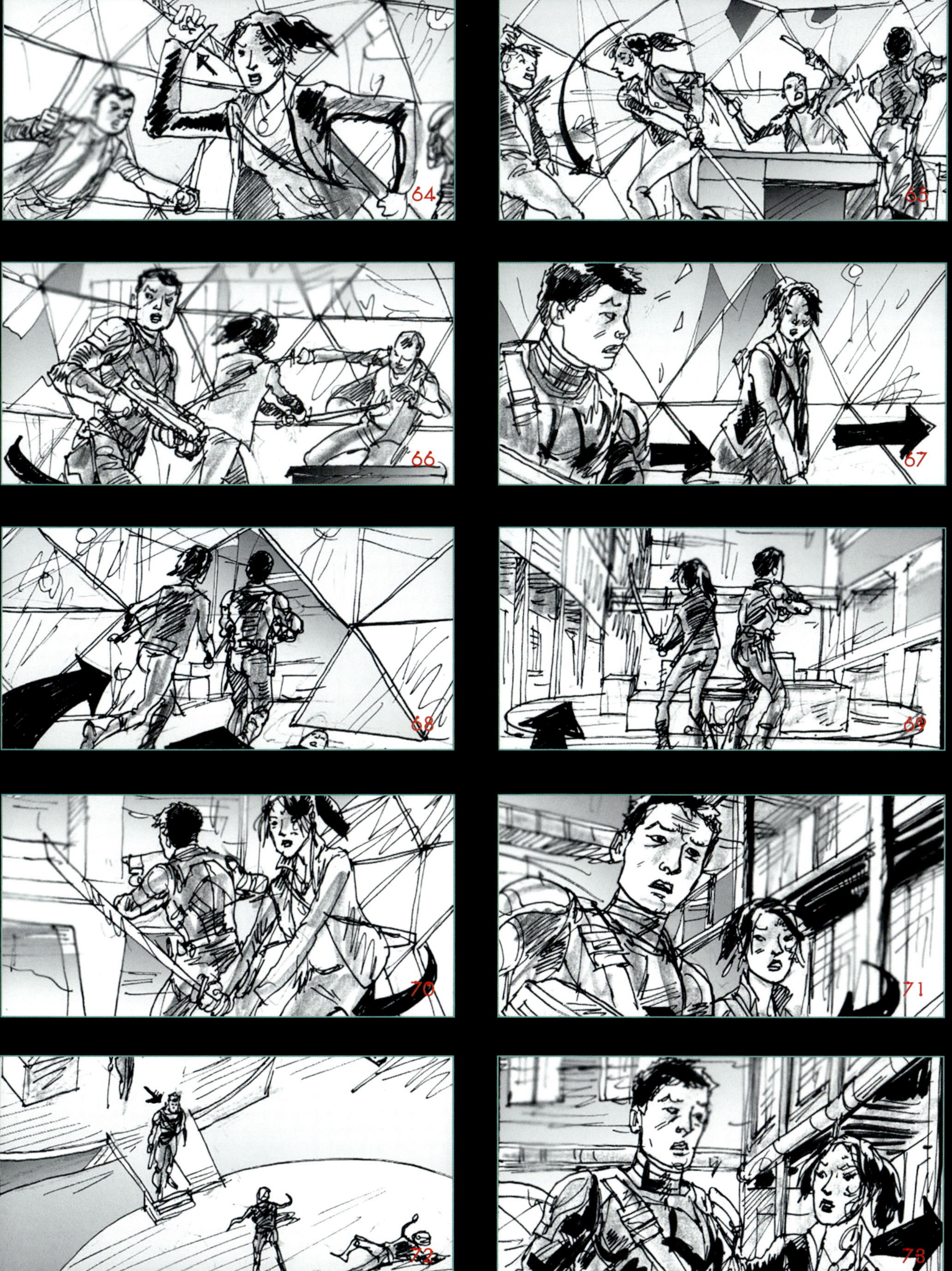
64
65
66
67
68
69
70
71
72
73

n this flashback sequence, we see Mary Lou Henchy's pivotal eap from Head in the Clouds into the San Francisco Bay. Mary Lou has just been traumatized by seeing Bancroft rape, murder, and destroy the stack of another prostitute in the same room; when Bancroft turns on Mary Lou, she flees. Pursued by Reileen, Mary Lou goes as far as she can on the external rim of Head in the Clouds before jumping. The details show how precarious her position is, and how vulnerable she is, walking in the thin atmosphere in a negligee with bare feet. Mary Lou doesn't know that the fall will kill her identity as well as her body, since Reileen has secretly had religious coding applied to Mary Lou's stack.

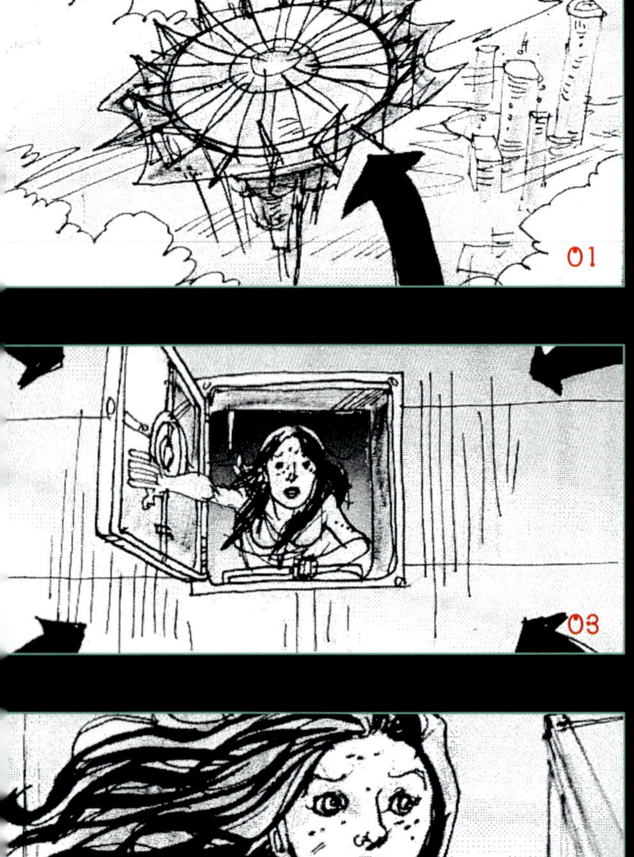

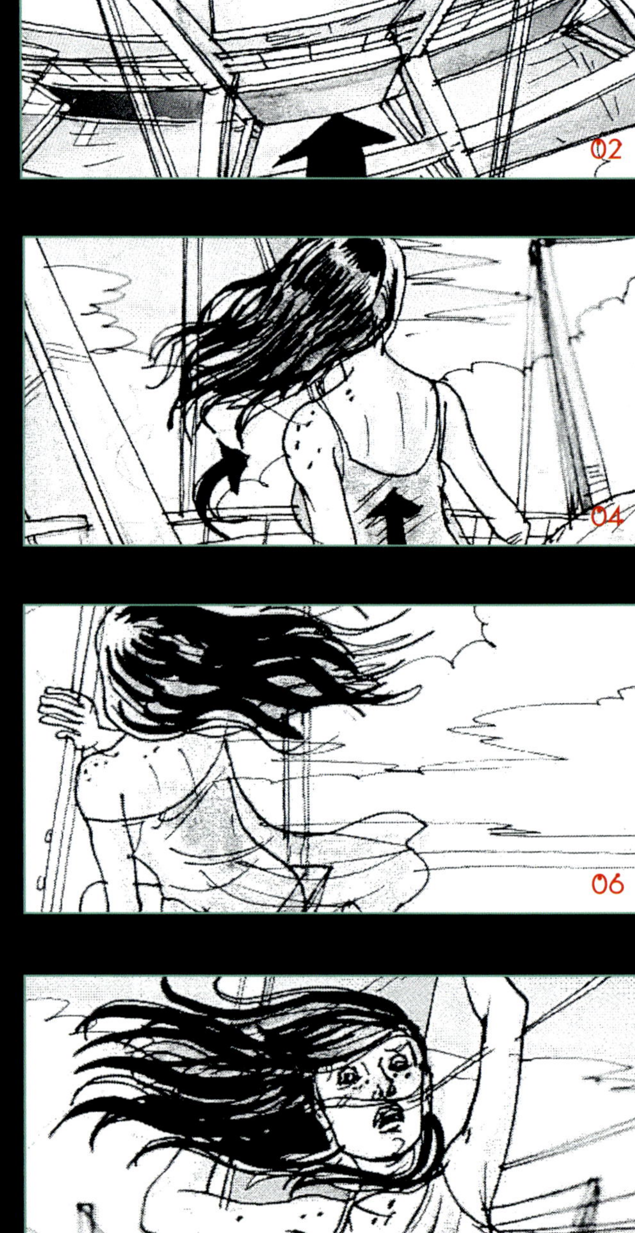

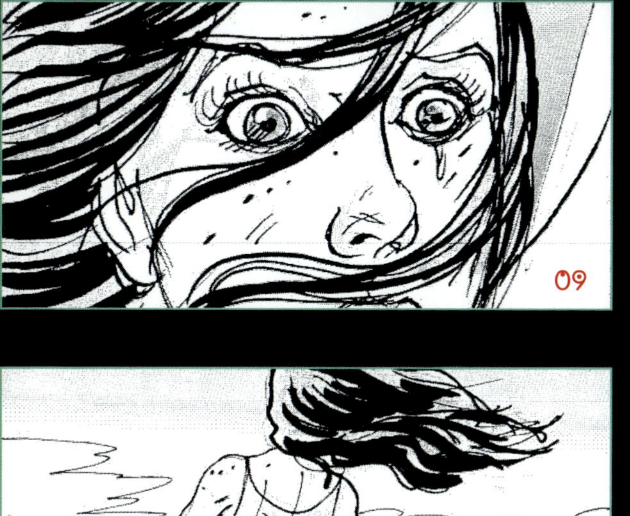
09

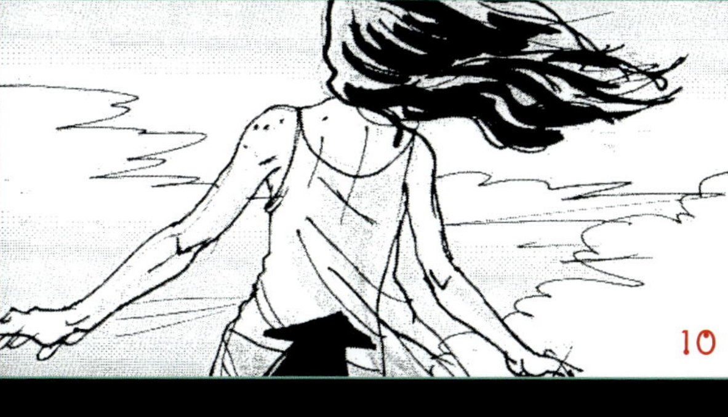
10

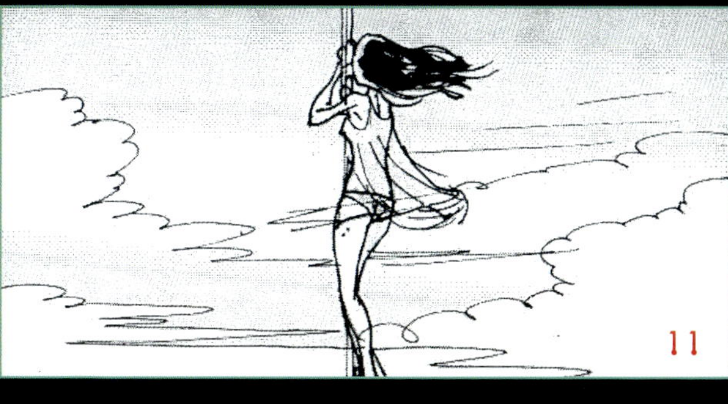
11

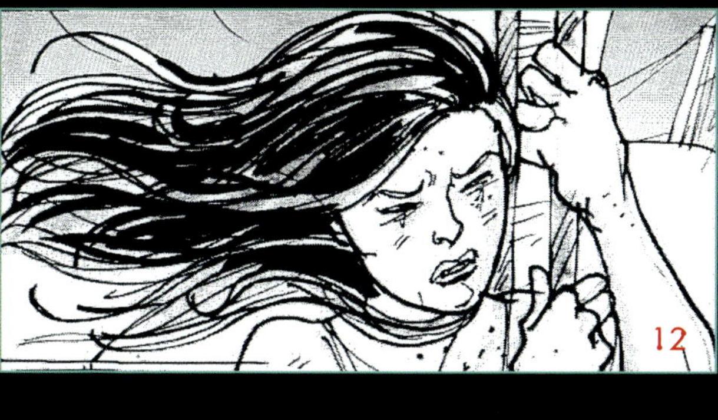
12

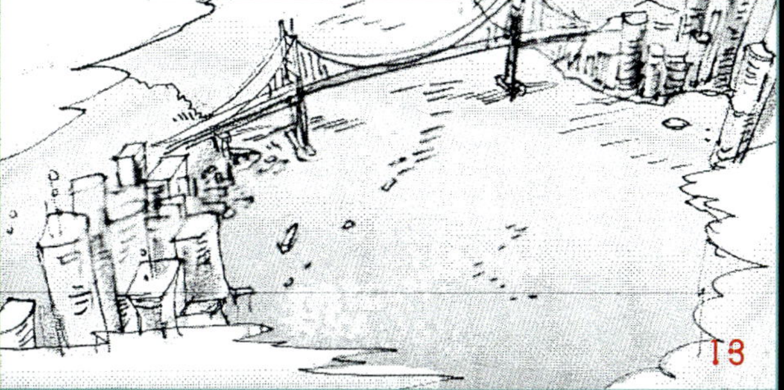
13

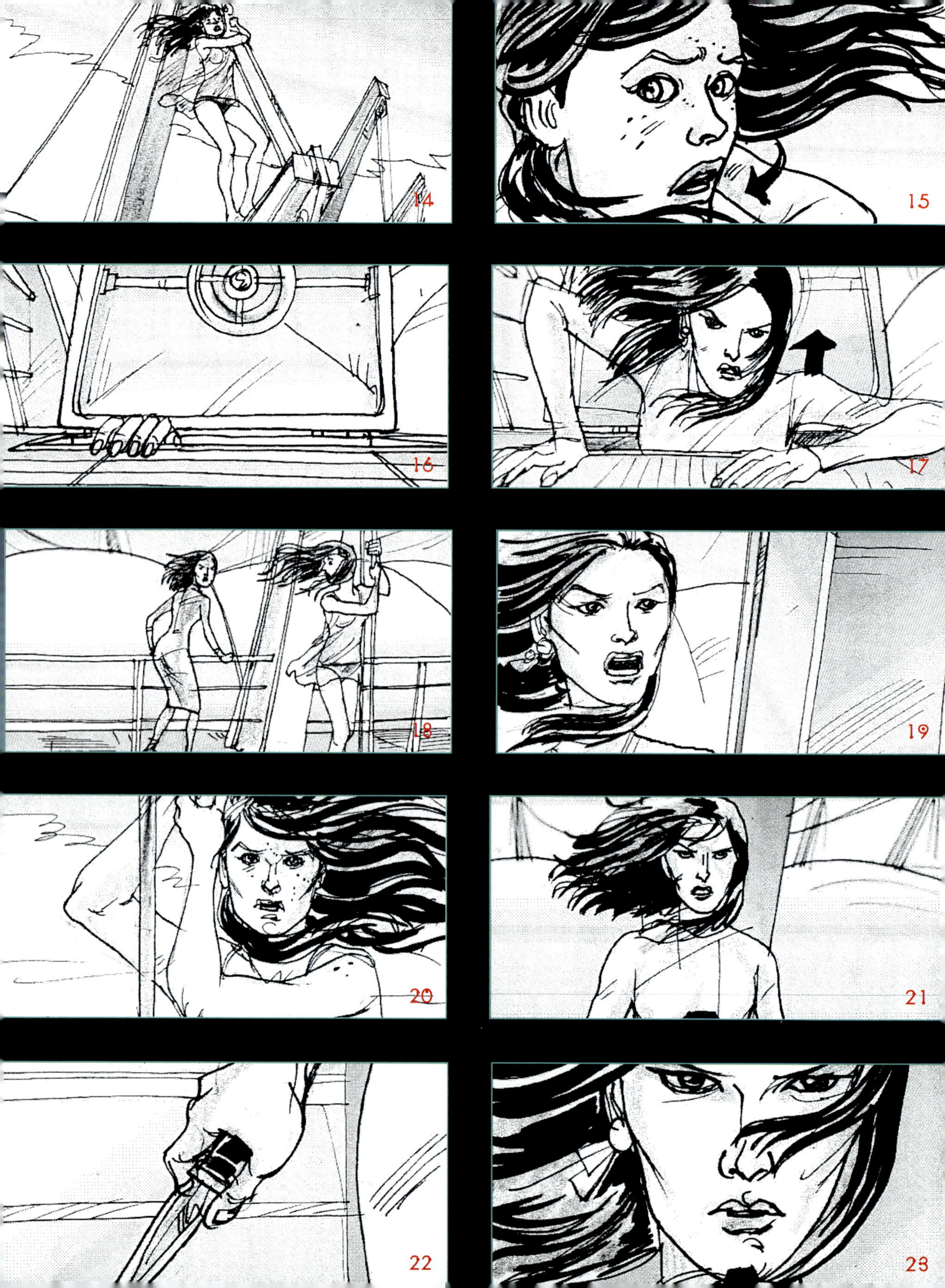
14
15
16
17
18
19
20
21
22
23

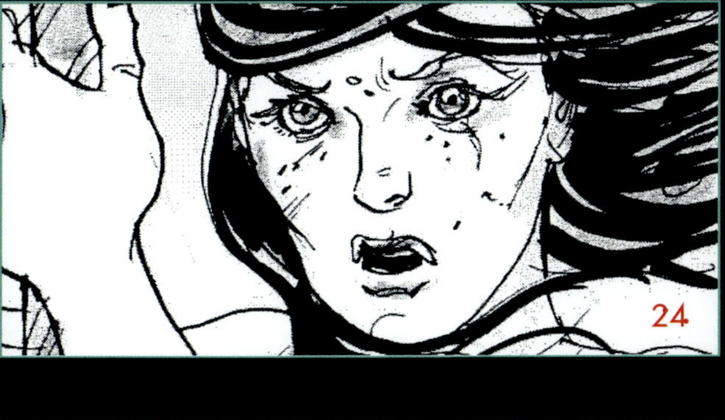
24

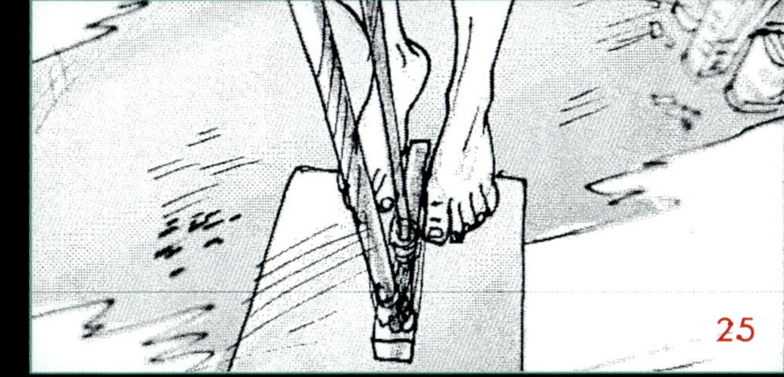
25

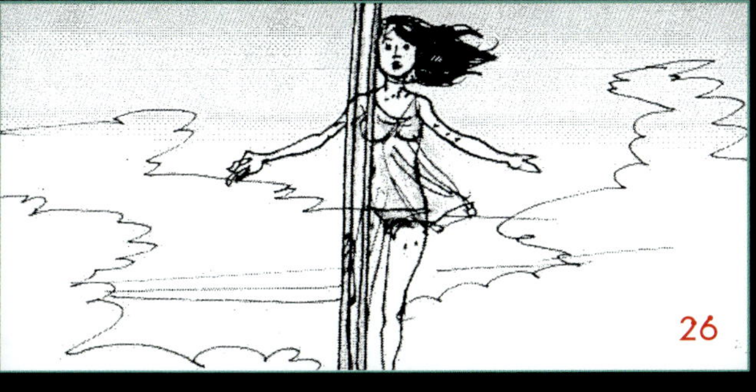
26

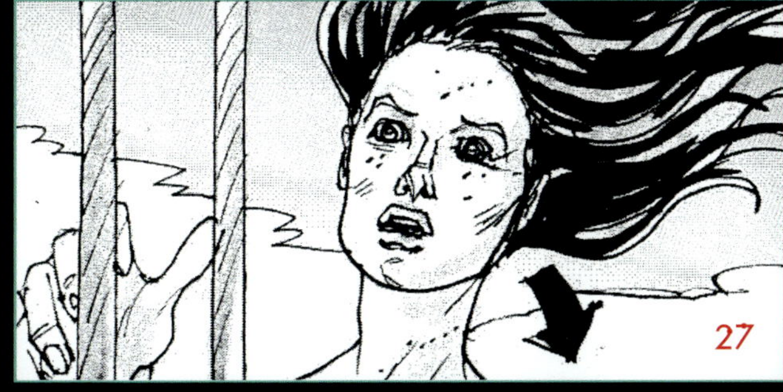
27

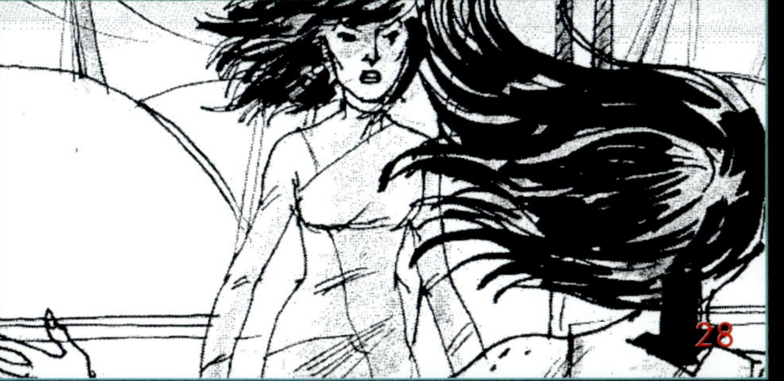
28

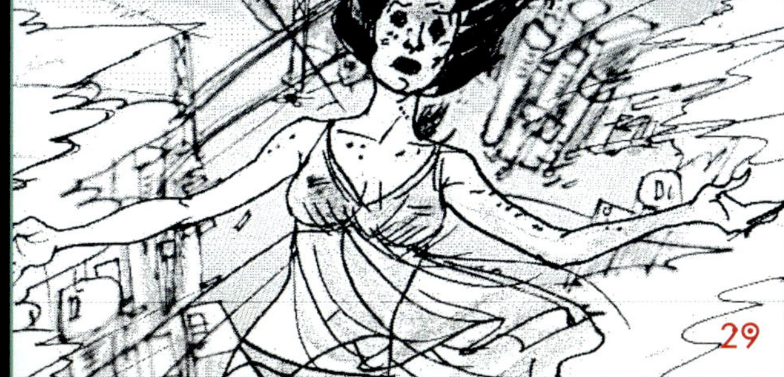
29

SEASON ONE EPISODE TEN SCENE FIFTEEN

In this sequence, Lizzie Elliot has just transferred her consciousness from her virtual room in the Raven into a naked female synth body at Head in the Clouds. This is the first step in the rescue of her parents. When a guard there sees that the synth is 'awake,' he assumes she will comply with his rape fantasies and forces her legs apart. When he criticizes the synth for not looking at him with the proper respect and enthusiasm, Lizzie is able to change the synth's appearance to match her own real look. Before the guard can begin to fathom what's happening, Lizzie snaps his neck, steps over his corpse, then goes to the wardrobe rack to put together a striking outfit that suits her purpose.

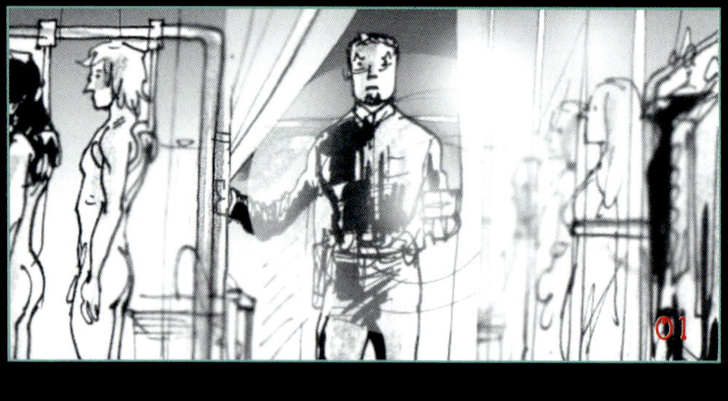

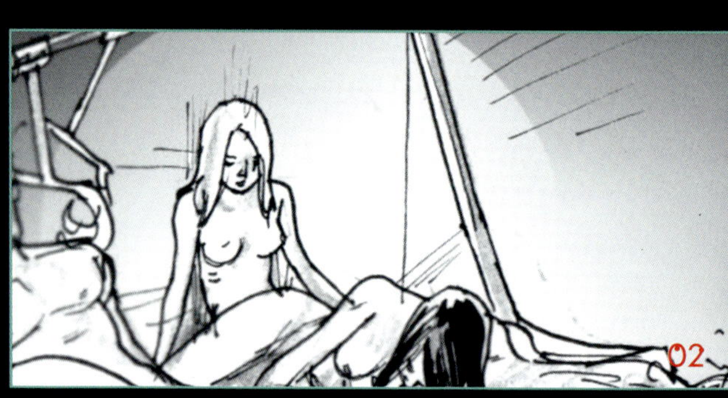

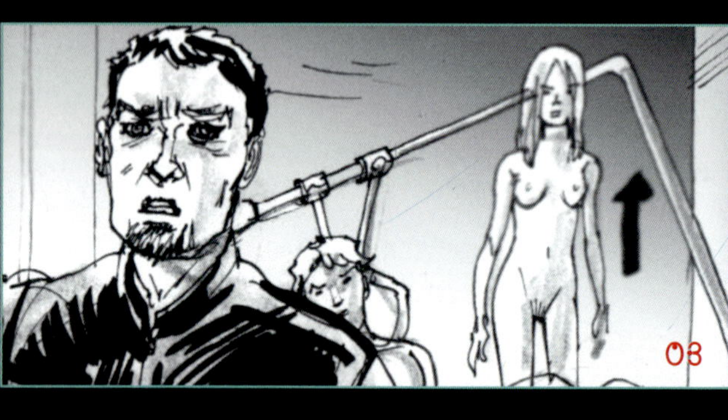

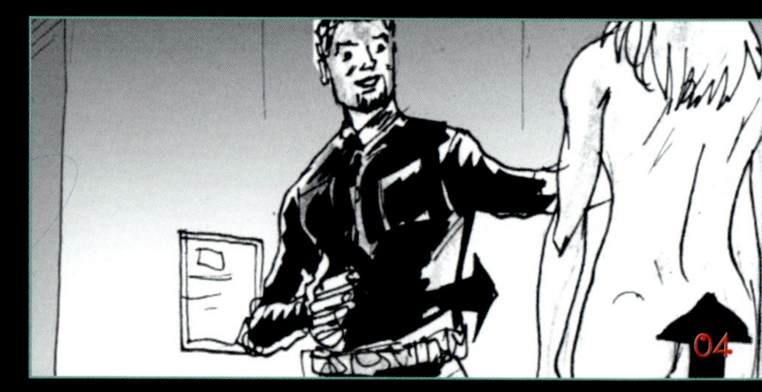

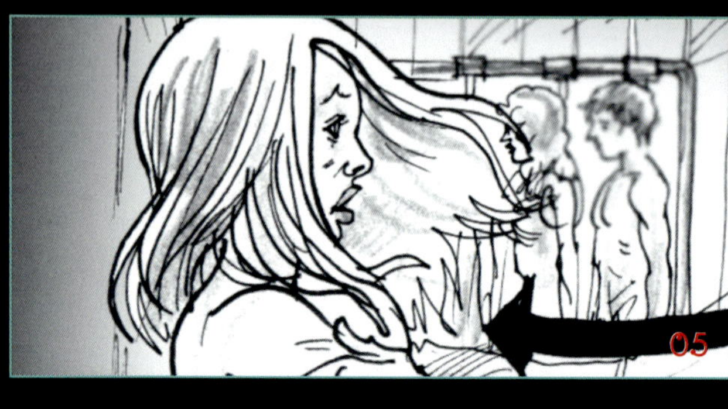

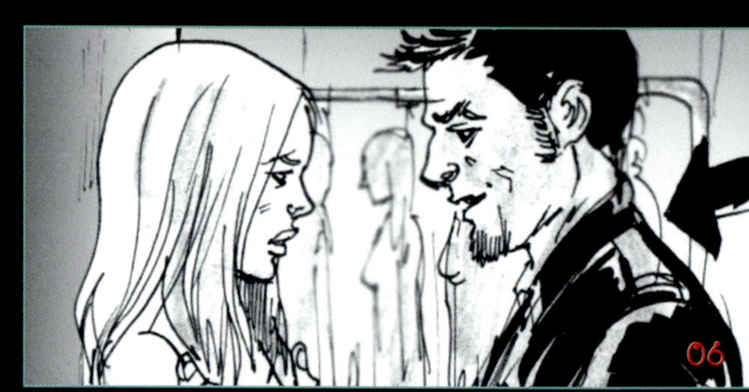

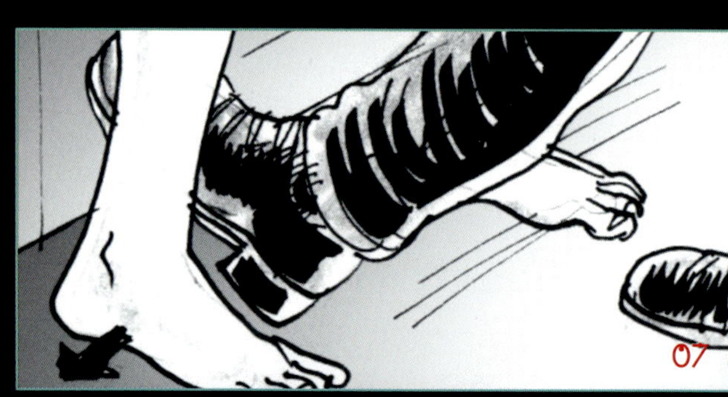

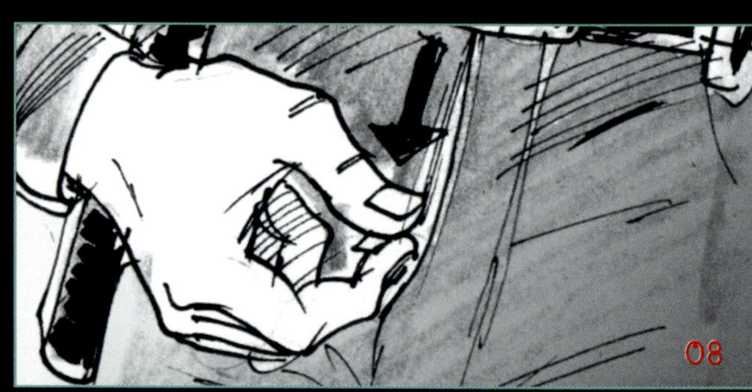

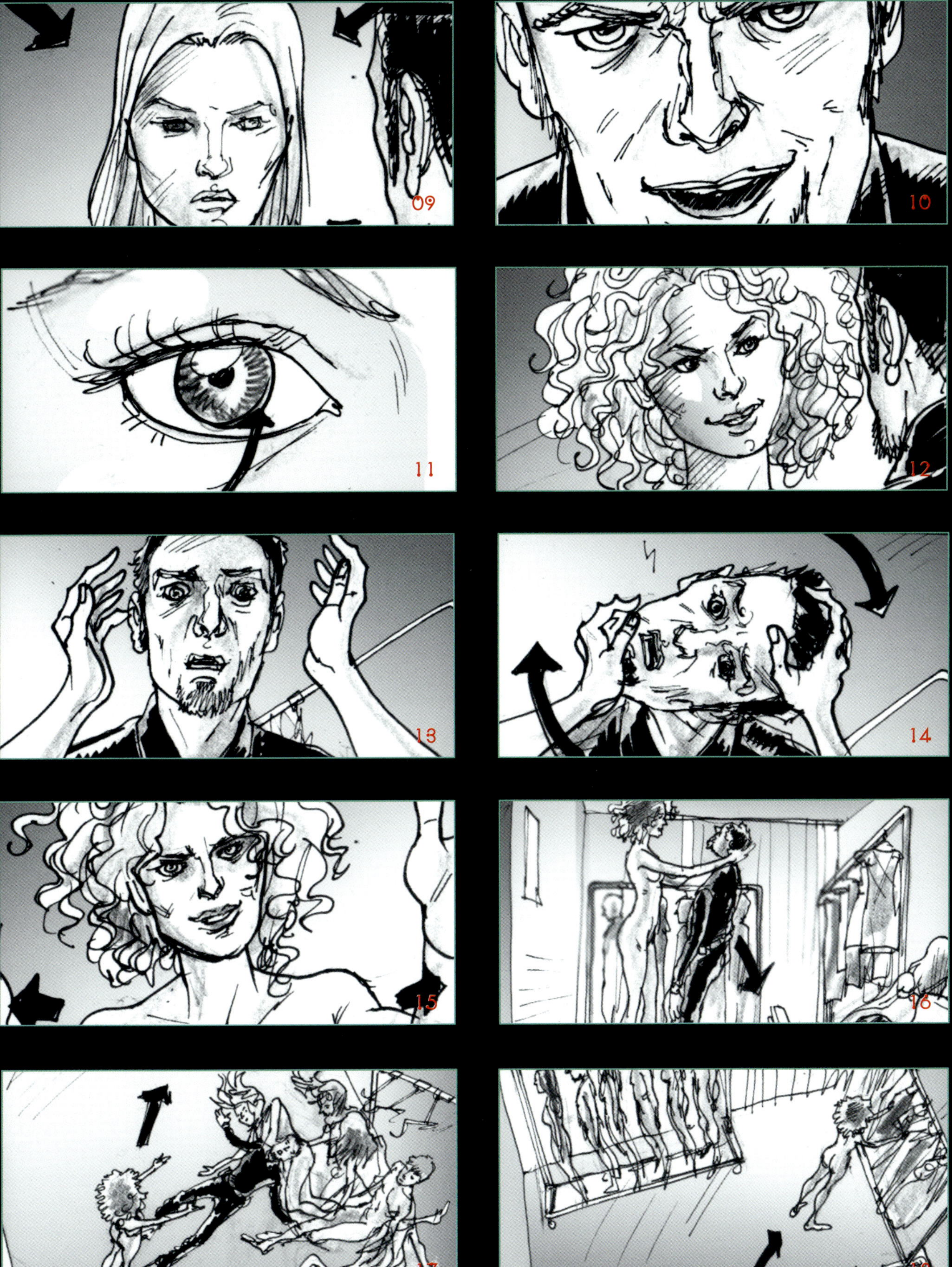
09
10
11
12
13
14
15
16
17
18

SEASON ONE EPISODE TEN SCENE TWENTY-ONE

izzie Elliot, with Poe's help, has overcome her own brutalization nd become a powerful new entity. She will no longer tolerate buse, either of herself or of others. As Lizzie makes her way long one of the Head in the Clouds corridors she looks into a oom where a male guest has partaken of the premier Iridium xperience, where the customer gets to not only brutalize but stack-murder the prostitutes. This guest has crushed a femal prostitute's skull and stabbed a male prostitute through th throat with a knife. Lizzie closes the victims' open eyes, retrieve the knife, and briefly lets the guest believe that she's there t service him. Then she stabs the guest up through the chin destroying his stack and his brain.

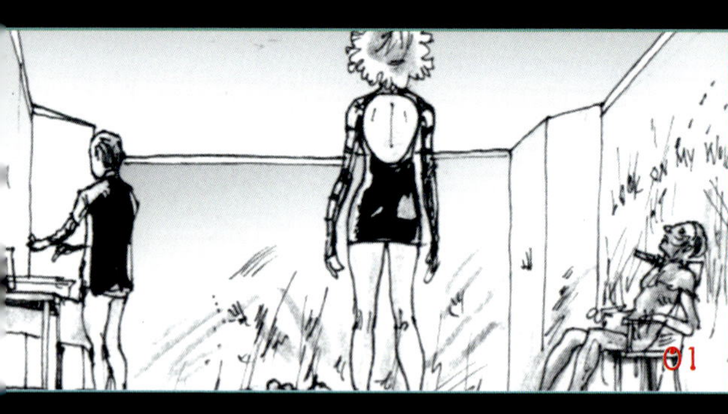

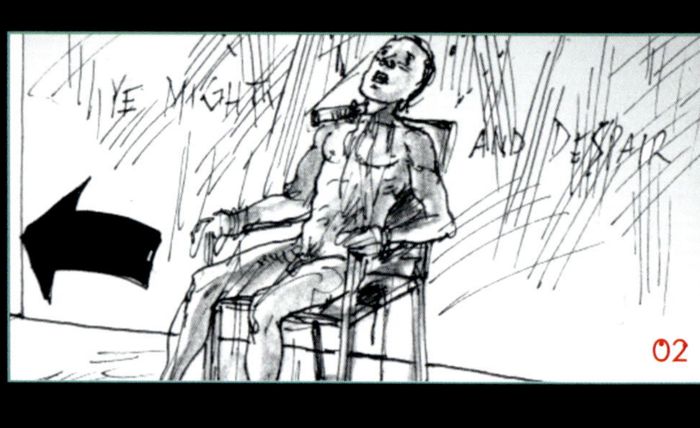

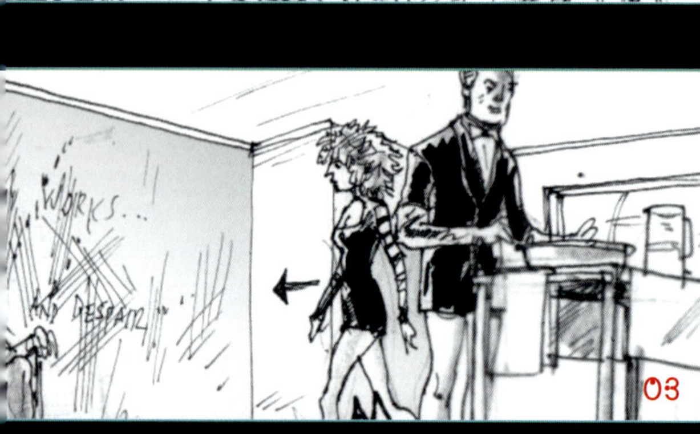

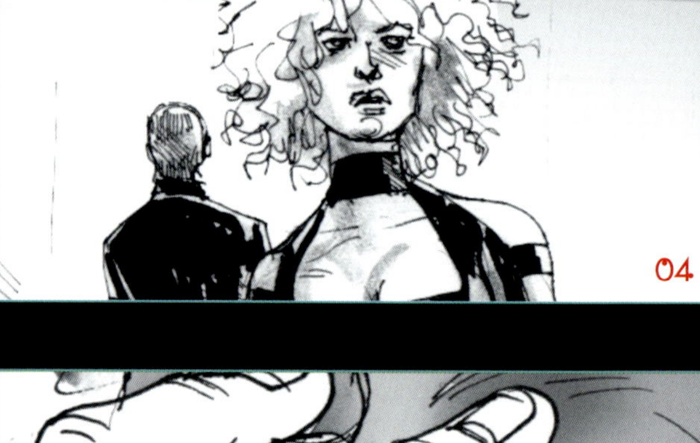

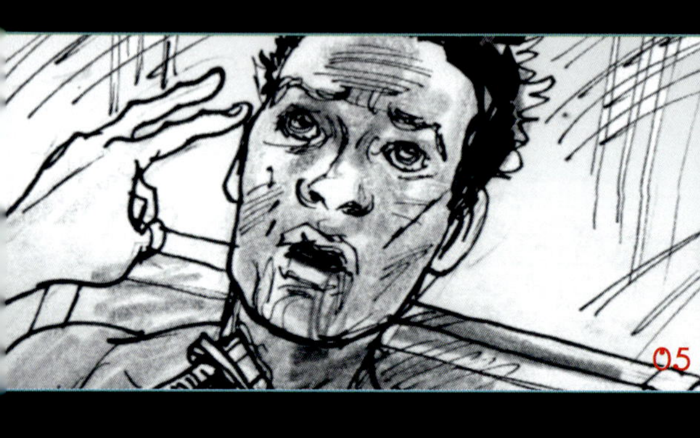

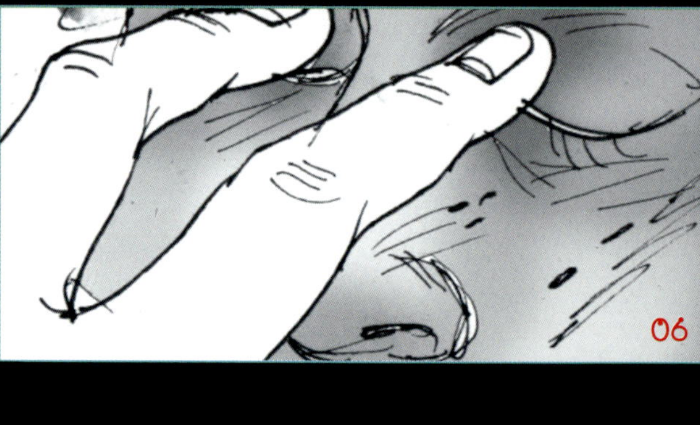

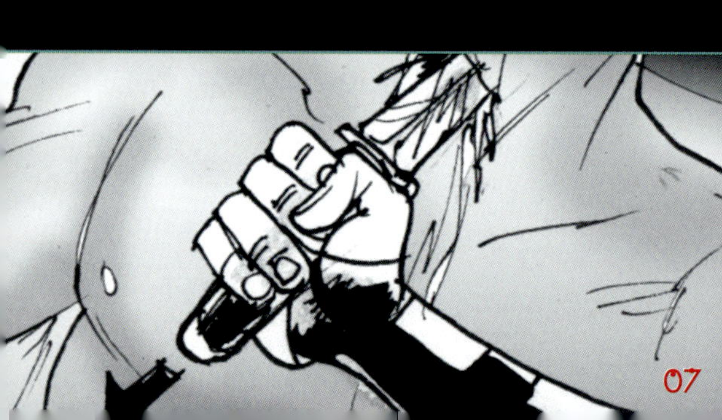

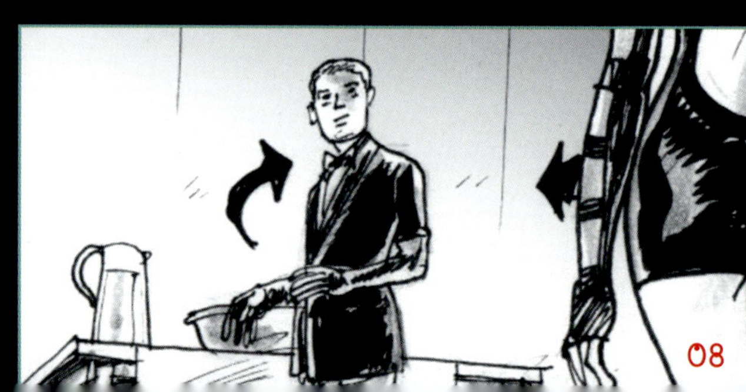

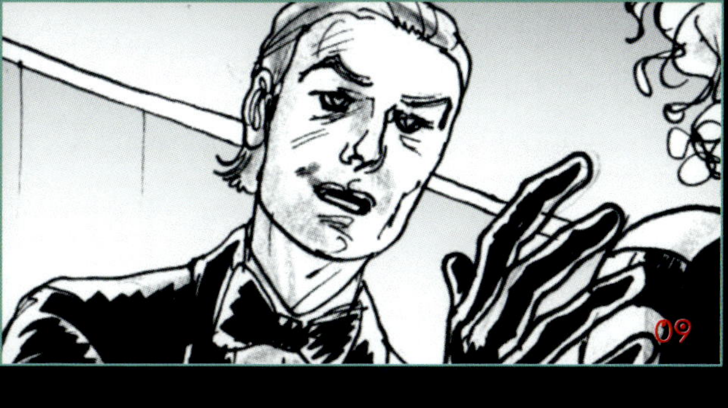
09

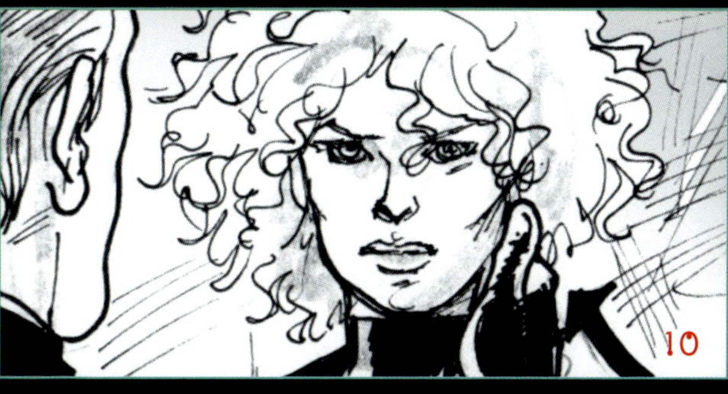
10

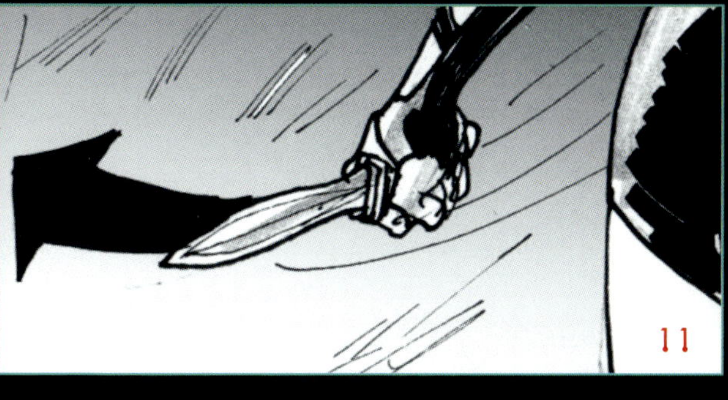
11

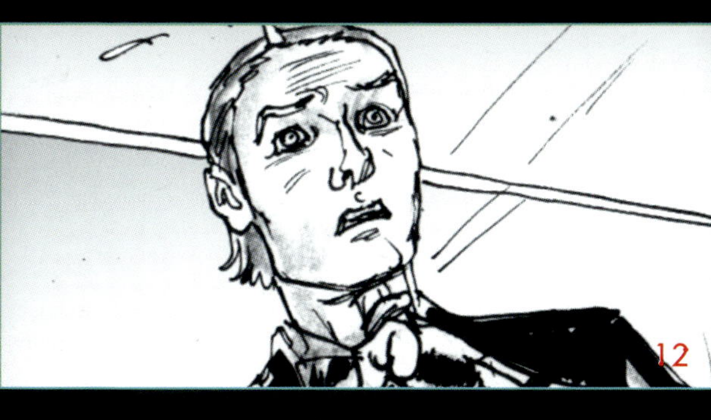
12

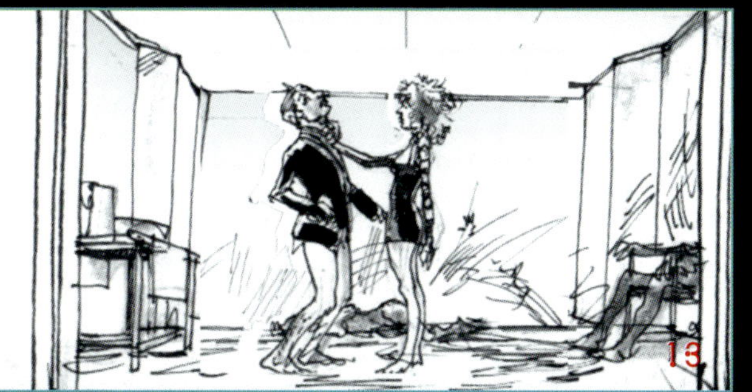
13

GLOSSARY

AI: Short for artificial intelligence. The majority of AIs started off as hotel owners, but once the AI hotels fell out of style, most of them moved on to more profitable industries.

BROADCAST BLOCKER: Holographic adverts are broadcast straight to a user's stack but placing a device named a broadcast blocker over the stack prevents this.

CONTAGION BOMB: A warfare weapon used to spread disease.

CORTICAL STACKS: A small disk that fits at the base of the neck that can hold a person's DHF.

CTAC PRAETORIAN: An acronym for colonial tactical assault corps, a highly skilled trained-to-kill military force that works on behalf of the Protectorate.

DHF: Short for digital human freight. A person's DHF contains their personality and memories and is downloaded to a cortical stack.

DHF BACKUP: If the person can afford it, their DHF can be digitally backed up to ensure immortality even if their cortical stack is damaged.

DIPPER: Somebody who makes their money hacking into DHFs to download memories and sell them on.

DOUBLE-SLEEVING: Highly illegal and punishable by real death. Double-sleeving involves creating two copies of one DHF and simultaneously downloading them into two sleeves. Sometimes referred to as 'multi-sleeving' or 'twinning.'

DREAM TANK: Another term used for VR.

ELDER: The alien race that was supposedly extinct before humans discovered their technology on Harlan's World.

ENVOYS: The soldiers of the rebellion that were trained by Quellcrist Falconer to have heightened reflexes and withstand psychological damage from needlecasting.

FOUNDERS: Refers to a small group of people who discovered the planet Harlan's World and founded civilisation there.

GROUNDERS: People who live on Earth but cannot afford the high life of the Aerium.

HAWKEYE: A tracking device that the police use to track suspects. It can be placed on a broadcast blocker, as Kristin Ortega does to Kovacs, to disguise the device.

METH: Short for Methuselah (named after the biblical character), refers to the upper class of humans who use their wealth to gain immortality.

NEEDLECAST: Transferring a person's DHF digitally from one stack to another, anywhere in the universe. If a person is needlecasted into too many different bodies too often it can cause psychological damage.

NEO-CATHOLICS: Catholocism in the future includes new scripture that relates to the use of stack technology and proscribes that humans should have one life (and one body).

NEO-C CODING: A coding that New-Catholics can have added to their stacks to indicate they don't want to be spun up after death, even to help solve a murder or give evidence in their murder case.

OCULAR NEURAL INTERFACE: Also referred to as an ONI. A small gadget worn in one eye that functions like a smart phone.

ORGANIC DAMAGE: When a sleeve is wounded to the point of death but the stack and DHF are undamaged. Also referred to as sleeve death.

PERSONALITY FRAG: Short for 'personality fragmentation', sometimes further shortened to 'p-frag.' Personality frag is a side effect of needlecasting too many times and results in serious psychological damage.

PIL: A transport system, similar to metro trains, used on both Earth and Harlan's World. There are public and private versions of the PIL transport.

PROTECTORATE: The ruling government of Earth and the settled planets.

PSYCHASEC: The high-tech company, secretly owned by Reileen, that created and runs all of the advanced technology such as synthetic sleeves, VR torture and clones.

PSYCHOSURGERY: A form of virtual surgery performed on DHFs with psychological trauma.

RAWLING'S VIRUS: Is a deadly virus threatening both organic and artificial life. Attacking cortical stacks as well as AI, it can corrupt the information stored on both, making them useless. If a stack is infected while in a living person, it drives the person insane, while it drives AI's insane before melting their cores. Rawling's can even damage a stack's offsite backup if it's infected during the backup.

REAL DEATH: A term used to describe when a person has irreparable damage (e.g. a gunshot) to their stack.

RESOLUTION 653: A new piece of legislation brought in to allow murder victims the opportunity to give evidence against their killer.

SLEEVE: In a world where immortality is possible bodies are now referred to as sleeves as they're replaceable. A sleeve can be a person's natural birth body or a clone or a synthetic body.

SLEEVE DEATH: When a sleeve is wounded to the point of death but the stack and DHF are undamaged. Also referred to as organic damage.

SONGSPIRE TREE: A tree native to Harlan's World with mysterious properties – they glow a faint blue light and create a noise similar to singing.

SPIN UP: A stack is placed into a temporary sleeve, usually to be interrogated by police.

SYNTHETIC SLEEVE: An expensive body created in a lab. Synthetic sleeves have special abilities, such as customisable features.

UPRISING: The rebellion, led by Quellcrist Falconer, against the protectorate plotted to end the use of DHF and stack technology.

VR: Virtual reality or VR, also known as a construct or simulspace, is a space that police, military and criminals use to interrogate suspects. Technology has developed so far that VR is indistinguishable from reality.

CONCLUSION

FINISH THE MISSION

Laeta Kalogridis feels that *Altered Carbon* is ideally suited to Netflix. "We're a Netflix show because of our deep passion for the material, and because of Netflix's deep passion for the material, and because what we're making is different. They're so creator-driven, they're so vision-driven that everything you see feels original. And that's why I think we fit."

Those involved with *Altered Carbon* consider it a career high point. For Alison Schapker, "It is beyond exciting to take part in a series that brings to life such a complex and compelling sci-fi universe."

"It was one of the best shows I've ever done," says Peter Hoar.

Ann Foley relates, "The collaboration between the departments on this show has been absolutely amazing, probably one of the best I've ever had. Everybody works so seamlessly together, because it does take a village to pull off a show of this size. We all know what we're doing with this world and where we want to take it and what we want to do with it."

"It's just an amazing experience," agrees Everett Burrell, "the amount of detail in the world. Building that world was a lot of fun. Certainly working with some amazing crew, Carey Meyer the production designer, and I became very good friends. It was a lot of fun to be part of that process creatively."

"It's a perfect world for visual effects, stunts, special effects," says Nick Hurran, "and they have excelled beyond the call. Every day, the requisition is for explosions, or ships crashing, or fight sequences, and every day, they bring something special to the table." As for the storytelling, "There is humanity. *Altered Carbon* chose the human side to a character like Kovacs. 'Finish the mission' is embedded in his mind from his training with Quell. He is fighting for what he believes is right and humane."

Audience members agree, James Middleton observes. "The feedback we received from fans was amazingly positive and remains so. I think the audience loved our characters and the narrative surprises. There really is no show like it, with its mix of entertaining spectacle and sobering themes."

What does Middleton hope viewers will get out of season two? "I hope they are inspired by the resilience of Kovacs, Poe, and Quell. Despite mistakes, loss, and sacrifice, these characters never give up on each other."

Schapker concurs. "The heart of *Altered Carbon* exists in its characters, who struggle to make connection and meaning in spite of everything."

Kalogridis hopes for the series as a whole "that we didn't make it to purely fit in any particular box. I hope that it's a human drama that has a sci-fi framework and sci-fi elements. That's what it's meant to be. The technology is a really interesting factor in it. But it's just a way to tell the same human stories that we've been telling since we were sitting around campfires, passing them down from one person to another before we could even write them. We're hoping that that's what we're doing."

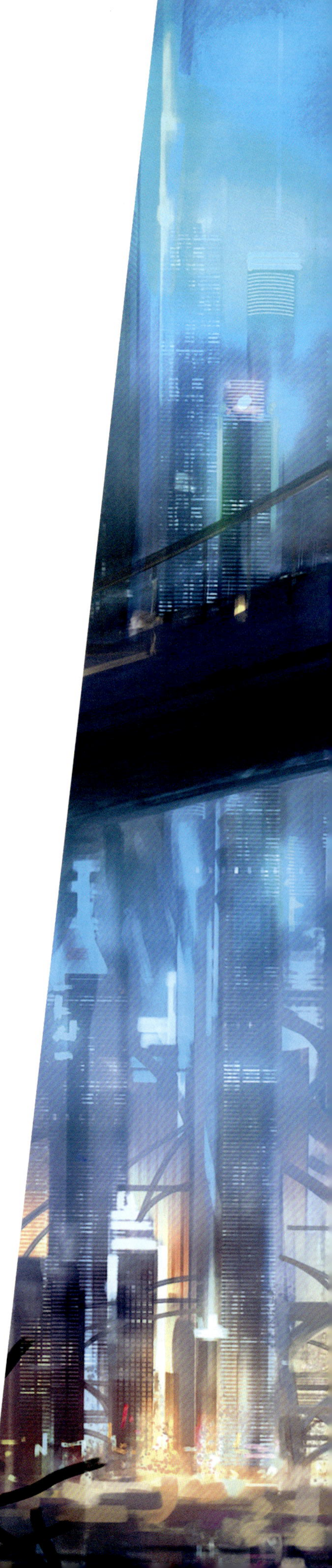

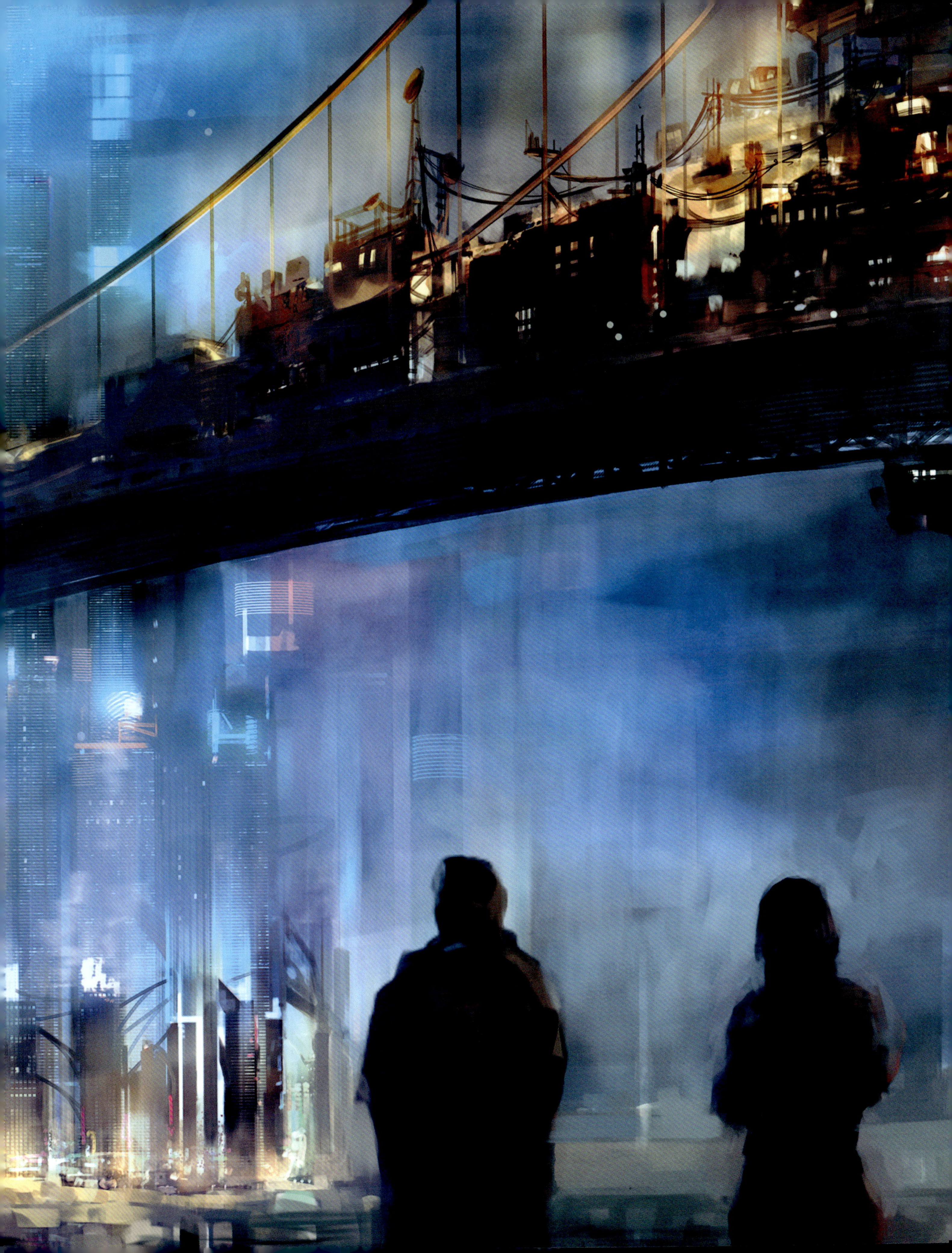

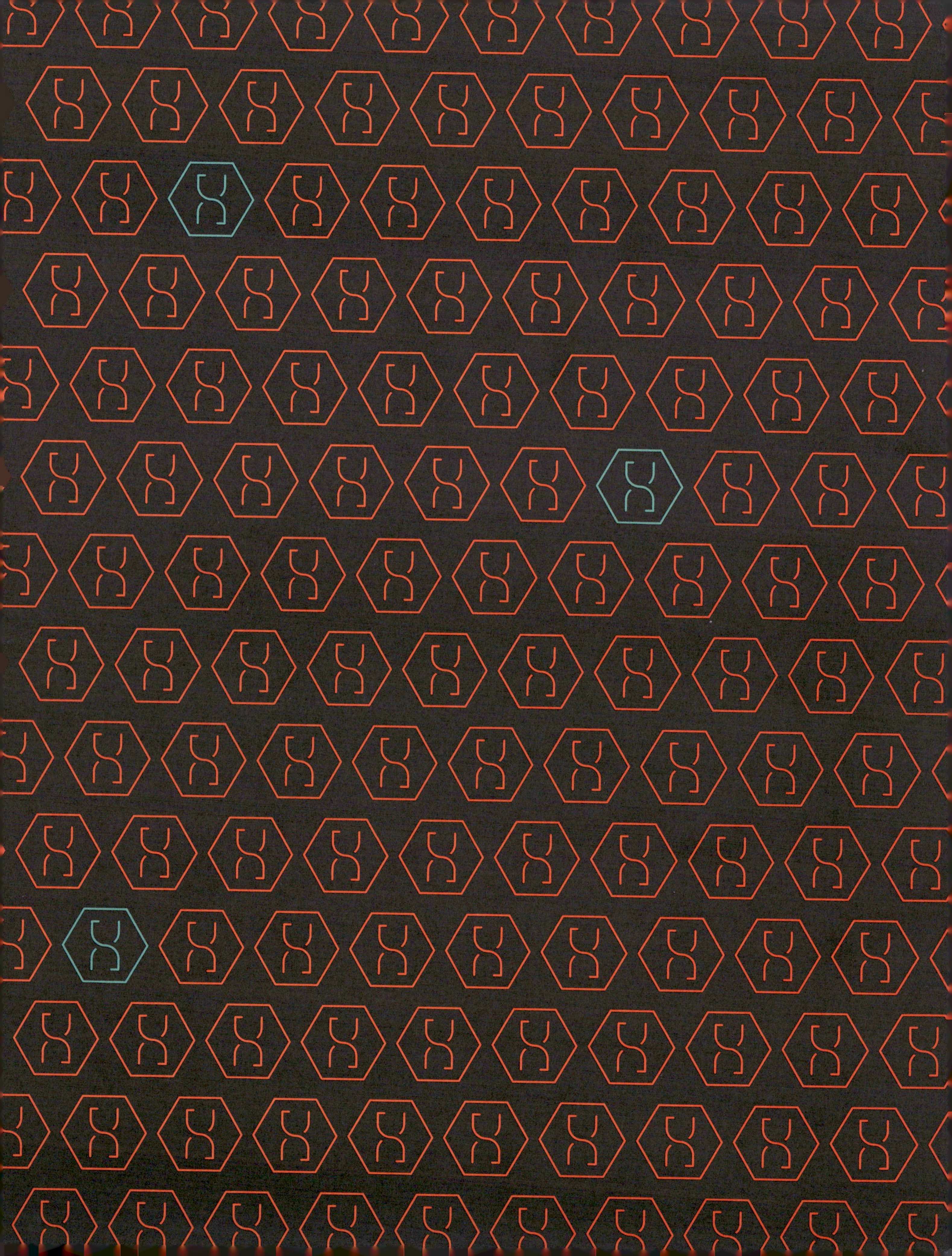